The Virginia Genealogist

Volume 5
1961

John Frederick Dorman, Editor

HERITAGE BOOKS
2009

HERITAGE BOOKS
AN IMPRINT OF HERITAGE BOOKS, INC.

Books, CDs, and more—Worldwide

For our listing of thousands of titles see our website
at
www.HeritageBooks.com

A Facsimile Reprint
Published 2009 by
HERITAGE BOOKS, INC.
Publishing Division
100 Railroad Ave. #104
Westminster, Maryland 21157

Copyright © 1961 John Frederick Dorman

— Publisher's Notice —
In reprints such as this, it is often not possible to remove blemishes from the original. We feel the contents of this book warrant its reissue despite these blemishes and hope you will agree and read it with pleasure.

International Standard Book Numbers
Paperbound: 978-1-55613-714-3
Clothbound: 978-0-7884-8208-3

THE VIRGINIA GENEALOGIST

Volume 5, Number 1   Whole Number 17

January-March, 1961

CONTENTS

Ohio County Legislative Petitions	3
Middlesex County, Virginia, Wills, 1713-1734 (Continued)	7
Amelia County, Virginia, 1800 Tax List	18
Bible of Jonathan Durrett, Spotsylvania County, Virginia Contributed by Mrs. Bert Harter	28
MacCarthy-McCarthy-McCarty Notes: Ireland, Virginia, Tennessee By John Insley Coddington	31
A Guide to the Counties of Virginia Berkeley County	33
Jane (Smith) Holbrook of New Jersey and Virginia Contributed by Robert Karl Peterson	36
Local Notices from the Virginia Gazette, 1780 (Continued)	37
Book Reviews	
King, The Register of Saint Paul's Parish	40
Shetler, Guide to the Study of West Virginia History	40
Knorr, Marriages of Orange County, Virginia	41
Knorr, Marriage Bonds and Ministers' Returns of Surry County, Virginia, 1768-1825	41
Lindsay, Marriages of Henrico County, Virginia	42
Lyman, The Belfield Family	42
Rudd, Shockoe Hill Cemetery, Richmond, Virginia, Register of Interments	43
Neel, The Wilford-Williford Family	43
Lockhart, Thompsons, Mainly of Hanover & Louisa Counties, Virginia	44
Ohio Records and Pioneer Families	44
Queries	45

Editor: John Frederick Dorman

Published quarterly by John Frederick Dorman
Business address: Box 4883, Washington 8, D.C.
Copyright 1961, by John Frederick Dorman

Subscription rates: $5.00 per year; single issue, $1.50
All subscriptions begin with first issue of year
V. 1, nos. 1-2, $2.50 each, only as part of entire set

Second class postage paid at Washington, D.C.

STATEMENT REQUIRED BY THE ACT OF AUGUST 24, 1912, AS AMENDED BY THE ACTS OF MARCH 3, 1933, JULY 2, 1946 AND JUNE 11, 1960 (74 STAT. 208) SHOWING THE OWNERSHIP, MANAGEMENT, AND CIRCULATION OF The Virginia Genealogist, published quarterly at Washington, D.C., for 9 September, 1960.

1. The names and addresses of the publisher, editor, managing editor, and business managers are: Publisher, Editor, John Frederick Dorman, Box 4883, Washington 8, D.C.; Managing editor, none; Business manager, none.

2. The owner is: (If owned by a corporation, its name and address must be stated and also immediately thereunder the names and addresses of stockholders owning or holding 1 percent or more of total amount of stock. If not owned by a corporation, the names and addresses of the individual owners must be given. If owned by a partnership or other unincorporated firm, its name and address, as well as that of each individual member, must be given.) John Frederick Dorman, Box 4883, Washington 8, D.C.

3. The known bondholders, mortgagees, and other security holders owning or holding 1 percent or more of total amount of bonds, mortgages, or other securities are: none.

4. Paragraphs 2 and 3 include, in cases where the stockholder or security holder appears upon the books of the company as trustee or in any other fiduciary relation, the name of the person or corporation for whom such trustee is acting; also the statements in the two paragraphs show the affiant's full knowledge and belief as to the circumstances and conditions under which stockholders and security holders who do not appear upon the books of the company as trustees, hold stock and securities in a capacity other than that of a bona fide owner.

5. The average number of copies of each issue of this publication sold or distributed, through the mails or otherwise, to paid subscribers during the 12 months preceding the date shown above was: (This information is required by the act of June 11, 1960 to be included in all statements regardless of frequency of issue.) 725.

John Frederick Dorman

Sworn to and subscribed before me this 14th day of September, 1960

Edwin Hoffman

[Seal]   My commission expires Nov. 30, 1962

The Editor is solely responsible for the general policies, printing, distribution and sale of this periodical. Neither the Editor nor The Virginia Genealogist assumes responsibility for errors of fact or opinion expressed by contributors.

The Virginia Genealogist will publish source material and accounts of the early generations of families of Virginia and West Virginia. Manuscripts which are submitted should be of general interest and thoroughly documented and should be accompanied by return postage.

Of the 725 subscribers at the end of 1960, 74 percent have volumes 1-4, 5 percent have volumes 2-4, 8 percent have volumes 3-4, and 13 percent have only volume 4, according to the publisher's records. The total number of subscribers has remained about the same at the end of each year, but about 150 persons drop their subscription each year and new subscribers must be obtained to take their place if the magazine is to continue successful operation.

OHIO COUNTY

LEGISLATIVE PETITIONS

The following five petitions are the earliest from Ohio County now preserved at the Virginia State Library. Among the names appended to the petitions are to be found some of the first settlers of this region along the banks of the Ohio River.

1785, December 10. Petition of Daniel Leet, one of the inhabitants late of the County of Ohio, stating that he had an appointment in 1776 as Quarter Master in the 13th Virginia Regiment and after about one year's service was preferred to Pay Master and continued nearly two years until the staff of the Army was reduced and taken from the Line. He was appointed Brigade Major to General McIntosh on the Western Expedition, at the close of which his service as a Virginia officer ended. He continued on the frontier, a volunteer at his own expence in every emergency and expedition against the Indians from Fort Pitt and its dependencies (save that of the Moravians) and was major to Col. Crawford at his defeat on the Sandusky Plains. He asks for an allowance of land equal to those of his rank.

29 November 1784. Dorsey Pentecost, John Canoy [Candy?] and Van Swearingen at Washington Co., Pa., certify the facts set forth in the petition are just and true.

Petition found reasonable and bounty land allowed him as a major.

1787, October 26. Petitioners have labored under great difficulties ever since 1776 by the incursions of the Indians. Some of them and others in the county are possessed of land that is now subject to tax which they cannot enjoy (nay, dare not go to see unless in the winter) yet they must pay their proportionable part of the public tax without defence, without trade or any humane means to get money. They ask that they may pay tax in hemp, flour or tobacco, that a warehouse be built on the Ohio River and inspectors appointed to receive the same, and that provisions furnished the militia may be allowed in their tax.

William Boggs	John Ross
Ezekel Boogs	James Caldwell
Francis Boogs	Saml. Caldwell
Alexander Boogs	Jas. Caldwell Junr.
Willm. McWilliams	David Jolly Junr.
Ebenezer Zane	John Jolly
Joseph Mc hendry	James McConnell
Isaac Martin	Hugh McConnell

James McConnell
David Jolly
John McConnell
Henry Jolly
Stephen Parr
Nathan Parr
John Jolly
Henry Baker
Lewis Grindstaff
Luis Bonet [?]
John McBride
Phillap Main [?]
Abraham Mercer
Henry Winters
Jacob Rose
Daniel Main [?]
John Mills
Moses Shepherd
Wm. Shepherd
Jno. Howell
David Howell
Henry Pechtall
John Howell Jur.
Aaron Howell
Jno. Grist
Jakem [?] Colman
Alexander Scott
Thomas Mamson
Moses Williamson
Moses Williamson Junr.
James Fugat
Jaramiah Williamson
George Beller
Edward Ritchson
Robert Griffin
Alexr. McDowel
John Williamson
Scott Travis
Willm. Travase
Saml. Michall
Willm. Myres
John Blackburn
James McMeekin
John Myres
Henry Cleyback
Danl. Gifin
Thomas Smith
William Chapman
John Williamson of John
William McMetchen
Henry Smith
James Smith
Am. McColloch
Ignatius Ogdin
John Boogs
James Bogs
David Barr
John Cross
Benjamin Cross
John Williams
Henry Clark
James Clark
Archibald Carr
Richard Hardesty

1787, October 29. Robt. Woods petitions for establishment of a ferry from the land whereon he now lives across the Ohio River to the northwest side thereof. There is no ferry near his place and the public road leading down through the County of Ohio by the Court House strikes the river on his land. The following join in the petition:

George McColloch
Levi Mills
Zach Bigg
James Dik
Andw. Woods
John Mitchell
John Connell
Shadrk. Williams
Jac. Sprigg
Reuben Farming
Saml. Glass
William May
Arnod. Evins
James Nevitt
Aaron Willson
Charles Hedges
James Hally
Jno. Liske
Joseph Nully
John Mc intyer
John Greer
James Caldwell

OHIO COUNTY LEGISLATIVE PETITIONS 5

    John Finley
    John Caldwell
    Jacob Paull
    Robt. McClure
    Richd. Spears
    Saml. McColloch
    Samuel Wilson
    Joseph McHenry
    Alexanr. Millhier

    John Bukey
    Joseph Moorhead
    James Black [?]
    George Stricker
    Benr. Uline
    James Mitthall [?]
    Moses Chapline
    John Atkison

1787, November 6. Petition of Reuben Foreman and Providence Mounts. In Dec. 1776 an election was held in the County of Ohio for the purpose of choosing a seat of justice, when it appeared by a majority of 28 votes that the place then known by the name of Blacks Cabbins but now by the name of West Liberty was the most centerical and convenient place. The petitioners in 1786 laid out West Liberty with convenient streets and alleys upon a tract of land granted to Reuben Foreman and Hannah Vanmater. They ask the Legislature to establish the town. The following ask the same:

    [ ]ae Sprigg
    Isaac Meek
    Chas. Wells
    John Mitchel
    James Caldwell
    Wm. Griffith
    Van Swearingen
    Moses Chapline
    George McColloch
    John Caldvill
    William Pearc
    Andrew Fouts
    Silas Hedges
    Charles Hedges
    Benjn. Davis
    James Mitchel [?]
    Alexr. Fulton
    George Stricker
    Jeremiah Williams
    Jonah Seaman
    Levi Mills

    Andw. Woods
    John McColloch
    Jacob Paul
    James MColloch [?]
    Abraham Wells
    Jos. [?] Miller
    John Gree[r?]
    John Connell
    Aaron Wells
    David Chambers
    John Vanmeter
    John Bucky
    Robt. McClure
    Allen Metcalf
    John Francis
    Charles Tiberghier [?]
    William Harrison
    John Anson
    Wm. McKinly
    Joseph Biggs

1789, November 16. Petition of John Henderson of Ohio County. He is on his way to Richmond for the purpose of raising money in discharge of sundry orders drawn by the Auditor of Public Accounts on the Treasurer of the State for services performed by the scouts and rangers in said county, which came into his hands in consideration of his furnishing them with sundry necessary supplies in order to enable them to perform their duty. On 28 April last he put up at the house of Richard Taylor, tavern keeper in Fredericksburg, when he was robbed of his saddle bags containing the orders, sundry military and other certificates and about 65 pounds in cash. Mrs. Taylor, the wife of Richard Taylor, saw William Clarke go out of the house with the saddle bags in his possession and directed some of her servants to pursue him, but Clarke went down the river bank and joined company with another man who called himself Captain Hall and they went off together. The petitioner went very early the following morning to Clarke's lodgings and apprehended him upon a warrant from a magistrate. Clarke was convicted of robbery at the ensuing District Court. Hall, calling himself Evans, was apprehended in Hanover County. In his possession was between 30 and 40 pounds cash, a pinchbeck watch and a gold ring. He asks for a law authorizing the Auditor of Public Accounts to issue duplicates of the orders.

MIDDLESEX COUNTY, VIRGINIA

WILLS, 1713-1734

(Continued from V. 4, p. 152)

Pages 267-68. Will of William Daniell, dated 27 Feb. 1722.

Unto my son Willm. Daniell my plantation with the track of land I live on, and for want of heirs to Eliz., Sarah, Mary, Ann and Agatha Daniell my daughters.

Unto my son Willm. Daniell my brandy still and a table and carpitt belonging to it.

Unto my sons Mosely, John, Robeart, Obadiah Daniell all my track of Jemeco land equally, and for want of heirs to my daughters.

Unto my daughter Elizt. Daniell a young Negro boy Ben.

Unto my daughter Sarah Daniell my feather bed that I lye upon with all the furniture and L 3 sterling to buy her a suit of cloths.

Unto Mosely and John Daniell a feather bead that stands in the closit with the furniture.

Unto Elizt., Mary, Ann and Agatha Daniell two feather beds and furniture, the one a trundel bed, the other at Jemeco.

Unto Mosely, John, Robeart and Obadiah Daniel a Negro woman called Katte.

My three youngest daughters Mary, Ann and Agatha Daniell live at Jemeco upon their brothers' plantations till they are marry'd and their Negro wench that their unkle John Moseley byes for them to have ground to work upon to make cropes for their maintenance with the help of their brother.

All the rest of my whole personal estate to be equally divided among my seven children Mosely, John, Robeart, Obadiah, Mary, Ann and Agatha Daniell.

None of my estate be appraised but my children have it to live upon.

My sons William, John, Robeart and Obadiah Daniell executors.

Will Daniell

Wit: David (D) George, John George, Ann (A) Gardner.

2 July 1723. Produced by Wm. Daniel. Proved by the witnesses.

Pages 268-69. Will of Benj. Taylor, dated 4 June 1723.

Unto Jonathan Herring all my wearing cloths made and unmade, and all my goods, my horse, bridle and saddle, and my bed cloths, 50 shillings current money to be paid by Coll. Henry Armestead and halfe a barrell Indian corne.

Residue unto Collonell Henry Armsteed.

Collo. Henry Armsteed executor.

2 July 1723. Verbal will produced in Court by Coll. Henry Armsteed. Proved by George Hardin and Richard Steevens.

Page 269. Charles Lee. Additional inventory. 2 April 1723. Consists of tobacco due in 1721 from Thomas Kidd, Senr., Thomas Kidd Junr., Nicholas Bristow, John Ridd, William Norcutt, Wm. Daniell Senr., Samson Betts and Thomas Chaney. Signed by Dorothy Lee. Admitted to record 2 April 1723.

Page 269. Mattw. Crank. Estate account. Payments made to Mr. John Robinson, James Walker (sheriff), Jos. Hardee, Dr. Walford, Mr. Stanard. Signed by Eliza Gardner and Wm. (W) Gardner. Produced in Court 4 April 1724 by Wm. Gardner and Anne [sic] his wife, executrix.

Pages 270-71. Will of William Daniel in the County of Middx. and parish of Christ Church, being sick and weak, dated 16 Aug. 1723.

To my son James Daniel all my land lying on the Bryary Swamp containing 150 acres with two plantations thereon.

To my son James Daniel one Negro man Jack and one brandy still and worme and tub as likewise one table and carpett, one mare colt, one small ovall table.

Unto my eldest daughter Jeane one Negro girl Nan, one small oval table.

To my youngest daughter Constant Daniel one young Negro girle Kate, one new feather bed tick.

To my three child James Daniell, Jane Daniel and Constant Daniel one Negro wench Judy equally.

My whole estate may be kept upon my said plantation to be lookt after for the maintenance of my three children.

My loveing cousin Robert Daniel executor. He shall have the management of James Daniel and Constant Daniel till they shall come to age and the other to be with Mr. Daniel till she shall come to the age of 18 years.

My estate shall be brought to no appraisement.

My youngest children have schooling.
                                        William Daniel
Wit: Garrett Daniel, Elizabeth Daniel, Jos. Haulee.
3 Dec. 1723. Proved by the witnesses.

Pages 271-73. Robert Perrett. Inventory. Made pursuant to order of 3 Sept. 1723. No total valuation. Signed by Catharine Perrott, admx. Appraised by Robt. (R) George, Wil Segar, Thos. (T) Chancy. Admitted to record 3 Dec. 1723.

Page 273. Will of John Mayo, weake in body and sick, dated 3 Feb. 1723.
All my whole estate unto my dear and loving wife only I except ₤ 20 current cash to be given to put such poare children to schoole so far as the ₤ 20 shall proceed as my executors shall think fitt, after my wife's decease if she cannot without prejudice pay it before.
If my wife marry my whole estate be equally divided into two parts, my loving wife to take her first choice, and the second to Ruth Rowe the dafter of Benjamin Rowe and Mary his wife being my wife's sister, when she arive to the full age of twenty one years.
If Ruth Rowe shall dye then equally between John Owin and William Owin his brother who are now both bound to me by indentures.
My wife exexetor. Mr. Mathew Kemp and Mr. Christopher Sutton to aide and direct and assist her.
                              John Mayo
Wit: Jos. Goare, William Owen.
7 April 1724. Ruth Mayo and Mathew Kemp produced this will in Court. Proved by the witnesses.

Page 274. Will of Chichester Curtis of the County of Middlesex being sick and weak in body, dated 6 Jan. 1723.
All my estate equally divided between my loving wife Mary and Augustine her son. If Augustine should dye without heires, to my brother Charles Curtis.
If my Negro wench Phillis should have any children, they to be equally divided.
The care of my son Augustine to my loving wife Mary and Mr. Richard Walker of Urbanna without their giving security.
My said son shall be put in possession of his share at the age of eighteen.
My loving wife and my good friend Mr. Richard Walker executors.
                          Chichester Curtis
Wit: Bar. Yates, Joh. Robinson, Avarilla (X) Curtis.
7 April 1724. Mary Curtis and Richard Walker presented this will in Court, Richard Walker refusing to stand executor. Proved by John Robinson, Esq., and Bartholomew Yates, Clk.

Pages 274-75. Chichester Curtis. Inventory. Appraised pursuant to order of 7 April 1724 by Stokley Towles, John Alldin and Samuel Batchelder who were sworn before Mr. John Price. Total valuation ₤ 101.0.8, including three Negroes valued at ₤ 85. Signed by Mary (X) Curtis, executor. [No entry of recording.]

Page 275. Elizabeth Ingram. Inventory. Appraised 2

May 1724 by Robt. George, Ed. Mickleburrough and John (J) Williams. Total valuation L 1.12.0. Signed by Jno. (J) Johnson. Admitted to record 5 May 1724.

Page 275. Will of Thomas Cheadle in the County of Middlesex and Parish of Christ Church, dated 19 Dec. 1720.
Unto my well beloved wife Frances Cheadle all my estate during her life. My wife Frances executtor.
One cow and calf to Robt. Cheadle after my death.
        Tho. Cheadell
Wit: Jos. Harden, Mary (X) Godbey, John (X) Guttrey.
2 June 1724. Proved by the witnesses.

Pages 275-76. Thos. Cheadle. Inventory. Estate not valued; includes two Negroes. Signed by Frances (X) Cheadle. Admitted to record 4 Aug. 1724.

Pages 276-77. Will of Patrick Kelly of the County of Middlesex, being sick and weak in body, dated 6 May 1724.
All my estate to be equally divided between my loving wife Kathrine Kelly and Thomas Hackett Junr. the son of Thomas Hackett, and James Murry son of David Murry of King William County.
My wife shall have my Negro girl Lewsey in her part of my estate.
My loving wife Kathrine Kelly and Thomas Hackett executors.
       Patrick (O) Kelly
Wit: John Alldin, Charles (X) Cooper.
4 Aug. 1724. Produced in Court by Thomas Hackett, Kathrine Kelly refusing to prove the said [will] or stand by the same. Proved by the witnesses.

Page 277. James Curtis Junr. Additional inventory. Signed by John Robinson and John Smith. Admitted to record 4 Aug. 1724.

Page 277. Abraham Trigg. Estate account. Signed by Henry Borck. Admitted to record 4 Aug. 1724.

Page 277. Partrick Kelley. Inventory. Appraised pursuant to order of 4 Aug. 1724 by Stokly Towles, Samuel Batchelder and Wm. Southwarth who were sworn before Mr. Price. Total valuation L 71.17.9. Signed by Thos. (T) Hackett. Admitted to record 1 Sept. 1724.

Page 278. Wm. Davis. Inventory. Appraised pursuant to order of 5 May 1724 by John Alldin, William (W) Southworth, Stokly Towles and Charles (X) Cooper who were sworn before Major Edwin Thacker. Total valuation L 99.18.7, including John Harris and his wife at L 2.10.0 and John Grange, servant, at ₤ 6. Signed by George Chowning, admr. Admitted to record 1 Sept. 1724.

Pages 279-80. Thomas Smith. Inventory. Estate not valued. Signed by Ann Smith and T. Waring. Ann Smith presented this inventory 3 Dec. 1723. Thomas Waring Gent. made oath to this inventory 7 April 1724.

Pages 280-81. Jno. Rowe. Inventory. 30 Aug. 1724. Appraised pursuant to order of 5 Aug. 1724 by Jacob Stiff, John Berry and John Davis. Total valuation ₤ 15.0.2. Signed by Tho. Read, admr. Admitted to record 6 Oct. 1724.

Pages 281-82. Eliza. Elliott. Inventory. Total valuation ₤ 52.18.7½, including receipts from or sales to Edward Couch, Aquila Sneling, William Tignal, Ann Sims, Edward Whitaker, Thos. Inichan [?], Augn. Smith, Sarah Larrance, Robert Taliafor, Capt. Bell, Sarah Hevens. Signed by Robt. Dudley. Admitted to record 3 Nov. 1724.

Page 282. Eliz. Elliott. Estate account. 26 Dec. 1718. Payments made to Jno. Roads, Richd. Esterby [Esterly?], James Walker, Jno. Walls, Phill. Potts, Tho. Inichan, Jno. Dudley, Thos. Read Junr., Wm. Stanard. Signed by Robt. Dudley 3 Nov. 1724. Admitted to record 3 9ber [Nov.] 1724.

Pages 282-83. Wm. Anderson. Inventory. 10 Dec. 1724. Appraised pursuant to order of 1 Dec. 1724 by Wm. Wood, John Alldin and Stokly Towles. Total valuation ₤ 71.18.0½, including one Negro valued at ₤ 20. Signed by Wm. Anderson, admr. Admitted to record 5 Jan. 1724 [1725].

Pages 283-84. Pinchback Hamerton. Inventory. Appraised pursuant to order of 1 Dec. 1724 by Thomas Montague, Tho. (T) Chuney, Wil Segar and Tho. Haselwood. Total valuation ₤ 22.15.3. Signed by Paul Thilman, admr. Admitted to record 2 Feb. 1724 [1725].
List of debts received by estate 25 March 1725 from John Wigglesworth, Robert Brown, William Gardiner, Richd. Curtis and John Moseley.

Page 284. Will of Ann Anderson of Xt. Church Psh. in the County of Middx., dated 27 April 1724.
For reasons best known to myself I deprive my son Wm. Anderson of any power in settling my goods and chattells, house and lott. Wm. Anderson receive from my executors one shilling. All claims he shall make otherwise to be invalid and of no force or effect.

To my grandson Harry Anderson (the son of Wm. Anderson) my house and lott in Urbanna. All my goods and chattles to be put to publick sale within the space of three months after my decease (excepting one trunk of linnen, 6 plates, two dishes, one porringer, one bason new pewter) and the value for the use of my grandson when he comes to the age of twenty and one. My son Wm. Anderson might have the use of my house and lott and the service of my Negro girl (if he keeps the house in good repair) till my grandson Harry Anderson comes to the age of twenty and one and then both house and lott and Negro girl with her increase be delivered to my grandson Harry Anderson.

To Wm. Linton (for making this my will and settling and ordering my accounts) a silver snuff box.

Upon the decease of my son Wm. Anderson, Sarah Anderson his wife (provided she lives unmarried) to have the use of my house and lot till my grandson Harry Anderson comes to the age of twenty and one, but should she marry the house and lott to be rented.

If in case my grandson should die, my son Wm. Anderson be made sold possessor. If it should please God to visit him and leave his wife Sarah, she shall then have possession. Upon her decease without heirs of the body of Wm. Anderson, I constitute Henry Robinson son to Collo. John Robinson Esqr. my lawful heir.

Appoint Xtopher Robinson and John Grimes Esqrs. executors.

Ann (X) Anderson

Wit: Wm. Linton, Robert Crawford, John Livingston.

1 Dec. 1724. Christopher Robinson and John Grymes, Esqrs., relinquished their executorship. Proved by Wm. Linton.

2 Feb. 1724 [1725]. Proved by Robert Crawford.

Page 285. John Mayo. Inventory. Includes five Negroes, not valued. Receipts from Mr. Augustin Smith, Robt. George Junr., Thos. Falkner, Mr. George Hardin and John Grymes Esqr.

Book debts not received: Mr. William Gordon, dec., Mr. Harry Beverly, Jonathan Johnson, Benja. Stratten, Wid: Mathew, James Hipkings, Mr. Armistead Churchhill, Jonathan Herrin, Angia Cumings' note of John Grymes Esqr.

Signed by William Owen, Ruth Owen and M. Kemp.

2 Feb. 1724 [1725]. William Owen, Ruth Owen and Matthew Kemp, Gent., presented this inventory.

Pages 285-86. Anne Anderson. Sale of estate. Ordered by Court 2 March 1724 [1725]. Christopher Robinson, Sheriff, reports that John Grymes Esqr. sold 145 pounds of bacon. Mr. Wm. Pain of Lancaster County stated

account due but not paid 30 sh. 6 d.
   I am creditably informed that the said Ann many years ago intermarryed with one Wm. Anderson who had children by her; that the said William being much indebted ran away from his creditors and his said wife and children and was so absent several years and the said Ann and her children all that time destitute of any releafe, provision or assistance from her said husband; that after some years the said Wm. did return but did never cohabit with the said Ann but they did ever after his first leaving as above live separate. Ann did during the said separation acquire some small estate by her own care and industry without any aid or assistance of her said husband. I am further informed that one William Anderson of this county, blacksmith, hath lately obtained administration of the before mentioned William Anderson's estate (the last mentioned Wm. Anderson being son to the before mentioned Wm. and Ann Anderson) by virtue of which administration he hath possessed himself of all the other estate of the said Ann acquire as is set forth above and the same doth detain claiming it as his father's estate.
                    Ch. Robinson

Page 286. Angelo Cummings. Inventory. Appraised pursuant to order of 1 Feb. [1725] by James Smith, Francis (F T) Timberlake, John Larke and Augustin Owen who were sworn before John Grymes. Presented by Eleanor the widow and administratrix. Total valuation ₤ 36.4.3½ except the crop of corn and stock of hoggs, both of which are applyed to the support of myself and children. Signed by Eleaner Cummings. Debts due the estate from Mr. James Skelton, Harry Wright, Edmond Ryan and Saml. Low. Admitted to record 5 April 1726.

Page 287. Will of John Gibbs of the County of Middlesex in the parish of Christ Church, dated 14 June 1725.
   Unto my dear and loving wife Mary Gibbes all my land.
   All the rest of my estate to my abovesaid loving wife during her natural life only one piece of coined silver called twelve pence to my grand daughter Elizabeth Roye. At her decease equally divided amongst my children.
   My estate be neither inventoryed nor appraised.
                    John (J) Gibbs
   Wit: Elizabeth (W) Walker, Anne (A) Finney, George Wortham.
   5 April 1726. Mary Gibbs presented the same in Court. Proved by the witnesses.

Pages 287-88. Will of Robert Williamson of the County of Middlesex, being sick and weak in body, dated 9 Aprill

1726.

To my daughter Martha Williamson my Negro woman Hanah. Also two cows and the bed whereon she usually lyes on and my loome and a four gallon pot and a pestle after the decease of my wife. And have a living on my land as long as she hath occasion and to work her Negro on. And if she like not to live with her brother Benjamin my will is that he build her a twenty foot dwelling house any where on my said land that she shall appoint.

To my son Benjamin all my land and plantation and my Negro man Jemey after the decease of my wife. And two cows and the bed where he usually lyes.

To my loving wife all my whole estate during her natural life. After the decease of my wife all the remainder of my estate that is not already given to my son and daughter Benjamin and Martha equally amongst all my children.

My loving wife and my son Benjamin Williamson executors.

        Robert Williamson

Wit: Jno. Lewis, Hennery Tugel Junr., William (W) Gutrie.

5 June 1726. Proved by the witnesses.

Page 288. Will of Benjamin Williamson of the County of Middlesex, being sick and weak in body, dated 23 April 1726.

Unto my sister Martha Williamson of Middlesex County all the land father Robert Williamson took up and pattented after he was marryed to my mother. All the land that was not my mother's before hir marriage to my sister Martha. Also my Negro man Jemey and the two cows that my father gave me by his will.

To my cuzen Robert Williamson son of my brother Robert Williamson all my other lands that was my mother's before hir marriage to my father.

Unto my sister Martha Williamson my young horse.

To my cuzen Elizabeth the wife of John Smith my riding mare and sadle and bridle.

All the remainder of my estate that was given me by the last will and testament of my father to my sister Frances the wife of John Alldin and my sister Martha Williamson and my cuzen Robert Williamson son of my brother Robert Williamson to be equally divided.

My brother John Alldin and my sister Martha Williamson executors.

        Benjamin Williamson

Wit: Henry Tugel, Jno. Lewis, Powell Stamper.

5 June 1726. Produced by John Alldin, Martha Williamson refusing to stand executrix. Proved by the witnesses.

MIDDLESEX COUNTY WILLS 15

Page 289. Will of Robert Blackley of the County of Middlesex, being sick and weake in body, undated.
Unto my eldest son Robert Blackley one shilling.
Unto my son George Blackley all my land and plantation.
All my personal estate equally amongst my loving wife Anne Blackley and the rest of my children to be equally divided.
My friend John Alldin and my son in law Thomas Cardwell executors.
                        Robert (O) Blackley
Wit: John Smith, Randolph (X) Rhodes, John Terbet.
2 Aug. 1726. Presented in Court by Ann Blackley, executrix within named [sic]. Proved by John Smith and Randolph Rhodes.

Pages 289-91. Robert Williamson. Inventory. 24 Aug. 1726. Appraised pursuant to order of 5 July 1726 (also naming Stokeley Towles) by Henry Thacker, Jno. Lewis and Henry Tugel. Total valuation Ł 123.7.7½, plus legacies at Ł 61.6.0, and including five Negroes valued at Ł 81. Signed by John Alldin, admr. Admitted to record 6 Sept. 1726.

Page 292. Wm. Robinson. Inventory. 5 Sept. 1726. Appraised by Joseph Goare, Wm. Owen and John Davis. Total valuation Ł 3.3.3. Signed by Alexr. Middleton, admr. Received of Thos. Tuke Ł 0.10.0. Admitted to record 6 Sept. 1726.

Pages 292-93. Robert Blackley. Inventory. Appraised pursuant to order of 2 Aug. 1726 by Marvell Moseley, John Moseley and George Chowning. Total valuation L 29.19.4. Signed by Ann (O) Blackley, admx. Admitted to record 6 Sept. 1726.

Page 293. John Denoon. Inventory. 6 Sept. 1726. Consists of receipts from Captain Blackburn, Robert Holderness, John Bery, Henry Wright and Thos. Tuke. Signed by Alexr. Middleton. Admitted to record 6 Sept. 1726.

Pages 293-94. At Court held 2 Aug. 1726 in the suit by attachment between Henry Fleet plt. and Theo. Bere deft. for Ł 12.10.- current money by account proved before Lancaster Court, the defendant not appearing judgement is granted to the plaintiff. Jacob Rice confest that he had 39 rheames of paper belonging to the said Theo. Bere. Ordered that the Sheriff deliver so much thereof to the plaintiff as will satisfy the judgement and costs. Executed by Jno. Curtis, SSMC. Admitted to record 6 Sept. 1726.

Page 294. Will of John Dodson alias John Hackney Dodson being very weake, dated 7 April 1726.

All my lands and tenaments to my two sisters Rachel and Mabell to be equally divided between them by my good friends John Rhoads and William Hackney.

All my personal estate unto my sister Rebekah Dodson.

My three sisters Rachel, Maball and Rebekah executors.

       John Dodson
Wit: John (X) Sanders, William (D) Baker.
4 Oct. 1726. Proved by the witnesses.

Pages 294-95. Will of John Price of the Parish of Christ Church in the County of Middlesex, being sick and weak in body, dated 24 Sept. 1726.

Unto my son Thomas Price my plantation and all my land in this county together with the mill and appurtenances thereto belonging.

Unto my sons Robert and James Price all my tract of land in Essex and King and Queen County to be equally divided.

Unto my other three sons John, Samuel and William Price each of them sixty pounds sterling to buy each of them a tract of land.

To my daughter Jane Price sixty pounds sterling after her marriage to be paid on demand with her other part of my estate.

As for all the rest of my estate, vizt. my Negros and moveable estate, equally divided amongst my six sons and one daughter. If any children should dye their parts of my moveable estate to be equally divided among the survivors.

My son Thos. Price shall have the care and tuition of my other children so long as he shall do well by them.

My son Thomas Price be of age at my death to act or do anything concerning my estate.

When the first of my children is qualified to demand their part of my estate, it shall be appraised and what it comes to a share paid each of them.

My son Thos. Price executor. In case he should die my son Robt. Price executor. My two friends Mr. Humphrey Jones and Mr. Oliver Segar my trustees.

To each of my trustees twenty shillings to buy them a ring.

       John Price
Wit: Thos. Greenwood, William Mountague Junr., Cathrine (E) Perrott.

20 Sept. 1726. Whereas it is mentioned that if any of my children should dye before they come to age then their part of my moveable estate to be equally divided amongst the survivors, my Negroes in such case shall go to the survivors in the same manner.

MIDDLESEX COUNTY WILLS 17

                    John Price
   Wit: Wm. Mountague junr., Cathrine (X) Perrott.
   6 Dec. [1726]. Will of John Price, Gent., produced
by Thomas Price executor. Proved by the witnesses.

Page 296. John Vivion. Additional inventory. 2 Dec.
1726. Total valuation [£ 17.4.0] and 2017 pounds of
tobacco, including £ 11.2.7 in England in Mr. J.
Bradley's hands. Signed by Eliza Vivion. Admitted to
record 6 Xber [Dec.] 1726.

Page 296. Will of John Berry in the County of Middlesex,
dated 6 Dec. 1726.
   Unto my two sons John and William Berry all my land
belonging to me in King and Queen County to be equally
divided.
   Unto my loving wife Mary Berry one Negro man Peter
during her naturall life and after her decease to my
daughter Ann Berry.
   Unto my sone John Berry Negro man Cuffy and boy Tom.
   Unto my son William Berry Negro woman Nan.
   Unto my daughter Ann Berry my two mulatto girls Betty
and Lucy. They shall remain with my wife for her use
and service untell my said daughter shall com to the
age of eighteen or day of marriage.
   My Negros given two my two sons John and William
Berry shall remain with my wife untill they shall each
come to the age of twenty one years.
   The remaining part of my estate shall remain in the
hands of my wife untell my children shall come to the
age as aforesaid and then to be equally divided between
my wife and my two sons John and William Berry and my
daughter Anne Berry.
   My loving wife Mary Berry executrix and my loving
friend Capt. Matthew Kemp executor.
                    John Berry
   Wit: William Burditt, Thomas (X) Jones, John (X)
Tilly.
   7 March 1726 [1727]. Produced in Court by Matthew
Kemp, Gent., surviving executor. Proved by William
Burditt and John Tilley.

                (To be continued)

AMELIA COUNTY, VIRGINIA

1800 TAX LIST

In the following entries, the first number after each name is that of the white males over age twenty-one, the second the number of horses owned, and the third and fourth, if given, the number of tithable slaves aged over sixteen and between twelve and sixteen.

District of George Baldwin

Anderson, James 1-1-3-1
Adams, Dancy, Senr.
  1-3-5-0
Ashurst, Jacob 1-9-6-0
Atkinson, Joshua 2-6-6-0
  1 2-wheel carriage
Anyan, George 1-0
Asselin, Francis 1-2-4-1
Adams, Dancy, Jur. 1-0
Atkinson, James 2-3-2-0
Anderson, Churchel
  2-3-5-0
Allen, Samuel 3-2-2-0
Anderson, Henry, Senr.
  2-2-3-1
Anderson, Ralph C. 1-1-2-2
Adams, Wily 1-1
Anderson, Henry, Jur. 1-5-15-3 2-wheel carriage
Adams, Frederick 1-0
Archer, John Jur. 1-5-2-2
Anderson, William 1-2-1-0
Archer, Peterfd. (Powhatan)
  2-14-22-2
Archer, Richard, Est.
  1-6-11-0
Archer, John Senr.
  3-12-21-5
Allen, Richard (F.C.)
  1-3-1-0
Allen, Hamblin 1-0
Aston, Samuel 1-0
Adams, William 1-0-1-0
Allen, William 2-4-6-0
Archer, William 1-2-2-0
Archer, Peterfield
  1-10-11-0
Anderson, Charles 1-0
Asselin, Sally 0-0-1-0
Avory, Hannah 1-3-9-1

Anderson, Francis, Est.
  1-16-29-4
Anderson, Claiborne
  1-13-14-2
Adams, David, Est. 0-1-1-1
Allen, Richd. (son of
  Danl.) 3-3-2-0 ordinary license
Allen, Daniel Senr.
  2-4-6-2
Avory, Joel 1-3-1-0
Anderson, Francis
  1-9-15-2
Bedel, Thomas 1-4-6-3
Bradshaw, John 1-1-2-0
Butler, William Senr.
  1-2-1-0
Boothe, Matthew 1-3-1-3
Bell, John 2-3-3-0
Bell, Claiborne 1-1
Bass, Edward 1-3-5-0
Bott, James 1-5-3-2
Bott, Miles 2-10-12-0
  1 stud horse
Barden, William 1-1
Booker, William M.
  2-12-16-1
Bevil, Claiborne 1-2-3-0
Burton, William 1-3-2-2
Booker, Efford, Est.
  0-3-11-5
Broaddus, Richard 1-8-3-1
Butler, Isaac 1-1
Berry, Peter 2-9-7-0
Berry, Thomas 1-1
Burton, Samuel 1-0-1-0
  1 stud horse
Booker, Davis 1-1-1-1
Bass, Alexander 1-1
Brian, Banister 2-2-1-0

AMELIA COUNTY 1800 TAX LIST

Booker, Pink D.   1-4-4-1
Bradley, James A.
   0-15-22-3
Bentley, Efford   1-7-11-4
   4-wheel phaeton or stage
   wagon
Bass, John   1-3-5-1
Broadway, Thomas   3-3-1-0
Brown, Bennet   1-14-22-3
   4-wheel coach or chariot
Booker, Daniel   1-4-8-3
Bass, Mary (Genito)
   0-3-8-3
Bass, Edward, Est.   0-11-
   21-4   4-wheel coach or
   chariot
Bracket, Ben, Est.
   2-5-6-0
Bentley, William   0-7-9-1
Booker, John   3-11-17-5
Broadfoot, Charles
   1-5-11-2
Baugh, William   1-0
Belcher, Thomas   2-2
Belcher, John   1-1
Bevil, Joel   1-2-3-0
Bevil, Susanah   2-2-2-1
Burton, Allen   1-3-2-0
Brumskil, John   1-2-14-4
Booker, Richerson   0-8-10-3
Booker, Parham   1-8-13-0
Blankinship, Thomas   1-0
Booker, Sarah   0-5-6-1
Boothe, John, Est.   0-2-4-1
Butler, Zachariah   1-2
Boothe, Thomas   1-0
Bass, Mary (H)   0-2-6-1
Brackett, Ludwell
   2-8-14-5
Brooking, Vivion   5-13-34-3
Brooking, William   1-1-2-2
Bolling, Thomas T.
   1-15-19-2
Bevil, Lucy   0-1-1-0
Bowles, Henry   1-2
Burton, Abel   1-4-7-1
Burton, Abraham   1-1
Burton, John   2-1
Burton, Peter   1-0
Brawton, John   1-0
Bradshaw, William   1-0-1-0

Bottom, John   1-7-6-0
   2-wheel chair
Bottom, William, Est.
   0-0-4-0
Bottom, Lydda   0-2-5-1
Baldwin, George   2-4-5-0
Baldwin, John   1-1
Baldwin, William A.   1-1
Baldwin, George W.   1-1
Booker, John E.   1-0-0-1
Claybrook, Mary   0-1-1-0
Claybrook, Lucia   0-1-1-0
Claybrook, Samuel   1-0
Craddock, Claiborne
   1-2-3-0
Coleman, Daniel   3-4-5-1
Clay, David   1-3-4-0
Chapman, Benjamin   1-5-3-1
Clayton, Henry   1-2-2-1
Clay, Edward   1-0
Crenshaw, Antho., Est.
   0-4-4-0
Chandler, Martin   2-4-3-0
Chappell, Abner   2-4-2-0
Coleman, Archer   2-4-4-0
Cox, George   0-5-15-2
Craddock, James   1-3-2-0
Craddock, Wm. C., Est.
   2-5-5-5-
Craddock, Charles   3-5-6-2
Do for Mary Jeter   0-3-7-0
Chappell, John   1-3-6-1
Craddock, Asa C.   1-3-3-0
Chaffin, Joshua   2-7-5-2
Crowder, John M.   1-3-4-0
Chapman, William   1-3-3-0
Compton, Jeremiah   2-1-1-0
Cousins, Elizabeth   0-5-6-1
Cousins, John C.   1-1-2-0
Cliborne, Leonard   1-2-1-0
Cousins, John (Carpt.)
   2-4-5-2
Clark, Benjamin   1-0-0-1
Coleman, Burwill   1-3-6-1
Chapman, John   2-3-4-1
Clements, Joseph   1-1-1-0
Clay, Thomas   1-1-1-0
Clements, Isham   2-6-8-2
Carpenter, Benjamin Senr.
   1-0
Chappell, Robert   1-2-5-0

Craddock, Jean H. 0-3-4-0
Coleman, Solomon 1-2
Coverley, Thomas 1-2-1-1
Cassels, William 1-11-12-3
  2-wheel chair
Craddock, Samuel 1-0
Crittenton, John 1-5-4-1
Coleman, Robert 3-2
Coleman, Abraham, Est.
  1-3-6-0
Crowder, Herod T. 1-2-0-1
Coleman, William 1-3-2-0
Clements, John 1-7-9-1
Coleman, Ebenezer 1-3-2-3
Clay, Charles 1-2-1-0
Coleman, Joseph 1-1-1-0
Cobbs, John C., Est.
  1-6-12-0
Cobbs, Thomas M. 1-2-2-0
Cobbs, John C. 1-0
Clements, William 1-1-1-0
Colley, Thomas 3-7-2-0
Clay, Jesse 2-5-8-0
Crowder, William 1-8-11-2
Cox, Ann 2-7-12-1
Clough, Richard, Est.
  0-7-11-1
Craddock, Richard C. 1-0
Chappell, Bob (F.N.) 1-2
Coleman, Jesse 2-6-9-3
Cousins, John Jur. 1-2-6-1
Cousins, Richard 1-3-4-1
Cardwell, Richard 2-5-5-1
Carrel (F.N.) 1-0
Craddock, Robert 1-0
Cooper, John L. 1-8-12-3
  2-wheel chair
Clark, Lewis 1-0
Cocke, Stephen, Est.
  2-22-45-9
Deaton, Levy, Est. 1-3-2-0
David, Thomas 1-1
Dunnavant, Philip Jur.
  1-4-3-1
Dunnavant, Samuel 1-1
Dunnavant, Hodges 1-5-8-1
Dunnavant, Thomas 1-2
Dier, Thomas 2-3
Dunnavant, Philip Senr.
  1-4-3-1
Dunnavant, Abner 1-1-2-1

Delany, David 1-0
Deaton, John 1-0
Dalby, John A. 1-3-2-0
Deaton, George 1-1
Durham, Thomas 1-0
Dearen, William 2-2-1-0
Dier, Daniel 1-2
Dickey, Robert 1-1
Dier, William 1-5-1-0
Daniel, Stephen 1-0-3-0
Deaton, James 1-0
Dowdy, Benjamin 2-0
Drake, Boswell 1-3-1-0
Drake, James 1-1
Drake, William 1-0
Dunnavant, Frederick 1-0
Dupriest, Nathan 1-0-1-0
Eggleston, Edward 2-7-9-0
Elmore, Thomas 1-4-5-3
Ellis, James 1-1
Easter, Matthew 1-1-1-1
Ellis, John 1-0
Eanes, Henry Senr. 1-6-5-2
Edmunds, John 1-2-1-0
Eanes, Henry Jur. 1-0
Eggleston, William T.
  1-2-1-0
Eggleston, Richard, Est.
  1-17-28-1
Eppes, John 2-3-3-1
Edmunds, William 1-0
Eggleston, Joseph 1-27-
  49-6 4-wheel coach or
  chariot
Ellis, Thomas 1-0-1-0
Foster, Richard (Carpt.)
  1-2-2-0
Foster, William (N.P.) 1-4
Foster, Robert 1-0
Foster, John 2-6-7-0
Farley, William (D.C.)
  1-4-2-1
Ford, Waller 1-1-1-0
Farley, Matthew 2-11-9-2
Finney, William 1-7-6-0
Finney, Nancy 0-3-6-1
Friend, William 0-5-10-2
Foster, Joel 1-1
Farmer, Charles 2-1-3-0
Foster, Richard Senr.
  1-9-6-0

AMELIA COUNTY 1800 TAX LIST

Freeman, Will (S.M.) 1-0
Farley, Peter Senr. 1-1-5-0
Ferguson, William 1-0
Foster, Claiborne 1-3-3-0
Fisher, William 1-0
Foster, Booker 2-6-4-1
Farley, Stephen 1-4-3-2
Farley, William (F.C.) 1-4-3-0
Foster, Larkin 1-2-1-1
Foster, Anthony 2-3-1-1
Forrest, Josiah 1-3-3-1
Farrer, Samuel 1-6-8-0
Ferguson, Robert 1-0
Ford, Samuel 1-4-7-1
Featherston, Charles 1-6-16-4
Farley, Peter Jur. 1-1
Ford, John 1-4-7-2
Ferguson, Joseph 1-2
Ford, Hezekiah 1-3-3-1
Fagg, William, Est. 0-2-1-0
Faris, William 2-3-3-0
Fleming, Robert 1-1
Green, William 1-4-7-1
Gibbs, Miles 1-0
Gibbs, William 3-4-6-3
Gill, John 2-6-5-3
Gill, James 1-3-3-0
Goodwyn, Solomon 2-2-1-0
Green, Thomas 3-8-8-2
Goodwyn, Francis 1-1
Goodwyn, Jesse 3-0
Gordon, Charles, Est. 0-3-2-0
Green, Abraham 2-14-29-9
 4-wheel coach or chariot
 2-wheel chair
Gibbs, Thomas 0-1-1-0
Green, Caleb 1-0
Gilliam, William 1-7-12-1
Gregory, William 1-4-6-5
Grant, William 1-0-0-1
Goode, Mary 1-4-5-0
Giles, William B. 1-17-40-6 4-wheel coach or chariot; 2-wheel chair
Green, John 1-2-1-0
Hendrick, John Jur. 1-2-1-0

Holt, Jesse 2-2-2-0
Holt, William 1-0
Howell, Spencer 1-0
Henderson, James 1-4-7-0
Hewlings, Jacob W. 1-0
Hill, James (overseer) 1-0
Hall, Bolling 1-0
Hudgings, Burwell 1-0
Hamm, John 1-1-1-0
Hannah, Salley 0-6-3-3
Hudson, William 1-1
Holt, Sarah 0-2-5-0
Harris, Benjamin, Est. 0-2-3-0
Hendrick, James 1-0
Hendrick, Benjamin 1-4-5-0
Hendrick, Zach. 2-2-1-0
Hughs, Blackburn 1-3-7-4
Hamm, William 2-3-1-1
Hughs, John 2-4-5-1
Hilsman, Jose 1-2-1-0
Hall, John 1-1
Hood, Allen 1-0
Harrison, Nathaniel 2-12-13-2
Hendrick, Garland 1-2-3-1
Hall, Instant 1-2-4-0
Hern, Peter (F.N.) 1-0
Hamlin, William B. 2-8-16-3
Harrison, Edmund 4-20-49-6
 4-wheel coach or chariot
 2-wheel chair
Harrison, William 1-1
Hudson, William C. 2-6-11-2
Harper, John Senr. 3-5-6-4
Harper, John Jur. 1-3
Hill, James 2-15-17-5
 4-wheel coach or chariot
Holloway, John 1-0
Hill, John (overseer) 1-0
Hudson, Francis E. 1-0-5-0
Hayes, James 2-11-20-2
 2-wheel chair
Hood, Edward 1-3-6-0
Hood, Abraham Jur. 1-1
Hudson, Leweling 1-2-3-2
Hardaway, Daniel 1-15-27-5
 4-wheel coach or chariot
Hughs, Nancy 0-2-9-0

Hubbard, Christopher 1-1
Hilsman, James 1-1
Howel, John 2-3-1-0
Hood, John 1-0
Holt, Richard 1-3-2-2
Holt, John 1-1
Hughs, Benjamin 1-0
Hurt, Anderson 1-1-2-0
Hutcherson, Charles
 1-3-2-0
Hundley, Joshua 1-2
Hilton, Moses (F.N.) 1-2
Hilton, Matt (F.N.) 1-0
Hawkins, David, Est.
 0-2-3-0
Hastins, Clayton 1-1-1-0
Hastins, Elizabeth 1-2
Hood, Abraham Senr. 1-2
Hood, Joshua 1-0
Hood, Solomon 1-1
Hall, Thomas 1-1-3-0
Hall, William 1-1-1-0
Harrison, William (W.C.)
 1-3-4-3
Howlett, William 1-5-11-4
Hodgson, Richard 1-1-1-1
 2-wheel chair
Johnson, Richard Jur. 1-2
Johnson, Bennet 2-3-2-0
Jackson, Abel 1-1-1-0
Jones, Richard (W.C.)
 1-1-5-2
Jeter, John 1-4-4-0
Johnson, Allen 2-3-5-1
Jeter, Allen 1-6-3-1
Jackson, Samuel A. 1-4-5-0
Jeter, Rodofil 1-3-3-2
Jones, Henry W. 1-1
Free Tom (Jones) 1-2-3-0
Free Joe (R. Nassers) 1-2
Jones, Samuel 1-1-3-0
Johnson, James Jur.
 1-1-2-0
Free Jim (Johnson's) 1-0
Jolly, Henry 1-0-3-0
Jeter, Ambrose 1-8-4-4
Jones, William (F.C.)
 1-5-8-1
Johnson, Thomas 1-3-2-0
Jackson, Francis 1-6-4-1
Jones, Francis 2-3-7-2

Jones, Peter (Sher.)
 2-9-8-2
Johnson, James Senr. 2-4-4-0 ordinary license
Jones, Littleberry H.
 1-11-12-2
Jones, Agnes 0-1-1-1
Jones, John, Jr. 1-3-4-1
Jones, John, Senr.
 2-9-14-2
Jones, David C. 1-3-10-2
Free John (Hughes) 2-3
Jones, Alexander 1-15-35-7
 2-wheel chair   1 stud
 horse
Free Jemmy (J. Booker)
 1-1-1-0
Jones, Colo. John 2-7-21-0
 2-wheel chair
Jones, Susanah, Est.
 1-5-9-1
Jackson, Wily (hatter) 1-0
Jones, George 1-0
Jones, Archer 1-16-34-5
Free Jemmy (Prides) 1-1-2-0
Jolly, Susanah 0-1-1-0
Jones, Peter (W.C.)
 1-7-10-1
Johnson, Richard Senr.
 2-6-5-1
Johnson, Robert 1-2
Jones, Richard (B) 2-13-14-4 4-wheel coach or
 chariot
Jones, Robert 1-10-28-5
 4-wheel coach or chariot
Jefferson, John G. 1-1
Jones, William (D.C.)
 2-9-25-7
Kerr, John 1-2-0-1
Kersy, Edward 1-1
Kid, George, Est. 2-3
Kid, George 1-1-1-0
Locket, James 1-1
Ligon, Richard 1-5-8-0
League, James 0-1
Lovern, Moses 2-2
Lovern, James 1-2
Leigh, Zachariah G.
 1-2-0-2
Locket, John 1-1

AMELIA COUNTY 1800 TAX LIST

Locket, Josiah 1-2
Locket, Jacob 1-0
Ligon, Thomas (son of Wm.)
   1-1
Ligon, Joseph 1-2-2-1
Ligon, William 2-6-3-2
Lacy, John 1-1
Leath, Jesse 1-4-9-2
   2-wheel chair
Lester, Riland 1-1-0-1
Leslie, Alexander 1-2
Litle, Harmon 1-1
Ligon, Thomas Senr.
   3-12-9-2
Mitchell, John 1-4-3-1
Marshall, John 1-3-4-1
Mottley, Joseph 1-1
Miller, Dabny 1-4-5-1
McClarren, John 2-3-1-0
Meglason, James 2-5-6-1
Meglason, Thomas W. 1-1
Meglason, William 1-2-2-1
Marshall, William 1-0
McCan, John 1-0
Mann, Joel 1-2-5-1
Mayes, Garner 1-1
Maddera, John 1-1-1-0
   2-wheel chair
Munford, Mary 1-0-4-2
Marshall, Abraham
   1-11-13-1
Mann, Field 3-8-10-2
Moor, Edward 1-0
Meadors, Hezekiah 1-1
Meadors, Benja., Est.
   1-4-4-0
Morris, Moses, Senr.
   2-3-5-0
Morris, William 1-0
Morris, Walter 1-1
Meadors, Ambrose C. 1-1
Meadors, Isaac 1-1
Morris, Zachariah Senr.
   3-6-6-1
Morris, John 2-5-7-0
Morris, Tabitha 0-1-2-1
Mann, Abner 1-0
McNeil, Hector 1-7-9-2
Marshall, Robert 2-8-11-2
   4-wheel coach or chariot
Morgin, Simon 4-4-6-1

Morgin, William Senr.
   2-4-3-0
Morgin, John 3-6-9-0
   2-wheel chair
Meriweathers, William
   1-8-8-2   4-wheel coach
   or chariot
Mead, David 1-5-12-0
   2-wheel chair
Morris, Silvanus Jur.
   1-0-0-1
Mead, Everard 1-12-21-3
   2-wheel chair 4-wheel
   coach or chariot
Murray, William 1-16-23-9
   2-wheel chair 4-wheel
   coach or chariot
Morris, Isaac 1-3-1-0
Mann, William 1-7-5-1
Mann, Cain 1-1-6-1
Mann, Mary 0-3-5-2
McDowel, John 1-1
Mann, Daniel 1-3-3-0
Morton, Edmund 1-1-0-1
Martin, William 1-3-2-0
Free Mark (Hught[?]) 2-1
Morgin, William Jur.
   1-4-4-1
Morgin, Martha 0-2-2-0
Mitchell, James C. 1-1-2-2
McVea, Christopher 1-0-1-0
Mann, Abel 1-1
More, Carter 2-5-5-1
Mills, Henry 1-2
Mottley, John Senr.
   1-5-6-1
Meadors, Anderson 1-1
Maxy, David 1-0
Mottley, John Jur. 1-4-6-2
Neil, Archer 1-3-4-1
Nevils, Levy 2-wheel chair
Noble, Joshua 1-1
Noble, John 1-4-3-2
Noble, Joseph 1-3-2-0
Noble, Austin 1-1
Neil, John 2-4-6-0
Newman, Rice 2-5-9-2
Newman, John 1-4-2-0
Newby, Jesse 1-3-3-0
Noble, Stephen 1-2-4-0
Overton, Moses 1-6-5-1

Overton, Richard 1-1
Overstreet, Benoni 1-3-2-1
Ogilby, Richard, Est.
 1-9-8-0 2-wheel chair
Overton, Mary 0-2-5-0
Osborne, John 1-0
Osborne, Joseph 1-13-16-1
Osborne, Abner 0-3-7-1
Old, Winney 0-5-7-1
 2-wheel chair
Perkinson, Thomas 1-9-8-0
 2-wheel chair
Pollard, Zachariah 1-1-0-1
Pollard, Leah 1-3-4-2
Pride, Francis 1-1
Pride, John Senr. 1-1
Pride, Thomas 1-5-6-4
Ponton, John 1-2
Page, Francis 1-0
Pollard, Thomas Jur.
 1-2-2-0
Pollard, Thomas Senr.
 0-3-4-0
Pollard, John Senr. 1-1
Pollard, Ambrose 1-1-1-1
Powell, William 1-3-8-0
Perin, Isaac 1-2
Paulett, Thomas 1-3-2-0
Pollard, Thomas (son of
 Joe) 1-2-2-0
Ponton, Francis 1-3-2-1
 ordinary license
Pitchford, John 2-1
Powell, Robert 1-1
Perkinson, John Senr. 2-3
Perkinson, Claiborne 1-0
Perkinson, John Jur. 1-1
Perkinson, Elizabeth (B
 Bridge) 1-2-1-0
Pilkinton, William 1-0
Perkinson, Isham 2-2
Perkinson, Archer 1-2
Pride, Elizabeth 1-4-6-3
Pride, John Jur. 1-3
Phillips, Lucy 0-6-5-2
Powell, Winney 0-1-5-0
Powell, Richard 1-1-1-0
Powell, John 1-2-1-1
Powell, Abraham 1-3-1-1
Pollard, George 1-2-4-1
Pollard, John Jur. 1-1

Perkinson, Elizabeth (W.C.)
 0-0-1-0
Parsons, Major 1-0
Parton, William 1-0
Quarles, Isaac 0-4-7-1
Robertson, Nathan 1-3-2-0
Rison, John 1-0
Roberts, John 1-0
Robertson, William Jur.
 1-2-2-3
Robertson, John Jur.
 1-1-2-1
Roberts, Jacob 1-6-5-1
Raiborne, George 1-3-1-0
Royall, John Jur. 1-6-9-0
Rucker, Joshua 1-2-1-0
Rucker, Reubin 1-0
Rucker, Pleasant 1-0
Risin, Elery 2-4-1-1
Robertson, Elizabeth
 0-4-8-0
Roberts, Alexander 1-1
Reins, William 1-1-1-0
Rogers, William, Est.
 0-2-3-0
Rucker, Lemuel 1-0
Rogers, William 1-2-2-1
Rucker, Brice 1-0
Robertson, James (G.J.)
 1-7-10-1 4-wheel coach
 or chariot
Roach, John 1-1
Rowlet, Thomas 1-3-2-2
Robertson, George, Est.
 0-6-12-2
Rowlet, George 1-5-4-1
Robertson, George 2-6-7-0
Robertson, Bridge 3-3
Robertson, John Senr.
 1-11-17-6
Risin, Richard 1-0
Robertson, James (K)
 2-7-16-5
Royall, Joseph, Est.
 1-10-14-3
Royall, John Senr. 2-8-
 25-4 2-wheel chair
Robertson, John (son of
 Matt) 1-4-2-1
Robertson, William Senr.
 1-3-2-1

AMELIA COUNTY 1800 TAX LIST

Robertson, John A. 2-9-13-4 4-wheel phaeton or stage waggon
Randolph, Thomas 1-6-9-0
Roach, Elizabeth 1-2-1-0
Robertson, Peter 1-0-1-0
Roach, Joseph 1-0
Roberts, Pleasant 3-17-12-4 4-wheel coach or chariot
Sudberry, John Senr. 1-2-2-0
Sudberry, John Jur. 1-2
Southall, Henry H. 1-5-2-0
Simmons, Vinson 1-1
Scott, Thomas 2-2-2-0
Free Sam (Negro) 1-2
Scott, Thompson 1-3-2-2
Smith, John 1-0
Stott, James 1-4-3-1
Stott, Rawleigh 1-3-1-0
Smithey, Joshua 1-4-3-1
Smithey, John 1-0
Smith, Sterling 1-0
Seay, Dudley 1-2-0-1
Seay, Moses 2-4-7-1
Seay, Abraham 1-2-5-0
Sadler, Samuel 1-0
Sadler, Anna 0-0-1-0
Sadler, Robert 1-3
Sadler, James 1-0-1-0
Shuffield, Stephen 1-0
Scott, Sarah 2-3-6-1
Smith, Thomas 1-0
Southall, Stephen 1-1
Scott, George 1-10-14-1
Scott, Samuel 1-0
Scott, Joseph 2-2-7-0
Sandifer, Matthew 1-1-4-1
Southall, John 1-3-1-0
Scott, John L. 1-2-2-0
Seay, James 2-4-4-0
Free Suky (Crawley's) 0-3-3-1
Southall, James 2-4-5-1
Spinner, John 2-3
Stanback, John 1-1
Smithey, Robert 1-1
Sayre, Daniel 1-7-4-2
Smith, Anthony 1-0
Smith, Covington 1-6-4-4
Stringer, Daniel 2-1-1-1
Sneed, Claiborne 1-0
Thompson, David 1-2-2-1
Trent, Alexander (B Pond) 0-3-7-3
Do at B Bridge 1-4-10-2
Free Tom (J. Booker's) 1-0
Townes, James (Clk.) 1-11-8-1 2-wheel chair ordinary license
Truly, John 1-15-14-3 2-wheel chair
Tanner, Robert 2-3-2-1
Talley, Grief 1-4-10-3 2-wheel chair
Taylor, Blackgrove 1-0-1-0
Tucker, Nelson 1-1
Tucker, Thomas, Est. 1-3-1-0
Townes, John Senr. 1-10-14-2
Tucker, Anderson 1-1-1-0
Townes, James Senr. 1-7-16-4
Townes, John Jur. 1-4 4-wheel coach or chariot
Townes, Armistead 1-1
Free Tom (G. Booker's) 1-1
Townes, Allen 1-3
Talley, Peyton 1-1-0-1
Talley, Abner 1-0
Talley, John 1-2
Thompson, Thomas 1-1
Tucker, John 1-2-1-0
Tucker, Absalom 4-5
Talley, Robert 1-3-3-0
Tabb, John, Est. 0-50
Tabb, Frances 0-19-63-13 4-wheel coach or chariot
Tabb, Frances C. 0-0-15-8
Tabb, Polley 0-0-15-4
Tabb, Seigniora 0-0-17-7
Tabb, Harriot 0-0-15-6
Tabb, Marianna 0-0-19-5
Townes, John (Sher) 1-13-11-4 1 stud horse
Truly, Sam (F.N.) 1-0
Vaughan, John (F.C.) 1-3-2-0
Vaughan, Lewis 2-2-2-0
Vaughan, James 2-9-6-1

Vasser, Peter 1-1-5-1
Vasser, Richard 2-6-6-2
Vaughan, Willis 1-0
Vaughan, Robert 1-4-5-1
Vaughan, Patrick 1-1-2-0
Vaughan, Nicholas 1-3-1-0
Vaden, Henry 1-2-2-0
Wright, Samuel 1-0
Woodson, Joseph 3-3-2-0
Winston, John 1-1-1-1
Wray, Thomas 1-1
Walthal, John 1-0
Whitworth, Rowland 1-0
Willson, John 2-2-1-0
Webster, Anthony Jur.
   2-2-1-1
Warriner, William 1-0
Worsham, Peter 1-3-3-1
Walker, George 1-3-2-1
   4-wheel phaeton or
   stage waggon
Walker, Mary 0-4-8-0
Webster, William 1-0-1-0
Worsham, George 1-1-2-0
Ward, Rowland 2-8-24-2
   2-wheel chair
Worsham, Elizabeth 1-1
Walke, Hannah 0-10-13-2
Webster, Peter Senr.
   2-5-5-3
Webster, Edward Jur.
   1-1-3-1
Webster, Anthony Senr.
   2-10-8-4
Webster, Anthony Jur. (F.C)
   1-1
Wright, Reubin 1-7-5-3
Wright, Stephen, Est.
   0-5-4-1
Walthal, Francis 1-2-1-0
Wright, Thomas Senr.
   2-3-3-1
Wright, Pleasant 1-0
Waltrip, Joseph 1-0
Walthal, Daniel Senr.
   1-3-4-2
Walthal, Daniel Jur. 1-0
Waddil, Carter 1-1
Wright, John 1-1
Ward, William 1-7-10-0
Walden, John 4-4-3-1

Willson, Richard 1-1-1-0
Willson, Thomas 1-0-1-2
Walthal, Christopher
   1-0-1-0
Walthal, Richard 1-1
Wood, William Jur. 1-5-9-2
Weatherford, William 1-0
Wingo, John (K.W.) 2-3-4-0
Wingo, Churchel 0-0-0-1
Wingo, John (P) 1-3-4-0
Wright, Robert 1-2-2-0
Wilkinson, Edward 1-7-10-1
Wilkinson, William 1-1-1-0
Willson, Daniel Senr.
   1-10-18-4 4-wheel
   coach or chariot
Willson, Archer 1-8-9-1
Willson, Daniel Jur.
   1-4-7-1
Webster, Edward Senr. 2-5-
   8-1 1 stud horse
Willson, Tom B. 1-6-15-3
   2-wheel chair
Willson, Tom F. 1-9-15-5
   1 stud horse
Willson, William, Est.
   1-19-26-8 2-wheel chair
Williamson, Jacob 2-7-15-2
Worsham, Henry, Est.
   1-4-6-1
Wilkinson, Joseph 1-8-10-2
Walthal, William 1-4-3-0
Wills, John 1-0
Walthal, Bartlet 1-3-1-1
Walthal, Peter 1-5-6-1
Walthal, John 1-1
Waugh, Andrew 1-3-5-0
Walthal, Henry 1-11-25-4
   2-wheel chair
Walthal, Richard Senr. 1-0
Willson, Alexander 1-5-3-0
Webster, John 1-5-5-1
   ordinary license
Wray, James 1-2
Wily, John 1-10-12-2
Waters, William 1-1-1-0
Williamson, Lancelot
   1-2-1-0
Williams, Frederick H. 1-0
Wood, William Senr. 3-10-
   14-3 2-wheel chair

AMELIA COUNTY 1800 TAX LIST 27

Willson, John, Est.
  0-1-3-0
Willson, Matthew 1-2
Worsham, William 1-0
Wilkinson, Daniel 1-1-1-0
Wills, Thomas F. 2-2-7-2
Walthal, Lucy 0-2-3-0
Williams, Philip Senr.
  1-7-4-0
Williams, Philip Jur. 1-1
Winston, William Senr.
  2-2-4-0
Walton, Sherwood 1-10-
  15-2 2-wheel chair
Worsham, Thomas 1-5-6-3
Worsham, Betsy G. 0-1-1-0
Worsham, Daniel 2-13-24-3
Walton, Jesse 2-2-2-2

Watkins, Peter 1-0
Waddel, Jacob 1-0
Worsham, David 1-0
Wright, Thomas Junr.
  2-3-4-0

Retail merchants who have
applied for licence:
  Thomas Perkinson
  John Mottley Jur. & Co.
  John Holloway
  William Mann
  William Cassels
  Parham Booker & Co.
  Thomas Colley
  Thomas Ligon & Co.
  Joseph Royall & Co.
  John & Francis Pride

BIBLE OF JONATHAN DURRETT

SPOTSYLVANIA COUNTY, VIRGINIA

Contributed by Mrs. Bert Harter
Doylestown, Ohio

This Bible was published at Philadelphia by M. Cary. The Old Testament title page bears the date 1817 and the New Testament is dated 1816.

Births

Jonathan Durrett was born	April 4, 1771
Polly H. Durrett, his wife	June 28, 1784
Albert Durrett	July 19, 1805
William Hines Durrett	Feb. 27, 1807
Oscar Fitzallen Durrett	Dec. 25, 1808
Abigail Durrett	Feb. 5, 1816
Braxton Byrd Durrett	Nov. 16, 1819
Jonathan Jackson Durrett	June 24, 1824
Mary Elizabeth Durrett	Sept. 3, 1829
Nancy Hodges	Aug. 7, 1797
Mary Ann Johnson Durrett	Dec. 4, 1828
Martha Ellen Durrett	Oct. 6, 1830
Judith Terrell Durrett	Feb. 24, 1833
Elliott Vermanet Durrett	Sept. 24, 1834
Maria L. Hester	June 15, 1837
Mary Ann J. Carter	Jan. 15, 1836
William Porter Carter	Nov. 28, 1837
Wallis Marion Carter	April 28, 1838
Ellenorah Hassentine Carter	Nov. 24, 1840
Jonathan Melzar Carter	March 13, 1849
Kate Baker Durrett	Oct. 16, 1856
Cliveous Albert Baker	Nov. 15, 1856
Charles Lewis Durrett	Apr. 14, 1859
William Albert Durrett	Mar. 30, 1868
Judith T. Durrett	May 13, 1870
Everett Vermanet Durrett	Apr. 18, 1872
Robert Henry Durrett	Mar. 18, 1874
Mary Virginia Durrett	Nov. 10, 1875
Ann Lewis Durrett	Oct. 9, 1877
Laurence Blanton Durrett	Mar. 25, 1880
Harvey John Thomas Durrett	Oct. 18, 1881
Ann Elizabeth Blanton	Oct. 9, 1878
Joseph Hart Baker	Jun. 24, 1879
Emmet Todd Blanton	Jun. 11, 1880
Albert Riftin Baker	May 22, 1881
Richard Alfred Blanton	May 26, 1882
Herman Cliveous Baker	Mar. 28, 1885
Andrew Ellis Baker	Mar. 6, 1888

BIBLE OF JONATHAN DURRETT

Marriages

Jonathan Durrett and Polly H. Lively were married	Oct. 25, 1804
Albert Durrett and Nancy Hodges	Feb. 22, 1827
William H. Durrett and Mary I. Dumkum	May 15, 1832
Melzer Carter and Abigail Durrett	Oct. 16, 1834
Braxton Byrd Durrett and Ann E. Williams	May 30, 1844
Jonathan J. Durrett and Susan E. Jones	Aug. 20, 1848
Abner Hines and Mary Elizabeth Durrett	Sept. 5, 1855
Bushrod W. Baker and Judith T. Durrett	July 26, 1855
Elliott V. Durrett and Maria L. Hester	Dec. 20, 1855
Andrew Hart and Mary A. J. Durrett	Jan. 16, 1867
E. V. Durrett and Mary A. Blanton	May 16, 1867
Jonathan J. Durrett and Margaret J. Tompkins	June 7, 1866
Cliveous Albert Baker and Marie Lou Hart	Dec. 19, 1877

Deaths

Oscar Fitzallen Durrett		Feb. 25, 1816
Abigail Carter		Apr. 22, 1851
Polly H. Durrett		May 2, 1851
Jonathan Durrett	9 O'clock AM	Mar. 23, 1855
Mary E. Hines		Apr. 26, 1856
Judith T. Baker		Aug. 14, 1857
Maria L. Durrett		Sept. 21, 1861
Susan E. Durrett		Sept. 16, 1862
Nancy Durrett		[ ] 17, 1883
Albert Durrett		Sept. 26, 1889
Mary Ann Johnson Hart		Aug. 12, 1900
Martha E. Durrett		Nov. 26, 1916
Andrew Hart		Oct. 21, 1877

This Bible is now owned by Herman Baker of Woodford, Va.

Jonathan Durrett is shown by the personal property tax books of Caroline Co., Va., to have been a son of William Durrett, a tailor of Caroline County, who about 1809 moved away, probably to Kentucky. The Bible of Martin Durrett, Jonathan's brother, which has been printed in Mississippi Genealogical Society, Mississippi Cemetery and Bible Records, v. 2, p. 50, states that William Durrett (born 28 July 1745, died 11 Aug. 1813) married Elizabeth Hines (born 2 Sept. 1746, died 11 Oct. 1821) on 2 Sept. 1766. Martin Durrett was born 8 Jan. 1783 and died 16 March 1848; his wife Rebecca White was born 9 May 1799.

Other children of William and Elizabeth (Hines) Durrett were John Hines Durrett (see Caroline County chancery suit Durrett vs. Bibb), Elizabeth Durrett (who married William White 22 May 1790 in Caroline County) and Ferenia Durrett (who married Thomas Marshall 11 Jan.

1804 in Caroline County). It is probable Mary Durrett (who married William Miller 2 Aug. 1791 in Caroline County) and Claiborne Durrett (who married Elizabeth --- prior to 1801) were also children.

Martin Durrett and Rebecca White were married in Roane Co., Tenn., 10 Sept. 1822. Alex Nesmith, J.P., attached the following to the marriage record:
    This day wedded Rebecca White to Martin Durrett,
    He hugged her tight, she loved him for it,
    It is somewhat a curious case,
    He her uncle, she his niece,
    If it was wrong I'm not to blame,
    Being kept ignorant of the same,
    Until the marriage knot was tied,
    He a husband, she a wedded bride.

The children of Braxton Byrd Durrett and Ann Elizabeth Williams are named in his diary which was given by this contributor to West Virginia University, Morgantown, W.Va.: John Hines Durrett, born 22 Feb. 1845; William Alfred Durrett, born 25 Oct. 1846; Francis Braxton Durrett born 1 April 1849; Mary Sophia Durrett, born 15 June 1855, Oscar George Price Durrett, born 9 Feb. 1863.

The children of Jonathan Jackson Durrett are named in a letter written in 1874 by his daughter Mildred to Mary Sophia Durrett, grandmother of the contributor: By his first wife Susan Jones, Mildred Durrett, born 23 April 1854 and Minor Durrett, born 27 Nov. 1856. By his second wife Margaret J. Tompkins, Thomas Jackson Durrett, born 11 June 1868; Robert William Durrett, born 23 Sept. 1870; Fannie Durrett, born 1 Jan. 1873. Another child, Ellis Durrett, was born after 1874.

The children of William Hines and Mary Jane (Dunkum) Durrett, who went to Missouri in 1834, and named in his Bible (record sent by Mrs. Marie Parrish of Johnstown, Colo., whose husband was a descendant): Eleanorah Ann Hazzeltine Durrett, born 12 April 1833; William Jonathan Durrett, born 13 April 1835; Mary Elizabeth Tule Durrett, born 7 Feb. 1837; Oscar Hines Durrett, born 27 Jan. 1839; Susan Pauline Durrett, born 9 Nov. 1841; Charles Henry Bland Durrett, born 21 Feb. 1844; Jane Richard Durrett, born 5 June 1846; John Dunkum Durrett, born 2 Oct. 1848; Cammillus Durkee Durrett, born 6 Aug. 1852; and Avah Durrett (the youngest daughter, married --- Stephenson and was living in Colorado in 1923).

Mary Elizabeth (Durrett) Hines died without issue.

MacCARTHY-McCARTHY-McCARTY NOTES:

IRELAND, VIRGINIA, TENNESSEE

By John Insley Coddington

Like most Irish families, the great house of MacCarthy or McCarthy lacks a proper and scholarly genealogy. The best that can be offered is The MacCarthys of Munster, by the late Samuel Trant McCarthy, D.L., J.P., M.R.I.A., who styles himself "The MacCarthy Mor." This work, of 399 pages, was published at Dundalk, Ireland, in 1922, during the most serious period of the "Troubles," which may account in part for the book's lamentable lack of organization, and for the fact that the thing at the end, which purports to be an index, actually lists less than half the names in the book. For instance, the surname O'Driscoll appears not at all in the so-called Index, yet it may be found at least ten times in the text (pp. 101, 117, 118, 129, 140, 171, 224, 236, 319, 365).

A large number of McCarthys appear in the "index," but none bearing the Christian name Darby. Yet at least one of this name is to be found in the text, on page 74. This man, Darby MacOwen MacCarthy, Lord of Duhallow (Co. Cork), was one of those who claimed to be "MacCarthy Mor" and head of the family in 1599. It is apparently this same man to whom the author, S. T. McCarthy, refers on pages 253-61 as "Dermod MacOwen MacCarthy, Lord of Duhallow," in quite a lengthy description of his turbulent career, which was ended by his death "in or before 1627." It is quite probable that Dermod was this chieftain's Irish name, and Darby the name by which he was known to his English contemporaries. Such instances are not rare, but a more careful author than S. T. McCarthy would have drawn attention to this fact.

At all events, the given name Darby was used in the Duhallow branch of the MacCarthys, and it may well be that Darby McCarty who was progenitor of the McCarty family of Mr. Prentiss Price's "McCarty Bible Records" in The Virginia Genealogist, v. 3, pp. 23-26, came from Duhallow. Readers of that article will recall that the marriage of "Darby Carty" and Hannah Richardson was recorded at the First Presbyterian Church of Philadelphia on 4 July 1736, and that Darby McCarty appeared in the land records of Frederick Co., Va., in 1754, and on a Poll List there in 1758, and in Dunmore County in 1774.

To all this we have a footnote, which may or may not pertain to the family of Darby and Hannah (Richardson) McCarty. Among the many valuable and fascinating records kept at the Historical Foundation of the Southern

Presbyterian Church, Montreat, North Carolina, there is a manuscript volume of the "Records of Ebenezer Church, Bigbyville, Columbia County, Tennessee, 1824-1921," which contains the following:

Andrew McCarty & his wife Ruth & their Family (Removed 1824)

Names of Children	Births
Minerva Cowan	June 23rd 1809.
David Franklin	July 1st 1810.
James Reese	Decr 12th 1811.
William Wriley	Jany 6th 1813.
Andrew Hervey	March 9th 1814.
Ruth Lovenah	Decr 4th 1815.
John Leroy	Jany 10th 1817.
Elizabeth L.	Sept. 29th 1818.
Sarah Susannah	April 24th 1820.
Nancy Caroline	August 2nd 1821.
Jane Moriah	Sept. 4th 1823.

Since Andrew McCarty and his family moved away from Bigbyville in 1824, there may have been more children, born after that time.

A GUIDE TO THE COUNTIES

OF VIRGINIA

BERKELEY COUNTY
West Virginia

Berkeley County was formed in 1772 from the northern part of Frederick County. It then included all of its present area, all of Jefferson County and the eastern part of Morgan County. The southeastern border was Loudoun County, the southwestern was Frederick County and there was a short common border with Hampshire County on the west. The Potomac River formed the northern border, separating Berkeley from Frederick (after 1776 Washington) Co., Md.

In 1801 Jefferson County was erected from the part of Berkeley east of a line from the point where Opeckon Creek crossed the Frederick County line to Wyncoop's Spring Run on the Potomac.

In 1820 Morgan County was created from the northern part of Berkeley and the western part of Hampshire. At this time Berkeley attained its present boundaries.

In 1862 the Virginia Assembly consented that Berkeley County should be in West Virginia if the voters agreed, but in 1865 this Act was repealed and in 1866 the Virginia Attorney General was authorized to bring suit to stop West Virginia's exercise of control, provided the U.S. Congress gave consent thereto. The arguments were heard before the Supreme Court.

Several histories of the county have been written, including F. Vernon Aler, Aler's History of Martinsburg and Berkeley County, West Virginia (Hagerstown, Md., 1888), Willis F. Evans, History of Berkeley County (Wheeling, 1928), and Mabel Henshaw Gardiner and Ann Henshaw Gardiner, Chronicles of Old Berkeley (Durham, N.C., 1938). Other material appears in Thomas K. Cartmell, Shenandoah Valley Pioneers and their Descendants ... 1738-1908 (Winchester, 1909), J. E. Norris, ed., History of the Lower Shenandoah Valley Counties of Frederick, Berkeley, Jefferson, and Clarke (Chicago, 1890) and Historical Hand-Atlas, Illustrated, Containing ... Histories of Berkeley and Jefferson Counties, West Va. (Chicago, H. H. Hardesty, 1883).

COURT RECORDS (at the Court House at Martinsburg; records after 1860 are not inventoried in detail): Wills are complete from the formation of the county with the exception of five books. The missing periods are 1832-1836, 1849-52 and 1854-60. There is a General Index of Wills, Inventories, Etc., 1772-1953. The W.P.A.

Historic Marker Project prepared "Berkeley County, West Virginia, Wills, Inventories, Sale Bills, Etc." (2 v.; typewritten; n.p., 1936).

Deeds are also complete from 1772 except for eight books. The missing periods are 1797-98, 1809-11, 1816-1817, 1827-30, 1837-38, 1853-55 and 1861-64. There are grantor and grantee deed indexes, 1772-1925. Superior Court Deed Book 1 covers the years 1809-24. A "List of Conveyances Lying in the Clerk's Office Awaiting Further Proof" is dated 1819.

Volumes of administrators' bonds exist for 1773-89, 1792-1817 and 1825-47, and volumes of executors' bonds exist for 1774-1823, 1828-47 (with more than one volume covering the same period in some instances).

There are volumes of guardians' bonds for 1776-1847. The first volume, 1776-96, has been abstracted in The Virginia Genealogist, v. 4, pp. 3-7, 60-63.

Order and minute books exist for 1772-86, 1789-1862, with some duplication. The majority are rough minutes rather than the more formally written orders.

A volume of marriage returns covers the years 1781-1854. There are five volumes of marriage bonds, 1797-1834, and marriage licenses from 1834 to date, with the exception of a missing book for 1852-64. The W.P.A. Historic Marker Project prepared "Berkeley County, West Virginia, Marriages" (3 v.; typewritten; n.p., 1936) which covers the years 1816-99. The D.A.R. Library, Washington, D.C., also has "Marriages in Berkeley County, West Virginia" (typewritten; n.p., 1936), apparently prepared by the Historic Markers Project, which covers the years 1797-1816.

Birth and death records begin in 1869 and continue to the present.

Volumes of Ordinary license bonds cover the years 1792-1847. Constables' bonds, 1845-47, are in one volume. A volume of Certification of Strays exists for 1775-92. There is a Mill Book (naming persons who had corn, etc., ground) for 1824-25.

Executions cover the years 1772-83, 1798-1800, 1810-1817, 1821-36; rule dockets, 1796-99; a judgement docket 1815-25; a fee book 1803-04.

The Minutes of the Board of School Commissioners are for 1818-46 and the Records of the Berkeley County Bible Society cover 1821-61.

Some miscellaneous notes from the court records appear in Kentucky Historical Society Register, v. 50, pp. 276-283.

CHURCH RECORDS: Episcopal. Norborne Parish was created in 1769 and when Berkeley County was formed in 1772 the boundaries were adjusted to make it coterminous

GUIDE TO THE COUNTIES OF VIRGINIA   35

with the county.
Baptist. Photostats of the records of Mt. Zion
Church, 1835-90, and Mill Creek Church, 1805-1928, are
at the Virginia State Library.

TAX LISTS: The personal property tax books of Berkeley County at the Virginia State Library cover the years 1782-1861. There are two books 1787-1820 except for 1790, 1795-96 and 1807 when there is but one book and 1801 when there are three books. Volumes of land tax records at the Court House are for 1782-1805, 1810-39, with some omissions.

CENSUS RECORDS: 1810 census, a single list. Martinsburg is designated.
1820 census, lists for Martinsburg, Darkesville, Middle Town, and the county.
1830 census, a single alphabetical list.
1840 census, a single list. Martinsburg is designated.
1850 census, a single list. Martinsburg is designated.
1860 census, a single list (post offices, Martinsburg, Hedgesville, North Mountain Depot, Little Georgetown, Falling Waters, Hainesville, Vancleavesville, Scrabble, Mill Creek, Darkesville, Gerardstown, Tomahawk, Jones Springs, Shanghai, Glengary). Martinsburg, in two sections, is so marked.
1870 census, for Arden Township (P.O. Martinsburg), Falling Waters Township (P.O. Falling Waters, Hainesville), Gerardstown Township (P.O. Shanghai, Gerardstown, Martinsburg), Hedgesville Township (P.O. Hedgesville, North Mountain, Little Georgetown), Martinsburg (city), Mill Creek Township (P.O. Mill Creek), Opequon Township (P.O. Martinsburg).
1880 census, for Opequon District, Martinsburg, Arden District, 13th District (Mill Creek District), Gerardstown District, Hedgesville Township (includes village of Hedgesville), Falling Waters District.

POST OFFICES (established before 1890): Arden (1851-1852, 1853-62).
Beddington (1831-51; name changed to Hainesville); Bedington (1875-   ; formerly Hainesville); Berkeley Springs (1803/5-   ; fell into Morgan County 1820); Bunker Hill (1879-   ; formerly Mill Creek).
Darksville (1819-1905); Dunnington's Depot (1848-50; name changed to Van Clevesville).
Falling Waters (1815-66, 1867-   ).
Ganotown (1880-   ); Gerardstown (1820-   ); Glengary (1851-58, 1859-   ), Greensburgh (1863-68).
Hainesville (1851-64, formerly Beddington; 1865-75, name changed to Bedington); Harper's Ferry (1800-   ;

fell into Jefferson County 1801); Hedgesville (1833-46, name changed to North Mountain; 1846-   ); Holton (1889-1903; changed into Morgan County 1889/97).
    Jones Springs (1852-66, 1868-   ).
    Lightsville (1855-57); Little Georgetown (1854-1900).
    Martinsburg (1793-   ); Mill Creek (1804-79; also called Bunker's Hill; name changed to Bunker Hill).
    North Mountain (1846- ; formerly Hedgesville).
    Oakton (1873-78, 1879-81, 1882-95).
    Scrabble (1851-54); Shanghai (1854-1920); Soho (1886-1901); Spring Mills (1885-1900).
    Tabler (1889-   ); Tomahawk Spring (1844-94; name changed to Tomahawk).
    Van Clevesville (1850-1908).

JANE (SMITH) HOLBROOK

OF NEW JERSEY AND VIRGINIA

Contributed by Robert Karl Peterson
Washington, D. C.

The following record, which appears in Salem Co., N.J., Deed Book 1715-97, page 349, identifies the family of Jane Smith, wife of the Rev. John Holbrook who was a missionary of the Society for the Propagation of the Gospel at Salem, N.J., 1723-31, minister of St. George's Parish, Harford Co., Md., 1726-27, and rector of Hungar's Parish, Northampton Co., Va., 1729-47. He died testate in the latter year leaving descendants. See F. L. Weis, The Colonial Clergy of the Middle Colonies (Worcester, American Antiquarian Society, 1957), p. 241.

Rec'd. Aug 26th 1742 by me Jane Holbrooke wife of the Rev. John Hollbrooke of Virginia and County of North Hampsted [Northampton] of Samuel Smith my father and John Smith my brother of New Jersey and County of Salem, the sum of 60 pounds current money of New Jersey as being a legacy given unto me the said Jane Hollbrooke aforesaid by the said Samuel Smith aforesaid in and by his last will and testament of which said sum of 60 pounds and all other debt, duties, sum and sums of money and demands whatsoever I the said Jane Hollbrooke do acquit and fully discharge the said Samuel Smith and John Smith ...
                                        Jane Hollbrooke
    Witness: Sarah Turner
    Recorded 6 June 1753.

LOCAL NOTICES FROM THE

VIRGINIA GAZETTE, 1780

(Continued from V. 4, p. 178)

6 September 1780

 Proclamation by Gen. George Washington at Orange, N.Y., 15 Aug. 1780, stating that many soldiers belonging to the regiments raised by the Commonwealth of Virginia for the army of the United States have most wickedly and shamefully deserted. Those who have left the army in such manner will receive full pardon if they return.
 Benjamin Wilks advertises a bull taken up in Charlotte County on Dannivant Creek.
 Wills Cowper & Co. advertises for sale at Suffolk all the rigging and materials from the Suffolk packet lately stranded to the southward of Cape Henry.
 William Claiborne advertises for sale his seat, Putney, on Pomunkey River eight miles below New Castle, formerly the property of Hon. G. Webb, Esq. Webb's Ferry, which has become very valuable since the removal of the seat of government to Richmond, is annexed to the land. There is every necessary building for a large and genteel family, a fine fishery and wild fowl in abundance at the door.
 C. Russel, L.M.P.& R.C., at Petersburg, advertises for all soldiers formerly belonging to the 1st Virginia Regiment who have not received full wages and deficiencies of clothing due them for 1777 and 1779 to attend at Blandford personally.
 Order of H. Goar, Deputy Clerk, to the Sheriff of Halifax County to summon Henry Woodward, heir at law of William Woodward, to answer a bill in chancery exhibited against him by Joseph Gill.
 Daniel Vanduvall advertises a tobacco note containing two hogsheads lying on Pomunkey River at Meriwether's Warehouse, found in Richmond.
 William Pointer advertises for a horse stolen from Mr. John Swepston's near Mecklenburg Court House. To be delivered to Mr. Swepston or to Pointer at Osborne's Warehouse.
 William Rose, K[eeper] P[ublic] J[ail] at Richmond, advertises that Luke Linley who broke out of jail is retaken.
 Proclamation of Gov. Thomas Jefferson, 29 Aug. 1780, relating to the redemption of money in circulation and the emission of new bills of credit.
 Thomas Cary at Hanover Town advertises Madeira wine

for sale.

William Call, at Petersburg, advertises for sale two tracts in Mecklenburg County lying on the waters of Butcher's and Bluestone Creeks, about 80 miles from Petersburg, good for tobacco, wheat and corn, and convenient to mills. The one has about 30 acres of cleared land (not tended for several years) with an overseer's house. The other is wood land. Additional wood land adjoining both tracts can also be purchased. He will exchange for land nearer Petersburg.

Richard Burnley and Alexander Burnley at Hanover Town advertise they intend for Statia [St. Eustatia] soon and have appointed Mr. Joseph Brand their attorney.

Galvan de Bernoux at Fredericksburg advertises he intends shortly to France. Mr. Bajien Laporte, his partner, will attend to his business.

William Pitt at Williamsburg advertises that he gave Dr. Baker, late of that city, two bonds in Sept. 1778, each for ₤500. He will pay no interest after the last day of September when due.

13 September 1780

Last Sunday [10 Sept.] was interred in the churchyard of this place Robert C. Nicholas, Esq., of Hanover County, after a lingering illness. ...

Andrew Marr at Williamsburg demonstrates "that a square number measures the circle by a square number; consequently the circle is squarely square."

Nicholas B. Seabrook advertises for sale at his house in Hanover County near the New Bridges, a quantity of silk and medicines.

Mary Sullivan at Fredericksburg advertises that she has stopped the sale by a suspicious person of a piece of plate on which is engraved a castle and griffin and from which a name has been scratched.

Col. George Muter at the War Office, Richmond, requests that all former officers who bore command in the regular army, are now out of employment, and are willing to serve again, notify him.

Richard Burnley at Hanover Town advertises that he purchased land of Mr. Thomas Cartwright and sold it to Mr. Adam Byrd. He gave Cartwright a bond for ₤4500 and now finds Mr. Thomas Doncastle has a mortgage on the land for ₤500. He warns all persons from taking assignment of the bond as he will not pay it until the dispute is settled.

Thomas Napier offers ₤300 reward for a gelding strayed from Fluvanna County.

James Taylor offers ₤100 for return of run away Negro boy to him or Samuel Smith in Richmond.

LOCAL NOTICES FROM THE VIRGINIA GAZETTE

Amos Harris advertises three cattle taken up in Southampton.

Richard Mason advertises a horse taken up in the upper end of Stafford County.

John Barret advertises a cow and calf taken up in the town of Richmond.

William Black advertises sale of stud horses Regulus and Agamemnon at Tredway's Ordinary in Manchester; also a number of mares including Mary Grey and Jenny Cameron.

Thomas Hughes at Richmond advertises he intends for Saint Eustatia. He has for sale an elegant eight day clock.

James Gray of the ship Gloucester informs Capt. William Morris of Gloucester County that he has a Negro Gabriel captured in a whale boat of Goodrich's, going to New York, by the schooners Antilope and Felicity.

Richard Davenport offers $100 reward for apprehending runaway Negro Joe.

John Harmanson and John Burton, executors, advertise for sale at Northampton Court House 270 acres, a mile and a half from the Court House.

John Banks at Richmond offers $200 reward for horse strayed from Richmond. He bought him at Surry Court House.

John Mason, D[eputy] S[heriff], states a Negro woman called Hannah Jackson was taken from some travellers passing through Botetourt County about 12 months ago going to Kentucky. She had a certificate from John Hundley certifying she was set free in Goochland Court by Col. Martin and others. She says she has two children, one living with Mr. Mawbry of New Kent and the other with Mr. Martin. She lived some time with Mr. Revley at the foundry. He, Mr. Foster of Prince Edward, Mr. Martin and Mr. Lewis of Goochland know her to be free. She wishes certification of her freedom.

Jeremiah Overbee advertises that linen, blankets and other things were taken from the camp of runaway Negroes in Dinwiddie County.

Clayborne Whitworth advertises two colts taken up in the upper end of Amelia County.

John Phelps advertises a mare taken up in Buckingham County.

Richard Wilton advertises a mare taken up in Mecklenburg on Blackstone Creek.

William & Mary College has for sale a considerable quantity of scantling, originally intended for an additional building.

John Cobbs advertises for sale 2000 acres on James River about 45 miles above the town of Richmond.

(To be continued)

BOOK REVIEWS

<u>The Register of Saint Paul's Parish, 1715-1798</u>, Stafford County, Virginia, 1715-1776, King George County, Virginia, 1777-1798. Arranged alphabetically by surnames in chronological order by George Harrison Sanford King. Fredericksburg, Va., 1950. xxxiii, 157 pp. $10.00.

Saint Paul's has been one of the few extant colonial parish registers which remain unpublished. This is, therefore, a most welcome volume, prepared by an eminently qualified genealogist.

Mr. King begins his introduction with a description of the register when he first saw it: "The back had all but disappeared, the first dozen pages were completely loose and many pages had crumbled around the edges into the writing." It was restored in 1940 by the John Lee and Lillian Thomas Pratt Foundation. Mr. King has used his considerable knowledge of King George and Stafford County residents in the eighteenth century to reconstruct entries which are partially worn away and to identify items which are not clear.

There are many discrepancies between the Register entries and other records owing to carelessness on the part of the ministers. Examples of a number of these are given. We might add to this list the birth of William, son of Jesse and Sarah Bowling (Bolling), given in the Register as 17 June 1772 and in family records as 8 June 1773.

The historical sketch of the parish is an important part of the book. Every reader will do well to study it. There is an additional list of vestrymen 1720-1857. The texts of the memorial tablets in the church are given and there is a photograph of the church.

The highest praise is justly due.

Copies may be secured from the compiler at 1301 Prince Edward Street, Fredericksburg, Virginia.

<u>Guide to the Study of West Virginia History</u>. By Charles Shetler. Morgantown, West Virginia University Library, 1960. vii, 151 pp. $6.00.

There are certain basic tools which genealogists will do without only to their detriment. Mr. Shetler's new volume is one of these. Anyone with West Virginia interests should have this volume on his desk.

The contents are divided into two parts. In the first there is a listing of materials by counties and regions. This reviewer hangs his head in shame when mentioning that not a single one of the five entries under Barbour County was listed in his own "Guide" in this magazine, v. 4, pp. 127-28.

Part Two has a topical arrangement. Of special interest to the genealogist will be the sections of Biography and Autobiography, Boundaries, Land and Land Companies, Military History and State History.
There is a very full index.
Copies may be secured from the West Virginia University Library, Morgantown, West Virginia.

Marriages of Orange County, Virginia, 1747-1810. Compiled and published by Catherine L. Knorr. [Pine Bluff, Ark., 1959] 122 pp. $5.00.

This, the thirteenth of Mrs. Knorr's books, is an especially fortunate choice. The imperfection of the printed lists of Orange County marriages, all of which were based on a twentieth century compilation in the County Clerk's Office, has long been known. Mrs. Knorr has carefully checked each entry in her book against the original marriage bonds and ministers' returns and all information of genealogical import is given in this book. The vicissitudes she encountered are narrated by George H. S. King in his preface, which also includes historical information relating to the county.
Copies may be secured from the compiler, 1401 Linden Street, Pine Bluff, Arkansas.

Marriage Bonds and Ministers' Returns of Surry County, Virginia, 1768-1825. Compiled and published by Catherine Lindsay Knorr. [Pine Bluff, Ark.] 1960. 112 pp. $5.00.

Mrs. Knorr's books of Virginia marriages have always been greated with pleasure. This time there is gloom and sadness, not because the quality of her work and the importance of the publication of Surry marriages is any less, but because this is the last of her series. It is hard for this reviewer and her many friends to realize that Kitty Knorr is retiring. In eleven years she has given us fourteen volumes; how could such a good thing end!
There is another sadness about this book - the story of the difficulties in compiling the marriages which Mrs. Knorr recounts in her preface. Marriage bonds are supposedly public records, open to the examination of interested persons. The friend in Virginia who tried to check discrepancies for her at the Surry Court House was refused access to the bonds. When Mrs. Knorr made a special 1200 mile trip to Virginia to attempt to do this work of comparison herself, she was permitted to look at the bonds - but she could not touch them.
The frontispiece is a photograph of Mrs. Knorr. We

are glad that those who have never had the pleasure of knowing Kitty Knorr will in this way be able to see in her features the sweetness and generosity which make up her character.

Copies may be secured from the compiler, 1401 Linden Street, Pine Bluff, Arkansas.

Marriages of Henrico County, Virginia, 1680-1808. Compiled and published by Joyce H. Lindsay. [Richmond, 1960] 123 pp. $5.00.

Henrico, one of the original Virginia shires, has lost some of its early records. The marriage bonds begin in 1781 but there are references to marriages in the 1680's among extant records. These and marriages by inference found in the records of the Orphan's Court have been included by Mrs. Lindsay.

The arrangement is that with which we have become familiar in using Catherine Lindsay Knorr's books. There is an index of brides. Parents, securities and witnesses are not indexed. There are about 1600 marriages in this book.

Searchers for Henrico families should not fail to note that Richmond had separate courts beginning in 1782. The Richmond city marriage records were published in 1939 by Ann Waller Reddy and Andrew Lewis Riffe.

An attractive feature is the use on the cover and title page of the seal of Henrico County's 350th anniversary, 1611-1961 - the first use that has been made of it.

Copies may be secured from Mrs. James R. Lindsay, 303 Gilmour Courtway, Richmond 21, Virginia.

The Belfield Family. A Record of the Descendants of Dr. Joseph Belfield, Immigrant to Virginia About 1700. Compiled by John Lyman. Washington, D.C., 1960. 20 pp. $1.00.

This outline of about seven hundred descendants of Joseph Belfield of Richmond County is concerned chiefly with the family of his grandson John Belfield (1725-1803) who married Ruth Sydnor. In most instances only names are given, although some dates and places of burial do appear.

This is an excellent first step toward a Belfield genealogy and descendants will find it useful in determining family connections and degrees of relationship. Mr. Lyman has met one of the chief requirements for a good genealogy by providing a full name index.

Copies may be secured from the compiler, 7801 Gateway Blvd., Washington 28, D.C.

BOOK REVIEWS 43

Shockoe Hill Cemetery, Richmond, Virginia, Register of Interments, April 10, 1822 - December 31, 1950. Compiled and edited by A. Böhmer Rudd. Volume One, April 10, 1822 - December 31, 1850. Washington, D.C. [1960] 98 [3] pp. $12.50.

Shockoe Cemetery opened in 1822 and thereafter for many years a large number of Richmond residents were buried within its confines. The importance of this book is that it includes the records of all interments, not just those persons to whose memory gravestones were later erected. In many instances the reader can secure further information from newspaper obituaries, using the date of burial as a guide.
The entries contain three items, name of deceased, age, and date of burial.
The foreword, written by Dr. E. G. Swem, gives a brief history of the cemetery and a number of gravestone inscriptions taken from an article which appeared in the Richmond Whig in 1866. There are photographs of several stones and the inscriptions on ten which were moved to the cemetery in recent times are given.
A second volume will complete the interment records. It is to be hoped that Miss Rudd will publish a third volume giving all gravestone inscriptions for this cemetery. The typescript list prepared by the W.P.A. (there are copies at the Virginia State Library and D.A.R. Library) has many errors.
Copies may be secured from the compiler, 1819 G St., n.w., Washington 6, D.C.

The Wilford-Williford Family Treks Into America. By Eurie Pearl Wilford Neel. [Nashville, Tenn.] 1959. xxvi, 437, 320, 319, 94, 13, 13 pp. $12.50 plus 29¢ postage and 38¢ state tax.

This is a book in two parts. The first 437 pages comprise Mrs. Neel's second volume of the history of the Wilford-Williford family, chiefly the descendants of John Williford of Isle of Wight Co., Va., and old Albemarle Co., N.C. Some of his descendants later moved to western Kentucky. Much information about them and allied families is given by Mrs. Neel.
Chapter 7, comprising some 30 pages, gives information about Revolutionary, 1812 and Mexican War soldiers who lived in Christian and Trigg cos., Ky. Chapter 8 contains a history of the Edmund Bacon house in Trigg County and some information about the Bacon family.
The arrangement of the Williford section is not always easy to follow and much extraneous information has been interjected in some of the sketches, but the index will

facilitate the location of connecting links and we cannot complain about Mrs. Neel's inclusion of such data as the records of Burnett's Chapel Methodist Church or nine pages listing residents of Christian County in 1810-11. There are a number of maps and illustrations.

Part Two of this volume will have a wide interest. It is a reprint of William Henry Perrin's <u>Counties of Christian and Trigg, Kentucky. Historical and Biographical</u>, published originally in 1884. There is a lengthy account of the history of each county and in addition the copy from which reproduction was made contained the biographical sketches of Trigg County residents. The Perrin histories are to be found in very few libraries and it is good to have that of Christian and Trigg counties made available again. No library with Kentucky interests should be without this book.

There are three indexes, one to the Williford section and two surname indexes for the Perrin histories of Christian and Trigg counties.

Copies may be secured from Mrs. Courtland Moore Neel, Neelwil Place, 2110 Lone Oak Road, Paducah, Kentucky.

<u>Thompsons, Mainly of Hanover & Louisa Counties, Virginia</u>. By Henry Lockhart. Oxford, Md., 1960. 53 pp. $3.50.

Mr. Lockhart has gathered notes on the Thompson-Thomson families of Hanover, Louisa and adjoining counties from various published materials and has included in his book many of the notes of the Rev. S. O. Coxe and Judge Leon M. Bazile from unpublished county and state records. This is not a formal genealogy but persons interested in these families will find many helpful clues in establishing relationships.

Several copies containing additional data have been presented to the Library of Congress, Virginia State Library, Virginia Historical Society and Sons of the American Revolution Library in Washington, D.C. The copy which we review is an abbreviated one and a number of these are available for sale for the benefit of the Hanover County Police Benevolent Association.

They may be ordered from the compiler, R.F.D. 1, Oxford, Talbot County, Maryland.

<u>Ohio Records</u> and <u>Pioneer Families</u>. Volume 1, 1960. Published quarterly by Esther Weygandt Powell. $5.00 per year; single issue $1.50.

The subtitle of this magazine, "The Cross road of our nation," explains the important niche it fills. Ohio settlers came originally from all parts of the country,

BOOK REVIEWS

New England, the middle states, Virginia and even further south. Many of them stayed a while and then joined the trek to newly opened territory to the west.

Mrs. Powell has gathered together in her first volume material relating to many sections of the state. There are innumerable names. Our only objection is that there is not enough about any area, generally no more than two or three pages to a county. We belong to that school of thought which believes it is better to abstract ten wills in detail than to give only the names of a hundred testators. There are those, however, who prefer many clues which they can follow up to just a few items telling the full story. We cannot complain of the validity of their arguments, when viewed from their standpoint, and they, in turn, should have no complaints about this fine magazine.

Subscriptions may be entered with the editor, 36 N. Highland Avenue, Akron 3, Ohio.

QUERIES

Each subscriber to The Virginia Genealogist is entitled to have one or more queries published, free of charge, but limited to a total of fifty words per year, exclusive of name and address. All queries must have a Virginia connection.

432. EMERSON. Want parents, ancestry and data of Sarah Emerson who became second wife of Daniel Cowgill on 10 June 1793. He was born Burlington Co., N.J., 9 Oct. 1755, moved with parents to Culpeper Co., Va., fought in Revolution from Va. and Ky., in 1785 married first Elizabeth Martin of Orange Co., Va., and had Joseph, Martin, and Nancy Cowgill. Daniel and Sarah (Emerson) Cowgill had Elizabeth, George Washington and Frankie Cowgill. They moved via Ky. to Ohio where he reared his children. In old age he lived in Fayette Co., Ky., with son George W. He died Grant Co., Ky., 1843, aged 88; his wife was then dead. Mrs. Charles DeSpain, Box 54, Anchorage, Ky.

433. DEANE-PANCOAST-GRAY-MOHLER-CROOK-CHURCHMAN-DOGGETT. Want any data on Deane (of Caroline Co., Va.); Gray (of Northern Virginia); Pancoast (am compiling a family history); Mohler (of Loudoun, Jefferson and other northern cos. of Va.); Churchman and Doggett who married into Jones family; James Crook who married Mary West (where?). Have data to exchange. Mrs. W. A. Dean, Magnolia, Texas.

434. LONG. Want parents of Catherine E. Long, born 11

Feb. 1813, Va., died 31 Aug. 1855, buried Burke's Garden, Va.; married Patton James Thompson 18 July 1829, Washington Co., Va.

WINSTON. Want parents of Robert Winston, born 1828, Mississippi, married 18 Jan. 1849, Tazewell Co., Va., Mary Ann Gillespie.

BURKE(BURK). Want parents of Thomas Burke (Burk), born ca.1736, Augusta Co., Va., married Cleary (Clara) Fleming; eldest son Henry, born 8 Aug. 1758, married Mary McKinney. Mrs. Ella Burke, 251 Shoshone Ave., Lovell, Wyo.

435. SCOTT-SPENCER. Mildred (Milly) Scott, dau. of Capt. James and Frances (Collier) Scott of Prince Edward Co., Va., married --- Spencer (where? when? given name?) and lived in Augusta, Ga. Want names and residence of his parents (Charlotte Co., Va.?). Mrs. Lynn T. Webb, Porto Bello, Box 817, Aliceville, Ala.

436. JONES. Want any information regarding two daughters of David Jr. and Angelina (Hatcher) Jones: Timandra E., born 1846, Bedford Co., Va., wife of S. F. Perry, died 1874, place unknown; Julia R., born 1849, died 1893, buried in Sheldon Cemetery, Milo, Mo., wife of W. P. Clark. Mrs. Leona A. Clark, 433 W. Washington, Macomb, Ill.

437. PIERCE. Desire parentage and given name of --- Pierce who married James Ledgerwood (bapt. 11 Dec. 1740 Tinkling Spring Church) son of emigrants William and Agnes Ledgerwood of Augusta Co., Va. James was in battles of Brandywine and Germantown with Washington's troops and when his three years' enlistment expired remained in the South and served with Sumter and Marion until the close of the war. Mrs. W. L. Ledgerwood, 948 North Road, n.e., Warren, Ohio.

438. BATEMAN. Want parents and ancestors of Rebecah Bateman, born 14 Jan. 1799, died 11 April 1881, wife of Thomas Warden (Worden), born 1 Feb. 1798, of Wythe Co.,Va.

BOLT-SUTPHEN. Want parents of William Amos and Catherine (Sutphen) Bolt, who lived in Carroll and Grayson cos., Va., about 1830. Children: Charles, Harrison, Ellis, William, Catherine, Elmyra and Loretta. Miss Helen K. Bolt, 1804 Front Street, Blair, Nebr.

439. BOMAR. Want to correspond with descendants of the Bomar (Bowmar or Bomer) and related families wherever now located. About 1800 or 1810 many migrated southward and westward from Halifax Co., Va. Have information to exchange. E. B. Wood, Sr., Box 83, Oak Hill, W. Va.

QUERIES

440. DENT-HERBERT-GIBBENS. Want name and parents of --- Dent who married 1st Benjamin Gibbens (settled before close of Indian Wars on South Branch of Potomac River), 2nd Benjamin Riggs. Two known Gibbens sons: James (married whom?), John (m. ca.1795 Catherine Herbert who m. 2nd Col. Anthony Buckner; who were her parents?). Will exchange. Mrs. Lindley J. McFarland, 828 Stratford Ave., South Pasadena, Calif.

441. TORR-TARR. Want information about William Torr, from England 1830; operated ferry across Potomac prior to Revolution; married Mary Troxel; lived Frederick Co., Va., 1785. Sons Levi and William, probably others. Son William settled in James River, Va. (what county?) in late 1700's. Mrs. M. B. Rowan, 342 Beechwood Road, Ridgewood, N.J.

442. DONALDSON-MOREHEAD-LOUREY-SIBLEY-HILDEBRAND. Want information on and parents of Daniel Donaldson (born where? died Ky. where?) married Karenhappuck Morehead, Fauquier Co., Va., 1786. Parents of Jean Lourey of Caroline Co., Va. (will probated Ky. 1804), Robert Sibley of Charlotte Co., Va., 1782, and John Hildebrand (born 1812 Pa., died 1882 W.Va.). Mrs. R. E. Sibley, 64 Irving, Pryor, Okla.

443. WALKER. Want family of Jacob Walker, born 1809 on Walker Creek near Roanoke, Va. He ran away aged 13 with David Crockett on lumber raft to Tennessee, being unhappy with a step-parent (stepmother? stepfather?) named Nichols. In 1880 two Nichols kin visited him in Corinth, Miss., on way to Texas; my mother, aged 86, remembers visit. Mrs. Vivian P. Harrison, 1572 Overton Park, Apt. 11, Memphis 12, Tenn.

444. GUTHRIE. Want parents and birthplace of Henry Guthrie who died Franklin Co., Va., 1786. Was he from Middlesex Co.? Also maiden name of wife Penelope. Their children were Mary, Agg, James, John, David, Sally Ann, Penelope, Milley, Henry, Benjamin, Ruth. Wayne T. Guthrie, 4828 Oakwood Ave., Downers Grove, Ill.

445. CRUTCHER-POLLARD. Want parents of Revolutionary soldier William Crutcher and of his wife Elizabeth Pollard. Both Amherst Co., Va., families, where they were married in 1782. Mrs. Eugene A. Stanley, 135 E. 50th St., Savannah, Ga.

446. COLLIE-HALL-GOOLSBY-MARTIN. Want ancestry and data on Carter Collie, born (supposedly) 1812 near Chatham, Va., and his wife Gidem Hall, born Pittsylvania Co., Va.

Known children, not in order of birth (same mother?):
J. W., Confederate soldier; Nannie; "Miss Johnnie"; Dona; William R., of Richmond; James Hall, sheriff of Pittsylvania Co.; Mary Elizabeth (Mollie), born 1861, died 1919, married William Edward Goolsby, born ca.1844, Nelson Co., Va., son of A. M. and Nancy Goolsby. Wish full name of A. M. Goolsby and maiden name of his wife, ancestry and data on families of both. Was Rawley Martin, Confederate soldier of Chatham area, related to Collies or Goolsbys? Mrs. Anne G. Greene, Girard College, Philadelphia,21, Penn.

447. BUNTING. When did Richard Bunting, immigrant to Norfolk Co., Va., arrive? Desire to contact descendants. Mrs. Lea F. Duholm, Secretary Bunting Research, Main Street, Austin, Minn.

448. TOMKIES-READE. Elizabeth Tomkies, will dated 4 Dec. 1778, proved 24 Nov. 1783, Middlesex Co., Va., married Dr. John Reade of Middlesex. Issue: Charles (student, William and Mary College, 1770; married Ann ---; had Elizabeth, born 24 Sept. 1779); and John (died before 1778; married Elizabeth ---; had Charles mentioned in grandmother's will). Want information on this line. D. Simpson Tomkies, 166 Woodland Dr., Huntington 5, W.Va.

449. JOHNSON-BROWN. Want ancestry, name of wife, brothers and sisters, of Dennis Johnson, sea captain, Robert Brown, a cooper, and William Johnson, shoemaker, all in 1799 census of Alexandria, Va. Miss Bessie Z. Edwards, 2312 Enfield Rd., Austin 3, Texas.

450. McBRIDE-LANCASTER. Robert McBride, born 13 June 1794 in Va., married ca.1823 Elizabeth Lancaster, born 10 Feb. 1808, Hanover Co., Va., according to her death certificate. Both died in Logan Co., Ill. Where in Va. was Robert born and who were his parents? Who were Elizabeth's parents? According to obituaries, their eldest son, John (born 5 Oct. 1825) was born in W.Va., while another son, Warren, was born 2 Jan. 1830, Staunton, Va. A daughter, Martha, was born between these two brothers. I cannot reconcile their places of birth. Was Robert's father in the Revolution? Mrs. Jerry Drennan, 1002 Park Ave., Omaha 5, Nebr.

451. KING. Will exchange information on King family. Allie King, died 1802, Bucton, Warren Co., Va., married 17 June 1775 "Rich" John Catlett of Frederick Co., Va. Miss Jennie Allensworth, 1102 Linden Ave., Memphis 4, Tenn.

THE VIRGINIA GENEALOGIST

Volume 5, Number 2   Whole Number 18

April-June, 1961

CONTENTS

Editor's Page	50
The Booker Family of Petsworth Parish, Gloucester Co., Va., and South Farnham Parish, Essex Co., Va. By Cameron Allen	51
Middlesex County, Virginia, Wills, 1713-1734 (Continued)	65
Griffin Family Bible, Gloucester County, Virginia	75
A Guide to the Counties of Virginia	
Bland County	77
Boone County	78
Corrections and Comments	79
Amherst County, Virginia, 1800 Tax List	80
Local Notices from the Virginia Gazette, 1780 (Continued)	85
Book Reviews	
Cocke, _Parish Lines, Diocese of Southwestern Virginia_	89
Edwards, _Genealogy of the Henton Family_	89
Walker, _New Hanover County Court Minutes_	90
Baer, _The Vandeveers of North Carolina, Kentucky and Indiana_	90
Greer, _Early Virginia Immigrants_	91
Bidlack, _Letters Home_	92
Queries	92

Editor: John Frederick Dorman

Published quarterly by John Frederick Dorman
Business address: Box 4883, Washington 8, D.C.
Copyright 1961, by John Frederick Dorman

Subscription rates: $5.00 per year; single issue, $1.50
   All subscriptions begin with first issue of year
V. 1, nos. 1-2, $2.50 each, only as part of entire set

Second class postage paid at Washington, D.C.

EDITOR'S PAGE

During the first four years of publication fewer than one-fifth of the individual subscribers inserted a query in The Virginia Genealogist. In the same period approximately 75 pages were devoted to queries. The Editor would like to have an expression of opinion from his subscribers regarding the desirability of continuing the Query section. Is the use of this space for more abstracts of Virginia records preferred? Does the query section enable a sufficient number of subscribers to locate material not previously found by them? No precipitate action will be taken but comments are welcomed. Should the section be discontinued, it must be remembered that the magazine does not carry paid advertisements and there would be no means available for inquiries through its pages.

The Virginia Magazine of History and Biography for October 1960 contains three articles showing European antecedents of Virginia families. Peter Walne's "Henry Filmer of Mulberry Island, Gentleman" and Frank Tyrer's "Richard Blundell in Virginia and Maryland" contain family letters. Milton Rubincam's "The Noble Ancestry of the Revercomb Family" concerns the German forebears of the great-grandmother of Jacob Revercomb of Virginia.

In The American Genealogist for October 1960 Dr. George E. McCracken's article, "Thomas Pursell and His Earlier Descendants," includes the branch of Thomas Pursell (1720-1779) who came to Loudoun Co., Va., from Bucks Co., Pa., and gives reasons for believing he is the Thomas who was baptized in Hunterdon Co., N.J. Valentine Vernon Purcell, Thomas' grandson, gave his name to the town of Purcellville, Va.

Welch-Welsh-Walsh for September 1960 contains abstracts of a number of Virginia wills and inventories.

The Daughters of the American Revolution Magazine for October 1960 includes the Bible record of John Bass (born 1738) and his wife Tabitha, and also records of the Bukey family of Ohio Co., W.Va.

The Austin Genealogical Society (c/o Robert E. Lee, Texas State Library, Austin) published the first issue of a very helpful quarterly bulletin in November 1960

The Editor is solely responsible for the general policies, printing, distribution and sale of this periodical. Neither the Editor not The Virginia Genealogist assumes responsibility for eryors or fact or opinion expressed by contributors. Manuscripts which are submitted for publication should be of general interest and thoroughly documented and should be accompanied by return postage. Report of non-delivery of magazines must be reported within one month after the quarter they are dated.

THE BOOKER FAMILY

OF PETSWORTH PARISH, GLOUCESTER CO., VA.
AND SOUTH FARNHAM PARISH, ESSEX CO., VA.

By Cameron Allen,
East Orange, New Jersey

Virtually all published references to James and Lewis Booker of Essex County very quickly and neatly assign James as a son of Richard Booker (1688-1743) of Gloucester, James City and (at his death) York County by his first wife Margaret (Lowry). That this error, for error it is, was a natural one is easy to understand, for James is known to have come from Gloucester County to Essex County and Richard's sons are known also to have resided in Essex County for varying periods of time, though likewise born in Gloucester. This error was likewise a human one, for the Richard Booker family through the maternal line went straight back to the Purefoy family, one of the identifiable First Families of Virginia.[1] Unfortunately the linking of James Booker to Richard Booker was compounded more of wishful thinking (that omnipresent genealogical phenomenon) than of concrete, legally satisfactory proof.

On 14 March 1747 (1747/8), James Booker of the County of Gloucester first appeared in the Essex records when he bought 35 acres in the Parish of Southfarnham, Essex County, from Francis Brown. The deed refers to "the Line of the said Booker that Divides the said land the sd. Booker purchased of James Younger."[2] By 19 June 1753 James Booker had definitely become a resident of Essex County and South Farnham Parish when Francis Brown sold him additional land.[3]

The other Bookers from Gloucester County appear in Essex deeds covering the period 1707-1732. For example, on 24 Oct. 1709 "Richard Booker of Glo. County do give unto my son Richd. Booker ... the one moiety or halfe of a certain Tract of Land lying in Essex County on Portotobacco Swamp ..."[4] On 8 July 1713 "Edward & Richard Booker of Essex County do give unto our welbeloved Brother Edmund Booker ... 100 acres of land ... in Essex County upon the head of a branch of Portobacco Swamp."[5]

---

[1] Annie Lash Jester and Martha Woodroof Hiden, Adventurers of Purse and Person, Virginia, 1607-1625 (Princeton, N.J., 1956), pp. 275-78.
[2] Essex Co., Va., Deed Book 24, p. 207.
[3] Ibid., Deed Book 26, p. 253.
[4] Ibid., Deeds &c 13, p. 258.
[5] Ibid., Deeds &c 14, p. 146.

The Richard Booker family were long identified with the Parish of Abington in Gloucester County.

James Booker's family, on the other hand, were long identified with Petsworth (Petso) Parish in Gloucester County. The Gloucester Quit Rent Rolls of 1704/5 list:

    Petso Parish   Mary Booker   100 acres
    Abbington Parish   Capt. Booker   1000 acres[6]

The next reference to the Bookers of Petsworth Parish occurs 3 July 1722 when James Booker witnessed the indenture of Danell Moore, orphan, to Francis Easter.[7] At a vestry meeting 1 Oct. 1729, James Booker was chosen sexton of the church, succeeding Thomas Easter, decd.[8] James Booker occupied the position of sexton from that time down to 9 Nov. 1750, when the last vestry minute reference to him occurs.[9] Scattered references to his wife also appear: e.g., 6 Oct. 1731, "To James Booker's Wife for Washing the Scurplis 5 Times."[10] Presumably this wife was the Amy Booker who succeeded James Booker as sexton 16 Oct. 1751.[11] On 14 Nov. 1752 she was herself succeeded as sexton by John Blasingame.

A younger generation of Bookers gradually appears in the vestry minutes. Thomas Booker is mentioned 7 Oct. 1730[12] but not again until 16 Oct. 1749.[13] Seemingly he was too old to be a son of James, but conceivably he was a brother. James Booker Jr. appears only once, under date of 16 Oct. 1749, for assuming responsibility for John Spratt by indenture.[14] Presumably his disappearance from the Petsworth vestry minutes is accounted for by his removal about this time to Essex County.

Mr. Lewis Booker appears for the first time 4 Sept. 1751 when he is ordered to procession land in his precinct. He appears regularly thereafter. Eventually, on 1 Dec. 1767, "Mr. Lewis Booker is Chose Vestryman in the room of John Fox who refuseth to serve As a vestryman."[15] On 15 Nov. 1770 it was ordered that "Mr. Lewis Booker be church Wardin in the room of Mr. John Wiatt."[16] On 28 March 1785 Lewis Booker, being re-elected to the vestry of Petsworth Parish, subscribed to a paper along with the rest of those so elected professing "ourselves to be Members of the Protestant Episcopal Church."[17]

---

6 Polly Cary Mason, Records of Gloucester Co., Va., v. 1 (Newport News, Va., 1946), pp. 86-87.
7 Churchill G. Chamberlayne, ed., The Vestry Book of Petsworth Parish, Gloucester Co., Va., 1677-1793 (Richmond, 1933), pp. 161-62.
8 Ibid., p. 218.
9 Ibid., p. 281.
10 Ibid., p. 225.
11 Ibid., p. 285.
12 Ibid., p. 221.
13 Ibid., p. 280.
14 Ibid., p. 279.
15 Ibid., p. 337.
16 Ibid., p. 344.
17 Ibid., p. 374.

THE BOOKER FAMILY

In 1787 by the annual parish election, both Lewis Booker Senr. and Lewis Booker Ju. became members of the parish governing body.[18] On 14 July 1787 the vestry elevated Cap[n]. Lewis Booker (i.e., Lewis Booker, Jr.) to the post of churchwarden.[19] By 17 Nov. 1791 Lewis Booker, Sr., was dead, for it was "Order'd That M[r]. Meux Thornton is appointed a Vestryman in the room of the late M[r]. Lewis Booker, Deceas'd."[20]

From the foregoing Rent Roll and Petsworth Vestry Book the following genealogy may reasonably be constructed:

1. ---- Booker of Petsworth, left widow Mary (1704/5).
   Issue:
    2   i. (possibly) Thomas Booker
   *3 ii. James Booker, Sr., born say 1695.

3. James Booker, Sr., born say 1695, dead or in declining health by 1751; married Amy ----. (Can she have been a Lewis? There were Lewises in the parish.) Issue:
   *4 i. Lewis Booker, Sr., born say 1726, died
       by 1791.
   *5 ii. James Booker, Jr., born say 1723, died
       1793.

4. Lewis^3 Booker (James^2, ---^{1}), born say 1726, first mentioned in the Petsworth Parish vestry minutes in 1751 when he is referred to as "M[r]. Lewis Booker." Subsequently he became vestryman and churchwarden of the parish. On 5 Sept. 1755 Lewis Booker advertised finding a black horse in Gloucester County.[21] In 1771 a vacant plantation was offered for sale in Gloucester by Nelson Jones, terms to be learned "by applying to Mr. Lewis Booker, in Gloucester."[22] Several years later Wilson M. Cary offered for sale a tract in Petsworth Parish, "lying upon Poropotank river," to "be shewn by Mr. Lewis Booker, of whom the terms may be known."[23] It would seem that Lewis Booker was, among other things, an early-day realty agent. Lewis Booker, Sr., was dead by Nov. 1791, as we have seen. Issue by unknown wife:
   *6 i. Lewis Booker, Jr.
    7 ii. (possibly) William Booker, listed in 1782
        in Petsworth Parish for taxes on one free
        male, one horse, one cow.[24]

---

18 Ibid., pp. 378-79.
19 Ibid., p. 380.
20 Ibid., p. 384.
21 Virginia Gazette, 5 Sept. 1755, p. 4, col. 2.
22 Ibid., Purdie and Dixon, 4 July 1771, p. 3, col. 2.
23 Ibid., Rind, 23 June 1774, p. 4, col. 2.
24 Mason, op. cit., v. 1, p. 9.

8 iii. (possibly) James Booker, Surveyor of Mathews County in the 1780s and 1790s.[25] Listed in Kingston Parish, 1782.

9 iv. (possibly) John Booker, sheriff of Gloucester in 1789;[26] listed in Petsworth Parish in 1784; served as private in the Company of "Gloster" militia commanded by Capt. Thomas Baytop, 31 May-5 June 1781.

Note: One or more of the last three Bookers <u>could</u> be descended from Thomas Booker (#2).

6. Lewis[4] Booker, Jr. (Lewis[3], James Sr.,[2] ---[1]). Not until 1787 do we become aware in the parish records of both a senior and a junior Lewis Booker. On 11 July 1793 Mr. Lewis Booker "having been elected on Easter Monday last past being the 1st day of April by the members of the protestant Episcopal Church, in Petsworth parish, to act & serve as Vestryman" agreed in writing to "be conformable to the Worship, Doctrin, & Disciplin of the protestant Episcopal Church."[27] He was presumably the Lewis Booker who in 1785 was serving as surveyor in Gloucester.[28] Presumably, also, it was the junior Lewis who was commissioned assistant Inspector at Poropotank Warehouse in the County of Gloucester on 6 Feb. 1777.[29] On 30 Sept. 1784 Lewis Booker was commissioned inspector of tobacco, assisted by Richard Taliaferro.[30] On 11 Sept. 1777 Lieut. Lewis Booker was serving in the "Gloster" County Militia.[31] From 31 May to 5 June 1781 he served actively in the Gloster County Company of Militia commanded by Capt. Thomas Baytop.[32] This Lewis Booker of Gloucester County with militia service has been confused with his first cousin Lewis Booker (#12) of Essex County, with service in the Continental Line. In 1782 Lewis Booker was listed for taxes in Petsworth Parish with 541 acres, 2 free males, 15 Negroes, 3 horses and 24 cattle.[33] This last reference is presumably to his father as head of the family, and not to the junior Lewis Booker.

5. James[3] Booker, Jr. (James[2], ---[1]), born say 1723, died 1793, Essex Co., Va., migrated from Gloucester County

---

25 Ibid., v. 1, p. 122.
26 Ibid.
27 Chamberlayne, op. cit., p. 388.
28 Mason, op. cit., v. 1, p. 122.
29 H. R. McIlwaine, ed., Journals of the Council of the State of Virginia, v. 1 (Richmond, Virginia State Library, 1931), p. 329.
30 Ibid., v. 1, p. 379.
31 The Virginia Magazine of History and Biography, v. 7, p. 148.
32 Tyler's Quarterly, v. 8, p. 270.
33 Mason, op. cit., v. 1, p. 91.

to Essex between 1747 and 1753, and gradually added to
his holdings in South Farnham Parish until the entire
tract was of sufficient extent that he might properly
call it "Laurel Grove." His home, a modest one by the
standards of later generations, is yet standing near
Miller's Tavern, at the end of a few last vestiges of an
avenue of laurels.

James Booker married first ----- (name nowhere recorded), the mother of his children, and second Mrs. Elizabeth
Wright, ca.1775. It is a not unreasonable supposition
that his first wife was named Elizabeth H---, for in the
five groups of her grandchildren whose names are known,
there is an Elizabeth in each, two of whom were named
Elizabeth H., typically in each group an older daughter.
(Examine below.) Nor does it seem likely that these
granddaughters Elizabeth were named for the second wife
of James, their step-grandmother, for one or two of them
were born prior to their grandfather's second marriage.
It is uncertain whether this Elizabeth H--- came from
Gloucester County or Essex County, but the chances are
that she was from Gloucester. In glancing over the
families of Petsworth Parish whose surname begins with
"H", one finds that the name which would seem to offer
the greatest possibilities of this tie-in with the Bookers
is the Hubbard family. A Mrs. Johannah Hubbard is mentioned in a vestry record of 1720, and the apparently
oldest child of James Booker was named Joanna, a comparatively distinctive name for the age and locality.
Furthermore, the second wife of James Booker, Mrs.
Elizabeth Wright, was apparently a Sheppard from Petsworth, whose paternal grandmother was a Hubbard. The
Bookers, Sheppards and Hubbards of Petsworth seem to
have had multiple connections with one another.

On 30 Nov. 1775 James Booker and Mrs. Elizabeth Wright,
widow, drew up Articles of Agreement in anticipation of
a "marriage shortly intended between" them: "Elizabeth
to have free liberty to dispose of her estate and shall
not claim dower right in the estate of the said James."[34]
She was apparently the widow of Ambrose Wright, for on
24 July 1777 James Booker of Essex County caused to be
published an announcement that "All Persons who have any
Demands against the Estate of Ambrose Wright, deceased,
or against my Wife are desired to bring in their accounts
by the 1st Day of September ..."[35]

This Mrs. Elizabeth Wright, apparently the widow of
Ambrose Wright, is presumably the Elizabeth Sheppard who
had married Archibald Wright, according to the statement
of her brother Samuel Sheppard, made in 1792. She was

---

34 Essex Co., Va., Deed Book 31, p. 270.
35 *Virginia* *Gazette*, Dixon and Hunter, 15 Aug. 1777, p. 7, col. 2.

the daughter of Samuel and Mary (Kavanagh) Sheppard of Petsworth and granddaughter of Robert and Jessica (Hubard) Sheppard. Her brother Samuel Sheppard, born 3 Feb. 1730, married Anne Burwell and named a son James Booker Sheppard. Further, the William Shapard (Sheppard) who married James Booker's daughter Mary was either Mrs. Wright's brother or more probably nephew.[36]

In his will made 3 May 1790, probated 18 June 1793, James Booker named "my Daughter Mary Shapard, my grandchildren by my Deceased Daughter Joanna Woodson, my son Lewis Booker, my Grand Daughters by my Dec^d. Daughter Ann Wild and my Daughter Elizabeth Jeffries" and appointed as executors his son Lewis Booker and "my Sons in Law Jno. Webb and Richard Jeffries and Capt. Thomas Wood."[37] The inventory of his estate listed inter alia 20 slaves, 2 Bibles, 1 Dictionary, the Universal Gazetteer and a parcel of Old Books.[38]

Issue of James and [?Elizabeth (Hubbard)] Booker:
- *10   i. Joanna Booker, born say 1750, married John Woodson of Cumberland Co., Va.
- *11   ii. Amy Booker, born 27 Aug. 1752, died 25 March 1835, married 20 Feb. 1772 in Essex County to John Webb; migrated about 1782 to Granville Co., N.C.
- *12   iii. Lewis Booker, born 21 May 1754, died 23 Dec. 1814, married 7 Feb. 1788 Judith Dudley; inherited "Laurel Grove" where he lived and is buried.
- 13   iv. Mary Booker, born say 1756, married William Shapard (Sheppard); migrated to Granville Co., N.C. Issue, inter alia: 1) Thomas Shapard, married Fanny Bailey of Person Co., N.C., and migrated to Tennessee; 2) John S. Shapard, married 1808 Elizabeth Vass, daughter of Philip and Elizabeth (Webb) Vass; 3) Elizabeth H. Shapard, married 6 May 1789, Granville Co., N.C., Francis Royster.
- 14   v. Ann Booker, born say 1758, married ---- Wild (Wyld). She was deceased by 1790. Issue: 1) Elizabeth H. Wyld (Betsy), born 7 Sept. 1785; 2) Ann B. Wyld (Nancy), born 9 Jan. 1788.
- 15   vi. Elizabeth Booker, born say 1760, married Richard Jeffries.

10. Joanna^4 Booker (James^3, James^2, ---^{1}), born say 1750, married as his first wife John Woodson of Cumberland

---
36 William and Mary College Quarterly, 2nd ser., v. 7, pp. 174-80.
37 Essex Co., Va., Will Book 15, p. 101.
38 Ibid., p. 206.

THE BOOKER FAMILY 57

Co., Va., born there ca.1747, son of John and Mary (Miller) Woodson. Presumably John Woodson met Joanna on visits to his mother's Miller relatives in Lancaster and Essex counties. Joanna died about 1780 and Woodson married second Mrs. Elizabeth (Raine) Venable, widow of John Venable.

Issue of John and Joanna (Booker) Woodson:[39]

- 16   i. Booker Woodson, born ca.1768, married Patsy ---; resided in Cumberland Co., Va.
- 17   ii. Peter Woodson, born 27 Dec. 1770, Cumberland Co., Va.; married 14 Nov. 1799 Elizabeth Harrison Hobbs. In 1805 they migrated to Robertson Co., Tenn. (that portion now Cheatham Co.). He died there 30 June 1847.
- 18   iii. Benjamin Woodson, born ca.1772, Cumberland Co., Va.; married ca.1793 his step-sister Martha Ann Venable. They migrated to Rockingham Co., N.C.
- 19   iv. Joseph Nathaniel Woodson, born 1774, Cumberland Co., Va., died 1852, Montgomery Co., Tenn; married Elizabeth ---.
- 20   v. James Woodson, born ca.1776, Cumberland Co., Va., married Sukey ---; shortly d.s.p. in Cumberland Co., Va.
- 21   vi. Elizabeth Woodson, born ca.1778, Cumberland Co., Va., married ca.1798 William Wright.

11. Amy[4] Booker (James[3], James[2], ---[1]), born 27 Aug. 1752, was married in Essex Co., Va., 20 Feb. 1772 to John Webb, born 18 Jan. 1747, son of James and Mary (Edmondson) Webb of Essex County. John Webb early identified himself with the Revolutionary cause. On 8 Feb. 1776 a Warrant was issued to Griffin Fauntleroy "for the use of Capt. John Webb for £72 for the recruiting service in the Essex District, James Edmondson's Letter lodged as Security for a proper application ..."[40] On 13 March 1776 Commissions were issued and delivered by the Council to Capt. Webb and his subaltern officers, dated 5 March.[41] Numerous references appear in the Journals of the Council to warrants issued Capt. Webb for his company's arms and necessaries. Muster rolls exist from 29 Dec. 1776 for Capt. John Webb's co., 7th Va. Regt. of Foot, commanded by Col. Alexander McClenachan. The muster roll dated 7 Aug. 1777 notes that Webb was left at Middlebrook sick.

---
39 Henry Morton Woodson, Historical Genealogy of the Woodsons and Their Connections (Columbia, Mo., 1915), pp. 129-30.
40 McIlwaine, op. cit., v. 2 (Richmond, 1932), p. 408.
41 Ibid., v. 2, p. 451.

The roll dated 1 Sept. 1777 records him sick at Philadelphia. His company's muster for Feb. 1778 was dated 7 March 1778 at Valley Forge. The muster roll of "Capt. John Webb's company, 7th Va. Regiment, commanded by Lt. Col. Holt Richeson" taken at Valley Forge 4 June 1778 notes that Webb was "on furlough, Virginia." He was, however, present on 4 Aug. and 1 Sept. 1778 when musters were taken at White Plains. On 26 Jan. 1778 he had been advanced to the rank of major. Succeeding muster rolls find him at White Plains, Middlebrook, Smiths Cove, Ramapough, Haverstraw and Morristown. On 4 July 1779 he was made Lieutenant Colonel. When on 27 Jan. 1783 certificate for his final pay was given, it was received by a family connection, Capt. Henry Young.[42]

Among the above papers is one order that "Capt. Webb 7th to go to Virg^a. to bring up Recruits." On one of his tours of duty in the recruiting service, "John Webb, Capt." advertised: "Deserted from my co. of the 7th Va. Regt. on their march from Williamsburg to Fredericksburg, the following soldiers ..." named and identified as being from Essex, King and Queen and Middlesex counties.[43] A second advertisement for the deserters was inserted by "Henry Young, lieut." in Capt. John Webb's Company.[44]

Webb was back in Essex County by 14 July 1781 when he wrote from there to "the Executive" of Virginia "in regard to the claim of Mrs. Webb for her negro Slave 'Robins,' carried off by Capt. Carre and his crew, who were afterwards captured by a party of volunteers under Webb's command."[45] The following year he was temporarily under a cloud for on 20 May 1782 Governor Harrison wrote to Isaac Smith, William Roane and Thomas Gaskins, county lieutenants of Richmond, Essex and Northumberland counties, respectively:

> The Executive have received information that Col^o. Webb was concerned in a vessel that had committed an act of hostility by taking a vessel from New England, and that she afterwards came up Rappahannock river to him and loaded at Hobbshole; notwithstanding the fair character this Gentleman has always borne and the probability there is of his innocence, yet you must be sensible how much it is our duty to have the matter strictly enquired into that Justice may be done as well to his reputation as to the public. We ... request that you will call on Col^o. Webb for a full account of his transactions with the Captain or any other person on board this vessel and the interest he has in her ...[46]

---

42 Military service record, Lt. Col. John Webb, 5th and 7th Va. Regts., National Archives, Washington, D.C.
43 Virginia Gazette, Purdie, 28 Mar. 1777, supplement, p. 2.
44 Ibid., Purdie, 13 June 1777, p. 1.
45 Calendar of Virginia State Papers, v. 2, p. 218.
46 H. R. McIlwaine, ed., Official Letters of the Governors of Virginia, v. 3, Letters of Thomas Nelson and Benjamin Harrison (Richmond, Virginia State Library, 1929), p. 228.

THE BOOKER FAMILY

Very shortly on the heels of this episode, concerning which we know nothing further as to his implication therein, John Webb moved to Granville Co., N.C., where his brother William Webb had preceded him before the outbreak of the Revolution. Prior to this, on 1 Jan. 1782, he had bought 316 acres from his brother-in-law Philip Vass in Granville County.[47] His residence was two miles north of Oak Hill. With his removal from Virginia, if not before, he severed his affiliation with the Anglican Church, and in his new home became an elder in the Grassy Creek Presbyterian Congregation. Later, in 1822, he was instrumental in organizing a daughter congregation, Spring Grove Church, nearer his home. John Webb died in Granville County 29 Aug. 1826, having made his will 12 June 1826, the same being proved in November Court 1826. By it he gave "to my beloved wife the sum of $500 to carry interest from this date ... in lieu of the sum of about that amount which came to her by the will of one of her sister's daughters."[48] Presumably this refers to one of the Wild nieces.

Amy (Booker) Webb appears to have had ideas of her own as to religion, for she did not follow her husband into the strong Presbyterian congregation of his locality. Several years after the move to Carolina, she became a member of Ebenezer Methodist Episcopal Church at Oak Hill. The sermon preached at her funeral refers to the fact that she had been a member of the Methodist Episcopal Church for 48 years.[49] She died 25 March 1835.

Issue of John and Amy (Booker) Webb, the first three or four born in Essex County, the remainder in Granville Co., N.C.:

22 i. Elizabeth Webb, born 4 March 1773, died 6 Sept. 1829, married 1794 Thomas Owen, Jr., son of Thomas and Isabella (Allin) Owen, natives of Hanover Co., Va.; migrated to Breckinridge Co., Ky.

23 ii. Thomas Webb, born 26 Dec. 1776, married 1800 Mary Jane Thomas, a native of Charles Co., Md., daughter of Philip Thomas. Thomas Webb was one of the first students to enroll at the young University of North Carolina; was merchant at Hurdle Mills, Person Co., N.C.; represented Person County in the North Carolina State Legislature.

---
47 Granville Co., N.C., Deed Book O, p. 254.
48 Ibid., Wills, Inventories, Etc. 10, p. 254.
49 A Funeral Sermon Occasioned by the Death of Mrs. Amy Webb, Delivered ... at Ebenezer Church, Granville County, N.C., by Rev. Jesse Rankin (Richmond, T. W. White, printer, 1835), copy in Webb family papers, North Carolina Department of Archives and History, Raleigh, N.C.

24	iii.	James Webb, born 21 Nov. 1779, died 3 Aug. 1827, Person Co., N.C., married 17 Feb. 1803 Ann Hunt Smith, born 5 Sept. 1784, Granville Co., N.C., daughter of James and Amy (Pomfret) Smith.
25	iv.	Mary Webb, born 22 June 1782; second wife of her cousin James Webb Smith, born 18 May 1770, son of Col. Samuel and Mary (Webb) Smith; migrated to Jackson Co., Tenn.; no issue.
26	v.	Ann Webb, born 24 June 1784, died 29 Jan. 1825, Granville Co., N.C.; married 1808 John Franklin Patillo, son of Rev. Henry and Mary (Anderson) Patillo.
27	vi.	John Webb, born 1 April 1786, married Elizabeth Moorman; settled in Breckinridge Co., Ky.
28	vii.	William Webb, born 17 Oct. 1787, married 1812 Elizabeth Pulliam, daughter of John and Elizabeth (Wilson) Pulliam; migrated to Lafayette Co., Miss.
29	viii.	Lewis Webb, born 15 July 1789, married 1818 Ann Nutall; merchant at Richmond, Va.; resided in the historic former home of Judge Spencer Roane there.
30	ix.	Isaac Webb, born 29 Dec. 1790, married 1816 Harriet Phillips Dickins, daughter of Jesse and Frances (Moore) Dickins; settled in Smith Co., Tenn.
31	x.	Amy Webb, born 3 July 1792, died 7 July 1793.
32	xi.	Amy Webb (II), born 31 Aug. 1794, married 1829 as his second wife her cousin Col. Maurice Smith of Granville Co., N.C., son of Col. Samuel and Mary (Webb) Smith.
33	xii.	Susanna Webb, born 4 Oct. 1796; never married.[50]

12. Lewis[4] Booker (James[3], James[2], ---[1]), born in South Farnham Parish, Essex Co., Va., 21 May 1754, the only son of the family apparently to reach adult years. On 13 Jan. 1777 the Council of the State of Virginia "being prepared to go upon the Business of recommending proper persons to Congress for Subalterns in the Regiment of Artillery to be raised in this State proceeded thereon and came to the following Resolutions ... that Lewis

---

[50] Vital dates of the entire above family are taken from the photostats of the Webb family Bible preserve: at the North Carolina State Department of Archives and History, Raleigh. For information on descendants of the above children, see W. J. Webb, *Our Webb Kin of Dixie* (Oxford, N.C., 1940).

THE BOOKER FAMILY

Booker ... be recommended as proper Persons to be appointed Second Lieutenants."[51] Lewis Booker appeared as "Captain-Lieutenant" in Capt. Wm. Murray's Company of Artillery under the command of Col. Charles Harrison in a muster roll dated 21 Oct. 1777. Lewis Booker, Capt. Artillery, advertised in the Virginia Gazette of 1 May 1778 to advise that the "heirs of Dudley Taylor are desired to apply to Mr. William Mitchell, quartermaster in York garrison for a small box of clothing, &c which I left in his possession with an inventory."[52]

Thereafter Lewis Booker held the rank of Captain-Lieutenant in Capt. Samuel Edden's Company, same regiment, in a muster roll dated 3 June 1778 at Valley Forge. During the succeeding year and a half he was entered consistently on muster rolls of the company dated at Camp White Plains, Camp Fredericksburg, Pluckemin, Middlebrook, Camp Smiths Clove, New Windsor ("Park of Artillery near Chester"). From Nov. 1779 through March 1780 he was noted as "on furlough" on the "Muster Roll of Capts. Pierce's, Burwell's, Dandridge's and Edden's Cos., incorporated and commanded by Capt. S. Eddens in the 1st Battn. of Artillery Comd. by Col. Charles Harrison," Morristown. From Jan. through May 1782 he commanded a detachment of Artillery from the 1st Regiment, stationed near Bacon Bridge, S.C. On 1 Jan. 1783 he signified his wish to retire, and on 30 Sept. 1783 received his final pay certificate.[53]

In 1796 Booker applied for and received a bounty land warrant, lost under the following circumstances:

> I (Anthony New) hereby certify that in the year 1796 while attending a session of Congress in Philadelphia, I received a power of attorney from Capt. Lewis Booker of Essex Co., State of Virginia, authorizing me to obtain a warrant for his continental bounty in land. I accordingly applied for and received a warrant for 300 acres, which at the request of the said Booker I inclosed in a letter addressed to him then in Lexington, Ky., but which did not reach him during his stay in that state.[54]

In 1803 Booker received a replacement warrant for his services in the company of Capt. Samuel Eddens. By his will, dated 23 Dec. 1814, probated 20 Feb. 1815, Booker directed his executors "if any of my land in the State of Ohio is still unsold" to sell same "for ready money" and referred to "money now due to me in that state for land hitherto sold."[55] The inventory of his

---

[51] McIlwaine, Journals, v. 1, pp. 312-13.
[52] Virginia Gazette, Purdie, 1 May 1778, p. 3, col. 2.
[53] Military service record, Lewis Booker, Capt.-Lt., Virginia Line, National Archives, Washington, .D.C.
[54] Revolutionary bounty land warrant 8-200, Lewis Booker, National Archives, Washington, D.C.
[55] Essex Co., Va., Will Book 18, p. 139.

estate, 1 April 1815, listed 18 slaves.[56]

Lewis Booker was married 7 Feb. 1788 to Judith Dudley, born 1 Jan. 1765, died in Essex County 16 Oct. 1817, daughter of George and Dorothy (Tabb) Dudley.

Issue of Lewis and Judith (Dudley) Booker:[57]

 34 i. Dorothy Booker, born 24 Feb. 1790, died 29 Oct. 1850, married 12 Nov. 1812 William A. Garnett who died 31 May 1835. Issue: 1) George S. Garnett, born 26 Feb. 1818, died 19 Oct. 1836. The mother and son are buried at Laurel Grove.

 *35 ii. James Booker, born 26 June 1791, died 20 March 1861, married Ann Throckmorton.

 36 iii. Elizabeth Booker, born 7 March 1793, died 22 Jan. 1874 at the home of her nephew Booker Garnett; married Henry H. Baughan; no issue.

 37 iv. Mary Booker, born 26 May 1796, died 7 Sept. 1818, buried at Laurel Grove; married 3 June 1818 Dr. Henry Fauntleroy (1794-1859), son of Robert and Sarah (Ball) Fauntleroy; no issue. Dr. Fauntleroy married second 1822 Annette Lorhelle Sisson. He inherited Naylors Hole from his father.[58]

 *38 v. George Tabb Booker, born 15 Oct. 1797, married 20 Dec. 1838 Caroline Richardson.

 39 vi. Lewis Booker, Jr., born 15 May 1799, died 9 March 1832; never married.

 *40 vii. Sarah H. Booker, born 1 Nov. 1802, died 19 Dec. 1837; married 29 March 1827 Muscoe Garnett of "Ben Lomond."

 41 viii. William Booker, born 31 Jan. 1807, died 17 April 1828; never married.

 42 ix. Judith Booker, born 29 Feb. 1808, died 1895; married 24 June 1830 John L. Cox; no issue.

35. James[5] Booker (Lewis[4], James[3], James[2], ---[1]) was born 26 June 1791 and died 20 March 1861. He married 11 Jan. 1814 Ann Throckmorton who died 12 July 1849. The couple settled at New Market, Shenandoah Co., Va. In 1838 they moved to Ohio, near Columbus, and settled upon a portion of his father's military land warrant. Later

---

56 Ibid., p. 196.
57 Booker-Garnett-Lyell family Bible, Essex and Richmond cos., Va., 1754-1956 (Philadelphia, Samuel Eckstein, pub., 1833), photostats at Virginia State Library, Richmond, Va.
58 Robert H. Fauntleroy, The Fauntleroy Family (Washington, D.C., 1952), p. 40.

THE BOOKER FAMILY 63

they moved to Vermillion Co., Ill., where they died and
are buried. Issue:
    43   i. Elizabeth Booker married --- Fitzgerald.
    44   ii. William L. Booker, died without issue 27
             Oct. 1844, Vermillion Co., Ill.
    45 iii. James Webb Booker.
    46   iv. George Albert Booker, died 16 Nov. 1849,
             Vermillion Co., Ill.
    47   v. Erasmus Darwin Booker, born 10 Sept. 1825,
             married first Olivia Carrington Anderson,
             second Elizabeth Eubank.
    48   vi. Emily Booker, died 22 Jan. 1859 near
             Springfield, Ohio; married George Browning.
    49 vii. Samuel Marion Booker, died 27 June 1858,
             Vermillion Co., Ill.

38. George Tabb^5 Booker (Lewis^4, James^3, James^2, ---^{1})
was born 15 Oct. 1797 and married 20 Dec. 1838 Caroline
Richardson, daughter of Thomas and Elizabeth (Coleman)
Richardson. They resided in Richmond, Va. Issue:
    50   i. Ellen Booker, born 30 April 1840.
    51   ii. Lewis Booker married Lucy Landon Page.
    52 iii. Thomas Booker, never married.
    53   iv. Elizabeth Taylor Booker married Robert
             F. Jennings.
    54   v. Mary Garnett Booker, never married.
    55   vi. Carrie Booker married the Rev. Robert
             Douglas Roller.

40. Sarah H.^{5} Booker (Lewis^4, James^3, James^2, ---^{1})
was born 1 Nov. 1802 and died 19 Dec. 1837. She married
Muscoe Garnett of "Ben Lomond" on 29 March 1827. He was
born 17 March 1808 and died 5 Oct. 1880. He was a
member of the Virginia House of Delegates and a judge of
the county court.[59] Sarah (Booker) Garnett is buried at
"Laurel Grove" where her tombstone is extant.
Issue of Muscoe and Sarah (Booker) Garnett:
    56   1. Lewis H. Garnett, born 28 Dec. 1827 at
             Hopkinsville, Ky., died 20 Sept. 1895,
             Essex Co., Va.; served in Company F, 9th
             Virginia Cavalry, C.S.A.; Commonwealth's
             Attorney.
    57   ii. George William Garnett, born 21 Aug.
             1829 at Dunbars, King and Queen Co., Va.,
             died 18 June 1903, Essex Co., Va.;
             Treasury Department, C.S.A.; prisoner of
             war at Forts LaFayette and Delaware.
    58 iii. Muscoe Garnett, Jr., born 1 Jan. 1832 at

---
59 Information from marble tablet on the wall of the Essex
County Court House.

"Farmers Retreat," King and Queen Co., Va.; Company F, 9th Virginia Cavalry, C.S.A.

59 iv. David S. Garnett, M.D., born 3 Oct. 1834 at "Ashland," Essex Co., Va., died 3 Oct. 1862 at "Ben Lomond." Surgeon, C.S.A.

60 v. Booker Garnett, born 4 Dec. 1837 at "Stock Hill," Essex Co., Va. 2nd Richmond Howitzers, C.S.A.; member of the Virginia House of Delegates.

MIDDLESEX COUNTY, VIRGINIA

WILLS, 1713-1734

(Continued from V. 5, p. 17)

Page 296-97. Will of Augt. Owen of Middlesex County, planter, being sick and weak, dated "this 28th day 1726/7."

To my well beloved Wm. Owin one Negro man Sharp. For want of heir to the next heir.

To my well beloved daughter Clemonds Owin Negro wench Betty. For want of heir to the next heir in law.

To my well beloved daughter Sarah Ball one Negro girl Marga[ret].

To my well beloved daughter Sarah Ball twenty shillings to be paid by 22 Jan. 1726 [1727].

To my well beloved son Augt. Owin twenty shills.

To the rest of my beloved children vizt. Christopher Owin, John Owin, Mary Owin, Anne Owin, James Owin, Jacob Owin, and Constant Owin twenty shills a peace to be paid them when they shall come to the age of twenty one.

The remainder of my estate equally divided between my well beloved son and daughter Wm. and Clemonds Owin.

My well beloved son Wm. Owin my sole executor.

Augustine Owin

Wit: John Larke, Jos. Smith.

7 March 1726 [1727]. Produced by William Owen. Proved by John Larke and Joseph Smith.

Pages 297-98. Will of David George in the County of Middlesex and Parish of Christ Church, being sick and weak, dated 28 Nov. 1723.

Unto my son John George all my land and plantation that I am now possessed with.

All my Negroes to be equally divided between my three soons onely my son John to have teen pounds les in the vallew of the Neagrows then Harry and James.

Unto my son Harrey my gun that I used to hunt withal.

Unto my son James one oval table which is now in my house.

Unto my daughter Jeane five pounds as likewise one cow and calf, desiring it may be all that she may have of my estate by reason of her disobedience.

All my personable estate, goods and chattles to be equally divided among my three sons John, Harry and James George.

My three sons John, Harry and James executors.

David (D) George

Wit: Joseph Hardee, John Seager, Robt. (R) Brown.

7 March 1726 [1727]. Presented in Court by John

George. Proved by John Segar and Robt. Brown.

Pages 298-300. Mr. John Price. Inventory. Estate not valued. Includes servant man named David Wilson, mulatto servant boy named Wil Whistler, two mulatto servant girls named Ann and Betty Whistler and ten Negro slaves. Signed by T. Price. Admitted to record 7 March 1726 [1727].

Pages 300-02. Mr. Humphrey Jones. Inventory. 21-22 Dec. 1726. Appraised pursuant to order of 6 Dec. 1726, by John Mosley, George Chowning, James Meacham. Total valuation ₤ 418.8.3 including 11 Negroes valued at ₤238. Signed by Humphry Jones, administrator. Admitted to record 7 March 1726 [1727].

Pages 303-05. Will of Richard Walker, merchant in Urbanna, being very sick and weak in body, dated 1 March 1726 [1727].

Unto my nephew James Walker the son of my brother James Walker all my lands lieing in Spotsilvania County commonly known by the name of Staggland containing 1400 and odd acres with all the Negroes, white servants, stock and utencils of the said plantation. The produce of the said servants and slaves shall be shipt from year to year for the use of my said nephew James by my executors and consigned to Mr. John Maynard, merchant in London, under the same mark they used to be in my lifetime.

Unto the said James a lott in Urbanna which I bought of Pinchback Hammerton bounded on the east by Parson McKenny's and on the west by Mr. Robinson's lott and on the south by Virginia Street. Also the lott my stable now stands upon being a corner lott fronting the Market place. Also the lott at the water side bounded on the east by the creek, on the west by a lott of Robert Logan, on the north by Virginia Street, on the south by a lott belonging to James Walker.

Unto the said James the sum of ₤ 500 current money to be let out at interest.

Unto my neice Ann Walker the daughter of my brother James Walker as much money as will make up the share she has of her father's estate the compleat sum of ₤ 500 current money.

Unto my neice Cathrine Walker the daughter of my brother James Walker as much money as will make up the share she has of her father's estate ₤ 500 current money.

I leave my said neices Ann and Cathrine Walkers my chaice and harness and sixteen pounds to buy them a couple horses.

To my brother John Walker at Ashbourn in Derbyshire

₤ 20 sterling to buy him a suite of mourning.
Unto my brother Thomas Walker at Ashbourn in Derbyshire ₤ 20 sterling to buy him a suite of mourning.
Unto my brother David Walker at Ashbourn in Derbyshire ₤ 20 sterling to buy him a suite of mourning.
Unto my sister Jean Locket at Leeke in Staffordshire ₤ 20 sterling to buy her a suite of mourning.
To my good friend Mr. Thomas Nelson in Yorktown my bay horse, broad hurst and ₤ 20 current money.
To my well beloved friend Mr. Bartholomew Yates, Rector of Christ Church in Middlesex County, ₤ 20 current money.
To my good friend Charles Burgess of Lancaster County ₤ 10 current money.
To my good friend William Wood a mourning ring of twenty shillings value.
To my good friend Doctor Mark Bannerman a mourning ring of twenty shillings value.
All the tobacco that can be got ready under the mark of L&M may be shipt on board the Sarah and Mary and consigned to Mr. Humphry Bell, merchant in London, upon my own proper accompt.
It is my will and desire to ship on board the Forward Friggot, Daniel Russell, master, ten hogsheads tobacco to be consigned to Mr. John Maynard, merchant in London, as those six hogsheads that are markt on board the Sarah and Mary already after this manner AC.
Likewise to get freight on board the Princess Amelia for eight hogsheads tobacco to be consigned to Mr. Edward Tucker, merchant in Weymouth; five of them I have bought of Mrs. Payne already at 12/6 per hundred Cask and she is to give me the casks.
Likewise if Capt. John Watkinson come in to ship twelve hogsheads tobacco on board his ship and to consign them to Mr. Foster Cunliffe, merchant in Leverpoole.
Likewise to have you keep buying tobacco till the last day of March allowing 12/6 per hundred cask and 16/8 goods.
Likewise I would have ten hogsheads tobacco that is good and large shipt on board the Mary, James Hopkins, master, and to be conveyed to Mr. Humphry Bell, merchant in London.
The rest of my tobacco to be shipt by my executors but I would have them be advised by my servants what market it is proper for.
All the women's shooes, stockings, aprons, headdress, edging, quilted coats and hoop coats that is in the house shall equally be divided betwixt my two neices.
The sum of ₤ 10 current money shall be paid to my neice Ann Walker for her better maintainance out of my estate untill she arrives at the age of twenty five years.

To my neice Cathrine Walker an annuity of ₺ 10 current money until she arrives at the age of twenty five years, but in case either of my two neices shall marry, from that day their annuity shall cease.

It is my will and desire to send home my nephew James Walker in Capt. John Watkinson or some other shipp bound that way to the care of Mr. Foster Cunliffe, merchant in Liverpool, to learn Lattin about three years, then to be taken from the Lattin School and be put to learn arithmetick and merchant's accompts, navigation or any other part of the mathematicks he inclines to.

To my man George Dennis ₺ 20 current money and desier they'l ask his advice about my affairs.

To my man George Dennis my gray suite of broad cloth, my Duroy coat and breeches with flatt buttons, my brown duffill coat, my regular and my leather breeches. The rest of my cloaths I give to my servants Joseph Bell and William Mckintosh excepting my stockings and my holland work waiscoat, Joseph Bell being to have two shares and William Mckintosh [one].

My nephew James Walker and my nieces Ann and Cathrine Walker shall have decent mourning such as my executors shall think fitt.

Unto my nephew John Walker, the eldest son of my brother James Walker, all the rest of my estate.

My trusty and well beloved friends the Reverd. Mr. Bartholomew Yates, Mr. Thomas Nelson and Mr. Charles Burgess together with my nephew John Walker executors.
R. Walker

Wit: Joh: Robinson, Benja. Robinson, Richard Moulson, George Dennis.

4 April 1727. Produced in Court by Charles Burgess. Proved by George Dennis.

Pages 305-06. Augustin Owin. Inventory. 25 March [1727]. Appraised by Tho. Machen, John Fearn and Jonathan Johnson. No total valuation; includes two Negroes valued at ₺ 33. Signed by Wm. Owen. Admitted to record 4 April 1727.

Page 306. Will of Thomas Norman of the County of Middlesix, being sick and week in body, dated 9 Jan. 1726/7.

Unto my son Robert Norman all my lands and plantation.

My Negroes Carty and Phillis with all their essues or increase equally divided betwext my son Robert and my daughter Elizabeth.

All my personal estate to be equally divided amongst my loving wife and my son Robert Norman and my daughter Elizabeth.

All my right and property of a slave now in the possession of Mr. William Mountague to my son Robert Norman

and my daughter Elizabeth.
My wife have use of all my estate during widowhood provided no wast be made.
My son Robert to be at age at the years of seventeen to act and do for himself.
My loving friend James Meacham and my loving wife and my neighbors George Chowning and William Chowning executors.
        Thomas Norman
 Wit: John Alldin, Ed. Mickleburrough, Elisabeth Kidd.
 4 April 1727. Jane Norman executrix refused to stand by the provision made for her and denied to prove the same as did also James Meacham. George Chowning made oath thereto and the will was further proved by Edmund Mickleburrough and Elizabeth Kidd.

Pages 307-08. John Berry. Inventory. 17 and 20 March 1726 [1727]. Appraised pursuant to order of 7 March 1726 [1727] by Geo. Hardin, Jacob Stiff and John Davis who were sworn before Edmd. Berkeley 17 March 1720. Total valuation ₤ 267.4.9¼, including four Negro slaves and two mulatto servants valued at ₤ 100. Signed by Matt Kemp. Returned 4 April 1747 by Matthew Kemp, Gent.

Page 309. Will of Francis Timberlake of the County of Middlesex in Virginia, being sick and weak of body, dated 17 Jan. 1726.
 To my loving wife Sarah Timberlake all my whole estate during the time of her widdowhood and if she marries she be put to her thirds. The remainder equally divided amongst my children Benjamin Timberlake, Frances Timberlake, John Timberlake, Henry Timberlake, Elizabeth Timberlake, Sarah Timberlake junr., Richard Timberlake.
 My loving wife Sarah Timberlake executrix.
        Francis (F) Timberlake
 Wit: Thos. Machen, John Larke, Archi Courdy.
 4 April 1727. Produced by Sarah Timberlake executrix. Proved by the witnesses.

Page 309. Will of Mary Berry of the County of Middlesex in Virga. being sick and weeck in body, dated 18 Dec. 1726.
 All my land in Gloster County to my son Robert Dudley.
 Unto my soness James and Robeart Dudley all my personal estate to be equally divided, which Berry gave me by his will.
 My Negro man Peter to be equally divided between them both.
 My two sones executors.
        Mary (M) Berry
 Wit: Danl. Sweny, William Burdett, W. Blackburne.

4 April 1727. Produced in Court by James Dudley. Proved by Wm. Burdett.

Page 310. Hezekiah Ellis. Inventory. Appraised by Tho. Machen, William Gray, Jonathan Johnson. No total valuation; includes five slaves valued at ₤ 80. Signed by Mary Ellis, who made oath to the inventory 1 Aug. 1727.

Page 310-11. Thomas Kidd. Inventory. Appraised pursuant to order of 4 July 1727 by Marvill Mossley, John Mosley, William Chowning. Total valuation ₤ 26.15.6. Signed by John Kidd, who made oath to the inventory 1 Aug. 1727.

Page 311. Will of Thomas Kidd, being sick and weak in body, dated 6 May 1727.
Unto my son Thomas Kidd all my plantation and land lying in this county on the west side of white oak swamp.
Unto my son John Kidd my land and plantation whereon I now live ... by the main road and running along Jos. Jacode's line to the mouth of the Spr[ing] branch ... to the white oak swamp ... to Marvel Moseley's line ... to the main road.
Unto my son Daniel Kidd all that percell of land on the south side of the Spring branch commonly called the Mill Neck.
Unto my son William Kidd all my land and plantation whereon my brother William Kidd formerly lived on excepting ninety acres joyning to the tree commonly called the halfeway tree which I desire should be sold.
Unto my son John Kidd my bay horse.
Unto my daughter Frances Kidd my gray horse.
The four smallest of my children shall live here upon my plantation untill my two youngest daughters comes to the age of sixteen years to be brought by my daughters Frances Kidd and Mary Kidd in case they do not marry. All the rest of my estate shall remain upon the plantation for the maintainance of my said children untill they come to the age aforesaid and then be equally divided among them all.
My son John Kidd and Frances Kidd my daughter executors.
        Thomas Kidd
Wit: John Godbee, Ann (A) Blackly, Janet Chowning.
4 July 1727. John Kidd and Frances Kidd made oath thereto. Proved by Jannet Chowning and John God[bee].

Pages 311-12. David George. Inventory. 14-15 March 1726 [1727]. Appraised pursuant to order of 7 March

MIDDLESEX COUNTY WILLS   71

1726 [1727] by John Segar, Mar. Moseley, George Chowning.
No total valuation; includes five Negroes valued at
₤ 53. Signed by John George, executor, who made oath
to the inventory 2 May 1727.

Page 312. Edward Farrell. Inventory. Appraised by Tho.
Machen, Jacob Stiff, Jonathan Johnson. Total valuation
₤ 7.0.9. Signed by Wm. Crutchfield, who made oath to
the inventory 2 May 1727.

Page 313. Jno. Merry. Inventory. 18 March 1726/7.
Appraised pursuant to order of 7 March 1726/7 by William
(W) Gardner, Tho. Haselwood, Thos. (T) Chaney. Total
valuation ₤ 21.1.5, including money due from Thos.
Mountague, Henry Nixon and Wm. Kidd's estate. Signed
by Peter Mountague, who made oath to the inventory 2 May
1727.

Pages 313-14. Francis Timberlake. Inventory. Appraised
by Tho. Machen, Jacob Stiff, John Fearn. Total valuation
[₤ 252.17.2½], including five Negroes valued at ₤ 84;
money in hands of John Berry, merchant in London, ₤ 20,
and due the estate from Jos. Smith 19 sh. Signed by
Sarah (X) Timberlake, who made oath to the inventory 2
May 1727.

Page 314. Will of William Tomson of Middlesex County,
overseer, being sick and weak, dated 21 Feb. 1726/7.
   To my cousen Mary Crouch three pounds towards paying
for her schooling.
   To my dear and well beloved wife Mary Tomson all my
estate for her widowhood. After marriage it is to be
equally divided, half to my loving wife Mary Tomson and
half to my loving son Samuel Tomson.
   My well beloved wife executrix.
                              William Tomsons
   Wit: John Weston, John Seblee (X).
   2 May 1727. Produced in Court by Mary Tomson. Proved
by John Weston.

Page 315-16. Will of John Alldin of the County of
Middlesex, being sick and weak in body, dated 23 Feb.
1726.
   Unto my loving wife Frances Alldin my plantation and
lands whereon I now live during her natural life. She
shall have any timber she shall have occassion of for
her own use of either side of the said plantations.
   Unto my son John Alldin my upper tracks of land and
all plantations thereto belonging.
   My loving wife and each one of my daughters shal have
the use of what timber they shall have occassion of out

of the Dragon Swamp for their own use and no others dureing their natural lives.

Unto my son Jo[hn] all my Dragon land and timber.

Unto my daughter Elizabe[th] wife of Jno. Smith all that parcel of land beginning at Edwin Thacker's line near above the corner of Davis [?] his land ... to the Green branch ... to Mr. Richard Willis his line ... In case my daughter shall dye without heirs of her body or her heirs should dye without issue, equally divided between my daughter Frances and my daughter Martha. My son in law John Smith shall have his natural life in the said land.

Unto my daughter Frances Alldin 220 acres beginning upon the line of Elizabeth wife of John Smith and running down between Richard Willis his road and Davis his line. In case Frances should die without heirs to be divided between my two daughters Elizabeth wife of John Smith and Martha Alldin but in case Frances should marry and dye without ishshew, husband shall have his natural life in the said land. My daughter Frances shall have 800 pounds of tobacco and caske and 5000 sortible house nails.

Unto my daughter Martha Alldin 220 acres beginning upon the line of Elizabeth wife of John Smith and so down Willis his road and Willis his land. For want of heirs, equally divided between my two daughters Elizabeth wife of John Smith and Frances Alldin. In case Martha should marry and dye without ishshew, her husband shall have his natural life in the land. She shall have 800 pounds of tobacco and caske and 5000 sortible nails for a house.

Unto my daughter Mary Alldin all my lands between John Burck line and the green branch. For want of heirs, two thirds of said land to fall to my son John Alldin and the other third to my daughter Elizabeth wife of John Smith. If Mary should marry and dye without ishshew her husband shall have his natural life upon the said land.

Unto my loving wife Frances Alldin one Negro man Tony. I lend unto my loving wife Frances Alldin one Negro woman Jaime, Negro woman Judy, Negro woman Beck, Negro George. After her decease to be divided among all my children.

Unto my daughter Elizabeth wife of John Smith, Negro boy Ned.

Unto my daughter Frances Alldin, Negro girl Hamar.

Unto my daughter Martha, Negro boy Sam.

Unto my daughter Mary, Negro girl Margry.

Unto my son John Alldin, Negro Bob, Negro Hamton, Negro Harry, Negro Phillis.

Unto my son John Alldin my great brandy still, cap and worm belonging to it. For want of heirs, equally

divided between my four daughters.
 Unto my loving wife my little brandy still, cap and worm dureing her natural life and after equally divided among my five chilldren.
 Unto my loving wife my sorrel mare.
 Unto my loving wife my gray riding horse during her natural life.
 Unto my daughter Elizabeth wife of John Smith one gray horse.
 Unto my daughter Frances Alldin one gray mare.
 Unto my daughter Martha Alldin one gray mare.
 Unto my daughter Mary one young gray mare.
 Unto my son John Alldin one young gray mare which did belong to the estate of Mr. Robert Williamson.
 Unto my loving wife Frances Alldin four cowes and calves and two four year old stears, one feather bed and furniture.
 Unto my son John Alldin one long trumpet mussle gun.
 What money can be raised out of my tobacco shall go to paying debts.
 The rest of my estate to be equally divided between my wife and five children.
 My son John Alldin shall be at age at the years of eighteen.
 My four daughters and their heirs shall have the use of what timber they shall have occasion of for their own use and no others for the space of forty years outt of the Dragon Swamp.
 My loveing wife Frances Alldin and my son in law John Smith and my son John Alldin executors.
John Alldin
 Wit: Robt. W^mson [Williamson], William (W) Mansfield, Thomas (X) Southworth.
 2 May 1727. Produced in Court by Frances Alldin and John Smith. Proved by the witnesses.

Page 317. Will of Joseph Goare of the parish of Christ Church in the County of Middlesex being sick and weak, dated 6 Dec. 1726.
 Unto my two daughters Elizabeth Goalder and Sarah Anderson each one shilling.
 Unto my daughter Mary Shelton one Negro boye Robin.
 Unto my loving wife all my land during her natural life.
 After her decease all my land unto my son Jose and if he dies without heirs unto my son Henry and if he dies without heirs unto my son William and if he dies without heirs unto my son John.
 All the rest of my estate equally divided between my loving wife and my six children John, William, Henry, Jose, Ann and Lucretia, each to possess their part as

they marry or come to the age of one and twenty. My wife's part shall be in lieu of her dower.
My loving wife executrix.
                                  Jos. Goare
Wit: Augustine Smith, Thos. Reade, Felix Bradshaw.
2 May 1727. Produced in Court by Lucretia Goare, executrix. Proved by Tho. Reade.

Pages 317-20. Mr. Christopher Robinson of Urbanna. Inventory. 28 March 1727. Appraised pursuant to order of 7 March 1726 [1727] by John Smith, Henry Thacker, Jno. Hipkins and W. Stanard. Total valuation Ł 1063.10.3¼, consisting of property in the room over the kitchen, in the room over the dining room, in the dining room, in the shed, in the kitchen, in Gordon's store, at the upper burnt house, at the lower burnt house, and including 12 Negroes valued at Ł 211.10.0 and one white servant Thomas. Signed by John Robinson. The appraisers were sworn before Edwin Thacker 28 March 1727. Admitted to record 2 May 1727.

Pages 320-21. Will of William Batcheder [sic], being sick and in body [sic], dated 26 March 1727.
My whole estate equally divided [among my] beloved wife and my three children Hannah, John and Sarrah.
My two loving brothers Samuel Batchelder and James Batchelder executors.
                              William Batchelder
Wit: John Shorter, John Mossley.
2 May 1727. Samuel Batchelder and James Batchelder produced this will. Proved by the witnesses.

Page 321. Mosis Norman. Inventory. Appraised by William Batcheld[er], John Guttry (X), and Nicholas Brish[ ]. No total valuation. Signed by William Chaing [sic]. Wm. Chowning made oath to this inventory 2 May 1727.

Page 321. Thomas Norman. Inventory. Appraised by Robt. W^{m}son [Williamson], Edmond Mid[ ] and Robt. George. No total valuation; includes two Negroes valued at Ł 25. Signed by George Chowning, executor, who made oath to the inventory 2 May [1727].

Page 321. Robert Blackley. Additional inventory. [Mutilated]

                                (To be continued)

GRIFFIN FAMILY BIBLE

GLOUCESTER COUNTY, VIRGINIA

The Library of the College of William and Mary owns a number of Bibles containing family records. The entries have been copied by Miss Donna C. Gaines of Alexandria, Va., a student at the College, and are submitted for publication by James A. Servies, Librarian of the College.

The family Bible of J. L. C. Griffin was printed at Philadelphia by Alexander Towar in 1833. The "Family record" is on two of the blank leaves between the Old and New Testaments. All entries, exclusive of the insertions as noted, were made in the same hand, presumably at the same time.

The record may have been copied into this Bible from that of Mrs. Nancy Chiswell Lewis which is published in The Virginia Magazine of History and Biography, volume 23, paged 430-34. Mrs. Lewis' Bible contains many more entries but there are variations between the data in it and in this Bible.

Marriages:

Samuel Stuart Griffin married to Sarah Lewis, of Gloucester Co., Va., Nov. 19th, 1808.

Stephen O. Wright married to Mary Louisa Griffin, daughter of Dr. S. S. & Mrs. S. Griffin, Nov. 23d, 1836, in Williamsburg.

J.S.B. Griffin married to Jane Hester Denning of St. Johns [Newfoundland], June 30, 1842.

J.S.B.G. married to Fannie Mary Denning of St. Johns, N.F., March 15, 1853.

M. Dulaney Ball married to Sallie Lewis, daughter of S.O. & M.L. Wright, Oct. 17th, 1860.

Births:

S. S. Griffin, born in Philad. Jan. 6, 1782.

Sarah Lewis, wife of S.S.G., born in Gloucester-Town, June 24 1787.

Cyrus Anstruther Griffin, son of S. S. & S. G., born July 26, 1810, at York-Town.

James Lewis Corbin, son of S. S. & S. Griffin, born March 17th, 1814, at Lewisville, Gloucester Co.

Mary Louisa, daughter of S. S. & S. G. born March 31st 1817, at Lewisville, Gloster Co.

Thomas Stuart, son of S. S. & S. G., born May 16, 1819, & died Feb. 24, 1822, at Lewisville, Gloucester.

John Mercer, son of S. S. & S. G., born at Lewisville,

Gloster Co., Aug. 24th, 1822, & died Sept. 3d, 1822 at the Birth-place.

Fayette, son of S. S. & S. G., born in Williamsburg, March 21st, 1824.

Julia Amy, daughter of S. S. & S. G., born June 3d, 1828, & died June 20 of the same year, in W^{ms}burg.

Mary Stuart, daughter of S. S. & S. G., born June 8th, & died on the 20th of the same month, A.D., 1830, in W^{ms}burg.

J. L. C. G., infant son of J. L. C. & J. H. G., born June 20, & died on 22d of the same month in Williamsburg.

[lower margin:] Henry Stuart, infant son of J.L.C. & F.M.G., born at Sharon, Miss., Sept. 28, 1856, & died in that village, Sept. 2d, 1857.

Deaths:

Samuel Stuart Griffin died in Williamsburg, Dec. 19, 1864, in the 83rd year of his age.

Sarah Lewis, consort of S. S. G. died in Williamsburg, Nov. 12th, 1846, in the 59th year of her age.

Jane Hester Griffin, consort of J. L. C. G., died in Williamsburg, July 28, 1848.

Cyrus Anstruther, son of S. S. & S. G., died in Williamsburg, Oct. 10, 1834.

Fayette, son of S. S. & S. G., died /near/ Williamsburg, Nov. 24, 1850, & was buried in the Episc. Ch. Yard of W^{ms}burg, bear his departed mother.

Stephen Orren Wright, son of Stephen & Abby W. of Norfolk, & husband of M. L. W., died in that city, Jany. 5, 1853, & was buried in the Family Cemetery, of Norfolk, near the remains of his father & mother.

Lady Christina, mother of S. S. G. died in W^{ms}burg, Oct. 8, 1807.

Cyrus Griffin, father of S. S. G. died at Yorktown, December 10, 1810.

[lower margin:] Sarah Tabb, mother of Sarah Griffin died at Gloucester-Town, Dec. 8, 1821, in 68th year of her age.

[upper margin:] John Griffin, brother of S. S. G. & eldest child of Cyrus & C. S. G., died in Philad., Aug. 3d, 1849.

[inserted on New Testament title page;] Mrs. Louisa Mercer relict of the late Col. Hugh Mercer of Fredericksburg, Va., daughter of Cyrus & Lady Christina Griffin, died in Savannah, Ga., 28th Dec. 1859, at the residence of her son, Hugh Mercer.

[also newspaper clipping from N.Y. Weekly Herald of 4 Oct. (year?) announcing death of Mrs. Mary Griffin, "relict of the late Maj. Thomas Griffin, of York Town, Virginia, and of the Revolutionary Army. ..."]

A GUIDE TO THE COUNTIES
OF VIRGINIA

BLAND COUNTY

Bland County was formed in 1861 from portions of Giles, Wythe and Tazewell counties. Its area has since remained the same except for a boundary adjustment in 1900 which transferred all of the land drained by Dry Fork Creek from Giles County into Bland.
No history of the county has been published.

COURT RECORDS (from Virginia State Library microfilm inventory; other and later records are at the Court House at Bland): Will Book I covers the years 1861-1904. There is no General Index of wills.
Deed Book I covers the years 1861-70. There is a General Index of Deeds, 1861-1907 for grantors and for grantees.
Order Book I covers the years 1861-69. There is a Bond Book for 1861-90.
The first Marriage Register is dated 1861-1929.

TAX LISTS: There are personal property and land tax books at the Virginia State Library for the years 1861-1863 and later.

CENSUS RECORDS: 1870 census, for Mechanicsburg Township (post office, Mechanicsburg), Rocky Gap Township (P.O. Rocky Gap), Seddon Township (P.O. Bland Court House), and Sharon Township (P.O. Sharon).
1880 census, for Mechanicsburg District, Rocky Gap District, Seddon Magisterial District (includes town of Seddon), and Sharon District.

POST OFFICES (established before 1890): Bland Court House (1868-94; formerly Crab Orchard; name changed to Bland); Byron (1889-97);
Ceres (1881-   ); Clear Fork (1870-1904; formerly in Tazewell County); Crab Orchard (1851-68; before 1861 in Wythe County; name changed to Bland Court House).
Grapefield (1886-   ).
Hicksville (1874-   ); Holly Brook (1875-78, 1879-1908).
Kimberlin Springs (1879-79); Kimberling (1886-   ).
Mechanicsburg (1837-   ; before 1861 in Giles County).
Point Pleasant (1874-97).
Repass (1883-87); Rocky Gap (1866-   ).
Sharon (1828/32-1876; before ca.1874 in Wythe County; name changed to Sharon Springs); Sharon Springs (1876-

1890; formerly Sharon).
Tilson's Mill (1873-   ; first in Smyth County for a short period of time).

BOONE COUNTY
West Virginia

Boone County was formed in 1847 from portions of Kanawha, Cabell and Logan counties. In 1867 its western area was cut off to form a part of Lincoln County.
Sigfus Olafson, "Historical Sketch of Boone County," appeared in West Virginia Review, v. 19, p. 101 et seq. (1942).

COURT RECORDS (at the Court House at Madison): No report on extant records has been received from the County Clerk. At the Daughters of the American Revolution Library there is "Boone County, W. Va., Births, Marriages, Deaths, Wills and Inventories, 1865-1899" (typewritten; Madison, Works Progress Administration, 1936).

TAX LISTS: The personal property tax books of Boone County for 1847-60, with the exception of 1848 and 1858-59, are at the Virginia State Library.

CENSUS RECORDS: 1850 census, a single list.
1860 census, a single list (post offices, Ballardsville, Peytona, Jarrell's Valley, Coon's Mill).
1870 census, for Crook Township, Peytona Township, Scott Township, Sherman Township, Washington Township (post office for all, Bald Knob).
1880 census, for Scott District, Washington District, Crook District, Sherman District, Peytona District.

POST OFFICES (established before 1890): Bald Knob (1854-   ); Ballardsville (1828-71; before 1847 in Logan County); Bias (1886-90); Big Cole (1851-58); Buffalora (1860-69; formerly Hewittsville; changed into Logan County 1860/66).
Chap (1885-1931); Coon's Mill (1851-53, 1858-66, 1874-96); Coons Store (1875-76), Crook (1866-1902).
Elk Run (1876-77).
Flat Creek (1860-66); Foster (1888-   ).
Giles (1884-85); Gordon (1885-   ).
Hager (1884-85); Handy (1883-83); Hewett (1875-75, 1877-   ); Hewit (1849-52); Hewittville (1854-60, name changed to Buffalora); Hill (1884-1910, name changed to Julian); Honey Farm (1873-76).
Madison (1871-   ); Mitchell (1884-84); Mouth Short

Creek (1868-74; 1875-79, name changed to Racine); Mud River (1858-66).
Nelson (1885-1916).
Orange (1883-1903).
Peytona (1849-   ).
Racine (1879-   ).
Slash Branch (1858-60); Sutton (1886-90).
Trace Fork (1873-74); Turtle Creek (1858-59).
Van (1883-95, 1898-   ).
West Fork (1854-54).

CORRECTIONS AND COMMENTS

V. 2, pp. 117-18. Mr. J. Ed Hill of Decatur, Ga., reports that a great deal of data on the family of Miles Hill and his wife Tabitha, who was daughter of Burrell Pope (1751-1800) and his wife Priscilla Wooten, is contained in Lodowich J. Hill, "The Hills of Wilkes County, Georgia, and Allied Families," a volume in the Georgia Department of Archives and History collection.

V. 3, pp. 23-26. Mr. Prentiss Price, Rogersville, Tenn., adds that the bond for $2000 of William McCarty as administrator of the estate of James McCarty, dec'd, with Benjamin McCarty and John Cocke as securities, was dated 15 Feb. 1802 (Grainger Co., Tenn., County Court Clerk's Office, File Box 55). The inventory lists one Negro girl, 17 years old. There is no division in the file. Mrs. James McCarty was killed by Indians in Washington District, Feb. 1788, according to Draper MSS, Tennessee Papers, 2XX28, Wisconsin Historical Society.

V. 4, p. 5, line 10. James Nourse was guardian of George Steptoe (not James Steptoe) Washington.

V. 4, p. 5, line 13. Susannah Washington was guardian of John Perring [Perrin] Washington, not John Penning Washington.

V. 4, p. 15, line 27. Mr. D. Simpson Tomkies of Huntington, W.Va., reports that Lewis Tonnkies should be Lewis Tomkies. Dr. Lewis Tomkies died in Abingdon Parish, Gloucester Co., Va., in 1727.

V. 4, p. 60, line 2. Briar should be Brian O'Banion.

V. 4, p. 173, line 32. Clarkmont should be Charlemont Township.

V. 5, p. 32, line 3. Ebenezer Church was in Columbia Presbytery, not far from Columbia, Maury Co., Tenn., according to information supplied by T. H. Spence, Jr., Executive Director of the Historical Foundation of the Presbyterian and Reformed Churches, Montreat, N.C., and by Prentiss Price, Rogersville, Tenn.

AMHERST COUNTY, VIRGINIA

1800 TAX LIST

In the following entries, the first number after each name is that of the white males over age twentyone, the second the number of horses owned, and the third and fourth, if given, the number of tithable slaves aged over sixteen and between twelve and sixteen.

Amherst Parish
District of James Montgomery

Adams, Richard 1-8-14-3
Arisman, Jacob 1-4
Abney, John 1-2
Allen, William 1-1
Anderson, Nelson 1-4-4-2
Austin, Thomas 1-0
Allen, Hiram 1-0
Allen, Joseph 1-0
Allen, Joseph Jr. 1-0
Arrington, Samuel 1-3
Alford, John 1-4-2-1
Alford, William 1-2-1-0
Adcocke, Joseph 1-1
Austin, Joseph 1-1
Alford, Thomas 1-1
Allen, Jesse 1-2-1-0
Arrington, John 1-0
Austin, Thomas 1-0
Bryant, Perminus 2-6-4-2
Becknal, William 1-0
Burnett, Edmund 1-2-1-0
  1 stud horse
Blain, George 2-4-4-0
Bradshaw, Shadrack 1-1
Barnett, Reason 1-0
Bebee, Peter 1-1
Blain, Alexander 2-4-0-1
Blunt, Charles 1-3-1-0
Bibb, James 2-4-2-3
Bibb, Cary 1-3
Bibb, James jr. 1-0
Bibb, Martin 1-1-1-0
Burnett, William 1-3
Burnett, Micajah 1-1-1-0
  1 stud horse
Bailey, William 1-4-5-0
Bethel, John 1-1-3-0
Bethel, Martin 1-1
Berry, John 1-0

Bryent, John 1-0-1-0
Burtin, James 1-4
Benner, Henry 1-1
Bibb, Thomas jr. 1-0
Barnett, William jr.
  1-7-3-0
Barnett, William senr.
  2-3-0-1
Breedlove, William 1-3-3-0
Ball, John 1-1-2-0
Barnett, Nathan and William
  1 stud horse
Bethel, John (ov^r) 1-2-3-1
Bryent, Martin 1-0
Bridgwater, William
  2-2-0-1
Bridgwater, Jonathan jr.
  0-2
Bridgwater, Jonathan
  2-5-3-0
Barger, Christian 1-2
Brock, Michael 1-1
Brumall, Thomas 1-1
Baber, Achillis 1-1
Branner, Peter 1-1
Barger, Phillip 1-0
Bowman, William 1-1-2-0
Brown Rives & Co., New
  Market 2-2-1-0
Brown, Thomas 1-4-4-0
Brown, Adam 1-0
Brydie Brown & Co. 4-3-1-0
Blain, William 1-3
Burnett, Richmond 1-1
Brooks, James 0-1-3-0
Burger, Joseph 2-4-1-0
Bridgwater, Samuel 1-4-3-0
Barnett, Alexander 1-1
Brown, Zachariah 1-1

AMHERST COUNTY 1800 TAX LIST 81

Brent, James 4-10-9-5
Boler, John 2-1
Bethel, Nancy 0-2
Bethel, John jr. 1-0
Becknal, John 1-1
Becknal, Nancy 0-1
Bibb, Henry 1-1
Brown, John R. 1-0
Bailey, Reubin 1-0
Boler, Austin 1-0
Boler, Larkin 1-0
Bryent, William 1-0
Bridge, James 1-0
Blain, George jr. 1-3-1-1
Bowman, William 1-6-6-1
Bowman, John jr. 1-0
Bailey, John 2-7-4-1
Bailey, Terisha 1-1
Bailey, Samuel 1-0
Bowman, Sherrod 1-0
Berry, Addamson 1-0
Ball, James 1-1-1-1
Bellow, Thomas 1-0
Ball, William 3-7-5-0
Burnett, John 1-0
Burnett, William 1-1
Breedlove, Richard 1-3-0-1
Barnett, Nathan 1-10-5-2
Bibb, Elizabeth 1-5-4-0
Bridgwater, Charles 1-4-2-1
Cabell, Nicholas 2-39-40-11   2 ferry men [Negroes] exempted from levies; subject to co. and psh. levies
Cabell, William H. 1-15-16-3
Cabell, Landon 1-16-16-3
Cabell, William 1-18-25-5   1 light waggon
Clarkson, David jr. 1-0
Coffey, William jr. 1-0
Clarke, John 1-1
Chase, Ambrose 1-0
Clarkson, David 2-6-8-0
Clasby, William 3-5-3-1
Campbell, George 1-1
Campbell, John (son of F) 1-2
Campbell, Francis 2-5

Campbell, Ambrose 2-3
Carr, John 1-1
Coffey, Edmund 1-4-5-0
Coffey, William (son of Ed^d) 1-1
Coffey, Edmund (son of Ed^d) 1-1
Coffey, Reubin 1-0
Campbell, John jr. 1-0
Camden, John jr. 1-0-0-1
Cooper, Robert 1-0
McCarter, John 1-1
Cash, Samuel 1-2
Cary, Solomon 2-1
Cary, Daniel 1-1
Calor, Charles 1-1
Cryser, John 1-2
Childres, Benjamin 1-4-2-1
Cabell, Frederick 1-1-2-0
Campbell, Peter 1-1
Coles, John 0-10-8-0
Cashwell, Henry 1-0
Carpenter, William 1-2
Clarke, Nathaniel 1-0
Camden, John 2-3-4-1
Camden, John 1-1
Camden, Benjamin 1-1-1-0
Collins, James 1-0
Campbell, Elizabeth 0-1
Campbell, William 1-2
Cocke, Absolem 1-1
Cabell, Hector 1-12-14-0
Coner, Daniel 1-0
Cabell, Margarett 0-10-17-0   1 chair
Clarkson, Jesse 1-2-8-0
Clarkson, James 1-3-3-1
Coffey, William 2-6-6-5
Crawford, Revd. William 0-2-3-0
Caubin, James 1-0
Church, Thomas 1-2
Campbell, Ambrose jr. 1-2
Campbell, Samuel 1-2
Clarke, David 2-1
Clarke, James 1-4
Carter, Apphia 1-7-18-2
Campbell, James 1-4
Chewning, John 1-1
Crawford, Nathan 2-6-9-1
Crawford, Ann 0-2-3-1

Campbell, Joel 1-3
Carter, Shadrack 2-2-2-0
Cole, John 3-3-4-1
Cattuk, Clarke 1-1
Crisp, William 3-3-4-0
Curry, William 1-0
Cheatham, Lenard 1-0
Cheatham, Robert 1-0
Cheatham, Josiah 1-4-2-0
Cunningham, James 2-1
Chisnal, Alexander 1-3-3-0
Dangerfield, Leroy 0-0-2-1
Digges, John 2-8-11-2
Davis, Edmund 1-1
Dold, William 2-2-1-1
Davis, Joel 1-2
Dickey, James 0-2-4-1
Dillard, James 1-6-5-1
   1 stud horse
Drummond, Henly 1-3-6-1
Demsey, William 1-0
Dawson, John S. 1-9-5-1
Depriest, Langsdon, Est.
   1-2
Damron, Littlepage 1-0
Damron, Michael 1-5-0-1
Dodd, John 0-1
Dodd, William 1-2
Diggs, William H. 1-3-5-3
Davis, William 1-1
Davis, Jabus 1-1
Davis, Phillip 1-1
Davis, Margaret 0-1
Davis, Jessee 1-0
Duncan, Joseph 1-1
Dixon, James 1-0
Dixon, John 1-1
Dixon, William jr. 1-0
Dawson, John 1-4-9-3
Dawson, Martin 1-3-4-2
Dennis, Jessee 1-0
Drumheller, Jacob 1-2
Demsey, Tandy 1-0
Demsey, William 1-0
Daubins, George 1-0
Durham, Isaac 1-1
Durham, James 1-2
Dinsmore, Thomas 1-0
Dinsmore, William Est. 0-1
Dickerson, Thurstin 1-0
Dawson, Henry 1-1

Dickson, William 1-4-2-0
Dixon, Enoch 1-1
Dillard, John 1-6-6-2
Dinwiddie, John 1-2-1-0
Dinwiddie, Ann 0-3
Damron, William R. 1-0
Cabell, Samuel J. 1-30-
   42-3   1 caachie
Coleman, Hawes, 1-9-13-3
Estep, Elisha 1-7-4-1
Evins, Charles 1-2
Eades, Isaac 1-2
Embly, Luke 1-2
Edmunds, Samuel 2-3-8-0
Eades, William 1-1
East, James 1-3
Ellis, Richard S. 1-4
Edmunds, Rolling 1-3-4-1
Edmunds, Charles 2-1-1-0
   ordinary license
Ens, Harbet 1-0
Edmunds, William 1-3-3-0
Evins, Charles 1-1
Enox, Mishek 1-1
Enox, David 1-0
Evins, John 1-1
Ewers, Thomas 1-4
Ewers, William 1-2
Edmunds, James 2-7-6-1
Evins, James 1-2
Edmunds, John 1-2-2-1
Fortune, Benjamin 2-1
Forkner, Spencer 1-0
Fortune, Eddy 1-1
Fitzpatrick, John E.
   1-3-1-1
Fitzjerrald, Jordan (alias
   Coffey) 1-0
Fitsjerrald, William 1-0
Fitzjerrald, James 2-3
Fortune, Zachariah 1-0
Fortune, Nicholas 1-0
Fortune, Thomas 1-7-6-1
Fitspatrick, Thomas
   1-3-6-0
Fitspatrick, Thomas (son to
   Jno.) 1-1
Farrer, Fleming 1-0-0-1
Fox, Samuel 2-6
Fox, William 1-0
Fox, John 1-1

AMHERST COUNTY 1800 TAX LIST 83

Fox, Joseph 1-1
Farrer, John 1-4-1-0
Fitspatrick, Thomas (son to Wm.) 1-0
Farrer, Joseph 1-0
Fitspatrick, William 2-4-4-0
Fitspatrick, William jr. 1-1
Fergason, Samuel 1-2
Flood, Charles 1-0
Forbes, William 2-1
Forbes, Alexander 1-1
Fenten, Zachariah 1-0
Farrer, Thomas 3-6-3-1
Fitspatrick, Joseph 1-1
Forbes, William (G Bent) 1-1
Freeman, Zachariah 1-0-1-0
Fitsjerrald, Hugh 1-0
Farrer, Parin, Est. 0-2-2-0
Fitspatrick, Edmund 1-0
Fitspatrick, John 2-8-6-1
Giles, William 1-1
Griffin, John jr. 1-2
Griffin, Thomas 1-0
Gregory, James 1-1
Going, Phillip 2-3
Going, Landon 1-0
Going, William 1-0
Goode, William 1-1
Griffin, Charles 1-0
Goode, Campbell 1-1
Goode, Phebee 0-1
Gant, Robert 1-0-1-0
Gaskins, James 1-1
Gandy, Elias 1-0
Garland, Anderson 1-0
Griffin, Thomas jr. 1-0
Graves, Richard 1-0
Goode, Daniel 1-2
Going, Aaron 1-0
Gillinwaters, Joshua 1-1
Graves, John 1-0
Gregory, James 1-0
Griffin, John M. 1-2-1-0
Gilbert, Ezekel 1-2
Griffin, John 1-4-2-0
Goodwin, Thomas 1-5-6-1
Haregrove, Hezekiah jr. 1-0
Hawkins, Thomas 1-6-4-2

Haregrove, Hezekiah 2-6-2-0
Hughes, John 1-4-4-0
Hawkins, John 2-1-3-0
Haregrove, Joseph 1-0
Haregrove, William 1-0
Hare, Richard 1-6-2-2
Hunly, James 1-1
Harris, William (son of Matt) 1-2-4-1
Hatter, John M. 2-4
Hatter, James 1-0
Hansborough, James 1-1-3-0
Hight, Matthew 1-2
Harris, James 1-1
Haycock, Ebnezer 1-2-0-1
Henderson, Stephen 1-0
Hill, Nathaniel 3-13-11-1
Harris, William Lee 1-4-5-0
Hight, George 1-2
Hollingsworth, Joseph 1-2-1-0
Helton, George 1-7-18-4
Harris, John 1-6-6-1
Harding, John 1-2-2-0
Harris, Benjamin 0-2-5-0
Harris, Edward 1-2-4-0
Harlow, Agustin 1-0-0-1
Harlow, Reubin 1-1
Hill, William 1-2
Howard, John 1-5-7-1
Handsborough, Samuel 1-0
Harris, William (son of Jno.) 1-2
Harris, Reubin 1-1
Harris, Elizabeth 0-1
Harlin, Jesse 1-1
Hare, William B. 1-5-9-1
Higginbotham, John 1-0
Higginbotham, Jesse 1-0
Horner, John 1-1
Hoofmire, John 1-0
Henderson, William 1-0
Hopkins, James 1-5-8-2
Hill, Pleasant 1-1
Henderson, Robert 5-5
Henderson, John, Estate 2-4
Hardy, Robert 1-7-6-1
Hail, Leonard 1-2
Harris, Nathan 1-3-2-2

Harris, William 2-11-18-4
Harris, William B. 1-1-3-0
Hareil, Thomas 1-2
Hambleton, William 2-0
House, James 1-0
Hambleton, Robert 1-0
Hambleton, Milley 0-3
Harper, Henry 1-4-2-1
Hays, Thomas 1-1
Hambleton, James 1-0
Hollingsworth, William
  2-2-1-0
Harris, Schuyler, 0-1-2-1
Horsley, Martha 0-2-4-1
Horsley, Robert 1-0-1-0
Horsley, William 1-2-1-0
Horsley, Joseph 1-1
Horsley, John 2-8-10-1
Hamlett, Susanah 1-2-2-0
Harding, Edward 2-3-5-0
Horsburgh, Alexander 1-1
Hudgens, Wilam 1-1
Hendricks, Peter 0-3
Hendricks, Jessee 1-1
Hudgins, Drewry 1-1
Harris, William (G Bent)
  1-1
Hays, Samuel 1-1
Harlow, Nathaniel 2-5-4-0
Harris, Mathew 2-13-14-2
Hansborough, Kezeah 0-2
Hughes, Moses 3-13-8-0
Harris, Mathew jr. 1-7-8-3
Jacobs, David 1-2-2-0
Jacobs, John jr. 1-6-3-0
Jones, Jessee 1-1
Johnston, Stephen 1-8-3-1
Jopling, Thomas 1-3-2-1
Jopling, James 2-3-3-1
Jopling, Josiah, Estate
  1-4-5-2
Innis, George 1-1
Innis, John 1-2
Jones, Thomas 2-6-3-1
Jones, Charles 1-2
Johnston, William (son of
  Stephen) 1-2
Johnston, Benjamin 1-0
Innis, John jr. 1-0

Johnston, Delinos 1-1
Johnston, William C.
  1-0-1-0
Jackson, Burwell 1-0
Johnston, William (son of
  Wm.) 1-1-1-0
Johnston, General 1-2
Johnston, John 1-2-4-0
Jopling, James 1-2-1-0
Johnston, Thomas 1-1-1-0
Jacobs, William 1-4-3-1
Jacobs, John 2-6-6-3
Johnston, Peter 1-1
Johnston, Saml. 1-0
Jopling, Thomas, Est.
  0-7-9-0
Johnston, William (Plt)
  2-5-4-0
Jopling, Jesse 1-1-5-2
Jordan, William 1-4-4-1
Johnston, Isham 1-1
Johnston, Benjamin 1-0
Johnston, William (Rock-
  fish) 1-4-6-1
Johnston, John (Plt) 1-0
Jopling, John, and Wm.
  Mathews 2-3-2-0
Killand, Thomas 1-1
Kidd, James 2-2
King, Majer 1-2
King, Jacob 2-2
Keey, Susanah 0-2
King, Zachariah 1-0
Kidd, Moses 1-1
Kidd, Zachariah 1-0
Key, William 1-1
Kerr, William 1-1
Loving, William (son of
  Jno.) 1-1-0-1
Loving, George 1-5-2-0
Loving, James (son of Wm.)
  1-2-3-1
Lewis, Charles A. 1-0-2-0
  1 stud horse
Layne, James jr. 1-0
Layne, James 2-1
Layne, Thomas 1-1
Layne, William jr. 1-1
London, Lavender 1-1-0-1

(To be continued)

LOCAL NOTICES FROM THE

VIRGINIA GAZETTE, 1780

(Continued from V. 5, p. 39)

20 September 1780

Richard James and Samuel DuVal Jun., in Manchester, offer for sale a vessel with oak timbers as high as her bends.

Philip Moody at Richmond advertises for carpenters and wheelwrights who are willing to serve the public.

Henry Peyton, escheator, advertises for sale at Dumfries, 7500 acres, late property of Robert Briscoe, Esq., of Great Britain, which now bring 30,000 pounds of tobacco as rent, 14 to 20 miles from Dumfries, which will be sold in lots of 400 acres or less. Also 500 acres within 14 miles of Dumfries, late property of Henry Ellison, Esq., of Great Britain.

William Carter at Williamsburg advertises for sale at his shop various drugs. He will fix up a complete apothecary and druggist shop in Richmond with anyone who inclines to practice physick and surgery at that place. "As the practice of physick and surgery is altogether disagreeable to me on account of my deafness, I would willingly give up one half of the profits from the shop (which are considerable) to any able and diligent Gentleman that may be willing to practice physick and surgery in Williamsburg."

Thomas Newton, Jr., and Preeson Bowdoin, executors, at Norfolk, advertise for sale the lands of Robert Tucker, dec., contiguous to Portsmouth.

George Muter, C., at the War Office, advertises that a number of houses are wanted to be built immediately at the foundery for public use.

Edmund Pendleton, Jr., Escheator, advertises for sale at Caroline Court-house, 200 acres about two miles from Chesterfield in said county, late property of Richard Goodall, a British subject.

Samuel DuVal advertises for sale at Mr. Galt's tavern [Richmond] his coal pits in Henrico County containing 1400 acres, 1000 of which are well timbered. The vein of coal extends two miles in length, and as to its width and debth, the labor of ten hands since 1760 has proved insufficient for a discovery. It is twelve miles from Richmond. Also 378 acres of tobacco and grain land on Flat Branch and Tuckahoe Creek, thirteen miles above Richmond. Also 500 acres on a main road ten miles above Richmond. Also a half acre lot in Beverly town on Westham. Also a number of Virginia born slaves.

John Moss at Richmond advertises for sale a new ship lying at Rocket's landing. Apply to Capt. William Skinner at Mr. Stephen Tankard's or to Moss.

William Herbert at Portsmouth advertises for sale 3/16 of the brig Venice, Robert Elliott master.

John Washington advertises that he purchased from Mr. Mordecai Cooke of Gloucester County a tract of about 600 acres in Westmoreland County for Ł 3000. Mr. Cooke has refused to make deeds. He intends to bring suit.

William Martin at Halifax Town, N.C., advertises his tavern is to be rented.

Catherine Park, administratrix, at Richmond, advertises for all persons indebted to the estate of Mr. Edward Park, dec., to make payment.

A. Slaughter at Portsmouth advertises that a mare, which was left with him by Major Allen M. Lane, was brought to Portsmouth by a fellow of suspicious appearance who was confined but has escaped. The owner may have the mare by proving possession. Any commissioned officer of the continental army intending in a short time for camp may have the loan of a saddle horse, the property of an officer in Major Lee's corps.

William Bailey, on Black Creek in New Kent County, advertises for a mare stolen from him.

William P. Mathews offers Ł 100 reward for a horse strayed out of Mrs. Stone's pasture in Osbornes and seen about Petersburg ferry. Bring the horse to Mrs. Stone's or to Mrs. Selden in Blandford.

William Pointer advertises for a horse stolen from Mr. John Swepston's near Mecklenburg C.H. Deliver to Mr. Swepston, Mr. Stephen Southall in Richmond or Pointer at Osborne's warehouses.

Francis Foushee at Stafford advertises a mare taken up in the Wilderness on his way to Kentucky and now at Potowmack run.

William Alford advertises two mares taken up in Amherst.

Benjamin Harrison and Co. at Osbornes advertises for sale a quantity of flour and ship bread.

William Hill advertises for a mare strayed or stolen from him at the College landing near Williamsburg.

27 September 1780

The enemy sent three armed boats yesterday morning to the house of Mr. George Turberville on Potomack, carried off three Negroes, his plate and stripped the house of everything they could lay their hands on, even the rings from Mrs. Turberville's fingers.

Advertisement of goods for sale at wholesale at Mr. Lambert's new house in the back street, Richmond.

George Jamieson Jun., at Newtown (Princess Anne), advertises for sale a ship and a brigantine.

Isaac Younghusband advertises various commodities for sale.

Monsieur Dubois has for sale in Williamsburg Scotch snuff.

M. Byrd at Westover advertises for sale at auction before Mr. Galt's door in Richmond, Mount Pleasant, 1408 acres in Powhatan County 35 miles above Richmond on James River, belonging to Robert Hare, Esq., of Philadelphia and at present in possession of Col. William Fleming. Has 100 acres of low ground with dwelling house with passage and three rooms below and two above, dry cellar with fire place, and new kitchen.

John Pleasants, executor, advertises for sale at the late dwelling house of Joshua Storrs, dec., within six miles of Richmond, all his personal estate.

John Baskerville advertises for rent in Mecklenburg County near Burton's ferry on Roanoke River, two plantations, one on the river with a large dwelling house, four rooms on a floor, apple orchard that will make 6000 or 7000 gallons of cider this year, and the other about a mile away on a large creek with about 90,000 corn hills, dwelling house, kitchen, crib and barn, two miles from a mill.

Anne Cowley, executrix, at Henrico, advertises for all who have demands against the estate of Capt. Abraham Cowley, dec., late of Richmond, to submit them.

Wilson Miles Cary advertises for rent all his plantations in Elizabeth City County, and also a plantation in Warwick County with 4000 acres of land. On the last tract are two dwelling houses with the proper offices, a fine spring and apple orchards.

W. Savage at Edenton advertises that the copartnership of Savage and Westmore has expired and he is to settle the business. Mr. Carr in Dumfries will pay the taxes on his land and property in Virginia.

Walker Maury at Orange advertises that he will give board and tuition to boys for three barrels of corn, 400 pound of nett pork and 2000 pounds of tobacco. For tuition alone, 1000 pounds of tobacco.

William Ramsey at Fairfax County advertises that Michael Gretter, jailer of the county, made oath that on 8 Sept. John Linch, about 24 years old, a blacksmith, James Lamb, about 26, a deserter, James Harris, a witness against said felons, Patrick Lawlen, a silversmith and engraver (served his time with Mr. Christopher Hughes in Baltimore), committed for debt, enlisted for a soldier.

Samuel Clark advertises a horse taken up in Charlotte County on Ward's Fork.

Martin Burton, near the Meadow Bridges, advertises a

silver table spoon found by his boy near the Meadow Bridges.

Archibald Robertson advertises a horse strayed or stolen from him at Blandford.

Richard Timberlake advertises to certify that on the day Mr. Robert Clopton was arrested in Richmond under suspicion of passing counterfeit money, he rode in company with Mr. Reuben Clopton from his [Timberlake's] house to Richmond and he had no saddle bags. Francis Ellis certifies he saw Reuben Clopton twice the same day and he had no saddle bags. Both sworn before William Winston. Reuben Clopton presents his own defense showing he was not involved with his brother. [He refers to the issue of 30 Aug. 1780 which is missing.]

4 October 1780

Deaths. John Lewis, Esquire, of Spotsylvania; one of the first lawyers in America. ...

Lieutenant Thomas Powell of the state artillery, at his father's in York town.

John Lennard of Henrico County, after a lingering illness, first occasioned by a fall from his horse. He was a kind husband, a tender father ...

Colonel William Harwood, of Warwick County.

Richard Booker at Chesterfield advertises for sale in Petersburg (opposite Mr. John King's) 1/3 of a lot on which are three houses, consisting of dwelling house (two rooms below, two above), store house and lumber house.

Archibald Blair, C[lerk of the] C[ouncil], in Council gives notice to Commissioners in sundry counties to stop taking spirits and to take rye only in those counties whose provisions were to be stored in the barracks at Albemarle.

Charles Carter advertises for sale 3000 acres known as the Puman's end tract in Caroline County, less than four miles from Port Royal and two from a mill. John Hart is resident there. Apply to Carter at Shirley, Charles City County. He has slaves to dispose of and would like to employ a young man as overseer.

Griffin Garland advertises for sale three blooded colts, and two fine fillies, part of the late Honourable Col. Tayloe's stud.

Joseph Pierce, Sheriff, advertises for sale at Westmoreland C.H., four slaves formerly property of William Campbell of Air in Great Britain, escheated by law.

(To be continued)

BOOK REVIEWS

<u>Parish Lines, Diocese of Southwestern Virginia</u>. By Charles Francis Cocke. Virginia State Library Publications, no. 14; Richmond, 1960. 196 pp. $4.00.

Mr. Cocke, who is Chancellor of the Diocese of Southwestern Virginia, has produced an extremely useful volume. Although he is concerned especially with the western counties of the state (west of the eastern line of Henry, Franklin, Campbell, Amherst, Nelson and Augusta counties) and with parishes which were not erected until the middle of the eighteenth century or later, he traces their descent from the beginnings of Virginia settlement and thus covers all of the state except the Eastern Shore, Northern Neck and the southeastern corner.

A few of the counties and parishes descend from Charles City and Henrico but the great majority, in the Valley of Virginia, trace back, by a circuitous route, to York County.

The Acts erecting various counties and parishes are quoted in detail, as are the actions of the Council of the Diocese in later years when the Episcopal Church was no longer the established church.

There are fifteen maps, carefully drawn and in color to show clearly the various boundaries. The maps facing pages 94 and 96 are especially useful, but two misconceptions are possible from their examination. It is true that the area between the forks of the Rappahannock River was in 1745 adjudged to be part of the Northern Neck. Culpeper, Madison, Page, Rappahannock, Warren, Shenandoah, Frederick and Clarke counties and their parishes, however, descend not from the early Northern Neck counties and parishes, but from York County through Spotsylvania County and St. George's Parish. It should also be noted that Fredericksville Parish, which comprises the northern half of Albemarle County, descends also from York (through St. Martin's Parish, Hanover County) rather than from Henrico, this territory having been added to Albemarle in 1761.

This is a "must" for any Virginia genealogical library. The careful reader will be rewarded beyond measure. We hope that studies of the parishes of the Dioceses of Virginia and Southern Virginia will be forthcoming shortly as Publications of the State Library.

Copies may be secured from The Virginia State Library, Richmond 19, Virginia.

<u>Genealogy of the Henton Family</u>. By Nell Henton Edwards. [Versailles, Ky., 1960] 32 pp.

The Henton family discussed by Mrs. Edwards descends

from George Henton who patented land in Berks Co., Pa., in 1720. His sons George, Thomas, John and William settled in Shenandoah and Rockingham cos., Va., and later generations moved to Kentucky and Indiana. Particular attention is given to the descendants of Thomas Henton III who married Mildred and Nancy Darnaby, sisters descended from the Ellises and Burbridges of Spotsylvania County and the Shackelfords of King and Queen and Gloucester cos., Va.

Mrs. Edwards has presented the information clearly and concisely.

Although all copies have already been distributed, a reprint is being considered. Interested persons may write the compiler, Mrs. A. L. Edwards, 130 Elm Street, Versailles, Ky.

New Hanover County Court Minutes, Part 3, 1786-1793. Abstracted, compiled and edited by Alexander McDonald Walker. Bethesda, Md., 1960. 121 pp. $5.00.

It is in the court proceedings, as in no other single series of documents, that we learn of the day by day activities and concerns of our ancestors. In this book we find reference to permission for Negroes to carry guns, a dispute over the lease of Wilmington Distillery, numerous licenses for taverns where its product was dispensed, naturalization proceedings, and the legal problems relating to manumission of slaves, to name but a few of the subjects of various court orders.

Mr. Walker has continued his careful and scholarly series of abstracts with the same attention to detail which marked his two previous volumes.

A map showing the early plantations in the lower Cape Fear region is a useful addition.

Copies can be secured from the compiler at 4887 Battery Lane, Apt. 21, Bethesda 14, Maryland.

The Vandeveers of North Carolina, Kentucky and Indiana. By Mabel Van Dyke Baer. Richmond, Whittet & Shepperson, 1960. 180 pp.

Mrs. Baer has prepared a well documented and handsomely printed account of the descendants of John Vandeveer, Sr., of Rowan Co., N.C., and his wife Amelia Speer, one of whom, W. W. Vandeveer, chairman of the Board of Directors of Vanson Production Corporation, commissioned the compilation of this genealogy.

In her foreword Mrs. Bear briefly surveys the history of the Van Der Veer family in New York and New Jersey, but she points out that it has been impossible to connect John Vandeveer of North Carolina with Cornelis Jansz

van der Veer who settled in New Netherland in 1659.
 In addition to the citation of sources in the text, there are thirty-nine appendices giving copies or abstracts of various pertinent documents. An address given by W. W. Vandeveer at the centennial celebration of Haubstadt, Ind., in 1955, and "Mergeritis," in which he discusses government pressures which tend to force the consolidation of small businesses, complete the book. There is a full name index.
 Although copies are not generally available for sale, interested persons may write W. W. Vandeveer, 55 Public Square, Cleveland 13, Ohio.

Early Virginia Immigrants, 1623-1666. By George Cabell Greer. Baltimore, Genealogical Publishing Co., 1960. 376 pp. $10.00.

 This is a reprint of a book which originally was published in 1912. At that time it was a very important contribution to Virginia genealogy but in recent years it has been somewhat superseded by Mrs. Nell Marion Nugent's Cavaliers and Pioneers, volume 1 (Richmond, 1934), which covers the same period and gives abstracts of patents of record in the Virginia Land Office rather than only a list of headrights.
 Mr. Greer, who was Clerk of the Land Office, arranged some 25,000 names in alphabetical order. The first entry reads: "Aaron, Rich., 1643, by John Freeme, Charles Co." Richard Aron (for so the surname appears in the original book) was a headright used by John Freeme when he secured a patent to land in Charles City County in 1643. It must be understood that the date is not the date of arrival in Virginia and the county is the location of the land rather than the place where Richard Aron settled. On the same page there are three identical entries for James Abbins, not because there were three persons of the same name but because he was entitled to fifty acres for each of the three times he came into the colony from beyond the Virginia capes. For a full explanation of the headright system the reader is referred to W. Stitt Robinson, Mother Earth, Land Grants in Virginia, 1607-1699 (Jamestown 350th Anniversary Historical Booklet no. 12; Williamsburg, 1957).
 Mr. Greer in his preface stated that his search had been systematic and thorough and that every name between 1623 and 1666 had been noted. A comparison with Mrs. Nugent's book and with the original volumes of land patents will show numerous omissions and a number of emendations of spelling, however.
 For those who do not have Cavaliers and Pioneers or access to the original patents, which are now at the

Virginia State Library, this will be a useful library addition.

Copies can be secured from the Genealogical Book Company, 530 N. Charles Street, Baltimore 1, Maryland.

Letters Home. The Story of Ann Arbor's Forty-Niners. By Russell E. Bidlack. Ann Arbor, Mich., Ann Arbor Publishers, 1960. 56 pp. $1.50 plus postage.

There is much more to genealogy than names and dates. If we are to have any purpose to our searches it must be to place our ancestors in the stream of history in order that their part in the events of past times, in whatever part of the world they found themselves, can be understood by us.

Dr. Bidlack's book is a contribution to the local history of Ann Arbor, Michigan, but anyone whose relatives crossed the plains or sailed by way of Cape Horn to the California gold fields will glean from its pages stories which must have been reenacted many times over. The hardships, the triumphs and the failures come alive.

There are delightful illustrations reproduced from a broadside of 1853 entitled The Miner's Ten Commandments, the text of which is also given.

Copies can be secured from Ann Arbor Publishers, 711 North University, Ann Arbor, Michigan.

QUERIES

Each subscriber to The Virginia Genealogist is entitled to have one or more queries published, free of charge, but limited to a total of fifty words per year, exclusive of name and address. All queries must have a Virginia connection.

452. BAILEY. Want Bailey ancestry of Joshua Lanier Martin Governor of Alabama, born 1799, Tenn., died 1866, Ala. His father was Warner Martin who married in Va. Martha Bailey, born 1761. Want given name of Martha's father who married ca.1740 in Brunswick Co., Va., Sarah Lanier, and the names of their children. Mrs. R. E. Ingersoll, The Kennedy-Warren, Washington 8, D.C.

453. SWAN-WILLIAMSON. Want parentage of Matthew Swan who died Surry Co., Va., 1703, and of John Williamson who married Abigail Bynum of Southampton Co., Va., bef. 1773. Will exchange information or pay for documented proof. Mrs. Raymond W. Barry, 7705 Glendale Road, Chevy Chase, Md.

454. NEWTON-WYATT. Want ancestry of Frances Newton of

either Stafford or Westmoreland Co., Va., who married as his first wife, William Wyatt (1750-1815), a Revolutionary soldier of Prince William and Fairfax cos., Va. I have a copy of the ancient Bible of William Wyatt. Leonardo Andrea, 4204 Devine St., Columbia 25, S.C.

455. SIMS-SHARP-STEWART-DAWKINS-GIBSON-PETTY-NALLE. Want parentage of Martha (Matthew), wife of William Sims who died Culpeper Co., Va., 1769; did she remarry? Also of Thomas Sim(m)s (wife Rebecca Petty) who died Culpeper Co. 1785; of Sarah Sharp(s) who married Clement Wheeler, Culpeper, 1810; of Sarah who married ca. 1770, John, son of James Stewart of Fauquier Co., Va.; of Nancy (Ann) wife of John Dawkins of Berkeley Co., W.Va., 1770-90; of Ann wife of Abraham Gibson, 1772-1800, Fauquier Co.; of Thomas Petty who died Orange Co., Va., 1750; and of Martin Nalle who married Mary Alden, 1705, Essex Co., Va. Mrs. L. D. Prewitt, 501 W. Carpenter St., Fairfield, Iowa.

456. DREISBACK-DAILY. Need names of children of Henry and Catherine (Ginder) Dreisback, buried Dutch Hill Cemetery, Columbia Co., Pa., 1828. Is Jacob, fourth son of Peter Daily (will proved 1804, Ohio Co., W.Va.) the same Jacob Daily who married Elizabeth (Baker) Rhodes probably 1809-11 and died about 1811, Belmont Co., Ohio? Mrs. A. V. Dailey, Route 1, Heyburn, Idaho.

457. OSBORNE. Want data on Christopher Osborne, born 1732, died 1789 in Mecklenburg Co., N.C.; member of Rocky River Presbyterian Church. He married Sarah Magruder of Va. in 1760. He had sons Christopher and Jonathan. Would like to know who father and brothers were and if related to Osbornes of Va. He was a soldier of the Revolution; will on file Raleigh, N.C. Mrs. Fred J. Wetzel, 2908 S. Quaker, Tulsa, Okla.

458. McRORY. Reward of $20 for first reasonable proof of parents of James Henry McRory, born Feb. 1820 in or near Lexington, Va., moved to Jacksonville, Fla., ca.1840, captain C.S.A., died 1862 near Jacksonville. Lt.Col. George W. McRory, Jr., 6950th R.G.M., APO 193, New York, N.Y.

459. BLANKS. Want parents, surname of wife and dates for both of Henry Blanks who died 1794, Pittsylvania Co., Va., naming heirs: sons John and Joseph of Va., William and James of Ga.; daus. Tabitha Farthing, Sarah Watkins, Polly Parsons, and Elizabeth Bayts; wife Naomi (died 1803, Pittsylvania Co., Va.). Will exchange data. Mrs. Blanford Towler Anderson, Chatham, Va.

460. JACKSON. Want subsequent residence and information generally of Isaac Jackson who acquired land in Amelia and Prince Edward cos., Va., in 1758-60; sold it with all farm equipment, livestock and household goods in 1760-62; and does not thereafter occur in the Amelia-Prince Edward records. Lundie W. Barlow, 255 Beacon St., Boston 16, Mass.

461. BERRY. Want parents of Morris Berry, born Va.(Del.) 1782, married 24 June 1806, Washington Co., Ky., Margaret Sims, dau. of John Sims. Had 14 children, including Docia and Matilda married Andrew and Larkin Nall, sons of George Nall from Culpeper Co., Va.; Steven, Wm. T. and Nancy Berry married Mary Jane, Catharine A. and John A. Lewis, children of James and Kitty Ann (Pendleton) Lewis from Culpeper Co., Va. Will exchange data. Mrs. Earl D. Berry, 912 W. Platt St., Tampa 6, Fla.

462. HUNTER-BENTLY. Want parents of Nancy Hunter (born Huntington, W.Va.) and of her husband Mortimer Bently (born Huntington or Columbus, Ohio, 17--). They had children Caroline (born 1837), Anna Salinda and Mortimer. Mrs. Cathryn Croker, 4618 Magoun Ave, East Chicago, Ind.

463. CRAWFORD-BUCHANAN. Margaret Buchanan married John Crawford 9 Aug. 1798, Davidson Co., Tenn. (MR 1, p. 36). Who were his ancestors; where did they live? Margaret was daughter of Andrew Buchanan (son of immigrant Samuel) of Washington Co., Va. Dr. James L. Crawford, 1701 Rosario St., Laredo, Texas.

464. WOODWARD-COX. Want ancestry of Elizabeth Woodward, born 9 May 1809, Lee or Washington co., Va., died 27 Dec. 1865, Athens, Tenn.; married Earl B. C. Shugart, born 12 May 1807, Lee Co., Va., died 5 Jan. 1878. Wish to contact descendants of Jacob Cox who married Lucy Estes, 3 Jan. 1803, Orange Co., Va. Will exchange data. Mrs. Edelle Cox Hignett, Box 824, Big Lake, Texas.

465. HUDSON-BOOKER. Want parents of William Hudson (died Ga. 1831) and Sarah Booker (died Ga. 1848), both born Va. 1775 or before and married 1795. Elbert Co., Ga., census shows several children, including Richard Hudson and Sarah Hudson (1816-1884, married 1st --- Holder, 2nd Thomas Cannon of Walton). Mrs. George B. Walker, 624 S. George Mason Dr., Arlington 4, Va.

466. MANNING. Want ancestors of my great-grandfather Michael (Micgha or Mike) Manning, born ca.1775. He and brother Ashley Manning came to Pitt Co., N.C., ca.1800, and married sisters. My mother said he came from Va.;

QUERIES   95

my aunt, from England. Mrs. Minnie Manning, Box 245,
Bethel, N.C.

467. CHEATHAM-HANCOCK-RUDD-BAKER. Information to exchange
on following: Obediah Cheatham, wife Margaret Rudd had
son Arthur (James?), born 1773, who married in Charlotte
Co., Va., Nancy Hancock, dau. of Anthony and Sara (Baker)
Hancock. The Cheatham and Hancock families migrated to
Ga. before 1803 and settled in Jefferson, Richmond and
Clark cos. Mrs. S. J. Nation, 655 Rutherford St.,
Shreveport, La.

468. WILLIAMS-WEST. Want names of parents, brothers,
sisters of Tobias Williams, born Oct. 1746, Chesterfield
Co., Va., who moved from Person Co., N.C., to Tenn.
Who was Robert West of Charlotte Co., Va., 1787 (parents,
wife, children, birth date and place, vocation, church
affiliation wanted)? H. H. West, 640 West Main St.,
Gallatin, Tenn.

469. PETERSON-LUNDY. Want parents of Martha K. Peterson
who married 3 March 1783, Southampton Co., Va., John
Taylor, son of Col. Henry and Temperance (Peterson)
Taylor. Want parents of Angelina Lundy who married
before Jan. 1809 William Taylor, son of John and Martha
K. (Peterson) Taylor of Southampton Co., Va. Mrs. James
R. Wooten, 2111 Grand St., Monroe, La.

470. NELSON-BURTON. Want information on parents and
families of Lucy S. Nelson, born 10 Feb. 1814, Orange
Co., Va., and Charles Burton, born 1 June 1812, Jefferson
Co., Ky. (when and where married?). Children born
Joplin, Mo., were: Thomas Nelson (b. 21 Oct. 1835; m.
Sarah Frances ---), Camillus, Belle, Vetura (b. 1841),
Laura, Minerva (b. 1846). Moved to California 1859.
Will exchange. Mrs. Elenor E. Poston, 4268 Ralph Lane
North, Fresno 27, Calif.

471. BLAND-WYNNE. Who were children of Theodorick Bland
and Anne Bennett of Charles City Co., Va.? Did they
have dau. Mary who married Robert Wynne, son of Thomas
Wynne (will 1718, Surry Co., Va.; Richard Bland executor).
Children of Robert and Mary Wynne: Lucretia, Martha,
Angelica, Cornelia, Anne; grandchildren: Richard and
Theodosia Raines. Mrs. Arnold Staubach, 3406 Windsor
Road, Austin 3, Texas.

472. LYLEEL. John Lyleel of Dinwiddie Co., Va., purchased land in Albemarle Co., Va., adjoining Revolutionary soldier William Martin, 16 April 1771.(Deed Book 5);
left a will in Albemarle Co. 1775 (executor John Napier;

witnesses Turner and Jno. Lisle, Jr.). Widow Sophia went to Clark Co., Ky. Will correspond.

KAY. Who were children of James Kay (born 169-, died 1795, King George Co., Va., son of James and Mary Pannill Kay). Probably married three times. No children by last wife whose husband James Peed died 1757. Sons John and James are mentioned only incidentally. Will correspond with anyone interested in Kay-Key-Kee-Keas, etc., in Va. and Md.

McKINNEY-CUNNINGHAM-WYLIE-ARMSTRONG-LAIRD-HARRIS-BLACK-WATKINS-McAFEE. Will exchange data on these related families from Lancaster Co., Pa., to Md., Va., S.C. Mrs. William H. Welch, 2700 Sea Island Dr., Fort Lauderdale, Fla.

473. CECIL. Samuel W. Cecil of Md. married Rebecca White ca.1750; moved to Va.; had 11 children. Anxious to learn parentage of Samuel Cecil, born 1797, Md., married Kezia Bryn (Bryan), born 1795, Va. Also want information on allied families of Ingram, Wysor, Witten, Boyleston, Mitchell. Miss Cleo A. Barry, 1706 N. Barton, Fresno 3, Calif.

474. WILLS. Want information on the children of Elias Wills of Warwick Co., Va., and wife Mary Condon, dau. of David and Elizabeth (Scasbrook) Condon. Elizabeth was dau. of Col. John Scasbrook of York County and wife Mary Martiau, dau. of Nicholas Martiau (1592-1657) who came to Va. 1620 on the Francis Bonaventure. Mrs. Cecil I. Small, 634 East 111th St., Los Angeles 59, Calif.

475. FLOWERREE. Want information on the Flowerree family, especially proof of the birth and death dates of Arianna Adolpheus Hanson, dau. of John Hanson of Md. and wife of Daniel Flowerree of Fauquier Co., Va. John K. Gott, 4204 S. 13th Road, Arlington 4, Va.

476. BURKS-ROWLAND. Isham Burks, Revolutionary soldier, born Va. 1759, married Elizabeth Rowland in Botetourt Co. 1781. He was son of John and Sarah Burks. Want last name of Sarah. Was John a son or grandson of Samuel Burks and Mary Davis of Albemarle County? Want ancestry of Elizabeth Rowland. Clyde Campbell, 1550 Hicks Ave., San Antonio 10, Texas.

477. RUNYON. Isaac Runyon (Runion) came from N.J. to Md. about 1755. He went from Frederick Co., Md., in 1779 to Rockbridge Co., Va., then to Montgomery Co., and died in Tazewell Co. after 1820. Want data and information on Isaac, his wife, and descendants. Robert Runyon, Box 11, Brownsville, Texas.

THE VIRGINIA GENEALOGIST

Volume 5, Number 3   Whole Number 19

July-September, 1961

CONTENTS

Editor's Page	98
Ann (Herndon) Lee	
By the late John Goodwin Herndon	
Contributed by Ross Boothe, Jr.	99
Middlesex County, Virginia, Wills, 1713-1734	
(Continued)	107
Local Notices from the Virginia Gazette,	
1780 (Continued)	117
Amherst County, Virginia, 1800 Tax List	
(Continued)	125
The Family of John Tomlin	
Contributed by Mabel Van Dyke Baer	130
A Guide to the Counties of Virginia	
Botetourt County	131
Book Reviews	
Servies, Earl Gregg Swem, A Bibliography	135
Williams, Marriages of Amelia County	135
Miller, Index to the Genealogical Department	
of the Daughters of the American Revolution	
Magazine	136
Moore and Simmons, Abstracts of the Wills of	
the State of South Carolina	136
Allison, Early Southwest Virginia Families	137
Walker and Wilson, Some Marriages in Montgomery	
County, Kentucky, Before 1864	137
Martha McCraw Chapter, Cemetery Records of	
Marion County, Texas	137
Spence, The Historical Foundation and Its	
Treasures	138
Queries	138

Editor: John Frederick Dorman

Published quarterly by John Frederick Dorman
Business address: Box 4883, Washington 8, D.C.
Copyright 1961, by John Frederick Dorman

Subscription rates: $5.00 per year; single issue, $1.50
   All subscriptions begin with first issue of year
V. 1, nos. 1-2, $2.50 each, only as part of entire set

   Second class postage paid at Washington, D.C.

EDITOR'S PAGE

A request was made in the last magazine for comments on the advisability of continuing the Query Section. The response has been overwhelmingly in favor of continuance. Since the Editor hopes always to meet the needs of his readers, there will be no changes in policy.

The Editor has appreciated all the comments about The Virginia Genealogist which he has received. The praise and encouragement was most gratifying and the unfavorable comments equally enlightening. He hopes, however, that each subscriber who feels a particular article or section constitutes wasted space will understand that the same article has been singled out by another subscriber as being especially helpful. The Editor will continue to attempt a balanced presentation of material and he hopes everyone will find something of interest in each issue.

The National Genealogical Society Quarterly for March 1961 contains "Research in the West Virginia Collection, West Virginia University Library," by Charles Shetler, a very useful survey. Copies of this magazine can be purchased for $1.50 from the Society, 1921 Sunderland Place, n.w., Washington 6, D.C.

Those interested in establishing European ancestry will find an article by Cameron Allen in The American Genealogist for April 1961 worthy of study. Its title is "The English Origin of Randall Holt and Edward Normansell of James City County, Virginia: A Suggested Method for Determining the Overseas Origin of Virginia Families."

Inscriptions from the Morrell Cemetery in Carroll Co., Va., are included in The Daughters of the American Revolution Magazine for April 1961.

Stirpes is the new quarterly publication of the Texas State Genealogical Society. The first issue, March 1961, contains 40 pages. Subscription $5.00; treasurer, Mrs. David C. Gracy, 2509 Harris Blvd., Austin 5, Texas.

The April 1961 Austin Genealogical Society Quarterly is a 50 page listing of the charter members and their ancestors, arranged alphabetically.

The Editor is solely responsible for the general policies, printing, distribution and sale of this periodical. Neither the Editor nor The Virginia Genealogist assumes responsibility for errors of fact or opinion expressed by contributors. Manuscripts which are submitted for publication should be of general interest and thoroughly documented and should be accompanied by return postage.

Report of non-delivery of magazines must be made within one month after the quarter they are dated.

ANN (HERNDON) LEA

By the late John Goodwin Herndon*

Contributed by Ross Boothe, Jr.
Gonzales, Texas

Through the cooperation of Miss Frances Powell Otken, of McComb, Mississippi, and Dr. Albert E. Casey, of Birmingham, Alabama, who are appropriately recognized as the two most serious students of the records of the Lea family of Virginia and North Carolina, the compiler of this genealogy has been able to discover the source of the misinformation that James Lea who died testate in 1788 in Caswell County, N.C., had married Ann Talbert (Talbort, Talbot, Tolbert, Tolburt, etc.).

About fifty years ago when certain descendants of James Lea first became interested in joining the Daughters of the American Revolution, they employed a woman professional genealogist to prepare the necessary papers. She sought information about lines of descent, dates and places of birth, marriage and death from various members of the family. From preserved correspondence we conclude that it was Mrs. A. Elizabeth (Yancey) Womack who furnished the name "Miss Talbot", but it was as the maiden surname of the mother of Mrs. Womack's maternal grandmother Nancy (Slade) Graves, not as the maternal grandmother of her grandfather John Herndon Graves.

In order to help the reader visualize the lineages involved, we add the following diagram:

```
JAMES LEA m. ANN --?--
            |
John    m. Isabella Lea    ---- SLADE m. Miss TALBOT
Graves  |                              |
        |                   _____|_____
        |                  |                       |
   John Herndon Graves m. Nancy        Hannah m. John C.
                       |  Slade        Slade  |  Lea
                       |                      |
   Bartlett Yancey Jr. m. Nancy Graves        son
                       |                      |
   ---- Womack m. A. Elizabeth Yancey         son
                                              |
                                        George A. Lea
```

---

* Dr. Herndon compiled five volumes relating to the Herndons, beginning with The Herndon Family of Virginia (Lancaster, Pa., 1947) which traced the first three generations. The manuscript relating to Ann (Herndon) Lea was sent to Mrs. C. W. Shields of Chapel Hill, N.C., the compiler of The Descendants of William and Sarah (Poe) Herndon (Chapel Hill, 1956), before his death in 1957. Although it does not appear that Dr. Herndon contemplated the

The genealogist carelessly added the Ann, mentioned in James Lea's will as his wife, to the Miss Talbot who married Mr. Slade, and thereby created Ann Talbert as the ancestress of the Leas of Caswell Co., N.C., descendants of James Lea.

Under date of 14 February 1898 Mrs. Womack wrote from her home in Yanceyville to her first-cousin-once-removed George A. Lea, of Danville, Va., a long letter, the concluding paragraph of which reads:

> The Slade family came from Maryland about the time the Graves [family] came from Virginia. Mother's grandmother, who was your great-[great-]grandmother, was a Miss Talbot of Maryland, a strong-minded woman; she brought cherry and apple slips with her and here is where the first Quirt [?] and blackheart cherries came from in this country [that is, neighborhood], Cousin John Slade has the old stone jar that she brought them in from Maryland.

While there are some errors in Mrs. Womack's letter, data so explicit are not lightly to be brushed aside. They bear the hallmark of authenticity. The Talbots were, as a matter of fact, a well known and highly regarded family early seated on West River, Maryland.

Miss Otken, in a letter dated 10 April 1949, written to the compiler, said:

> I have a number of old letters in which reference is made to the family connection between the Leas, Slades, Yanceys, Tolberts, etc., and one mentions particularly that one Ann Tolbert married a Slade; so it is possible that she was confused with the wife of James Lea ...

So we must reject as inaccurate the assertion that it was James Lea who married Ann Talbert. A painstaking inquiry by Dr. Casey, Miss Otken, Mrs. F. G. Harrelson of Yanceyville, and several others who are much interested in this subject has failed to produce a single item that shows support for that claim. It was first printed, so far as we have been able to learn, in Noted Southern Families[1] (no authority being stated or quoted), and has been copied consistently since as though proved to be true.

On the other hand, the evidence, though circumstantial, is overwhelming that James Lea married Ann Herndon.

---

publication of this manuscript, it represents the results of his careful study of the available records. It is published with the permission of his widow.

1 By Zella Armstrong (Chattanooga, Tenn., 1926), v. 3, p. 71.

ANN (HERNDON) LEA

It is circumstantial only in that no document showing the marriage has been discovered. In other aspects, we rely upon documents, classified below as (1) land ownership, (2) Spotsylvania interests, (3) family names, and (4) genealogical references.

(1) LAND OWNERSHIP: The following power of attorney from James Lea was recorded in Caswell Co., N.C.:[2]

STATE OF NORTH CAROLINA:
Know all men by these presents, that I, James Lea (the son and heir of William Lea, dec.) of the County of Caswell, have constituted, made, and appointed my true and trusty friend, Thomas Phillips of the County and State aforesaid, my true and lawful attorney for me [and in] my name and stead to ask, demand, sue for in law, so as to obtain a good and lawful right and title to a certain tract or parcel of land, lying in King and Queen County in the Commonwealth of Virginia, containing 25 acres on the waters of Matipone [Mattaponi], lying near Maddison Mill which said land fell to me by the line of heir-ship, and upon receipt or recovery of such land as aforesaid, I do impower him to contract, make sale or dispose of the said land, and sign, seal and execute lawfully to any person whatsoever a good and authentic deed of conveyance in fee simple and also all and everything needful and necessary whatever to be done touching the above premices [sic], I do include and perform as fully, largely and amply to all intents and purposes as myself might or could do if I was personally present.

In witness whereof I have hereto set my hand and seal this 16th day of March Anno Dom. 1784, in the Year of American Independence [the Eighth].
Signed, sealed and delivered
In the presence of   /s/ JAMES LEA
  Herndon Haralson, Jurat
  William Lea
March 1784:
  The above letter of attorney was duly proved in open court by oath of Herndon Haralson, one of the witnesses thereto, and ordered to be recorded.
                            TEST. A. C. MURPHY, C. C.

The land referred to was part of a tract of 100 acres on the north side of the Mattaponi River in St. Stephen's Parish, King and Queen Co., Va., granted to William Lea 16 December 1714.[3] It was in this immediate neighborhood that there had been patented to William Herndon in February 1673/4 land in New Kent County "on the north side of the Mattaponi River" and there his son Edward Herndon purchased another tract "in the fork of Mattapony" in St. Stephen's Parish, King and Queen County; and it was

---
2 Caswell Co., N.C., Deed Book B, p. 36.
3 Virginia Land Patents, v. 10, p. 214.

this land that Edward Herndon deeded to his son Edward Herndon who was later of Spotsylvania Co., Va.[4]

(2) SPOTSYLVANIA INTERESTS: From the intensive studies being made of the Lea family we learn that the aforementioned William Lea left (among others, probably) sons named John and James who are mentioned in the records of Spotsylvania County from which we summarize as follows:

John Lea had married by 4 February 1745 Ann, daughter of George and Elizabeth Carter, for on that date George and Elizabeth Carter made a deed of gift of 185 acres in St. George's Parish "in consideration of the natural love and affection they, the sd. George and Elizabeth, bear unto the sd. John Lea, their son-in-law, and Ann, his wife, their daughter." Seven years later, describing themselves as "John Lea, of Orange County, North Carolina, and Anne, his wife," they conveyed that land to Thomas Neal of Spotsylvania, for ₤24. (In 1770 John Lea was Sheriff of Orange Co., N.C.)

On 6 August 1745 there were recorded two deeds of interest to this study. James Lea, John Graves and Joseph Brock were witnesses to the first of these. It was from John Pain and Frances, his wife, to John Talburt, for 100 acres. The other was of adjacent property transferred by John Talburt and Margaret his wife to Jeremiah Stevens, 36 acres on Cattail swamp on the Mattapony River, joining the lands of Joseph Brock and near the Samms plantation. Five years later James Lea was a witness to the deed of sale of most of this land to James Samms by James Stevens and his wife Alice. The other witness was James Chapman. On 5 March 1753 James Lea and Ann his wife sold 200 acres in Spotsylvania to James Chapman.

James Lea and Edward Herndon were members of the Vestry of St. George's Parish, the former until he left for North Carolina about 1755, the latter until approximately the same date. James Lea was a witness in 1754 to the deed of trust conveying the land on which a new church was to be built. Edward Herndon was foreman of the November 1741 Grand Jury, one of whose members was James Lea.

Because Mrs. Hiden has carefully traced the Graves family of Spotsylvania Co., Va., and Caswell Co., N.C., in Tyler's Quarterly,[5] it is not necessary to repeat her data except to mention that the John Graves who married Isabella, daughter of James and Ann Lea, was of this family.

---

4 The original documents are quoted in The Herndon Family of Virginia, v. 1, pp. 1-2, 7.
5 Martha Woodroof Hiden, "The Graves Family of Spotsylvania," Tyler's Quarterly, v. 19, pp. 176-85, et seq.

(3) FAMILY NAMES: Not once among all the known descendants of James and Ann Lea does the name Talburt (or any other of the spellings of it) appear as a given name. On the other hand, we find that Nancy (Lea) Haralson, oldest of the children of this couple, named her eldest son Herndon Haralson; Isabella, the second daughter of James and Ann Lea, named her eldest son John Herndon Graves; and Major Lea, second of the sons of James and Ann Lea, named his eldest son Herndon Lea. Herndon was, moreover, the given name of numerous members of subsequent generations of this Lea-Haralson-Graves family.

(4) GENEALOGICAL REFERENCES: In addition to the genealogical references cited at the beginning of this sketch, the following is of significance in our opinion for it shows an independently arrived at conclusion that is in harmony with what we have been attempting to prove, namely, that James Lea married Ann Herndon:

> Mary (Graves) Kerr was born in James City County, Virginia, January 26, 1754, the daughter of Hon. John Graves (III) and Isabelle Lea of the Herndon family, their later home being in Caswel County, North Carolina, near Yanceyville, which he represented in the assemblies of 1788, 1791, 1792 and 1793, and the Federal Constitutional Ratifying Convention of 1788 and 1789. She died on February 22, 1831.[6]

> James Lea m Ann Talbert (or Talbot) of Maryland, of English descent. She is believed to have been Ann Herndon (dau. of William Herndon of New Kent Co., Va,) before her marriage to ---- Talbert.[7]

Mrs. P. W. Hiden in her "Graves Family of Spotsylvania County, Va., and Caswell County, N.C."[8] expresses the point of view that John Graves III married first a Miss Herndon. She was wrong in that assumption but it shows the way in which the mind of one of the keenest genealogists in this country was working. John Graves III had only one wife and she was Isabella Lea.

In addition to the foregoing, there should be cited another bearing on the Majors, because Major as a given name in the Lea family appears frequently. To cite a

---

6 John Motley Morehead, The Morehead Family of North Carolina and Virginia (New York, 1921), p. 54. Italics supplied.

7 Robert Murphy Williams, Williams and Murphy Records (Raleigh, N.C., 1949), pp. 121-22. As bad as the miscellaneous statements in the full write-up of James Lea are (saying he was the son of John and Rebekka Lea who came to America about 1740, that his daughter Lucy married Joseph Peterson, etc.), the quotation is of value in showing another person's view that James Lea's wife was an Ann Herndon.

8 Tyler's Quarterly. v. 19, p. 180.

few early appearances we mention that Major Lea, who was designated as executor of the will of his father James Lea, had a brother Reverend Luke Lea who named a son Major; that Herndon Haralson named a son Major and had a brother named Major Haralson; that Philadelphia Lea and her husband Joseph Henderson named one of their sons Major Henderson. Philadelphia was a sister of Nancy Lea who married Paul Haralson and of Luke and Major Lea, all of whom were children of James and Ann Lea. Whence came the Major into the family? We suggest the following.

Our first positive reference to William Lea with whom our story starts is dated 18 June 1711 when he was named one of the three appraisers of the estate of Lt. Col. Thomas Ballard of York County, deceased, whose daughter Anna (born 1689) had married about 1705 John Major (born 1677), a son of William Major (died 4 October 1716, St. Peter's Parish, New Kent Co., Va.) and his wife Elizabeth, daughter of Col. Lemuel Mason. His name was recorded as Lee, but later when the patent to land in King and Queen County was issued to him, it was written Lea. Did not William Lea marry a Miss Major?

From the foregoing evidence we have concluded that James Lea married Ann Herndon and not Ann Tolbert. Lacking the actual record of their marriage, we have shown now the error in the reading of Mrs. Womack's letter led to the unsupported, bald assertion that his wife was Ann Tolbert; that the Leas and Herndons had lived near each other from the early 1700's, first in King and Queen and later in Spotsylvania Co., Va.; that in the latter county they were active in the work of the Vestry of the Parish; that children of the Lea marriage named their eldest sons Herndon, a name that persisted among descendants for several generations, but that no child was named Tolbert; and that later students of the matter of family relationships have corrected the error of a descent from Ann Talbert and have asserted instead that the correct family name was Herndon.

In addition, it is appropriate to refer to the fact that the family of David Herndon also lived in Caswell Co., N.C., a few years, later being in Person County when it was created (as was also Herndon Haralson's family), and removed to Orange County a few miles to the south before he died there testate in 1811.

We have no information pertaining to Ann Herndon personally. We have assumed that she was the daughter of Edward Herndon and his second wife, Miss Leftwich, and that she was probably born about 1719. The birth year of her eldest child, Nancy, has been given as 1737, which would justify us in assuming that Ann Herndon

ANN (HERNDON) LEA

married at age 17 in 1736 and that she named her first baby Nancy for herself, since 'Nancy' is the diminutive of 'Ann.' We know nothing about the date of the death of Ann (Herndon) Lea, except that she was living when her husband made his will in 1771 and that a wholly unsupported record says that she died "upwards of ninety." As that record says that she and her husband were living together 75 years, we dismiss it as valueless, because we have the knowledge that James Lea was only 70 years old when he died.

James Lea was born in 1718 in King and Queen Co., Va., removed to Spotsylvania as a young man, lived there until about 1754, and after that date was in Orange Co., N.C., until Caswell was erected in 1771, and then until his death in Caswell County.

In the opinion of the professional genealogist who prepared the first D.A.R. applications for descendants of James Lea he was a private serving under his brother Capt. Gabriel Lea. This is probably incorrect. In the first place, James Lea was 60 years old in 1778. It is not likely therefore that he served in a military capacity. In the second place, the family historians have found no support for the claim that Gabriel Lea was his brother.

The difficulty of identification of what this James Lea did is borne in upon us when we consider that in 1773 when the petition for the creation of Caswell County (or more literally for the division of Orange County) was circulated the Lea signers included Edmund, Elliot, Garnett, Henry, four names James, Major, Thomas, William and William Jr., and Zachariah Lea. One of these was, it is reasonable to assume, the James Lea of this sketch.

James Lea founded Leasburg, now in Caswell County. There he and his brothers founded an Episcopal Church.

Among the Caswell County Minutes for 1777 we find that John Lea opened the Court at its June term; that Major Lea was appointed a juror for the next court of Oyer in Hillsboro; that John Graves, Esq. (usually referred to in family records as John Herndon Graves) produced his commission as Captain; that Major Lea, Gentleman, produced his commission as Lieutenant; and that James Lea, Jr., was appointed an overseer of one of the roads. At the term of Court beginning 9 September 1777 we find that Paul Haralson was granted leave to build a mill on his own land on Adams Creek; John Lea, James Lea (doubtless the James Lea of our search), Henry McCoy, Zachariah Lea and Edmund Lea were among those designated for road jury duty; John Lea was appointed surveyor for the County; James Lea (Little) was appointed overseer of a road; Major Lea was appointed patroller in the Richmond district; John Lea, William Lea, another John Lea and Zachariah Lea were appointed patrollers for St. Lawrence district; and Capt. William Lea was appointed overseer of a road.

The foregoing court items are cited as samples of the rich ore that may be dug out by a patient prospector.

The James Lea of this sketch was the owner of land in Orange County, on which he paid taxes regularly.

Note by the Contributor: The descendants of James and Ann (Herndon?) Lea are given in Dr. A. E. Casey's Amite County, Mississippi, 1699-1890, v. 3 (Birmingham, Ala., 1957), p. 561 et seq. Data on earlier generations of the Lea family begin on page 548. The ancestry of Ann Lea's alleged father Edward Herndon is traced with great care in Dr. Herndon's The Herndon Family of Virginia, v. 1 (Philadelphia, 1947).

Although members of the Herndon family have joined various patriotic societies on the records of the Digges family's distinguished American and English ancestry, it should be stated in all fairness that Dr. Herndon neither found positive proof nor ever stated positively that William Herndon married Catherine, daughter of Governor Edward Digges. Neither did he find proof that Ann Lea was a daughter of Edward Herndon, son of William. His theories, however, are of much interest and it is hoped that the publication of this article will inspire continued research among original records.

MIDDLESEX COUNTY, VIRGINIA

WILLS, 1713-1734

(Continued from V. 5, p. 74)

Page 322. Will of Hesekiah Ellis of the County of Middlesex in Virginia being very sick and of body [sic], dated 22 Dec. 1726.
To my dear and loving wife Mary Ellis all my whole estate during her natural life and after her decease,
To my son John Ellis twenty shillings,
To my daughter Elizabeth Ellis twenty shillings,
To my daughter Mary Ellis twenty shillings,
To my daughter Ellis Faulkner one shilling and to keep in her possession what she had already lent her,
To my daughter Anne Ellis twenty shillings,
To my son William Ellis five shillings.
Remainder be divided one half to my son Hezekiah Ellis and the other half to my son Robert Ellis and my daughter Sarah Ellis.
My loving wife Mary Ellis exeactrix. My friends Tho. Martin and John Fearn my trustees.
        Hesekiah Ellis
Wit: George (X) Sanders, Susanah (X) Curtis, Thomas Folkner.
6 June 1727. Produced in Court by Mary Ellis. Proved by George Sanders and Thomas Falkner.

Page 322. William Tomson. Inventory. 2 June 1727. Total valuation ₺ 69.[14.6]. [Names of appraisers are missing.] Signed by Mary (X) Tomson. Admitted to record 6 June 1727.

Page 323. Joseph Goare. Inventory. Appraised by Tho. Machen, Jacob Stiff, John Fearne and John Davis. No total valuation; includes six Negroes valued at ₺ 95.10.- Signed by Lucretia (X) Goare. Admitted to record 6 June 1727.

Pages 324-25. Wm. Batchelder. Inventory. Appraised by Robt. W[illia]mson, James Meacham and William Chowning. No total valuation. Signed by Samuel Batchelder and James Batchelder. Admitted to record 6 June 1727.

Page 325. Will of Richard Estree of Middlesex County, shooue maker, being declining, dated 17 April 1727.
To John Owen the son of Patrick and Mary Owen and servant to William and Ruth Owen my mair, with bridle and sadle and all my wearing close, wooling and lining and his first choice of my two beds with the furniture,

and half my other goods and half my cattle. In case the said John Owin should dye before he comes of age to return to his brother William Owen. In case these two brothers should dye without airs it is to be distributed to poor widows whom the executors shall think fitt.

To Christifor Owin the son of Augt. Owin one cow and calf.

To Ann Comings the daughter of Ealinies [?] Comings one cow and calf. In case ither of these should dye before they come of age to return to the executors.

To Ruth Owin the wife of William Owin five pound and her choice of a [   ] of my wife's close.

The remainder of my wife's close to Mary Yarrow and her daughter.

Six pound to be given three poor widows wim my executors shall think fitt of this county and parish.

The remainder of my estate to my executors.

To John Owin above named my working tools.

William Owin Senier my executor.

Richard Estree

Wit: [Jo] Weston, [   ] Weston.

6 June 1727. Produced in Court by William O[win].

Page 325. Will of Felix Bradshaw of the County of Middlesex in Virga. being sick and weeke, dated 18 Dec. 1726.

Unto my beloved wife Judith Bradshaw all my land in Gloster County and all my personal estate.

My beloved wife Judith executrix.

Felix Bradshaw

If my wife hath a child born in less than nine months after my decease I then give that child all my estate both real and personal except what the law doth give unto my wife.   Felix Bradshaw

Wit: Jno. Curtis, Jno. (X) Fulsher, Tho. (X) Freeman.

6 June 1727. James Dudley produced this will with the codicil annexed. Proved by John Curtis and John Fulsher.

Page 325. Will of Judith Bradshaw of the County of Middlesex, being very s[ick], dated 24 Dec. 1726.

All my lands in Gloster County or elsewhere which came by my dear husband Felix Bradshaw to James Dudley.

All my personal estate to my loving brother James Dudley.

My brother James Dudley executor.

Judith (X) Bradshaw

Wit: William Anderson, Richard Jones, Ann (X) Jones.

6 June 1727. Produced in Court by James Dudley. Proved by Wm. Anderson and Richard Jones.

Page 325. David George. Additional inventory. 13 May 1727. Appraised pursuant to order of 2 May 1727 by Mar. Mossley and George Chown[ing]. No total valuation. Signed by John George, executor. Admitted to record 6 June 1727.

Page 325. John Meacham. Inventory. 29 May 1727. Appraised pursuant to order of 2 May 1727; appraisers names are mutilated. Includes receipts from Henry Nixon, Thomas Lee and William [   ]. Admitted to record 6 June 1726.

Page 326. Heb^r [?] Whittingham vs. Richd. Parrott. Inventory of estate of Richard Parrott attached by the Sheriff (includes brandy per John Curtis) valued at 2808 pounds of tobacco. Appraised by Thomas (X) Haslewood, Wm. Mountague Jur., and Wm. Segar. Admitted to record 6 June 1726.

Page 326. Benja. Taylor. Inventory. Estate not appraised; includes Ł 17 sterling and tobacco received of Mr. Lewis Burwell and executor's obligation of Ł 56.14.7 sterling. Signed by Henry Armistead. Admitted to record 4 July 1727.

Page 326. Patrick Kelley. Additional inventory. 4 July 1727. Consists of 150 pounds of tobacco and 2½ barrels of Indian corn. Signed by Thos. Hacket. Admitted to record 4 July 1727.

Page 326. Thomas Smith. Additional inventory. Total valuation Ł 362.8.4, including cash in hands of Mr. Bell of London, merchant. Signed by Ann Smith, T. Waring and Matt Kemp. Presented in Court by Ann Smith and Matthew Kemp, Gent., 4 July 1727.

Pages 326-27. Thomas Hardee. Inventory. 26 June 1727. Appraised pursuant to order of 6 June by John Segar, Alexdr. Graves and George Chowning. Total valuation Ł 48.1.2. Signed by Margaret Hardee. Admitted to record 4 July 1727.

Page 327. James Cole. Sale of estate. 26 April 1727. Made pursuant to order of 4 April 1727. Signed by John Curtis.
    Purchasers were Jos. Sears, Henry Ball, Thompson Betts, Henry Daniel, Garret Daniel, John Hughs, Wm. Mansfield, Jno. Evins, Jno. Guttry, Jno. Rhodes, Edwd. Southren, Henry Nixon, Paul Thillman, Robt. Brown, Alexr. Graves, Jno. Sadler, Wm. Segar, James Daniell.
    Admitted to record 4 July 1727.

Pages 327-28. John Alldin. Inventory. 3 June 1727. Appraised pursuant to order of 2 May 1727 by Stokly Towles, Henry Tugel, Jno. Lewis and Saml. Batchelder. Total valuation Ł 407.4.11, including slaves valued at Ł 188.10.-. Legacies to wife, John Alldin, Mary Alldin, John Smith, Martha Alldin and Frances Alldin mentioned. Frances Alldin made oath to the inventory 4 July 1727.

Page 329. Powels Stamper. Inventory. Appraised by H. Tugel, Jno. Lewis and Lawr. Orrill. No total valuation. Signed by Mary (X) Stamper. Admitted to record 4 July 1727.

Page 329. William Kidd. Inventory. Appraised by Thomas Buford, Thomas Mountag[ue] and George Twyman. Total valuation Ł 8.18.3. Signed by Jno. Smith. Admitted to record 4 July 1727.

Page 329. John Hackney Dodson. Sale of estate, pursuant to order of 6 June 1727. Sold 3 July 1727 by John Curtis, Sheriff.
 Purchasers were Wm. Rhoads, Rebekah Dodson, Abra. Worton, Jacob Stiff, John Miller, Edm. Baker, Joshua Lewis, Richd. Stevens, John Curtis, Joshua Timberlake, Wm. Hill, Rebeckah Jonson, Richd. Smith, Richd. Stevens, Tho. Dudley, John Sanders, Wm. Hackney.
 Admitted to record 4 July 1727.

Page 330. Richard Eastree. Inventory. Estate not valued. Signed by Wm. Owen, executor. Admitted to record 4 July 1727.

Page 330. Felix Bradshaw. Inventory. 2 June 1727. Appraised by W. Blackburne, Wm. Owen, Geo. Barrick. Total valuation Ł 24.19.11. Signed by James Dudley. Admitted to record 4 July 1727.

Page 330. Will of Thomas Causer, dated 9 Jan. 1724/5.
 Unto my loving wife Alice Causer (whom also I constitute executrix) all my whole estate during her natural life. After her decease to be appraised and equally divided in two parts, one moiety or half to be bestowed as my wife shall think fitt and the other half to be returned to England and equally divided betwixt my son Wm. Causer and my daughter Anne Causer.
                                 Thomas (Tho) Causer
 Wit: [   ]mas Alldin, [   ]a Allford, [   ].
 Admitted to record 1 Aug. 1727.

Page 331. Wm. Kidd. Inventory. 31 July 1727. Appraised by Tho. Buf[ord], Thos. Mount[ague] and George

MIDDLESEX COUNTY WILLS   111

Twym[an]. Signed by Jno. Smith. No total valuation.
Admitted to record 1 Aug. 1727.

Page 331. Capt. John Degge. Inventory. Appraised pursuant to order of 6 Dec. 1726 by Geo. Harding, Robert Johnson and Chr. Sutton. No total valuation. Signed by Simon Degge. Admitted to record 1 Aug. 1727.

Page 332. William Smith. Inventory. Appraised by Geo. Barrick, Jno. Rhodes, William (W) Hackney. Total valuation ₤ 5.18.9½. Signed by Jno. Weston. Admitted to record 5 7br [Sept.] 1727.

Page 332. Will of Mark Bannerman of Middlesex County being at this in health of body, dated 4 Jully 1727.
To my dear wife my personal estate as long as she lives, earnestly recomending to her and adjuring her by the love she bore me to bring my child in the fear of God and the Christian Religion.
Unto my dear wife all my land in Essex County which I bought of William Winston to be occupied by her during the term of her natural life providing she remains a widow but if she marrys again which tis probable she will and from which I no ways restrain her then I leave her only the dwelling house, kitchen and all other office houses upon the said land and 200 acres of the land adjoyning thereto to be held and occupied by her during life.
To my dear daughter Margaret all the land in Essex which I bought of William Winston, decest, commonly known by the name of Nehocknay, excepting her mother before her death should bring a boy or at the time of my death should be with child of a son, then the land to the said son.
If my wife shall bring a male child after my decease he shall have all the stock of cattle, sheep and hoggs that shall be upon the said plantation of Nehockney.
The heire to my land should not possess the same during the life of his or her mother providing she remains a widow but if she marrys again then the heir shall be put in possession at the age of twenty one or sooner if my executors see it is for his advantage.
My wooling cloaths to be divided amongst my white servants as my wife shall think fitt.
To my very good friend Alexr. Fraser a handsome gold mourning ring of a guinia price, it being all the legacy my small estate will allow me to give him at this time.
To my dear friend Gilbert Hamilton if he comes in safe from Scotland my silver watch.
To William Gordon now my ward the carbine I bought of Mr. Christopher Robinson's estate.

All the rest of my personal estate to my dear daughter Margaret but she is not to enjoy the same til after her mother's decease.

My dear wife and my very good friends Gilbert Hamilton and Alexr. Fraser, as also William Gordon (now my ward) when he comes of age, my executors.

        Mark Bannerman

 3 Oct. 1727. Cathrine Bannerman produced the will in Court. Admitted to record.

Page 333. Mr. Josep Goar. Additional inventory. Aug. 1727. No total valuation; part not appraised. No signatures. Admitted to record 3 Oct. 1727.

Page 333. Eliza. Smith als. Morgan. Sale of estate. 30 April 1727. Made pursuant to order of 5 April 1726. Signed by Jno. Curtis, Sheriff.

Purchasers were Wm. Guhy, Wm. Batchelder, George Walker, John Smith, John Ridgway, Jno. Dunstall, Jno. Barnet, Jno. Sadler. Admitted to record 7 Nov. 1747.

Page 333. Robt. Blackley. Additional inventory. Consists of 1076 pounds of tobacco. Admitted to record 7 9br [Nov.] 1727.

Page 333. Willm. Batchelder. Additional inventory. 25 Sept. 1727. Appraised by Robt. W[illia]mson and Wm. Chowning. Admitted to record 7 Nov. 1727.

Pages 333-34. Will of John Smith of the Parish of Christ Church in the County of Middlesex, dated 1 Nov. 1727.

Unto my brother James Smith my horse named Trotman and all my wearing apparal.

Unto my nephew John Smith my Negro boy Robin and woman [ ], one bed and furniture which he shall chuse, six of my best chairs, the one half of my pewter, one iron pott, my be[st] kettle, one gun at his own choice, my sadle pistolls and holsters, my best rapier and his choice of fo[ur] head of cattle and two of my best chests.

Unto my nephew William Smith all my land and plantation together with one moiety of the mill, all my silver plate and my brandy still with its appurtenances, my chest of drawers and a great looking glass.

Unto my neice Phebe Lawson £ 15 current money when she comes to age or is married in order to buy her a young Negro.

Unto my neece Phebe Daniel £ 15 current money when she comes to age or is married in order to buy her a young Negro.

Unto my neice Jane Smith £ 15 current money when she comes to age or marrys in order to buy her a young Negro.

Unto my neece Elizabeth Smith my Negro woman Judy; also her choice of one of my beds and furniture.

Unto my neice Ann Smith daughter of my brother James one Negro woman Sarah. Also her choice of one of my beds and f[urniture].

Unto my neice Margaret Smith daughter of my brother James Smith one Negro woman Moll. Also her choice of one of my beds and furniture.

Unto Mary Freestone daughter of George Freestone, dec., one cow and calf when she comes to age or marrys.

All the rest of my estate to be equally divided between my three nephews Cary Smith, William Smith and Oswall Smith and my neece Dinah Smith as they severally come to age or marrys. If any should die their shares be divided among the survivors.

My Negroes not perticulary mentioned and given away by name be keept to work on my plantation or other rented plantations, the produce of their labour to be disposed of for the benefit of my abovesaid nephews Cary, William and Oswal and my neice Dinah.

My three nephews Cary Smith, William Smith, Oswal Smith and my nephew William Lawson, executors. My good friend Bartho. Yates, Clk., to be trustee.

John Smith

Wit: Edward Clark, Edward Smith, Wm. Bristow.

2 Jan. 1727 [1728]. Produced in Court by William Lawson. Proved by the witnesses.

Page 334. Will of Thomas Shurley of the parish of Christ Church in the County of Middlesex, being very sick and weak, dated 21 Dec. 1727.

Unto my God daughter Jane Williams one heifer viz. a black heifer with a white back and belly (unmarkt).

Unto my couzin William Moulson all the residue of my estate. It be taken care of for the use of my cousin until he be of age by his father Richard Moulson.

My loving brother Richard Moulson executor.

Thomas Shurley

Wit: Mary (M) Allen, Cathrine (X) Oneal, Benjamin Pace.

2 Jan. 1727 [1728]. Produced in Court by Richd. Moulson. Proved by Cathrine Oneal and Benjamin Pace.

Pages 334-35. Tho. Shurley. Inventory. 8 Jan. 1727 [1728]. Appraised by Robt. George, George Chownin[g], John Burk and Ed Micklebourrou[gh]. Total valuation ₤ 17.8.9. Signed by Richd. Moulson. Admitted to record 5 March 1727 [1728].

Pages 335-43. Mr. Richard Walker. Inventory. Appraised pursuant to order of [ ] May [ ] by W. Stanard,

Alexr. Frazer and Doctr. Mark Bannerman (since deceased). Total valuation ₤ 1352.18.[ ] including contents of chests, boxes, trunks and barrels in the store and below stairs, a parcel of pewter, items on the shelves and under the shelves on the floor, in the lower floor, in the new house and in the dwelling house, and two Negroes valued at ₤ 60. Signed by Cha. Burges. Charles Burgess made oath to the inventory 7 May 1728.

Pages 343-44. Will of Matthew Hunt of Christ Church parish in the County of Middlesex, being sick and weak in body, dated 3 March 1727.

Unto my loving wife Mary Hunt all my real and personal estate lying in the County of Mid[dlesex] dureing her natural life.

Unto John Lewis son of Eusabious Lewis after the decease of my wife all my land in the County of Middlesex.

Unto my daughter Mary Lewis Negro man Jack and Negro man Robin during her natural life and at her decease unto John Lewis, Jack, Robin and Negro girl Frank.

Unto Anne Lewis daughter of Eusabious Lewis one mollatto girl Beck.

Unto Mary Lewis daughter of Eusabious Lewis one feather bead and furniture.

Unto Eusabious Lewis son of Eusabious Lewis two cows and two calves.

Unto James Batchelder son of Samuel Batchelder ₤ 15 current money to be paid when he comes to the age of twenty one years.

Unto George Walker one Negro man Eyesom.

The said Negro named Yesom to William Lyall son of Ralph Lyall, deced, when he comes to the age of twenty one years.

Unto Josiah Daniell son of William Daniell ₤ 15 current money when he comes to the age of twenty one years.

Unto Hannah Batchelder daughter of William Batchelder ₤ 20 current money when she comes to age or marryed.

Unto Oliver Towles son of Stockley Towles Negro man James and woman Jenny.

Unto Clary Smith daughter of John Smith Negro girl Judy and girl Betty.

Unto Oliver Towles son of Stockley Towles and Clary Smith daughter of John Smith all m[y] personal estate to be equally divided after the decease of my loving wife.

My loving[wife M]ary Hunt and my [friends] Stokeley Towles, John Smith and Oliver Towles executors.

Matthew Hunt

Wit: Richard Moalson, John Smith Junr., Charles (C) Clark.

7 May 1728. Produced in Court by Mary Hunt, Stockley Towles and John Smith. Proved by the witnesses.

Page 344. Matthew Hunt. Inventory. 6 June 1728 [sic]. Appraised by Henry Tugel, Jno. Lewis, Law. Orrill. No total valuation. Signed by Mary (X) Hunt, Stokly Towles and John Smith. Admitted to record 4 June 1728.

Page 344. Mr. James Curtis Junr. Estate account. Entries dated 1720-27. Payments made to Mr. Richd. Walter and Mr. Daniel; receipts from William Kidd's estate. Signed by Jno. Smith. John Smith produced the account of his administration 4 June 1728.

Page 345. Will of James Smith of the Parish of Christ Church in Middlesex County, dated 11 April 17[2]7.
All my land unto my loving brother Oswald Smith. For want of heirse then to my loving brother Cary Smith. For want of heirse then to my loving brother William Smith.
All my sisters shall have their residence and abidence on my land or plantation until they are married.
My honoured father James Smith executor.
       James Smith
Wit: John Smith, Howard Williams, Ann (A) Smith.
4 June 1728. Proved by Howard Williams and Anne Smith. The two surviving witnesses to the will of James Smith depose:
Howard Williams maketh oath that he was desired to subscribe his name as a witness by Capt. John Smith which he accordingly did in the presence of the deced. but was unwilling to do so because that he coming to the said Capt. Smith's where the deced. was about an hour before the signing of the said will by the testator he observed that when nobody talked to him he spoke but did not talk sensibly, but when anybody spoke to him he talked sensibly and gave rational answers and that when Capn. Smith asked him if he would sign his will he answered he did not care and thereupon signed and sealed his will and declared it to be his last will. This deponent had no other reason to believe the said deced. was not in perfect sen[se] and memory than what he hath above declared.   Howard Williams
4 June 1728. Admitted to record.
Anne Smith declares that at the time of executing he was of perfect sense and memory to the best of her judgm[en]t.   Anne (X) Smith
4 June 1728. Admitted to record.

Pages 345-47. Doctor Mark Bannerman. Inventory. Produced by Mrs. Cathrine Bannerman. Appraised by Jno. Smith, John Smith Jur. and Henery Tugel. Total valuation ₤ 394.1.7½ including John Tenant, servant 4 years, and Don Sebastine Saunders, servant for 2 years 7 months.

Signed by Catharine Bagge. Catherine Bagge, executrix, made oath to the inventory 4 June 1728.

Pages 347-50. Mr. William Gordon. Inventory. Made by Chr. Robinson, Jo. Leatherbury and Edwin Thacker in the presence of Alexr. Frazier, John Bane and Bridget Waltham[?]. Estate not appraised.

Books are listed by title. Includes property in Mr. Gordon's closet, in the store, in the new hall, in the closet, in the room over the new hall, in the closet upstairs in the new house, the old house below stairs, in the old house upstairs, in the kitchen, the cellar under the old house, at the quarter in Middlesex County, in the old tobacco house, in the Negro quarter, and at town.

Also includes silver spoons marked CB, EM and MW, white servants named John Bean, Wm. McIntosh, James Edwards, James Tate, Tom Guine (a lad), Will Nisbitt and Christian Williams, and 32 Negroes. Also property at the quarter on the Eastern Shore, cattle in Accomack, and goods brought from the Eastern Shore.

Signed by Chr. Robinson. Ordered recorded 2 July 1728.

Page 350. Joseph Goar. Additional inventory. Account of money in England, Ł 19 the remainder of Joseph Goar's estate. Signed by Lucretia Goare. Ordered recorded 2 July 1728.

Page 350. John Gibbs. Inventory. Estate not valued; includes six Negroes, white servant named Roger, Samuel Markham an orphan boy, and property in the chamber, upstairs and in the dary [dairy]. Signed by Marry (X) Gibbs. Admitted to record 2 July 1728.

Page 351. Patrick Miller. Inventory. 18 June 1728. Appraised pursuant to order of 4 June 1728 by Richard Hill, John Marston, Thomas (T) Dudley and Wm. Crutchfield. Total valuation Ł 33.15.10. Signed by Elizabeth (C) Miller, administratrix. Admitted to record 2 July 1728.

Page 351. John Horton. Inventory. 15 June 1728. Appraised pursuant to order of 4 June 1728 by James Daniel, James Smith, John Larke and Wm. Owen who were sworn before Edwin Thacker, Gent. Total valuation Ł 44.12.10. John Grymes declares 10 July 1728 that a debt from Joseph Robins has also come into his hands. John Grymes, Esq., made oath to the inventory 6 Aug. 1728.

(To be continued)

LOCAL NOTICES FROM THE

VIRGINIA GAZETTE, 1780

(Continued from V. 5, p. 88)

4 October 1780

Thomas H. Talbot advertises for sale 200 acres on which he lives on James River about six miles above Richmond in Henrico County with dwelling and on the river side a warehouse.
Advertisement of a vessel for sale at Warwick (Chesterfield County). Apply to Jesse Roper at Warwick or Bernard Markham near Manchester.
J. H. Norton at Williamsburg advertises for sale at South Quay 7/8 of the brigantine Rachell.
John Brownlow at Fredericksburg advertises that he intends for France immediately, to return in a few months.
Advertisement for a pocketbook lost between Mr. Galt's tavern and Mr. Smith's ropewalk. It contained loan office certificates wrapped in a paper directed to Mr. Vesnel and tobacco notes of Pamunkey river. The loss concerns Mr. Honore Giroud at Hanover Town and reward of ₤ 1200 will be paid by him, Mr. John Hay or Mr. Benjamin Hedding in Richmond.
John Parke Custis at Abbingdon near Alexandria advertises for sale four mares in foal by Leonidas and other horses.
Henry Allen at Southampton gives notice that he gave a bond for ₤ 10,000 to Frederick Smith in consideration that he enter Continental service and thereby clear the 26th division of militia in which Allen is enrolled. Smith has probably deserted and Allen will not pay the bond.
Peter Harston in Henry County advertises that he has in custody a slave who belongs to Joel Coffee near the line between North and South Carolina.
Patrick Napier, Sheriff, at Fluvanna County advertises escaped slaves Joshua, property of Rene Woodson, and Frank, property of Patrick Woodson, both under sentence of death.

11 October 1780

Robert Lawson at Prince Edward quotes the order of Council declaring that volunteers for service in Carolina are to be free from militia duty when their division is called into service.
Margaret Edwards and John Edwards, administrators, advertise for sale at Pocohuntus the personal estate of

Mark Edwards, deceased.

Advertisement of stores and lumber houses now occupied by Messieurs Marsden and Smith which are for rent. Apply to Margaret Barnes at Richmond.

John Z. Lewis, Robert Lewis and Nicholas Lewis, executors, in Spotsylvania County, advertise for sale pursuant to the will of John Lewis of Spotsylvania County, dec., 1500 acres in Culpeper County at the Great Mountains on a branch of Staunton river. On this land is a rich mine of iron ore and good tobacco ground. Also for sale a complete assortment of law books. Persons who have borrowed books are desired to return them.

Daniel M'Carty, administrator, advertises for sale at the dwelling of the late Col. Peter Presly Thornton in Northumberland all his household and kitchen furniture, cattle, sheep, mares, colts and horses, two studs got by Yorick and imported by the late Honourable John Tayloe.

Advertisement of sale at Richmond of iron cannon, mostly four pounders, some with carriages, rammers, etc.

Samuel Beall advertises for sale the Schooner Liberty at Broadway (James River).

Alexander G. Strachan at Petersburg advertises 990 acres on both sides of Chickahominy River, known as Cowl's ferry. Apply to Mr. Jacob Rubsaman of Manchester, Mr. Christopher M'Connico or Strachan.

William Black offers $700 reward for slaves Caesar who belonged formerly to Capt. John Thompson late of Yorktown, and Landon, who formerly belonged to the estate of Armistead Lightfoot, Esq. (and sold from his plantation at Dover), who ran away from the Falls plantation in Chesterfield.

Benjamin Thrasher Edwards at Henrico County advertises that he intends to leave the state in a few weeks.

William Minitree at the long ordinary near Petersburg advertises articles taken from a Negro in Dinwiddie County.

Daniel Truehart at Hanover County offers £1000 reward for return of run-away Negro.

Richard Adams advertises for a colt strayed or stolen from his pasture in Richmond.

William Wright offers $1000 reward for mare purchased from Mr. Thomas Lorton of Prince Edward County, strayed from Manchester. Deliver to Mr. Lorton, Mr. Moses Tredway of Manchester, or Wright at Petersburg.

John Harwood advertises that a Negro Dick, who says he belongs to Christopher Branch of Chesterfield County, was committed to the jail of Charles City.

Benjamin Alsup advertises two heifers taken up in Spotsylvania County,

Samuel Hardaway advertises a horse taken up in Dinwiddie near Stony Creek.

Turner Richardson advertises a colt taken up in Hanover County.

Christopher Robertson advertises a horse taken up in Lunenburg County on Maherring River, near Willingham bridges.

18 October 1780

A Friend To Virtue comments on the failure of the magistrates to enforce the law to suppress excessive gambling.

David Goodwyn, executor, advertises for sale at the late dwelling of Henry Cox, deceased, in Chesterfield County on Buckingham road near the coal pits, all his personal estate.

The guardians of the orphans of Joshua Storrs, deceased, advertise for rent their houses and lots in Richmond. The dwelling house is at present occupied by Mrs. Park.

Thomas M. Randolph at Tuckahoe in Goochland County advertises for sale or trade the horse Shakespeare.

Francis Willis advertises for sale in Gloucester County three horses.

John M'Intosh, Lt. Col., advertises for all officers and soldiers of the Georgian brigade of continental troops to join Gen. Gates' headquarters.

William Linis advertises that the ship Renown from St. Eustatia will discharge at Osbornes. Gentlemen with freight on board are Ross, Shore and co.; Samuel Beall; Pierce and Wilson; Donald, Young, and co.; Basel Holmes; Kue and Roberts; Baird and Gordon; Richard Henry Lee; Samuel Rynes, John Hay; William Goosely and co.; Samuel Harrison; David Ross; James Maury; Paul Loyal; Capt. William Thwart; Benjamin Harrison and co.; Richard and Coleman; Richard Taylor; Lyle and Banks; Cornelias Colvert; William Call; John H. Norton; William Plume; Zachariah Rowland; St. George Tucker; Thomas Gordon; Thomas Newton; Wills Cooper; John Holloway; John Bowdoin; John Collins; Henry and Thomas Brown; Solomon Wilson; Stoddard, North and Kerr. Messrs. Hunter, Banks and co. of Richmond are authorized to settle and receive the freight.

Bernard Markham advertises for sale or exchange 1630 acres in Chesterfield County on James River, a good place for a mill, about two miles from Manchester. There is a dwelling house, two barns, garden and orchard.

Advertisement of sale by the Escheator of Berkeley County, 700 acres late property of Alexander Campbell and 770 acres property of Mr. Beall.

Richard Graham advertises that the snow Hero, late the Hero privateer of Liverpool, now lies at Fredericksburg and will take about 100 hogsheads of tobacco to St. Eustatia. Those inclined to ship may leave orders with Capt. Hallork on board, Mr. Samuel Roddey at Fredericksburg or Graham at Dumfries.

Thomas Craig advertises for a pocket book lost in Albemarle barracks with $200 and a certificate from the commissioners of Albemarle County for 264 pounds of beef.

John Wesson, executor, advertises for persons having demands against the estate of Mr. Randolph Price, dec., of Surry County to bring them for settlement.

Robert Rakestraw, jailer, advertises that a Negro Dinah who says she belongs to John Adderson of Northumberland is committed to Charlotte County jail.

Thomas Bolling, John Gilliam, Robert Gilliam, Nathaniel Harrison and William Robertson warn persons from hunting and fowling on their lands on Appomattox River or Swift Creek.

Robert Matthews in Gloucester County acquits Mr. John Corris of Hobbhole from payment of a note for ₤200 which he has received.

Thomas Stubbs in Gloucester County advertises that he intends to leave the colony soon to return in a few months.

Robert Rakestraw living at Charlotte C.H. advertises for runaway Negro Daniel who was purchased of Josiah Hunley of Amelia and formerly belonged to Mr. Dickerson of York County.

William Woodson and John Brumfield advertise for Negro Joe, of Indian breed, and woman Nan, who ran away from them in Goochland.

Nathaniel W. Dandridge in Hanover advertises for runaway Negro named Doctor, alias Will.

Thomas Pleasants Jun. offers $1000 reward for return to him at Curles in Henrico County of two runaway Negroes, one of whom served Peter Brown two years at the ship carpenter's trade.

25 October 1780

John Blair, Rector, requests the Visitors of the College of William and Mary to meet 21 November.

John Coles in Albemarle advertises for mare strayed or stolen.

John Wily advertises a horse taken up in Bedford near the long mountain.

Reuben Wilkinson, Capt. 3d N.C.B. [North Carolina Battalion?] at Bedford C.H. advertises that he has been charged in Bedford County at New London and suspected of being a Tory. He has been five years in the Continental Army.

David Galloway Jun. and Burditt Ashtore [sic] advertise

for sale Mount Pleasant, 500 acres belonging to the estate of Capt. James Blair, deceased, on Rosieurs Creek in the lower end of King George County about 1½ miles from Potowmack River, of which it commands a most extensive view for many miles both up and down, with dwelling house with four rooms below stairs, fire places to each, and two bed rooms and two closets above, laundry, kitchen, barn, two tobacco houses, overseer's house, Negro quarters, apple orchard; the court house within nine miles, church within one, several mills within three or four and Upper Macholock warehouse within 1½. Also 400 acres in same neighborhood four miles distant from Mr. Pleasant [Mt. Pleasant?] with overseer's house, tobacco house and quarters for four hands, about seven or eight miles from Gibson's Warehouse, upon Rappahannock river opposite the town of Port Royal.

James French advertises for sale the plantations named Freeman's and Marrable's which join, containing 2071 acres, extending near four miles along Nottoway River, not more than twenty miles from Petersburg. Apply to Mr. Robert Donald in Chesterfield or French in Dinwiddie.

John Seawell in Gloucester County advertises for sale 500 bushels of salt.

Advertisement of auction of barrels of West India rum at Mr. Galt's tavern.

Hezekiah Pigg advertises to trade for Negroes 1000 acres in Pittsylvania County near the Court House, on both sides of Banister River at the Three Forks.

P. Muhlenburg, B[rigadier] G[eneral], at Richmond advertises for officers of the Virginia line and Col. Gist's regiment to repair to Chesterfield Court House.

John Woodson in Cumberland advertises that he gave his bond to John Wright of said county for ₤ 400 which has been discharged.

Advertisement of money found lying on the table in the Treasury Office in Richmond.

Christopher Ford advertises for mare strayed or stolen from him in Richmond.

Joseph Smith advertises for a Negro John run away from Lunenburg Court House.

Joseph Smith advertises for a Negro Cato who formerly belonged to James Lyle of Manchester, run away from Prince Edward Court House.

John Mummey and George Bean advertise for horses stolen from them about eight miles from Baltimore on the Frederick road.

John Jarret Carter, jailer, at Williamsburg, advertises that he has committed to James City jail Negro Davie who says he is property of Mr. Bright Everidge of South Carolina and was formerly property of Mr. William

Eaton of said city.

Jesse Alexander, jailer, advertises that Dick, a Negro of John Scott of Gloucester County, was committed to the jail of Northumberland County.

Harmon Fishback advertises a mare taken up in Culpeper County near the Thoroughfare Mountain.

Charles Thompson advertises a horse taken up in the upper part of Hanover County.

Joseph Holt advertises a mare taken up in Charlotte County.

Vivion Brooking advertises a horse taken up in the lower end of Amelia County.

Frederick Coghill advertises a steer taken up in Caroline near Madison's ordinary.

William Thompson advertises a horse taken up in Pittsylvania County on Potter's Creek.

Rodham Tullos advertises a mare taken up in Fauquier near the head of Town run.

Edward Curd advertises a horse taken up in Henrico.

John Crutchfield Sen. advertises a mare taken up in Hanover near the town.

Edward Finch advertises a colt taken up in Mecklenburg near the Court House.

Gabriel Faulks advertises a heifer taken up in Amelia.

James Marks advertises two steers taken up.

Fortunatus Crutchfield advertises a horse taken up in Hanover town.

Edmund Booker Sen. advertises a mare and a colt taken up on Flat Creek in Amelia County.

4 November 1780

Proclamation of Samuel Huntington, President of Congress, 18 Oct. 1780, setting aside 7 December next as a day of public thanksgiving for the safety of the Commander in Chief and army from eminent dangers, at a time when treason was ripened for execution.

Archibald Blair, in Council, advertises that the Governor is advised to require all the officers of the first and second state regiments to join Gen. Muhlenburg.

G. Weedon, B[rigadier] G[eneral], at Richmond, advertises for all continental officers of the Virginia Line who are not stationed at points of rendezvous to receive new levies to repair to Richmond or to Gen. Muhlenburg's headquarters on the south side of the James.

Holt Richeson, colonel, requests that the commanding officers of each company where the militia are deemed to serve for eight months order them to attend at Richmond. All supernumerary officers and those resigned, who are willing to take command, are desired to attend immediately.

Nathaniel Irish, C.M.E., at Westham, advertises for

carpenters, gunsmiths, a wheelwright, a pair of sawyers and a lad to take care of horses and drive a cart.

Mr. Lowe of Fredericksburg advertises that he will close his grammar school at Christmas and will move to where Mrs. Dixon formerly lived where he will open a new academy. Young gentlemen will be taught Latin, Greek and French by him, and penmanship, accounts, drawing and practical mathematics by Mr. Philips. None will be admitted until they can read English tolerably well and none above the age of fifteen, as he proposes to conduct the plan of their education no farther than to qualify them for attending the lectures of the several professors in the University of William and Mary. Every scholar must furnish his own bed. The price of board, education, washing and mending will be thirty guineas per annum. Mr. Lowe has taught near eight years in Virginia and had near 200 pupils under his tuition. His present teaching rooms are in Col. Tylor's brick buildings, Fredericksburg.

Advertisement of the plantation of King William court house for sale or rent. Apply to Messrs. Lagarde and Co. at the Court House.

Thomas Shore at Petersburg advertises that he intends for St. Eustatia. In his absence Mr. Christopher M'Connico will settle all transactions of Ross, Shore and co. and prosecute the business of the firm of Shore and M'Connico.

Dudley Brooke advertises a new cure for dropsy. Afflicted persons may apply to him at Mecklenburg County near Finniewood, Va. Infirmity prevents his riding to them.

Any person having a letter for G. Anderson & Harrison which came by the ship Renown, Capt. Lewis, is requested to forward it to the Richmond Post Office.

David Ross at Petersburg advertises for sale 2000 acres in Mecklenburg County on Roanoke River joining the lands of Col. Robert Munford and Sir Peyton Skipwith, with 600 acres low ground. Also 1200 acres in Henry County on Pigg Run, with 200 acres low ground. Also corn, stock and fodder.

The executors advertise for sale the estate of John Redd, dec., of Caroline County, consisting of 300 acres, corn, fodder, plantation utensils, several Negroes, a good still, and stock.

Thomas Wall offers £400 reward for a gelding stolen from Mr. Goodman's plantation in Albemarle County

On Thursday last the following criminals were brought to the bar and received sentence: James Ober for felony; Benjamin Bryan for forgery; Charles Claxton for felony; Donald Warren for murder; Samuel Thomas for burglary; and Laurence Buckholder for horse stealing. All guilty.

Sentence, death.

Deaths. Mr. Robert Gates of Berkely County, only son of his Excellency General Gates.

Lately died near Portsmouth Capt. John Willis (formerly a resident of Bermuda) of a lingering illness.

Thomas Claiborne advertises for sale 420 acres whereon Brunswick court-house stands, with an ordinary.

John Ingram advertises for sale at the ferry landing near Richmond, a small schooner, burthen 16 tons.

Dorothea Arbuthnot advertises for sale at Henrico Court House 400 acres on Gillis Creek within two miles of Richmond.

Found, a silver watch near Westham. The owner on proving his property and paying the expence of the advertisement (and likewise a generous fee for the honesty of the person who found her) may have her, by applying to the printer hereof.

A blacksmith's anvil was found by the river side on Rappahannock. The owner may apply to John Green in Fredericksburg.

Deserted from the first and second battalions on their march from Chesterfield Court House: In Capt. Bentley's Company, Archibald Prayton, Jonathan Prayton, Joseph M'Donald, Bostin Martin, William Day, Henry Lower, James Sillies, James Turner, Andrew Lower, Lewis Butler, Lewis Thornton, Lewis Murrough, Peter Causanday, William Bates. In Capt. Harrison's Company, William O. D'Neal [sic]. In Capt. Scott's Company, James Smith, Peter Ledemon, James Bennett, Thomas Adderson [?], Ephraim Faircloth, Joshua Westbroke, Joseph Tunstall, John Jones, Thomas Winkfield, William Davis, Thomas Davis.

Andrew Reid, clerk of Rockbridge County, certifies order to sheriff to summon Samuel Norwood to answer a bill in Chancery exhibited against him by John M'Cawn and James M'Cawn son of Francis M'Cawn, deceased.

S. Southall at Richmond offers $1000 reward for runaway Negro James who also carried off two Negro women belonging to Mr. Ronald.

Job Carter, jailer, advertises that a Negro man Will, who says he belongs to Thomas Griffin Peachy of Amelia County, is in Lancaster jail.

11 November 1780

G. Muter, Commissioner, at the War Office (Richmond) requests those County Lieutenants who have not done so to send the returns of soldiers raised in their counties.

Stephen Southall, A.P.C., at Richmond advertises for 1000 pork barrels wanted immediately.

(To be continued)

AMHERST COUNTY, VIRGINIA

1800 TAX LIST

(Continued from V. 5, p. 84)

Amherst Parish, District of
James Montgomery, continued

In the following entries, the first number after each name is that of the white males over age twenty-one, the second the number of horses owned, and the third and fourth, if given, the number of tithable slaves aged over sixteen and between twelve and sixteen.

Lilley, William 2-1
Lobben, John jr. 1-2
Lobben, James 1-1
Lobben, John Senr. 1-2-1-0
Low, Benjamin 1-1
Lobbin, William 1-2-2-1
Loving, William, Estate 1-9-8-0
Loving, James 1-1-4-0
Layne, John 1-0
Lee, Richard 1-2
Lillard, Mordica 1-0
Lunsford, John 1-0
Lunsford, George 1-0
Lunsford, William 1-0
Lavinder, William 1-2-1-0
Lavinder, Anthony 1-1
Lanham, Benedict 2-2
Lanham, John 1-1
Lanham, Joseph 1-1
Lankford, Charles 1-0
Legin, Frances 0-3-5-1
Loving, John 1-6-8-0
Lemoin, Peter 1-2-1-2
Lyon, William 4-7-4-0
Loving, William 1-6-10-2
Loving, John jr. 1-9-4-0
Loving, Joseph 1-6-4-2
Lavender, George 1-2-2-0
Loving, Lunsford 1-0
Lyle, Joseph 1-3-1-0
Lavender, Allen 1-0
Lavender, Charles 2-4
Lavender, Allen, Estate 2-6
Layne, William (Water) 1-1-1-0

Layne, Thomas jr. 1-0
Lyon, Peter 1-3-4-1
Lyon, John 1-2
Layne, John 1-1
Martin, Moses 1-6-2-1
Moran, Nicholas 1-6-6-2
Moran, Elijah jr. 1-4
Moran, John 1-0
McGehee, Saml. 3-3-1-0
McAlexander, David 1-0
  1 stud horse
Mays, Charles 1-1-1-0
McAlexander, James 1-5-3-1
Mathews, John 1-3
McAlexander, John 2-3-3-1
McAlexander, Alexander 1-5-6-0
McDonald, Archibald 1-1
Mays, Jessee 1-2-3-0
Martin, James (son of Henry) 1-3-2-0
Masters, John 1-5-3-0
Mosbey, John 1-6-1-3
Mays, Robert 1-1-1-0
Mathews, William 1-1-2-0
Masters, Edward 1-1
Martin, Reubin 1-0
Mare, Alexander 1-2-2-0
Mosbey, William H. 1-4-4-1
McClain, Henry 1-3
Massie, John 2-3
Mays, Joseph, Estate 1-4-4-0
Mays, Lewis, 1-2-1-1
Morrison, James 1-10-6-1
Morrison, William, Estate 0-0-1-1

Martin, George (son of Peter) 1-2
Martin, Pleasant 1-1-2-0
Martin, William 1-1
McClure, John 2-5
Martin, Rebecca 2-2
Martin, Gideon jr. 1-1
Martin, Gideon 1-0
Martin, George (son to Sher^d) 1-3
McClain, James 1-2
Martin, John 1-0
McClue, Charles 1-0
Martin, Sherod jr. 1-0
McCulluck, Saml. 1-3
Moses, Samuel 1-2
Martin, Joseph 1-1
Martin, Hudson Esqr. 3-11-10-1
Montgomery, James 1-7-10-0
McCord, William 1-1
Martin, Henry, Est. 0-4-7-1
Martin, John T. 1-2-1-0
McAlester, Patrick 1-0
Murphey, James 1-3-9-0
Mathews, James 1-0
Murrell, Jessee 1-1
Martin, James 1-1
Mays, John 1-1
Martin, Hudson jr. 1-1
McDonald, Daniel 1-3-2-2
Montgomery, John Scott 1-0
Mays, James 1-6-9-1
Miller, Simon 1-2
Morris, Conrad 1-0
Martin, William (Doctor) 1-1
Mathews, William jr. 1-0
Murrel, Cornelious 2-3
Mathews, Joseph 1-2
Morris, John 1-1
Mathews, John jr. 1-0
McWane, Lewis 1-0
Monroe, Nelson 1-2
Massey, Thomas 1-4-6-2
Morrison, Robert 0-3-4-1
McDonald, William 1-0
Martin, Azariah 3-7-8-1
Martin, Sherrod 1-5-8-1
Morrison, Thomas 1-6-8-4

Murrel, John jr. 2-4-2-1
McNight, John 1-3
McNight, William 1-1
McCoy, Daniel 1-1
Martin, Peter 2-4-0-1
Martin, Charles 1-1
Martin, George (son of H.) 1-1-2-0
Mosby, Daniel 2-6-7-1
Moreland, Andrew 2-2
Moore, Lettisha 0-4-5-1
Melton, John 2-4-4-1
Nevil, James, Estate 1-6-10-3
Nevil, Zachariah 1-0-3-1
Nash, Thomas 1-3-1-0
Neice, Jacob 1-2
Newman, John 0-3-1-0
Nemon, Cutlip 1-1
Nimmo, William 1-1
Nimmo, Robert 1-0
Nevil, Lewis 1-6-7-0
Nevil, James 1-0
Nelley, Aaron 1-0
Nelley, Bennett 1-5-4-0
Owens, John 1-0
Owens, David 1-1
Owens, Mary 0-1
Owens, Levy 1-0
Oglesby, Jessee 1-0
Oglesby, Peter 1-0
Offutt, Nathaniel 1-0
Purvis, Charles 1-2
Phillips, Zachariah jr. 1-4-0-1
Phillips, John 1-4-2-2
Parrish, James P. 1-0-0-1
Parish, Saml. 1-2-0-1
Purckett, Jacob 2-4
Page, Gabriel 1-1
Puckett, Saml. 1-0
Powel, Benjamin 1-0
Penn, Thomas 1-4-2-1
Powel, Seymore 1-0
Ponten, Joel 3-3-1-0
Patterson, Charles 1-1-3-0
Ponton, William 1-1
Peters, Elisha 1-7-3-0
Peters, Zachariah 1-1
Patton, Thomas 1-3-0-2
Penn, Wilson 1-4-4-1

AMHERST COUNTY 1800 TAX LIST 127

Pugh, John jr. 1-2
Patrick, John 1-3-0-2
Plough, Henry 1-3
Plough, Phillip 1-1
Plough, Henry jr. 1-0
Panel, Luke 2-2
Pannel, Benjamin 1-2
Pasley, Hugh 1-2
Pasley, John 1-2
Pasley, Hugh jr. 1-1
Purvis, George 1-2-1-0
Pugh, John (WheelRight) 1-0
Phillips, Johnston 1-1
Patterson, David 0-4-6-0
Patters [sic], David jr. 0-2-1-1
Pigg, George 1-1
Parrock, David, Est. 0-3
Proffett, Randolph 1-0
Proffett, Jessee 1-0
Phillips, Leonard 1-1
Phillips, Nancy 1-2-3-0
Page, Linsey 1-0
Phillips, George 1-2
Parrock, John 1-4
Phillips, Emanuel 1-0
Page, Dillard 1-0
Pratt, Thomas 3-2
Page, Edmund 1-1
Purvis, William 1-3
Patterson, Elizabeth 1-1
Patterson, Alexander 1-1
Powell, Lucus 1-11-12-2
Page, Francis 1-0
Powell, Nathaniel 1-3-3-1
Powell, Mary 1-1
Pamplin, William 1-1
Peters, James 1-2
Proffett, John 1-3
Proffett, David 2-2-2-0
Pamplin, James 2-3
Pamplin, James jr. 1-1
Phillips, Zachariah 3-7-6-1
Phillips, Joseph 1-1
Pamplin, Robert 1-1
Phillips, Leonard 1-2
Pamplin, Leroy 1-2
Pugh, Thomas 1-3-1-0
Pugh, John Senr. 2-2-0-1
Pugh, Frederick 1-0
Pollard, Richard C. 1-6-4-2

Pugh, James 1-1
Perkins, Samuel 1-4-2-1
Pendleton, Micajah 1-5-8-3
Payne, Benjamin 2-4-1-0
Painter, John 1-1
Reves, Robert 1-8-18-5
Reves, Robert, & Co. 0-2
Reid, Henry 1-0
Rodes, David 1-2-2-1
Rhea, Archibald 2-3
Roberts, Alexander 1-4-1-1
Roberts, Joseph 2-13-6-4
Repeto, Peter 3-3
Roberts, John 1-5-4-3
Reid, Saml. 2-6-4-0
Repeto, James 1-1 1 stud horse
Rodes, Charles jr. 1-3-3-0
Roberts, Henry jr. 1-4-3-2
Rudicil, Jacob 1-2
Roberts, Henry 2-8-7-0
Ryon, Phillip 2-4
Ryon, Charles 1-3-1-0
Rose, Patrick 2-11-41-4
Rose, Margaret 0-0-2-0
Rains, Presley 1-1
Ramsey, James 3-4
Ready, Isham jr. 1-0
Ready, Isham 0-1
Repeto, James 0-0
Rose, John 3-21-55-10 1 cochee
Ryon, Winston 1-0
Rose, Charles 1-5-18-2
Rodes, Charles 1-7-13-2
Reed, Jonathan, Est. 0-4-3-0
Reed, Alexander 1-6-2-0
Robertson, Levy 1-1
Rossert, Henry 1-0
Robertson, Thomas 1-3
Roberts, Zachariah 1-5-9-1
Robertson, Leroy 1-0-1-0
Rucker, John 1-1-2-0
Spencer, John 1-1
Sanders, Richard 1-0
Seay, Abraham jr. 1-0
Sanders, Peter 1-3-2-0

Savage, John 2-2
Smith, Josias 1-1
Smith, Salley 0-2
Smith, William jr. 1-0
Stonham, Henry 1-4-1-0
Smith, Joseph 1-4-4-0
Smith, Childers 1-2-1-0
Shelton, Clough, Est. 0-9-8-1
Spencer, Saml. 1-6-5-1
Snider, John 1-2
Small, William 1-4
Stevens, John 1-1-2-0
Stevens, James Senr. 1-4-9-1
Smith, Austin 1-3
Scruggs, Saml. S. 1-2
Smith, William 1-1
Prince, Francis (alias Smith) 1-0
Siddens, William 1-2
Strickler, Joseph 4-5-2-1
Skelton, Joseph 1-11-10-2
Skelton, John 1-0
Shields, John 3-10-5-1
Shields, Robert 1-0
Shields, John jr. 1-1
Shields, James 1-2-1-0
Shields, James jr. 1-6-1-1
Shepherd, Augustin 1-8-7-2
Seay, Joseph 1-1
Statham, Thomas 1-1
Smith, John (R Gap) 1-2
Shields, John (R Gap) 1-2
Smith, Augustin 1-0
Seay, John 1-2-0-1
Scruggs, John 1-0
Sparrer, John 1-2
Shelton, Thomas 1 stud horse
Staten, Elijah 1-0
Statham, Charles 1-5-5-1
Seay, Abraham 1-3
Strutten, William 1-0
Sanders, John 1-1
Sutler, John 1-0
Seay, James 1-2
Stevens, James jr. 1-4-4-1
Spencer, James 1-1

Stricklin, Joseph jr. 1-1
Scott, Elizabeth 0-2-4-1
Smith, Henry 1-6-2-0
Smith, Abraham 1-1
Stockton, Thomas 1-1
Smith, William 2-3-6-0
Staples, John, Est. 1-4-3-1
Staples, Saml. 1-1
Scruggs, Timothy 1-2-1-0
Staples, Joseph 1-5-2-0
Spencer, William 1-11-27-4
Stonham, George 1-4-3-1
Shepherd, John 1-1
Snelson, Robert 1-0-1-0
Tilford, James 1-3-3-0
Trail, Charles 1-1
Townson, Charles 1-0
Thompson, Bartlett 1-1
Thompson, Pleasant 1-1
Tyree, Zachariah 1-0
Turner, James jr. 1-2-1-0
Turner, James 1-2-2-0
Tease, William 1-3-1-3
Tomes, Edward T. 1-1-1-0
Thompson, John (ovr^r) 1-3-3-1
Tyree, Nathan 2-2
Thomas, Cornelious 1-10-10-3
Tomes, Joseph 1-2
Tooley, John 2-1
Tooley, Elizabeth 0-2
Tooley, Charles 1-0
Thompson, Joseph 1-0
Thompson, James 1-3-3-0
Tryall, David 1-2-2-0
Turner, Terisha jr. 1-2-2-0
Turner, Stephen 3-5-14-2
Turner, James L. 1-1
Thompson, John (Mercht.) 1-10-9-3
Thomas, Norbon 1-8-9-5
Trusler, John 1-0
Thompson, James (son of Jno.) 1-0
Thompson, James jr. 1-0-1-1
Trail, Thomas 1-1
Tilman, Thomas 1-1
Turner, Terisha 2-5-7-0
Trail, Luraina 2-1
Taylor, Benjamin 1-0

AMHERST COUNTY 1800 TAX LIST   129

Thomas, John 1-0
Thompson, Charles 2-5
Thorp, William 1-0
Thorp, James 1-0
Thurmond, Charles 1-0
Thompson, Waddy 1-3-4-1
  1 stud horse
Thompson, John (R Gap) 1-2
Turner, John 1-3-1-1
Tyree, William 1-0
Tyree, Zachariah 1-0
Tyree, Reuben jr. 1-1
Tyree, Reuben 1-0
Tyree, Jesse 1-0
Thurmond, Goodrich 2-4-2-0
Taliaferro, Judith 0-3-6-1
Trail, Thomas 1-1
Trail, Charles 1-0
Trail, Abraham 1-1
Trail, Edward 1-0
Tindle, Lewis 1-8-8-0
Vaughan, George 1-3-2-0
Vaughan, William 1-2-1-0
Viar, Robert 1-1
Vines, John 1-0
Vigust, James 1-0
Viar, William 2-2
Wills, John 1-1
Wright, David 1-1-1-0
Wright, James 1-0
Watts, Charles (DC) 1-5-4-1
Witt, John 1-0
White, Conyers 1-3-3-0
Wright, John 1-3-4-1
Wright, William 1-1
Wright, William 1-3-2-0
Wright, Robert 1-3-1-0
Wright, Minos 1-1
Wright, Jordan 1-1-1-0
Wright, Richard 1-0
Wills, James jr. 1-3-4-0
Watts, Charles 1-4-7-0
Wright, Jesse 1-2
Wright, Linsey 1-0
Wright, Andrew 2-6-3-0
Wright, James jr. 1-2
Watt, Thomas 1-2
Walters, John 1-0
Winkfield, Robert 1-1
Winkfield, Josias 1-3-2-0
Wright, Jesse jr. 1-1-1-0

Wright, Benjamin, Estate
  0-2-2-0
Wilcox, Edmund, Estate
  0-16-17-1
Witt, Jenney 0-2-2-1
Wood, William 1-1
Ware, Thomas 1-1-1-0
Wright, John 1-0
Wood, Saml. 2-1
Warner, William 1-0
Woody, Augustin 1-0
Woody, Benjamin 1-0
Wills, Willis 4-4-4-1
  1 cheer [chair]
Watts, Stephen 2-6-12-4
Witt, David 1-4-3-1
Wills, James 2-11-14-4
Wright, Achilles 1-2-3-0
Westbrooks, William 1-1
Willoughby, Joshua 1-1
Woody, George, Est. 1-2
Woods, James 1-14-16-5
  1 stud horse
Wheeler, Jacob 1-3
Wood, William 1-0
West, James 1-3-2-0
Walters, James 1-3
Wright, James (son of
  Robt.) 1-0
Wright, Augustin 1-1-1-0
Wright, Thomas 1-1
Warner, James 1-0
Wood, Jessee 1-0
Wood, Richard 1-1-1-0
Wood, William (son of
  Richd.) 1-0
Warwick, Abram 1-9-10-0
  1 2-wheel [chair]
Watkins, Benjamin 1-0
Wade, Nathaniel 3-4
Warwick, John 1-2
Wood, Josiah 1-0-2-0
West, Bransford 1-3-3-0
Warner, Jacob 2-4-1-0
Wood, James 1-3-3-0
Watkins, John 1-2
Warner, William jr. 1-0
Watkins, William 1-1
White, Joseph 1-4-3-0
West, Francis 2-0
White, Zachariah 1-2-1-0

White, Conyers Senr.   List of merchants' licenses
   3-5-5-2   Brown Brown & Co.
Wingfield, Josiah 1-2-2-0   Brydie Brydie & Co.
Wright, James Senr. 0-0   Willis Wills & Co.
Yancy, Charles 0-2-5-2   ---- Jordey
                               Edward Braudus
                               John Fitzpatrick

THE FAMILY OF JOHN TOMLIN

Contributed by Mabel Van Dyke Baer
Washington, D. C.

John Tomlin was a Revolutionary soldier who died in 1815. His widow Jane resided in 1840 in Clarke Co., Va., where she applied for a pension which was granted.

In her pension file (National Archives, John Tomlin, Va., Jane, W6302) there is a charming small hand-sewn book, each page bordered with hand-drawn flowers and birds in color and a full page similarly decorated opposite each page of family data. The book was torn and has been hand-sewn through the middle of each page horizontally. The data contained therein follow:

         John Tomlin, born 15 March 1765
         Jane Chamblin [?] wife, born 19 June 1765
           [last four letters of surname illegible]
         Married 7 August 1784
Their Children:
   George Tomlin, born 7 October 1784
   Elizabeth Tomlins, born 2 [?] Nov. 1785
   William Tomlin, born 3 April 1787
   Reuben Tomlin, born 17 June 1789
   Mary Tomlin, born 9 Feb. 1791
   Sarah Tomlin, born [ ] Febr. [ ] [day and
     year obliterated]
   John Tomlin, born 2 May [year obliterated]

A GUIDE TO THE COUNTIES

OF VIRGINIA

BOTETOURT COUNTY

Botetourt County was formed in 1770 from the southern part of Augusta County. It then included all of Virginia and West Virginia west of the Blue Ridge and south of a line running through the center of Rockbridge County and west to include the southern parts of Pocahontas, Nicholas, Clay, Roane and Jackson cos., W.Va., and the State of Kentucky.

In 1772 when Fincastle County was created, Botetourt included its present area, the southern parts of Bath and Rockbridge counties, all of Alleghany, Craig and Roanoke counties, and the area of West Virginia south of the boundary mentioned above and north of a line running through present Monroe, Summers and Wyoming counties.

In 1778 Rockbridge County was formed from Augusta and Botetourt and Greenbrier County was formed from Botetourt and Montgomery.

In 1785 a part of Rockbridge County west of the top of Camp Mountain was transferred to Botetourt and in 1790 some of the southern portion of Botetourt was added to Montgomery County. Additional territory of Botetourt County was added to Montgomery in 1795 and there was a minor border change in 1796.

Bath County was created from Augusta, Botetourt and Greenbrier counties in 1791. Botetourt then comprised its present territory, all of Roanoke County, the eastern part of Craig County and the southern part of Alleghany County.

In 1802 part of Botetourt County was added to Monroe County.

Alleghany County was created in 1822 from Bath, Botetourt and Monroe counties. In 1838 Roanoke County was formed from the southern part of Botetourt County, and in 1851 Craig County was formed from Botetourt, Giles, Roanoke and Monroe counties.

In 1888 the boundary between Rockbridge and Botetourt counties south of James River was changed and a small part of Botetourt was transferred to Roanoke County.

Considerable material relating to the early history of Botetourt County appears in Frederick B. Kegley, Kegley's Virginia Frontier (Roanoke, 1938).

COURT RECORDS (from Virginia State Library microfilm inventory; other and later records are at the Court House at Fincastle): Deeds are complete from 1770 to 1869 and a general index of grantors and grantees covers the years

1770-1889. There is also a Circuit Court Deed Book for 1810-13. Deed Books 1-3 (1769-85) are abstracted in Lewis P. Summers, <u>Annals of Southwest Virginia</u> (Abingdon, Va., 1929).

There are five volumes of Surveyors' Records, 1774-1914.

Wills are complete from 1770 to 1869 and there is a general index, 1770-1952. Those before 1821 are briefly abstracted in Anne Lowry Worrell, <u>Early Marriages, Wills and Some Revolutionary War Records, Botetourt County, Virginia</u> (Roanoke, 1958). There are Circuit Court will books for 1835-54, 1855-1903. Some Botetourt County wills, 1834-37, are recorded in Roanoke County Will Book 1834-67.

There are Guardians' Accounts, 1799-1839.

Court Order Books exist for the years 1770-1813, 1815-17, 1820-25, 1828-46, 1851-67. There are three volumes of Chancery Orders, 1831-69. The court minutes from the first Court until Jan. 1800 are quoted or abstracted in Summers, <u>op. cit.</u>

Marriage registers cover the years 1770-1853, 1787-1844, both with indexes, 1844-53 and 1853-1913. There is an Index of Births, Marriages and Deaths, 1853-1913. Marriages 1769-1800 are printed in Summers, <u>op. cit.</u>, and in Annie B. McDowell, <u>Marriage Bonds of Botetourt County, 1769-1800</u> (Roanoke, 1933).

The Registers of Births and Deaths cover the years 1853-70.

CHURCH RECORDS: Presbyterian: The Virginia State Library has photostats of the Session Records of Locust Bottom Church, 1834-67, and of Galatia and Locust Bottom Churches, 1867, 1869-1898.

Episcopal. Botetourt Parish was formed at the same time as the county and remained the only parish within its bounds.

TAX LISTS: The Virginia State Library has lists of tithables 1770-90. The personal property tax books exist for 1784-1863, with two books for each year except 1784-86, 1791-95, 1797 and 1807. There are land tax books 1783-1863, with two books for each year except 1783-86 when there was only one and 1787-89 and 1838-39 when there were more. There is a list of alterations for 1782.

CENSUS RECORDS: 1810 census, a single alphabetical list.

1820 census, a single alphabetical list (area of residence is indicated beside each name).

1830 census, a single alphabetical list.

GUIDE TO THE COUNTIES OF VIRGINIA 133

1840 census, a single list. Fincastle is designated.
1850 census, a single list.
1860 census, a single list (no post office named). Fincastle is so marked.
1870 census, for Amsterdam Township (P.O. Fincastle, Amsterdam, Cloverdale, Troutville, Bonsack's Depot, Mountain Home), Buchanan Township (P.O. Blue Ridge, Waskey's Mills, Pattonsburg, Gilmore's Mills, Roaring Run, Fincastle, Jackson, **Saltpetre Cave**, Buchanan), Fincastle Township (P.O. Fincastle, Junction Store, Locust Bottom, Salt Petre Cave, Dagger Springs).
1880 census, for Amsterdam District (includes village of Amsterdam), Amsterdam District, Fincastle (10th) District, Fincastle District (includes town of Fincastle), Buchanan Magisterial District (includes Buchanan), and Buchanan Magisterial District (13th; includes laborers on Buchanan and Clifton Forge Railroad).

POST OFFICES (established before 1890): Air Mount (1803-1805/11), Amsterdam (1828-31; 1833-34; 1839-   ), Arch Mills (1887-1906; formerly Obenshain).
Baldwin Station (1886-1924), Barber's Creek (1833-34), Bellevue (1832-35), Big Lick (1798-1881; changed into Roanoke County 1838); Blue Ridge (1835-41; 1841-83, name changed to Obenshain); Blue Ridge Springs (1873-   ; formerly Flukes); Botetourt (1887-1906); Botetourt Springs (1827-85; changed into Roanoke County 1839); Breckinridge (1885-88, formerly Sheets, name changed to Eagle Rock); Brugh's Mill (1876-1906); Buchanan (1849-49, formerly Pattonsburgh, name changed to Pattonsburg; 1869-   , formerly Pattonsburgh).
Carolina (1881-85; name changed to Glen Wilton); Catawba (1847-59, before 1851 in Roanoke County, changed into Roanoke County 1853; 1858-59, formerly in Roanoke County, changed to Roanoke Red Sulphur Springs, Roanoke County); Cloverdale (1811-66, 1867-   ); Covington (1820-   ; fell into Alleghany County 1822); Coyners Springs (1886-1906); Craig's Creek (1831-32; 1843-66, fell into Craig County 1851).
Daggers (1880-80, 1881-81, 1882-1906); Daggers Springs (1849-69, formerly Rebecca Furnace; 1870-77; 1878-79); Daleville (1876-   ); Deisher's Mill (1868-74).
Eagle Rock (1879-80; 1888-   , formerly Breckinridge); Edgebrook (1881-83).
Fincastle (1793-   ); Flukes (1828-73, name changed to Blue Ridge Springs); Fork Dale (1872-74; name changed to Lick Run Bridge).
Gala (1881-   ); Glen Wilton (1885-   , formerly Carolina); Grace Furnace (1856-59; 1874-76).
Haymakertown (1875-   ); Henderson's (1821-36); Houston Mines (1883-83; 1884-96, formerly Mollie, name

changed to Nace).
Indian Rock (1871-   ); Iron Mound (1886-93; name changed to Oriskany).
James River (1840-43); Jennings Creek (1879-80); Junction Store (1848-68).
Kyle (1887-1903).
Lick Run (1884-   ;formerly Lick Run Bridge); Lick Run Bridge (1874-84, formerly Fork Dale, name changed to Lick Run); Lithia (1882-   ); Locust Bottom (1860-81).
Middle Mountain (1840-87; changed into Craig County 1858); Mollie (1884-84; name changed to Houston Mines); Mountain Union (1855-58); Mouth of Cow Pasture (1817-19; also known as Shirkey's); Munford (1886-   ).
New Castle (1821-   ; fell into Craig County 1851).
Obenshain (1883-87; formerly Blue Ridge; name changed to Arch Mills); Old Hickory (1851-90; formerly True Blue; name changed to Springwood).
Pattonsburgh (1805-49, before 1813/7 in Rockbridge County?, name changed to Buchanan; 1849-69, formerly Buchanan, name changed to Buchanan); Pine Dale (1876-81).
Rebecca Furnace (1828-49, name changed to Daggers Springs); Rio Mills (1858-58); Roaring Run (1843-1903); Rocky Point (1888-   ); Rocky Point Mills (1852-66).
Salem (1808-   ; fell into Roanoke County 1838); Salisbury Furnace (1881-1903); Salt Petre Cave (1858-1923); Sheets (1881-85, name changed to Breckinridge); Shirkey's (see Mouth of Cow Pasture); Silent Dell (1886-1907); Sinking Creek (1839-   ; fell into Craig County 1851); Strom (1880-1913); Sweet Springs (1795-   ; fell into Monroe County 1802).
Tinker Knob (1847-69; 1870-   ); Trinity (1886-96); Troutsville (1868-86; name changed to Troutville); Troutville (1886-   ; formerly Troutsville); True Blue (1851-51; name changed to Hickory).
Upper James (1874-74; 1878-78).
Waskey's Mills (1854-66, 1867-   ).

BOOK REVIEWS

Earl Gregg Swem, A Bibliography. Compiled by James A. Servies. The College of William and Mary in Virginia, Library Contributions, no. 1; [Williamsburg] 1960. 60 pp.

The name of Earl Gregg Swem is known to every person interested in Virginia history and genealogy. We may think first of the monumental Virginia Historical Index or of the second series of the William and Mary Quarterly but these are only two of many contributions to Virginia which Dr. Swem has made.

Mr. Servies has compiled this bibliography of Dr. Swem's writings on the occasion of his ninetieth birthday, 29 December 1960. It represents a panorama of research and thought in the field of Virginia history over the last half century. Included are many of the finding lists published in the Virginia State Library Bulletin during the years Dr. Swem was Assistant Librarian there and most notably his three part A Bibliography of Virginia (1915-19), five biographical sketches he prepared for the Dictionary of American Biography, the recent Jamestown 350th Anniversary Historical Booklets, and contributions to the American Antiquarian Society Proceedings, Virginia Magazine of History and Biography, Filson Club History Quarterly, William Parks Club Publications, and College and Research Libraries.

This record of his writings should be a source of pride both to Dr. Swem and to Virginia.

Marriages of Amelia County, Virginia, 1735-1815. Compiled and published by Kathleen Booth Williams. [n.p., 1961] 165 pp. $5.00.

Mrs. Williams' present book, like her previous compilations of Louisa and Goochland County marriages, is well arranged and carefully prepared. The importance of the preservation of early marriage records cannot be overemphasized and it is good that there are competent genealogists engaged in the work of publication.

The marriages are arranged alphabetically by the name of the husband. There is an index of brides and this is followed by the index of witnesses, sureties and others mentioned in the book.

In her Foreword Mrs. Williams quotes the Act creating Amelia County and discusses the division of its territory and of the parishes within its bounds. The condition and nature of extant marriage records is described and a list of officiating ministers is given with identification of their denomination where possible.

Copies can be secured from Mrs. E. Burton Williams, 2702 Russell Road, Alexandria, Va.

Index to the Genealogical Department of the Daughters of the American Revolution Magazine. Volume 92, 1958. Compiled by Martha Porter Miller. Washington, D.C., 1961. 54 pp. $2.00.

The Daughters of the American Revolution Magazine has over many years published an important body of genealogical material. While general guides to these data are available, there has until now been no way to locate specific names.

Both individuals and places are included in this index of more than 9000 entries. The data cover all parts of the United States. More than half of the Virginia counties are listed and there are numerous other Virginia entries. Early Rockbridge County marriages and a number of Virginia Bibles are among the contents of this volume.

Copies of this index and those for 1957, 1959 and 1960, each $2.00, can be secured from the compiler, 2311 Connecticut Avenue, n.w., Washington 8, D.C.

Abstracts of the Wills of the State of South Carolina, 1670-1740. Volume 1. Compiled and edited by Caroline T. Moore and Agatha Aimar Simmons. [Columbia, S.C., 1960] 346 pp. $25.00.

The early wills of South Carolina were preserved in the Journal of the Grand Council, Office of the Secretary of State and the Probate Court of Charleston County. An abstract of every known will prior to 1740 is included in this volume which is handsomely printed in an edition of 500 copies.

While this period is before the great migration from Virginia to the south, these wills reveal connections between the two colonies and with the islands of the West Indies.

The index is very full and includes references to portraits mentioned in the wills, to ships and to plantations. The abstracts provide the user of the volume with the basic information included in each will. All names and relationships are shown and bequests of land are mentioned. The necessity of conserving space prevented the compilers' giving the details of bequests, but the location of each will is shown and a full copy can be obtained by interested readers.

This is an important contribution to South Carolina history and genealogy. We hope that the succeeding volumes will not be long delayed.

Copies can be obtained from Abstracts of S.C. Wills, 307 Stono Drive, Charleston 43, S.C.

BOOK REVIEWS

<u>Early Southwest Virginia Families. Families of Kelly, Smyth, Buchanan, Clark and Related Families of Edmondson, Keys, Beattie, Ryburn, McDonald.</u> By Elizabeth Kelly Allison. Auburn, Ala., 1960. 135 pp. $5.00.

The earliest located records of most of the families discussed in this volume are to be found in Augusta, Montgomery and Washington cos., Va., although a few can be traced back to Pennsylvania and Delaware and the traditional origin of others is given.

Mrs. Allison begins her account of these related families with the statement that her compilation is an attempt to put on record for future generations a collection of family papers and other data she has gathered and is not intended as a history of these families. There is a great deal of material presented on the later generations of each of the families. A more thorough study of records prior to the American Revolution will undoubtedly provide new information about the progenitors of these families and we hope that Mrs. Allison will continue her research.

The book is well indexed. There are a number of photographs and in the front is a chart showing Mrs. Allison's ancestry and the connections of the several families.

Copies can be secured from Mrs. Fred Allison, Box 50, Auburn, Ala.

<u>Some Marriages in Montgomery County, Kentucky, Before 1864.</u> Collected by Hazel Mason Boyd. Compiled and edited by Emma Jane Walker and Virginia Wilson for the Kentucky Records Research Committee. [n.p.] Kentucky Society Daughters of the American Revolution, 1961. 120 pp. $5.00.

When the Montgomery County Court House burned in 1863 all marriage records were destroyed. Wills and deeds fortunately remain, as do the records kept by two early ministers. From these sources, the state vital statistics kept between 1852 and 1861, and numerous other published and unpublished materials, Mrs. Boyd compiled a record of marriages which she has now permitted the Kentucky D.A.R. to publish.

There are well over 6000 entries. The source of each entry is given.

Copies can be secured from Miss Virginia Wilson, 114 Woodland Avenue, Lexington, Ky.

<u>Cemetery Records of Marion County, Texas ... 1846 to June 1, 1960.</u> Copied & Published by Martha McCraw Chapter, Daughters of the American Revolution.

[Jefferson, Tex.] 1960. 331 pp. $6.00.

A great deal of work has gone into the preparation of this volume. Not only have the gravestones in the major cemeteries been copied, but out of the way family plots have been visited. The Death Records kept at the County Clerk's Office since 1903 have been copied, as have the burial records of Oakwood Cemetery in Jefferson, preserved since 1870 in the City Secretary's office.

Virginians are to be found in Marion County. Sarah Williams who was born in Richmond about 1819 died 22 Oct. 1886. Mrs. Lucy D. Bateman (1834-1862) was from Halifax County. Dr. Albert Butt (1830-1867) was born in Princess Anne County.

There is a map locating each cemetery and a plat of Oakwood Cemetery designating each lot. The index comprises 58 pages.

Copies can be secured from Mrs. A. K. Payne, 410 Delta Street, Jefferson, Texas.

The Historical Foundation and Its Treasures. By Thomas Hugh Spence, Jr. Revised ed.; Montreat, N.C., Historical Foundation Publications, 1960. 171 pp. $3.00.

T. H. Spence, Jr., the Executive Director of the Historical Foundation of the Presbyterian and Reformed Churches, has written an engaging history of the Foundation and its collections.

The genealogist will find much useful information about sources in this book. There is a list of church newspapers and magazines, some of which contain marriage and obituary notices, with indication of the Foundation's holdings. An appendix gives an abbreviated listing of the minutes of synods and presbyteries in the library. Some of the principal collections of manuscripts are mentioned.

Libraries will find this to be a helpful reference volume and all with Presbyterian ancestry will enjoy reading it.

Copies can be secured from the Historical Foundation, Montreat, N.C.

QUERIES

Each subscriber to The Virginia Genealogist is entitled to have one or more queries published, free of charge, but limited to a total of fifty words per year, exclusive of name and address. All queries must have a Virginia connection.

QUERIES   139

478. MOORE. Wish marriages of Thomas Moore (will 1676,
Northampton Co., Va., names chn. Gilbert, Thomas, John,
Matthew, Isabel and Cecil, dau-in-law Hannah McMullon)
and of Matthew Moore (will 1717/8, Northampton Co.,
names chn. Thomas, Elizabeth, Mathew, Zachariah, Frances,
John Lean and "son" William Satchel. L. H. Brown, 4510
Market St., Wilmington, N.C.

479. FORD-MILSTEAD-SPENCER-GRACE. Wish antecedents of
Thomas and Jane (Milstead) Ford who went from Charles
Co., Md., to Fairfax Co., Va., ca. 1725; Thomas died
there ca.1776. Wish proof their son John married 1st
Rachel Spencer; he married 2nd Catharine Grace in S.C.
and they went to Shelby Co., Ky., where John died 1803.
Mrs. Wm. H. Smith, 324 Queensway Drive, Lexington, Ky.

480. KITE. Henry Kite married Elizabeth Haestand, Rockingham Co., Va., 1793. His father was Philip Kite (who
were his parents; where did he come from?); want name of
Henry's mother. Who were wife and parents of John
Haestand; where did they come from? Who did Samuel Kite
(son of Henry), born S.C.,1797, marry? Mrs. Frank
Grass, 2506 N.W. 66th Street, Oklahoma City, Okla.

481. FLANIGAN. Want information on the Flanigan family
of Winchester and Frederick Co., Va. Mary Flanigan
married Samuel Tustin and lived first in Leesburg, Va.,
and is buried at Petaluma, Calif. Mrs. Georgia Hays,
Route 1, Box 125, Stayton, Ore.

482. DABNEY-GWATHMEY-CATLETT. Correspondence urgently
desired with descendants of the Gwathmey family of King
William Co., Va., and contact with owners of the old
Bible which belonged to Maj. Philip Gwathmey of "Bur-
lington." I descend from Philadelphia Gwathmey who mar-
ried William Dabney and Ann Gwathmey who married Thomas
Catlett, all of King William Co. Will exchange data.
Mrs. Margaret C. Bridges, 1411 Devon Rd., Winter Park,
Fla.

483. McNULTY-KLINE. Want information on parents of John
McNulty, family originally from Franklin Co., Pa., near
Chambersburg. He married Evelyn Orr, Wilkinson Co.,
Miss.; died 1837. Michael, Samuel and John McNulty
moved from Pa. to Va.; came to Wilkinson Co., Miss., ca.
1811. James McNulty married Catherine Kline, Green-
village, Pa.; the two families were related. Mrs.
James E. O'Donnell, Box 282, Woodville, Miss.

484. GRIGG, LOFTIN, WESTBROOK, WRAY. Want parents of
Augustin Loftin, born Va. ca1785, and wife Mary M. C.

Grigg (when, where born?), married in Greensville Co., Va., 12 Feb. 1812. Of Thornton Westbrook, born Va. (where?) 1806, married Elizabeth (Mabury?), born N.C. ca.1807. Of Thomas Jefferson Wray, born 25 Jan. 1797 (Va.?). Henry G. Wray, 10362 Margate St., North Hollywood, Calif.

485. HELM. Was John Helm who married --- Bosely 2 Sept. 1762 the same John who died 1776, Shelby Co., Ky.? Who was the John Helm who fought in Henrico and/or Pittsylvania Co., Va.? Mrs. Edward J. Bennett, R.R. 2, Box 373A, Carmel, Ind.

486. MARSHALL. Want parents, birth, death of William A. Marshall who moved to his farm in Rockingham Co., Va., 19 Feb. 1833. Was school teacher, miller. Married Mary Parker; 8 children. One son was Preston Holmes Marshall, born 7 April 1828, Rockingham Co., Va. Have a Marshall Bible. Mrs. H. R. Truxall, 161 W. Brighton Rd., Columbus 2, Ohio.

487. CULPEPPER. Sampson Culpepper and wife Eleanor Gilbert of Norfolk Co., Va., had children: John (born 1765, later U.S. Congressman from N.C.), Charles (born 1767), Agnes (born 1780), Elizabeth (born 1782), Sampson (born 1785, died Ga.), Joseph Mallory (born 1788, married Margaret Pickens Baskin; lived in Ga.). Want marriages of and data on first five children. Mrs. Paul F. Stinson, 303 8th Street, Jonesboro, La.

488. ENGLAND. Want parents and wife of Joseph England who died 1791, Franklin Co., Va. Will mentions son John who married Zippora Choate; son Charles, deceased; and Rhody and Isaiah Willis. Mrs. Frank S. Gray, 626 South McKinley, Harrisburg, Ill.

489. CLARKE-HOWARD. Diana Howard Clarke (1785-1851) who married 4 Dec. 1804, Mecklenburg Co., Va., George Washington Brame (born 22 Nov. 1779) was dau. of James Clarke (died Mecklenburg Co. 1785) and Sarah Howard (died 1809). Who were their parents? Mrs. Robert William Harper, 1321 North State St., Jackson, Miss.

490. BUCKLEY. Want parentage, date of birth, date and to whom married of Butler Buckley who was in 1st Va. Regt. in French and Indian War, tithable in Lunenburg Co., Va., 1764, living in Charlotte Co. 1767-84, moved to Burke Co., Ga., 1784. Admiral Ivan E. Bass, 3601 Connecticut Ave., n.w., Washington 8, D.C.

491. VAIDEN. Want information on family of Dr. Joseph C.

QUERIES

Vaiden (born 1830, New Kent Co., Va., died 1898, Goshen, Va.), son of William H. and A. Vaiden. He married 1st Martha Tyler of Richmond (no chn.), 2nd Dora Bell Critzer of Mt. Sidney, Va. (son Harry C.) who about 1905 moved to Ga. Harry C. Vaiden III, 2237 Cumming Rd., Augusta, Ga.

492. LINK-MOWREY-GRIFFIN-HOLLAND-MITCHELL-REESE. Want ancestry of John Nicholas Link (d. 1816, Augusta Co., Va.; wife Margaret [Rebecca] Pence); Lewis Mowrey (died 1825, Augusta Co.; wife Christiana --?--); Mary Anne Griffin (born 1799, Nansemond Co., Va.; married George Washington Holland; to Georgia); Joseph Holland (died 1804, Nansemond Co.; wife Elizabeth Anne Odom); Pleasant Mitchell (married 1791, Amelia Co., Va., Rebecca Coleman), Elizabeth Mitchell (born 1801, Va.; married Rev. John Hall Henry, Sumner Co., Tenn.; had brothers and sisters John, Henry, Robert, Nancy, Polly and Pleasant Mitchell); Isham Reese (born 1749, Petersburg, Va.; married Susannah Coleman). Want children of John Tayloe Griffin (born 1750; wife Mary Lightfoot; of Goochland Co., Va.). Will exchange. Mrs. W. R. Eckhardt, Jr., 4522 Willow Bend Blvd., Houston 25, Texas.

493. MORRIS. Want place of birth in Virginia (Monroe Co., W.Va.?) of Philip Morris who moved to Ohio before 1818. Also names of his wife and his parents. Mrs. H. A. Hallitrom, Box 655, North Bend, Ore.

494. FRANCE-FRANCEY-FRANCIS. Want information about Edward Francis, Capt. Dickey's Company, Augusta Co., Va. Was he the Edward France (Francis) of Rutherford Co., N.C., in 1790, 1800? Who were parents, wife; date of marriage and place? A. E. Scott, Jr., 3809 Lamont, Corpus Christi, Texas.

495. BURBRIDGE-CREEL-GOOCH. Want information on Burbridge family, especially identity and ancestry of Thomas (died 1807, Ky.) and his wife Easter; identity of Charles Creel and wife Sarah of Culpeper Co., Va. (in Fayette Co., Ky., ca.1780); identity of Thomas Gooch, born ca.1766 (what Va. county?), died 1854, Green Co., Ky. John Paul Grady, Box 1334, Roswell, N.Mex.

496. MOXLEY. Want information on Virginia-Maryland family. I believe William Moxley, born 1767, married Mary Spurling 18 July 1792 and, having brothers Daniel and Nathaniel, to have been born in Va. or Md. He died Wilkes Co., N.C., 1841. I have photostats of his family record from his Bible. Mrs. John C. W. Linsley, 305 Timberline Road, Mountainside, N.J.

497. WHARTON. Walker Wharton (aged 38, born Va.), wife Sarah (32, Va.) and children Elizabeth 10, William 8 and Susan 2, in Buffalo Lick Twp., and Leonard Wharton (aged 70, born Va.) and wife Elizabeth (60, Va.) in Clark Twp., Chariton Co., Mo., 1880 census. Who were parents? Want maiden names of wives. When did they leave Va. for Mo.? Want names of any other Whartons coming to Missouri. Miss Marie Perrin Lemley, 3210 West Pico Blvd., Los Angeles 19, Calif.

498. PATTERSON. Capt. James, William and Joseph Patterson were Revolutionary soldiers from Pendleton Co., W.Va. My gr.gr.father William Patterson, born 1804, married Mary A. Snider 1835. Children: Angelina, Virginia, Thomas, Elizabeth, Penelope, James, Frances, John. Can anyone help me connect William with above Revolutionary soldiers? Mrs. C. D. Osborne, 438 West George St., Carmichaels, Pa.

499. VAUGHAN. Thomas Vaughan who married Dorothy Jones lived Sussex Co., Va., where his will was proved 1788, hers 1796, naming children: sons William, Thomas Jr., Fielding; daughters Dorothy Hunt, Lucy Harwell, Elizabeth Rivers, Martha Locke, Anne Wilkerson. A daughter Judith Vaughan listed in Albemarle Parish Register has predeceased them. Thomas Vaughan was Justice and High Sheriff of Sussex and a large land owner there. Am very interested in any information on the parents of Thomas Vaughan and Dorothy Jones. Will gladly share information with anyone working on these lines. Laurence B. Gardiner, 1863 Cowden Ave., Memphis 4, Tenn.

500. COLE-BRYAN. Want information on Elizabeth Cole of Culpeper Co., Va., who married William Bryan of Fauquier Co. ca.1765. Was she daughter of John or Richard Cole, sons of John Cole (will 1757, Culpeper Co.)?
KENYON-WADDINGTON-THOMASIN. Want any information on these families of King George and Richmond cos., Va. Will exchange. Mrs. H. L. Benson, Box 569, Columbia, Mo.

501. McLAUGHLIN-TERRY-MADDING. Desire information on Charles and Barnet McLaughlin. Barnet witnessed deed to Charles from James Henry, 1772, Pittsylvania Co., Va. Charles married Sarah, dau. of Henry and Marget Terry. Who were Henry's parents? Want Marget's maiden name. Want parents of Thomas Madding (1790 census) and wife Rachel's maiden name. Miss Sarah McLaughlin, 715 Longview, Bluefield, W.Va.

502. SMITH-MORRIS. Need parents of Charles Smith, born 22 Jan. 1791, Va. (county?), married Lettice Gillam 1818,

QUERIES 143

Wayne Co., Ind.; think father was William or Joseph who served in Revolution from Va. Mark Morris served in Revolution 1781 with Gen. Morgan from Rockbridge Co., Va.; was he the same Mark Morris who died May 1823, Fayette Co., Ohio? Mrs. Edwin S. Brewster, 1000 East Glenwood Ave., Fullerton, Calif.

503. SCOGGIN-GREENE-KENNEDY-MAYSEY. Want parents and wife of Rev. John Scoggin, born Va., late 1700's; his son James W., born Va., 1805. Also wife of Jarvis Greene; her son was Rev. John Greene. Also information on Susan Kennedy, born Va. ca. 1820, of Scottish ancestry. Also parents of Mary Maysey (married Fairfax Co., Va., 1771). Mrs. William J. Doliante, 12 Tauxemont Road, Alexandria, Va.

504. JARVIS-HASELWOOD. Desire information on parents of Sarah Jarvis, wife of John Haselwood, born Va., moved to Kentucky ca. 1800. John C. Graves, Box 781, Escondido, Calif.

505. WILSON-LLOYD. Want ancestry of Mary Ann Luck (Wilson) Lloyd, first wife of Absalom Lloyd. She was deceased 24 April 1836 when father John Wilson wrote his will, Washington Co., Va. Also ancestry of Absalom Lloyd who married 2nd 1832, Carter Co., Tenn., Elizabeth Wells and moved from Lee Co., Va., to Missouri. Mrs. Joris B. Catron, 1410 Oakwood Ave., Pennington Gap, Va.

506. COLLIE-JENNINGS-SHELTON-HALL. Pittsylvania Co., Va. Want parents of Robert and Susanna Jennings (dau. Nancy married 1801 James Collie); Mark Shelton (1782 tax list) and wife Mary; son George Shelton's wife Mary; William H. Hall, born 1795, married 1817 Judith Shelton. Mrs. Anne G. Greene, Girard College, Philadelphia 21, Pa.

507. MARSHALL-SHANKLIN-SEAY-ENGLISH-DIXON-HOOD-FARRISS. Want parents and information on John Marshall, died 1733, Brunswick Co., Va.; Edward Shanklin, Rockingham Co.; Samuel Seay, born 1760, Amelia Co.; Edward English, born 1758; Henry and Elizabeth Dixon, parents of Tabitha who was born 1734; Nathaniel Hood born 1758; and James Farriss born 1758. Descendants to Tenn. and Ky. Will exchange. Mrs. Arthur A. Thompson, 722 Mathews, Union City, Tenn.

508. FRY. Want descendants of Col. Joshua Fry, Va., ca. 1700-1754, especially descendants of Robert Nelson Smith and wife Mary Margaret Fry; Thomas Walker Fry and wife Mary Ann Maury; Thomas Walker Fry and wife Elizabeth (Betsy) Speed Smith; Charles Meriwether Fry and wife Elizabeth Leigh; Thomas Slaughter Fry and wife Mary

(Mollie) Shorter. For tentative publication. George W. Frye, 5804 Bramble Ave., Cincinnati 27, Ohio.

509. LEWIS. Seeking ancestors and descendants of Robert Lewis, Campbell Co., Va., resident 1850; married twice, second wife Susan Haden, dau. of John Mason; children Mary Haynes, Emily Murrell (born Buckingham Co., Va.), Louisa, Harriet, Margaret, James, Sarah, Nancy, William. Will exchange county data, other families, for Federal census records. Miss Marion L. Dowdy, Evington, Va.

510. GIVENS. Want surname of Martha, wife of James Givens. Their oldest child Deborah, born Aug. 1749, Augusta Co., Va., married James Patterson 1766. Mrs. David Reichlein, Route 1, Box 53, Roy, Wash.

511. RANDOLPH. Want documented data on six different Henry Randolphs: 1) 1623-1673, Henrico Co., Va., wife Judith Soane who married Peter Field 1691; 2) 1650-1700, married Judith Lockey, York Co., Va., after 1667; 3) born 1675, married Ann Edwards of Surry Co., Va.; 4) 1665-1693, wife Sarah Swann who married Giles Webb 1699; 5) 1689-1726, wife Elizabeth Eppes; 6) born 1687, son of William Randolph of Turkey Island. Mrs. Gertrude L. Soderberg, Apt. 3-B, 405 E. 5th St., Greenville, N.C.

512. BURNETT-MAUPIN. Want names of children of Roland Burnett, living Albemarle Co., Va., 1785. Will proved Madison Co., Ky., 2 March 1790 names wife Margaret and children (not named). Was Margaret Maupin his second wife? Daniel Maupin's will names daughter Margaret Burnett and her daughter Lucy. Did Roland have a daughter Elizabeth? Mrs. J. C. Gillock, 2941 Bon Air, Louisville, Ky.

513. WALTON. John Walton, in Greenbrier Co., W.Va., by 1778, died 1808 leaving wife Ann and children William, George, James, John, Elijah, Elisha, Jane, Nancy, Elizabeth and Eleanor. James Walton also was there, and possibly Job Walton (married Margaret ---) and Amos Walton (married Mercy Laycock). Want ancestry of these Waltons. John Walton, 3435 Guilford Terrace, Baltimore 18, Md.

514. TOMKIES. Want to contact any descendants of 1) Sarah Jane Tomkies of Abingdon Parish, Gloucester Co., Va., who was married 21 Oct. 1793 by Rev. Thomas Hughes to Francis Smith Stubbs (1755-1820) brother of John Segar Stubbs; 2) Polly Tomkies (sister to Sarah Jane) who married John Stevens, ca. 1795. D. Simpson Tomkies, 166 Woodland Dr., Huntington 5, W.Va.

THE VIRGINIA GENEALOGIST

Volume 5, Number 4   Whole Number 20

October-December, 1961

CONTENTS

Editor's Page	146
Southside Virginia Austins	
By Janet Austin Curtis	147
Amherst County, Virginia, 1800 Tax List	
(Continued)	155
Edmunds Family Bible	161
Local Notices from the Virginia Gazette,	
1780 (Continued)	163
A Guide to the Counties of Virginia	
Boone County (Continued)	167
Braxton County	167
The Reverend David Mossom of Massachusetts	
and Virginia	
By Lundie W. Barlow	170
The Booker Family: Addendum	
By Cameron Allen	172
The Well Dressed Militiaman	
Contributed by James F. Lewis	174
Some Virginia Revolutionary Soldiers	
Contributed by William H. Dumont	175
Some Culpeper County Marriages	
Contributed by George H. S. King	176
Book Reviews	
Chapman, Wills and Administrations of Elizabeth City County; Isle of Wight County Marriages; Wills and Administrations of Isle of Wight County; Wills and Administrations of Southampton County; Davis, Surry County Records	177
Stewart, The Dulin Family in America	178
Boyd, The Broyles, Laffitte and Boyd Relatives	178
Queries	179

Editor: John Frederick Dorman

Published quarterly by John Frederick Dorman
Business address: Box 4883, Washington 8, D.C.
Copyright 1961, by John Frederick Dorman

Subscription rates: $5.00 per year; single issue, $1.50
All subscriptions begin with first issue of year
V. 1, nos. 1-2, $2.50 each, only as part of entire set

Second class postage paid at Washington, D.C.

EDITOR'S PAGE

The Virginia Genealogical Society, which was organized in October 1960, issued its first Bulletin in June 1961. Among the new officers are The Honorable Leon M. Bazile, President, Mrs. Grace Fuller Knowles, Vice-President, and Mrs. Edwina Warren Stine, Recording Secretary.

Projects of the Society at the present time are the microfilming of the records of Oakwood Cemetery, Richmond, and of loose Henrico County marriage bonds at the Virginia State Library, and publication of an index to W. R. Turner's Old Homes and Families of Nottoway.

From October through June meetings are held on the first Friday of each month in Richmond.

The address of the Society is Box 53, Richmond, Va., but interested persons should note that membership is by invitation.

Newsom News, published by Lloyd I. Showers, Route 3, Box 616, Mena, Ark., is a new family periodical. The first issues contain material on descendants of the Nusum-Newsome family of Greenbrier Co., W.Va. Several interesting letters written in 1851 by David Newsom while travelling to Oregon are reproduced.

The Daughters of the American Revolution Magazine for May and June-July 1961 carries Rockbridge Co., Va., marriages, 1788-93.

The National Genealogical Society Quarterly for June 1961 contains the records from the Bible of the Peyton family of Coles Co., Ill., beginning with Cuthbert H. Peyton (1762-1812) and his wife Catey Bronaugh, and notes on the Peytons of Prince William County. Also in this magazine is information on the Pinkston-Campbell-Bell families of Westmoreland and Northumberland counties taken from a suit in the English High Court of Chancery in 1797.

The Kentucky Genealogist for April-June 1961 contains information on the Harris, Davis and Foster families of Prince William County. Since January 1960 this magazine has been publishing entries in the reports relating to Virginia debts to British merchants which show migrations to Kentucky in the years after the American Revolution.

The Editor is solely responsible for the general policies, printing, distribution and sale of this periodical. Neither the Editor nor The Virginia Genealogist assumes responsibility for errors of fact or opinion expressed by contributors. Manuscripts which are submitted for publication should be of general interest and thoroughly documented and should be accompanied by return postage. Report of non-delivery of magazines must be made within one month after the quarter they are dated.

SOUTHSIDE VIRGINIA AUSTINS

By Janet Austin Curtis
Williamsburg, Virginia

It has been frequently stated that Stephen Fuller Austin of Texas descends from a Virginia family. It is true that he was born in Wythe Co., Va., 3 Nov. 1793, but his father Moses Austin was born in Durham, Conn., 4 Oct. 1761 and married in Philadelphia, Pa., 28 Sept. 1785, Maria Brown who was born in Sussex, N.J., Jan. 1768. Moses Austin was a fifth generation descendant of Richard Austin who arrived at Charlestown, Mass., in 1638.

There is, however, an Austin family in Virginia in which the name Stephen appears. The origin of this family is unknown but its members were closely associated with the Terry family of Halifax and Pittsylvania counties which came from Hanover and New Kent counties.

1 JOHN AUSTIN, born probably between 1680-1700. He first appears in the records in 1740 when he and a Richard Austin asked the Brunswick County Court to add them to the list of tithables.[1] In 1749 he was constable of Lunenburg Co., Va.[2] He owned at least 1000 acres in the part of Lunenburg County which later became Halifax and Pittsylvania County. John Austin made his will Sept. 1758, described himself as of Cornwall Parish, and named his wife Hannah and sons John, Valentine, Stephen, Richardson (also called Richard) and Joseph, mentioning that the first two were then married. The will was proved 5 Feb. 1760.[3]

Hannah, wife of John Austin, died before Feb. 1784 when a certificate to settle her estate was granted to Joseph Austin, Benjamin Sankford and Joseph Morton.[4] Some descendants claim her maiden name was Hannah or Honor Love, but this has not been verified.

Children:
    11 John Austin, Jr.
    12 Valentine Austin
    13 Stephen Austin
    14 Richardson Austin
    15 Joseph Austin

11 JOHN AUSTIN, JR., born ca.1720. He married before 1758 and perhaps as early as the 1740's. His wife may

---

1 Brunswick Co., Va., Order Book 1, p. 345.
2 Lunenburg Co., Va., Order Book 2, p. 253.
3 Ibid., Will Book 1, p. 308.
4 Pittsylvania Co., Va., Order Book 5, p. 64.

have been Mary, daughter of William Maybee who named a daughter Mary Austin in his will 20 Aug. 1758.[5] He moved away from Virginia about the time his father died[6] and in 1771 was in Rowan Co., N.C.,[7] in 1772 in Surry Co., N.C.,[8] and before 1782 had moved to Montgomery Co., Va.[9]

Children:[10]
- 111 Stephen Austin
- 112 Isaiah Austin
- 113 William Austin
- 114 Joseph Austin
- 115 Thomas Austin
- 116 John Austin

111 STEPHEN AUSTIN, born Nov. 1755, Pittsylvania Co., Va. He was a Revolutionary War soldier and in his pension application[11] stated that as a child, about age 2, he was taken to Grayson Co., Va. At the age of 21 he enlisted in the cavalry of Maj. William Armstrong and Col. Washington in the light horse dragoons in Gen. Greene's Division, in Surry Co., N.C. He spent five years in the Revolution but the last two years hired a substitute. After the war he went back to Virginia and lived there 20 years. He moved to Tennessee and lived in Warren, Giles, Wayne and Hardin counties, and also lived in Alabama three years.

Deeds of Grayson County[12] indicate that the Austins lived on the New River very close to the Virginia-North Carolina border. Stephen died 1850, Hardin Co., Tenn.[13]

Children:
1111 Saunders Austin. He was taxed in Warren Co., Tenn., in 1812 and was in Smith Co., Tenn., in 1816 when his son John was born. He is listed in the 1820 census of Wayne Co., Tenn. In 1840 he was a resident

---

5 Halifax Co., Va., Will Book O, p. 55.
6 Revolutionary War pension application, Stephen Austin, N.C., S.2040, National Archives.
7 Pittsylvania Co., Va., Deed Book 2, p. 204.
8 Ibid., p. 410.
9 Montgomery Co., Va., personal property tax books, 1782-87. He is listed as John Austin, Sr.
10 These Austins are thought to be brothers because of their association with each other. Stephen, William, Isaiah and Bartholomew were taxed in Montgomery Co., Va., in 1793. In 1795 Stephen and Isaiah were taxed in Grayson County. Bartholomew is probably a son of William.
11 Revolutionary War pension application, loc. cit.
12 Grayson Co., Va., Deed Book 2, p. 194, et seq.
13 Inscription on a government marker in Hollens Creek Cemetery, Hardin Co., Tenn.

of Hardin Co., Tenn., and his father was living with him. The family continued to live there. The 1850 census indicates he was born in Virginia 1784/5 and his wife Nancy was born there in 1791. They were probably married ca. 1805. He died before 1860 but she is listed in that census, although not in 1870. Their children were: two daughters born before 1810 (one of whom is probably Elizabeth Austin, born 10 Sept. 1810, who married first James Davis and second Elbourn Bowles, and who was living in Saltillo, Hardin Co., Tenn., in 1832), Stephen born 1810-12, John born 8 June 1816, David born 1818, William born 1820, Angeline born 1825 (married Henry Qualls), Archibald S. born 1826, and Robert born 1831.

1112 John Austin. He was in Wayne Co., Tenn., in 1820 and about the same age as Saunders.

1113 William Austin. He was in Wayne Co., Tenn., in 1820 as were Saunders and John Austin.

1114 Stephen Austin. He was in Smith Co., Tenn., in 1820, and in 1830 Stephen and Ransom Austin were living in McNairy Co., Tenn., which adjoins Hardin County on the west.

112 ISAIAH AUSTIN, born 18 Feb. 1759, perhaps in Surry Co., N.C. In 1832 he filed a claim for bounty stating he had served as an Indian spy in the Revolution.[14] His residence at this time was Grayson Co., Va., but he had lived in Surry Co., N.C., and enlisted there. He was taxed in Montgomery Co., Va., 1782-87, Wythe Co., Va., 1793, and in 1795 appears on the Grayson County rolls.

He probably married twice and had two sets of children (John, Daniel and James being by one wife and Bledsoe, Lacy and Franklin by a second wife).
Children:

1121 John Austin. He bought from Peter Coleman 174 acres on Little River, a branch of New River, in 1806[15] and sold this tract to Daniel Austin in 1809.[16] He was in Kentucky in 1823 according to the Grayson County land tax books. He may have moved to Athens, McMinn Co., Tenn., by 1831.

1122 Daniel Austin. He was taxed for the land bought from his brother John until 1822, but his residence according to the 1821 tax list was Ashe Co., N.C.

1123 James Austin. He paid taxes in Washington Co., Va., as early as 1811. His estate was appraised

---

[14] Revolutionary War pension application, Isaiah Austin, N.C., S.5259, National Archives.
[15] Grayson Co., Va., Deed Book 2, p. 194.
[16] Ibid., p. 473.

3 Oct. 1830 and Bledsoe Austin was administrator. On 10 Oct. 1831 Isaiah Austin, father and heir at law of James Austin, made a deed to John Austin of Athens, Tenn., conveying property belonging to James.[17]

1124 Bledsoe Austin, born 1807. He lived in Grayson County all his life, being listed in the 1850 census, in the 1860 census at Elk Creek and in the 1870 census at Independence. He was deeded land by Isaiah Austin.

1125 Lacy Austin, born 1808. He lived in Grayson County all his life, being listed in the 1850 census, in the 1860 census at Grayson Court House, and in the 1870 census at Old Town Township. He was deeded land by Isaiah Austin.

1126 Franklin Austin, born 1817. He lived in Grayson County all his life, being listed in the 1850 census, and in the 1860 census at Greeneville. His will was recorded in Grayson County, Dec. 1899.[18]

113 WILLIAM AUSTIN. Little is known of him. He appears on the Montgomery Co., Va., tax lists, 1782-87, and in 1793 paid for two tithables in Wythe County, indicating he had a son over 16 at that time. By a deed dated 25 July 17-- he bought from William Allison 250 acres on the New River in Ashe Co., N.C. This deed was witnessed by B. Austin, and when it was finally recorded in 1825 the witness was mentioned as Bat. Austin. On 2 Sept. 1826 William Austin deeded this land to Bartholomew Austin. He also purchased 300 acres on the New River, adjoining the lands of William Reeves and others, from Peter Whitaker on 2 May 1807.[19]

Child (presumably):

1131 Bartholomew Austin, born probably about 1768. The 1830 census of Ashe Co., N.C., places his birth 1760-70. He married ca. 1791 Anne Reeves, daughter of George and Jane (Burton) Reeves of New River Plantation, Grayson Co., Va. She was born 1773/4 and died 18 Feb. 1870, aged 96, at Pound, Wise Co., Va. Their children were: William born 1792, Isaiah born 1793, Jane born 1795 (married Bill Sanders), Jesse born 1797 (married Margaret Douglass and lived in Grayson Co., Va., in 1850), Andrew born 1799 (married Louisanne Bryant and lived in Ashe Co., N.C., in 1850), Lucinda born 1802, David born 1804, John born 1806, George born 1808 (married Eleanor Fields and died 1854, Grayson Co., Va.), Robert born 1811,

---

17 Washington Co., Va., Will Book 6, pp. 188, 237; Deed Book 12, p. 40.
18 Grayson Co., Va., Will Book 8, p. 469.
19 Ashe Co., N.C., Deed Book D, p. 41.

Prudence born 1813, Jackson born 1815, and Edwin born 1817.

12 VALENTINE AUSTIN. He was married before his father made his will in 1758. His father gave him 400 acres on Leatherwood Creek, then in Halifax Co., Va., and now in Henry County. Since Valentine is not a common name, it is reasonable to assume he is the Valentine Austin who is listed in the 1790 census of Beaverdam District, Granville Co., N.C. He paid taxes in Beaverdam District in 1788.

13 STEPHEN AUSTIN. He received 370 acres on Sandy River, then in Halifax Co., Va., and now in Pittsylvania County, from his father's estate. There is no record in Pittsylvania County of the disposition of his property there. He may be the Stephen Austin listed in the 1790 census of Nash District, Caswell Co., N.C.
   Children (probably):
      131 Mary Austin. She married Jonathan Davis in Caswell Co., N.C., the bond being dated 17 April 1781.

14 RICHARDSON AUSTIN. He was one of his father's executors and was bequeathed the family plantation after the death of his mother. His father spoke of him as both Richardson and Richard in his will. He may be the Richard Osten in the 1790 census of Salisbury District, Rockingham Co., N.C. There is, however, reference to Richardson Austin, Thomas Brumley and Austin Brumley in Augusta Co., Va., 27 Sept. 1763.[20]

15 JOSEPH AUSTIN, born probably ca. 1730-35, died ca. 1810, Pittsylvania Co., Va., when he was last taxed. In April 1811 Welthy Austin, his widow, was granted letters of administration on his estate.[21] He was probably married twice.[22] He married Welthy Prewett (Pruit) in Pittsylvania County 26 Nov. 1777. She was the daughter of Daniel Pruit who made his will May 1755, this will being witnessed by John Austin Sr. and John (X) Austin, Jr.[23] Welthy Prewett Austin died ca. 1818, Pittsylvania Co., Va., when she was last taxed. The family lived on Sandy River in Pittsylvania County, not far from the North Carolina Border.

---

20 Lyman Chalkley, Chronicles of the Scotch-Irish Settlement in Virginia, Extracted from the Original Court Records of Augusta County (Rosslyn, Va., 1912), v. I, p. 479.
21 Pittsylvania Co., Va., Order Book 14, p. 534.
22 His first wife is unknown but since his son Archibald Pruit Austin was born ten years before his marriage to Welthy Prewett (Pruit), he may have married first a Pruit also, perhaps Ann or Lucy, sisters of Welthy.
23 Halifax Co., Va., Will Book O, p. 71.

Children:[24]
    151 John Austin
    152 William Austin
    153 Archibald Pruit Austin
    154 Champness Austin
    155 Stephen Austin
    156 David Austin
    157 Fanny Austin. She married --- Covington.
    158 Lucy Austin. She married Thomas Kendrick.
    159 Pastsy Austin. She married Abraham Johns 21 Sept. 1801.
    15x Mary Austin. She married William Hankins 12 Jan. 1796.

151 JOHN AUSTIN, born ca. 1760-65, Pittsylvania Co., Va., died 4 Oct. 1827, Union Dist., S.C. He married 11 Sept. 1788 Polly --- who was aged 78 on 24 June 1840 when she made application for a pension.[25] She stated her husband was the oldest of five brothers and resided in Pittsylvania Co., Va., when he enlisted. He is listed in the 1790 census of Union Dist., S.C., with his wife but no children. The 1800 census indicates he had three daughters. The 1820 census shows him and his wife as aged over 45 with four males under 10, one female under 10, two aged 10-16, two aged 16-26 and one aged 26-45. The 1830 census shows a John Austin with a young family and the 1840 census shows James Austin and Joseph Austin, no doubt both of this family. The 1850 census places the birth of his daughter Nancy as 1793 in South Carolina, and of Martha Austin as 1800 and John Austin as 1827/8.

152 WILLIAM AUSTIN. He was taxed in Pittsylvania Co., Va., in 1787 with his father Joseph Austin and his age was given as over 21 on 30 April, so he was born before 1766. He was surety on the marriage bonds of his brothers Champness and David in 1796 and 1797. The 1820 census of Pittsylvania County shows him and his wife as over 45 and one male aged 10-16 and one under 10.

153 ARCHIBALD PRUIT AUSTIN, born 1767, Virginia (aged 83 in 1850 census of Grainger Co., Tenn.). He married Rebecca ---- who was born 1771, Virginia. She may have been the daughter of William Thompson whose will was recorded in Halifax Co., Va., 1780.[26] He was last taxed in Pittsylvania Co., Va., in 1795. On 19 July

---
[24] Pittsylvania Co., Va., Deed Book 22, p. 77.
[25] Revolutionary War pension application, John Austin, Va., widow Polly, R.325, National Archives.
[26] Maude C. Clement, The History of Pittsylvania County Virginia (Lynchburg, 1929), p. 152.

1794 he sold his horses, cows, furniture and his plantation to William Hankins, Sr.[27] William Austin and Champness Austin witnessed this deed. It is not known whether he went directly to Tennessee, but the family later owned a large plantation in what is now Hamblen County. The site was flooded by Cherokee Lake when it was formed as part of the T.V.A. His family is listed in the 1840 and 1850 censuses of Grainger Co., Tenn.
Children:
    1531 Clisby Austin, born 1802, Tennessee.
    1532 (perhaps) William Austin, born 1798, North Carolina, living in Knox Co., Tenn., 1850.
    1533 ---- Austin, a son who died before 1850, whose family was living in Grainger Co., Tenn., that year.

    154 CHAMPNESS AUSTIN, born ca. 1768/9, Virginia, died after 1850, probably in Rockingham Co., N.C., where he was living in 1850, aged 81. He married first, 27 July 1796, Pittsylvania Co., Va., Aincy Dear (widow), daughter of John Morton of Pittsylvania Co., Va. She was living as late as 1826 when she deeded to her sons G. A. Austin, John W. Austin and Daniel B. Austin 660 acres on Sandy River and Strawberry Creek which she inherited from her father.[28] He married second Elizabeth ----. He moved to Rockingham Co., N.C., prior to 1840.
Children:
    1541 Champ Austin, Jr., born ca. 1797. He went to Bedford Co., Tenn., before 1840.
    1542 ---- Austin, daughter, born 1797-1804.
    1543 ---- Austin, son, born 1797-1804.
    1544 Garland A. Austin, born 1799/1800. He lived in Pittsylvania Co., Va., in 1850.
    1545 ---- Austin, son, born 1802-04.
    1546 John W. Austin, born 1805. He lived in Henry Co., Va., in 1850.
    1547 Daniel B. Austin, born 1807. He lived in Henry Co., Va., in 1850.
    1548 James R. Austin, born 1804-10.
    1549 Jefferson Austin, born 1810. He lived in Henry Co., Va., in 1850.
    154x Robert J. Austin, born 1820.
    154a Lucinda Austin, born ca. 1821.
    154b Joseph Austin, born 1822.
    154c Francis Austin, born 1827.
    154d Elizabeth Austin, born 1830.
    154e William Austin, born 1833.
    154f Sarah Austin, born 1836.

---
27 Pittsylvania Co., Va., Deed Book 10, p. 31.
28 Ibid., Deed Book 28, p. 56.

155 STEPHEN AUSTIN, born Pittsylvania Co., Va., 1769 (aged 81 in 1850 census of Bedford Co., Tenn.). He married 23 April 1800, Pittsylvania County, Rebecca Hankins. They are listed in the 1830 census of Pittsylvania County with one male aged 20-30 and two aged 10-15 and three females aged 15-20 and one aged 5-10. They were living in Rutherford Co., Tenn., at the time of the 1840 census.

Children: The 1840 census indicated there were also three more daughters and two more sons
    1551 Owen Austin, born ca. 1800.
    1552 Eliza Austin, born 1801. She married Willis Dearing.
    1553 Mary W. She married 1827 Joseph Johns.
    1554 Sarah. She married 1844 Sampson Warren.
    1555 (probably) James Austin, born 1813, Virginia, living in 1850 in Rutherford Co., Tenn.

156 DAVID AUSTIN, born Pittsylvania Co., Va. He married 8 Jan. 1797, Pittsylvania County, Elizabeth Oliver. He was last taxed in Pittsylvania County in 1804 and subsequent records have not been located.

AMHERST COUNTY, VIRGINIA

1800 TAX LIST

In the following entries, the first number after each
name is that of the white males over age twenty-one, the
second the number of horses owned, and the third and
fourth, if given, the number of tithable slaves aged
over sixteen and between twelve and sixteen.

Lexington Parish
District of Peter P. Thornton

Anderson, Thomas 1-0
Alley, Isaiah 1-4-2-0
Arington, William 1-0
Anderson, Mary 0-6-16-2
Allen, Robert 1-0
Attkerson, Walker 1-5-0-2
Anguies, William 1-4-4-0
Aplin, Thomas 2-5-2-0
Armstead, William 1-4-3-0
Ambler, John 2-14-34-4
Allin, Thomas 1-1
Adams, Benjamin 1-0
Anguies, James 1-1
Armstrong, Benjamin 1-0
Alegan, John 1-1
Allcock, Joseph 1-1-1-0
Amus, Joseph 1-1-1-0
Allcock, Richard 1-2-1-0
Allcock, John 1-2
Allcock, William 1-0
Allen, Hannah 0-4-5-2
Andrew, William 2-2
Attkisson, Josiah 1-3-4-0
Brown, John 1-0
Brown, Henry 1-2-1-1
Barker, John 1-1
Burch, John 1-0
Ballinger, Henry 1-5-3-1
Burford, John jr. 1-4-3-0
Burford, Ambrose 1-3-2-0
Burford, Archerles 1-0-1-0
Burks, David jr. 1-3-2-0
Burks, William 1-3-4-2
Bibb, Martin 1-3-2-0
Burton, Philip 1-6-8-3
Burford, Philip 1-3-2-0
Biass, Roling 1-3-2-0
Briant, Lewis 1-1
Bolling, Bailey 1-1

Briant, Berry 1-1
Bailey, David 1-1
Burks, John jr. 1-0
Burks, Richard (Capt.) 1-5-5-3
Burks, Lindsey 1-2-1-0
Burks, Richard (SD) 1-3-1-0
Bacon, William 1-4-4-1
Ballard, John 1-0
Boothe, George 1-0
Bacon, Ludwell 1-1-0-1
Bacon, Langston 1-1-1-0
Brock, Rucker & Co. 1-1
Bagby, Daniel 1-0
Burnett, Jacob 1-1
Ballinger, James 1-1
Bell, Drury 1-4-6-0
Burford, James 1-5-3-0
Burrus, Charles 1-8-12-2
Burrus, Sarah 0-5-8-3
Burrus, Joseph 1-11-17-1
Byass, Larkin 2-2
Brydie, Brown & Co. 0-1
Bowles, Charles 2-2
Bolling, James 1-2
Bell, Samuel 2-2-2-0
Brown, James M. 1-2-2-2
Blair, Allen 1-2-4-1
Brown, William 1-2
Bobbitt, John 1-0
Bourne, Henry 3-6-8-2
Beck, Jessee 1-4-1-0
Bagby, Reuben 1-1-2-0
Bugg, Sherod 1-3-0-1
Brown, Leroy 1-1
Biass, John 1-1
Bowling, John 1-3-1-0
Brockman, John, Estate 0-2-3-0

Bettersworth, Richard 1-1
Brannum, Edward 1-1
Ballinger, Joseph 1-9-10-2
Burks, Samuel 1-2-3-1
Burks, David 4-4-8-1
Burks, John 3-8-10-0
Briant, William 2-1-1-0
Brown, Rachel 0-2
Burford, Daniel Senr.
 1-6-5-0
Burford, Daniel jr. 2-3-3-0
Burford, John Senr. 1-2-2-1
Burford, William 1-4-3-1
Bond, John 1-1
Bowling, Powhatan 0-4-8-1
Bailey, William 1-1-3-0
Blankinship, Abel 1-1
Burch, Francis 2-6
Bukley, Susannah 0-0-2-0
Burks, Charles 3-6-6-2
Brown, John Senr. 2-2
Biby, Jolley 1-0
Briant, Finney 1-1
Crawford, David jr. 1-1
Carter, William 1-4
Carpenter, Eaton 1-2
Cash, Joel 1-4
Carpenter, Enoch 1-2-1-0
Camden, Micajah 1-4-3-1
Cash, Howard 1-5-2-0
Carpenter, James jr. 1-2
Clarkson, William 1-4-1-0
Carter, Abraham 1-5-2-0
Clarkson, John 3-6-5-0
Clayton, John 2-3-2-1
Crews, Joseph jr. 1-1
Crews, Archerlis 1-1
Clements, David 1-0
Carter, Edward 1-4-4-1
Christian, Anthony 1-1
Crawford, Nelson 1-6-7-1
Clements, Drury 1-0
Cox, Reubin 1-1
Clayton, Thomas 1-0
Crews, Lewis 1-0
Crews, Anderson 1-0
Crawford, John 1-6-5-1
Cameron, Duncan 1-1
Carpenter, Benjamin 2-3
Cash, William 1-3
Campbell, James 1-0

Carpenter, Hensley 1-1
Cash, James 1-3
Cash, John 1-3
Cash, Peter 1-4
Cash, Bartlett 2-5-2-0
Cash, Randolph 1-2
Campbell, John 1-4-3-0
Carter, Edward jr. 1-1
Coleman, Benjamin 1-3-2-2
Coleman, Littleberry 1-1
Clements, James 2-1
Clements, William 1-4
Clements, William W. 1-1
Clark, William (CM) 4-5
Clark, James 1-2
Childress, Joseph 1-1
Carter, Peter 1-3-1-0
Clements, John 1-0
Childress, John jr. 1-2
Clements, John senr. 1-1
Childress, John 1-3
Crews, John 1-2
Christian, James (SG)
 1-3-3-1
Christian, John H. 0-7-6-0
Coats, Jeremiah 1-0
Cooper, Leonard B. 1-0
Christian, John (Capt.)
 1-8-10-1
Crews, Joseph Senr. 1-9-9-2
Crews, Thomas 1-3-6-0
Coleman, Lindsey 3-12-19-4
Camden, Henry 1-5-7-0
Coleman, Jessee 1-3-4-0
Campbell, Larrance 1-4-2-1
Campbell, Ambrose 1-2
Campbell, George jr.
 1-1-1-0
Campbell, Wiley 1-3
Campbell, Samuel 1-2
Campbell, George, Estate
 0-5-1-0
Carpenter, James (ST)
 1-3-0-1
Callaway, Nancy 0-0-2-0
Coulter, Michael 1-8-4-0
 ordinary license
Christia, Hugh 1-0
Callaway, Dudley 2-3-3-1
Carter, John 1-1-1-0
Clements, Thomas 1-0-1-0

AMHERST COUNTY 1800 TAX LIST   157

Cashwell, Peter 3-3-4-2
Crews, James 1-1
Crews, Reuben 1-0
Cheatwood, Daniel 1-1-1-0
Clark, Micajah 2-2
Clements, Gersham 1-1
Cooney, John 1-2
Campbell, Joel 3-6-4-0
Clark, George 1-0
Coleman, George, Estate
  0-0-11-3
Coleman, William 1-1
Camden, William 1-5-6-2
Camden, William jr. 1-1-3-0
Camden, Jabez 1-2-5-0
Campbell, James (SG)
  1-2-0-1
Cox, Valentine 1-6-5-2
Campbell, Aaron 1-3
Clements, Stephen 1-0
Clements, Jessee 1-1-1-0
Coleman, Elizabeth 1-7-5-0
Coleman, Samuel 1-1
Crawford, David 1-8-8-1
Campbell, Hugh 2-12-16-3
Crawford, John D. 1-3
Croacher, William 1-2-0-1
Christian, Drury 1-4-5-1
Christian, John (Buffalo)
  5-8-2-2
Carter, Charles 0-12-16-7
Crawford, William S. 1-9-
  12-2   1 rid[in]g
  carriage coach
Camm, John 1-1-0-1
Christian, Charles 2-4-3-1
Christian, Robt., Estate
  1-6-6-1
Christian, Robt. 1-1-1-0
Cashwell, Henry 1-0
Christian, Walter 1-1-2-1
Christian, James (SC)
  1-2-3-0
Clark, William (HC) 2-0
Clark, Joseph 1-0
Coleman, Thomas 1-2-2-0
  1 stud horse
Clayton, John W. 1-2-1-0
Clements, Francis 1-3
Carter, William, Estate
  0-4-4-0

Cooper, John 2-4
Crawford, Charles 1-4-5-0
Caufland, Benjamin, Est.
  0-1-0-0
Carter, Peter, Estate
  0-5-3-0
Carter, Solomon 1-0
Creamoore, Barnett 1-1
Christian, Henry 1-7-5-0
Cartright, John 2-4-11-0
Davis, James 1-1-1-0
Dawson, Pleasant 1-5-6-1
Duncan, Fleming H. 1-1-1-0
Dawson, Nelson C. 1-4-4-0
Day, Samuel 1-1
Day, Mary Ann 2-1
Davis, William (Cake)
  1-2-3-0
Dodd, John 1-1
Dodd, Joseph 2-3
Duncan, William 1-2-3-0
Davis, Arther L. 1-3-4-1
Davis, Nicholas C. 1-6-5-3
Dewauser, John 1-4
Dewauser, John jr. 1-0
Deen, Samuel 2-1
Deen, Jeremiah 1-3
Davis, Joshua 1-0
Davis, Lewis 1-1-0-3
Dehart, Jessee 1-0
Dawson, William 2-1
Dameron, William 1-6
Dewhitt, Thomas 1-0-1-1
Dawson, Martin 1-2-4-0
Davis, John F. 1-0
Dameron, Dunmoore 1-0
Davenport, Joseph 3-8-7-1
Dallill [?], John 1-0
Davis, Charles 2-6-4-1
Dillard, Joseph 1-3-4-1
Davis, John 1-2
Davis, Israel 1-0
Davis, Israel, Estate
  0-4-2-0
Davis, Richard 1-0
Davis, Elizabeth 0-1-2-0
Dillard, William 1-2-1-0
Dillard, James (SW) 1-0
Dillard, James 2-5-9-0
Dillard, George 3-6-8-1
  1 stud horse

Daverson, Giles 1-3-0-1
Dawson, Joseph 3-8-6-2
Devenport, William 1-2
Davis, Isham 1-2-3-1
Dunevent, Daniel 1-0
Devenport, Richard 1-3
Davis, William 1-1
Duncan, John 1-6-4-3
Dehart, John 1-0
Eubank, John 2-6-4-0
 1 stud horse
Ellis, Josiah jr. 1-1
England, William 2-3
Ellis, John 1-5-0-2
Evans, Elisha 1-0
Eads, Bartlett 1-2-1-0
Evans, William 1-3-1-2
Evans, Pleasant 1-0
Evans, Thomas 1-0
Edwards, Thomas 2-5-3-0
Ellis, William 1-0
Ellis, Samuel 1-0
Eubank, George 3-6-2-1
Ellis, Josiah 1-9-18-2
Franklin, Jeremiah 1-9-4-0
Fulcher, John 1-4-3-0
Franklin, James 1-9-19-2
Farnsworth, Henry 1-0
Flood, John 1-1
Franklin, Reubin 1-1-1-0
Franklin, Joel 1-8-6-2
Fulcher, James 1-3-1-0
Franklin, Samuel 1-3-2-0
Foster, William 1-2
Fletcher, Christopher
 1-3-1-1
Franklin, Peachery 1-1-2-0
Floyd, James 1-4
Frazer, Walter 1-3
Frazer, John 1-4
Franklin, James 1-1
Flower, William 1-0
Gatewood, Ransom 1-1
Garland, David & James
 2-1-0-1
Goodrich, Thomas (S James)
 1-0
Goodrich, John 1-4-1-1
Goodwin, James 1-3
Grant, William 1-0
Goodwin, Micajah 2-3-4-0

Goodwin, Cornelious
 1-2-2-0
Goodrich, Edmond 2-5-3-0
Gillespie, Sherod M. 1-0
Goodrich, Saml. 1-0
Gooch, Philip 1-5-7-1
Grooms, John 1-0
Goolsby, Samuel 1-3
Grimes, Moses 1-0
Garner, Joseph 1-0
Grisson, Thomas jr. 1-1
Grissom, Thomas 4-6-2-2
Gillespie, George 1-5-5-1
Gillespie, George jr.
 1-2-1-1
Gillespie, Alexander 1-0
Garland, Hudson M. 1-4-4-3
Gilbert, Ezekiel 1-2
Garland, David S. 3-9-8-3
 1 stud horse
Gregory, John 1-2
Guttery, David 1-0
Garven, James 1-0
Guttery, Edward 1-0
Galt, William 0-11-15-5
Guttery, William jr.
 1-4-3-0
Grimes, Thomas 2-5
Good, Benjamin 3-4
George, Salley 3-3-1-0
Gausney, Henry 1-4-3-1
Griffie, Benjamin 2-5
Gatewood, William, Estate
 0-0-2-0
Gatewood, William 1-1
Gatewood, Reuben 1-1-0-1
Garland, Spotswood 1-1
Gillinwaters, James 1-0
Gilbert, Henry 3-3-1-0
Gilliam, John 1-4-3-0
Gilliam, Jarrett 1-1-3-1
Gilliam, Archerbald 1-4-2-1
Goodrich, James 1-1
Goodrich, Thomas Senr. 1-0
Gilliland, Susannah 1-3-1-0
Goodwin, George 2-3-3-1
Guthery, William Sen. 1-2
Harrison, Josiah 1-1-1-0
Harrison, James 1-3-5-1
Harrison, Reuben 1-1
Hill, Ezekiel 2-2-1-0

AMHERST COUNTY 1800 TAX LIST

Hambleton, Andrew 1-1
Hambleton, Robert 1-4
Hamlet, Elias 1-0
Harrison, Richard 3-7-5-1
Harrison, Nicholas 1-1-2-0
Haynes, Hardin 1-4-8-0
Hansford, William 1-4-2-1
Higginbotham, William 2-4
Haynes, Jessee 1-1
Howard, William 1-2-1-0
Harrison, George 1-0-1-0
Howard, Binjamin 1-1
Hogg, William F. 1-1
Haynes, Charles 1-0
Harrison, John, Estate 2-2-4-0
Henley, Leonard 2-5-3-3
Hooker, William 1-0
Hartless, Henry 1-6-3-1 1 stud horse
Hall, William 2-4-2-0
Hamm, James 1-4-1-0
Hogg, John 2-5-1-0
Hughs, William jr. 1-2-1-0
Hardwick, Richard 1-2-0-1
Higginbotham, Joseph Senr. 1-6-5-1
Higginbotham, Joseph jr. 2-8-6-1
Hatton, Richard 1-2
Hartless, William 1-3
Hill, Samuel 1-11-9-2
Hartless, Richard 1-1-1-0
Hartless, James 1-1
Hall, John jr. 1-1
Hinson, Joseph 1-2
Hill, Thomas, Estate 1-3-3-0
Hill, James 1-6-3-0
Hughs, Harrison 1-1-1-1
Hudson, Rush 2-5-4-1
Hill, John jr. 2-1-1-0
Hudson, Joshua 1-2-6-0
Hughs, William 2-4-3-1
Hunter, David 1-3-2-0
Holloway, Robert 1-4-10-1
Howard, George 1-1
Hawkins, Jessee 1-0
Hutcherson, John, Estate 2-3-2-1
Hill, John Senr. 2-5-3-1

Higginbotham, Charles 1-0-0-1
Howl, Absolam 1-2-4-1
Hamm, William 1-1-0-1
Hill, Maddison 1-1-0-1
Howerton, Harritage 1-0
Hill, John (son James) 1-0
Hill, James (son James) 1-1
Hinson, James 1-5
Hall, John 2-4
Hudson, George 1-1-1-0
Hartless, Peter 1-1
Higginbotham, Aaron, Est. 1-6-5-1
Hudson, Reubin 1-1-1-0
Higginbotham, John 1-4-10-1
Higginbotham, Moses, Estate 1-4-5-0
Higginbotham, James 3-8-11-3
Harrison, Reubin Senr. 3-8-5-1
Hall, Moses 1-4-1-0
Huckstep, Samuel 2-4-4-0
Hawkins, Joseph 1-2-3-0
Henderson, Salley 0-1
Henderson, Peggie 0-1
Higginbotham, Joseph (SM) 2-6-4-2
Hager, John 1-1
Hogg, Randolph 1-1
Henderson, Nathaniel 1-1
Haywood, William 1-0
Hamm, Stephen 1-6-5-0
Hansford, John 1-5-5-1
Harrison, Richard (Poplar) 1-1-0-1
Jenkins, Lucy 1-0
Jenkins, Thomas 2-2
Isbell, William 1-3-3-1
Joiner, William 1-0
Joiner, Peter 1-3
Jones, William (the smaller) 1-2
Jones, Thomas 1-0-1-0
Jones, William (the larger) 1-1
Johns, Thomas 1-1
Johns, Robert 1-0
Johnson, John 1-2-1-0
Isbell, Zachariah 1-1

Isbell, Christopher 1-4-6-2
Jennings, Robert 1-1-1-0
Jarvis, Joseph 1-6
Jenkins, John 1-5-1-0
Jarvis, John 1-0
Irvine, William 1-0
Jones, Nicholas 1-4-2-0
Jenkins, Josiah 1-1
Jenkins, Bennett 1-0
Johns, William (or Patterson) 1-0
Johnson, Philip 1-5-5-1
Johns, John A. 1-2-1-2
Johnson, Ann 0-2-4-0
Jones, James 1-1-1-0 ordinary license
Kernal, William 1-0
Key, John 2-2-1-0
Kidd, John 1-1
Key, Rice 1-2
Knight, John 1-1
Knight, William, sadler 1-1-1-0 riding chair
Knight, William (B smith) 1-3-1-0
Knight, Augustine 1-1
Kennada, John 1-1
Kennada, Jessee 2-3-4-0
Kennerly, Joseph 2-1-1-0
King, Archerbald 1-0
Lockard, Philip 1-1
Lawless, Richard 1-1
Lane, Garrett 1-1
Lashell, James 1-1-1-0 1 stud horse
Lay, Gideon 1-0
Lee, James 1-5-3-1
Lawhorn, George 1-0
Lawhorn, William 1-1
Leigh, Ferdinand 1-1-1-0
Lawhorn, Henry 1-1
Lane, Henry 2-2-4-0
Lane, Henry jr. 1-2
Leonirgan, John 1-2
Lively, Mark 1-1-3-0
Lawless, William 1-3-1-0
Lockard, William 1-0
Lackey, John 1-1-2-1

Lane, William (Wagr) 2-3
Lee, Frank, Estate 0-7-6-1
Lusk, Robert 1-1
Liveley, James 2-4-4-0 1 stud horse
London, John 1-1-1-0
London, James 2-3-3-0
London, Larkin 1-2
Lavinder, John 1-1
Landram, Thomas 2-4-1-0
Lane, Joseph 1-2-0-1
Lane, William (s. Joseph) 1-2
Long, William 1-7-11-3
Lansdown, William 1-2
Mitchell, Archerles 1-1
Majah, John 1-1-1-0
Majah, Lucy 0-2-2-0
Miles, John 1-0
McGinnis, Hiram 2-2 stud horse; ordinary license
Muse, William 2-3-1-0
Merritt, Thomas 1-6
Morriss, Thomas 3-7-5-1
Magann, Joseph 1-3
Magann, John 1-1
Moore, John 1-0
Mays, James 1-2
Mays, John 2-3-1-0
Mays, Richard 1-1
Martin, James 1-0
Mays, William 1-0
Martin, Abraham 1-3
Marr, John 2-6-3-0
Mays, Joseph 1-0
Martin, John jr. 1-2
McCloud, Angus 1-5
McMurray, Samuel 1-0
Megginson, Joseph C. 0-0-1-3 ordinary license
Morriss, George 1-1
Martin, Obadiah 1-2
Martin, Peter 1-2
Mitchell, Archerles 1-1-2-0
Mitchell, Bolling 1-2
Milstead, Joseph 2-2-2-0
McLain, John 1-3
Mays, Robert 2-5-2-0

(To be continued)

EDMUNDS FAMILY BIBLE

The Edmunds family Bible was printed at Boston, Mass., by Lincoln, Edmands & Company in 1833. On the fly leaf are two inscriptions: "Sallie Daingerfield from her grandfather E. S. Edmunds Esq." and "Presented to W^m & Mary College by Sally Daingerfield Oct. 1936—grandaughter of Edwin Short Edmunds."

The records have been copied by Miss Donna C. Gaines of Alexandria, Va., and are submitted for publication by James A. Servies, Librarian of the College of William and Mary.

Births and Deaths:

Names	Births	Deaths
Thomas Edmunds		1791
Martha Short Edmunds m 1784	Jany 27 1763	Apr. 1789
John Edmunds	Mar 31 1785	July 27 1820
Eliza Kennon Edmunds	1787	1830
(who was E. K. Randolph)	1811	
Thomas W. R. Edmunds	Aug. 20 1809	Octob 9 1833
Jack B. F. Edmunds	Aug 27 1814	June 27 1835
Martha A. E. M. Edmunds	Mar 27 1817	27 April 184[ ]
Edwin S. Edmunds	Apl. 30 1819	27 July 1891
Edward R. Edmunds	Apl. 30 1819	Oct 22 1855
Georgia McAfee	Nov 7 1836	1911
Martha Eliza Nichol	Feb 23 1848	1857
Eliza H. Edmunds	Jan 4 1844	Aug 10 1932

Marriages:

Names	Dates	
Thomas Edmunds was married to Mary P. Green of Christian Co. Ky. on the by Rev^d. G. P. Giddings	b. Aug 20, m. Oct 3, d.	1811 1832 1833
Martha A.E.M.J.S. Edmunds was married to Rev^d. Geo. G. McAfee Nov. 21st 1835 by Rev. B. J. Wallace	Novr. 21st	1835
& to James Nichol	March 11,	1847
Edward R. Edmunds was married to Eliza G. Henry Apr. 28st 1841 by Rev^d. W^m. D. Jones & to	Ap^r. 28,	1841
Anna Greathouse		1853
Edwin S. Edmunds was married to Sally McAfee September 12, 1843 by Revd Wm D. Jones—	Sept 12,	1843

Names	Births	Deaths
Children of E. S. E. & Sally McAfee -		
America Edmunds	Jan 18, 1845	Dec 21 1935
George M. Edmunds no children	May 7 1847	Aug 14 1929
Thomas M. Edmunds I	Jan 23 1853	May 23 1911
Eliza Randolph Edmunds	Aug 16 1856	July 27 1857
Cornelia Edmunds	Dec 27 1859	Oct 6 1867
Grandchildren		
Marian Louise Daingerfield	Feb 16 1837	Jan 11 1875
Sally Daingerfield	Sept.21 1869	
Ealine Louise Edmunds	Mar. 2 1882	
Marguerite Edmunds m. Geo Parker	Dec 11 1889	
Thos McAfee Edmunds II m. Ethel Lauger	Dec 14 1891	
Thos McAfee Edmunds III	1926	

Georgia McAfee was married to
Dr C. S. Ratcliffe of Christian
Co Ky

b. Nov 7 1836
d. 1911
Sep 8 1853

Eliza H. Edmunds was married
to W. P. Wallace of Crittenden
Co Ky

b. Jan 4 1844
d. Aug 10 1932
Nov 10 1867
b. Mar. 1837
d. Feb 11 1881

America Edmunds was married to
J. F. Daingerfield M.D. of
Christian Co Ky
Thomas M. Edmunds
was married to
Nettie Van Vlear in
Stockton Cal.

d. Jany 21 1873
Feby 3 1869
d. Dec 21 1935
b. Jany 13 1853
d. May 23 1911
Apr 14, 1880
b. Nov 13 1858
d. Feb 17 1912

Geo M. Edmunds was married to Ida
Craig in San Francisco Cal.

b. May 7 1847
d. Aug 14 1929
Nov 22n 1883
b. Jan 6 1850
d. Apr 11 1914

America Edmunds formerly married
to J. F. Daingerfield was married
to H. V. D. Nevius DD of Peoria
Ill. in San Francisco by Dr. J. K.
Smith

Nov 28 1888

LOCAL NOTICES FROM THE

VIRGINIA GAZETTE, 1780

(Continued from V. 5, p. 124)

11 November 1780

Thomas Peyton at Richmond advertises for sale the horse Stephen.

Priller & Cary, importers, advertise for sale at auction at Chesterfield Court House, 5512 pounds of transfer tobacco at Cary's warehouse.

Elhannah Talley advertises for sale at Mr. John Beckley's tavern at the Green Springs in Louisa County, a large collection of books on various subjects and a light carriage well calculated for a peddlar.

William Ronald advertises for sale 600 acres in the lower end of Buckingham adjoining the noted tract of rich land of George Webb, Esq. Apply to Mr. John Hay in Richmond or to Ronald in Powhatan.

Francis Ellis advertises for rent the ordinary called the Cross Roads near the Meadow bridges, Hanover County.

John Pankey advertises for sale pit coal from Robert Wooldridge's pits, lying at Warwick on James River. Apply to Mr. Daniel Wiesegar who lives at the place.

Henry Reeves at Richmond advertises for sale a sulky with a bellows top and harness, and an East India slave who is a good waiting man and house servant. Apply to Mr. John Hay at Richmond.

William Hamilton advertises that he has taken the Sweet Springs in Botetourt County for a term of years.

Andrew Bell at King William advertises that he intends for St. Eustatia soon.

Charles S. Boush, esecutor, in Norfolk County, advertises for all persons having claims against the estate of Capt. William Ivy, sen., and Arthur Boush, deceased, to make them known.

W. Armistead, c.s., at Richmond, gives notice to the militia who marched into South Carolina in 1779 and did not return without permission, that the salt promised them by Act of Assembly of May 1780 is stored with Mr. James Belches jun. at Petersburg who will distribute it agreeable to a roll given in by Col. David Mason.

The wife of James Durham has behaved herself in such a manner that he refuses to answer for her debts. She has lived for some time past with another man. Dated Buckingham, 6 Oct. 1780.

John Fox advertises for two horses strayed from Mr. Samuel Duval's. To be delivered to him in Gloucester, John Ballentine Esq., or Capt. Thomas Booth near Westham.

George Boyd offers $1000 reward for delivery of runaway slave Walls to him at Boyd's ferry on Dan River in Halifax County.

Travers Daniel advertises a horse taken up by him in Stafford County on Potowmack.

Christopher Clark advertises two steers taken up.

E. Crutchfield advertises a horse taken up in Hanover town.

John Coles in Albemarle County advertises for a mare strayed or stolen.

Thomas Whitworth advertises a mare taken up in Mecklenburg.

18 November 1780

Advertisement of sale before Mr. Clarke's door in Richmond of a compleat [sic] set of house joiner's and cabinet maker's tools, lately imported from England.

Nathaniel Quarles advertises for sale at Gordon's tavern in Manchester a variety of household and kitchen furniture.

Thomas M. Randolph advertises for sale or rent, Salisbury, tract of 1326 acres in Chesterfield County, 16 miles above Manchester, with dwelling house, six rooms to a floor.

Griffin Garland advertises for sale three full blooded colts and two fillies, part of the late Honourable Col. Tayloe's stud.

William Anderson advertises for rent at Hanover Court, plantation in King William County about two miles from Hanover Town, belonging to the estate of Mr. John Smith, deceased.

Frederick Smith states that he agreed with Henry Allen to clear the 26th division in Southampton County for £10,000 but Allen did not comply with payment. Smith set out but was taken sick and Allen advertised him as a deserter and suspected him of being a deserter from the artillery. Smith states he has his discharge from Capt. Edward Moody, Commanding officer of York Garrison, and will fulfill this engagement as soon as Allen complies with his agreement.

Nathaniel Burwell advertises for sale 810 acres in King William County about three miles from the Court House, within six miles of navigation. Also forty head of cattle, fifty hogs, crop of corn and fodder.

Thomas Anderson in Buckingham County advertises for rent 150 acres on James River in the lower end of Amherst County, 80 miles above Richmond, with dwelling for overseer; 30 or 40 acres opposite part of aforesaid, in Buckingham County, with dwelling of two rooms on a floor; and an adjoining plantation with a ferry across the river

LOCAL NOTICES FROM THE VIRGINIA GAZETTE   165

with house for overseer.

John Bowyer advertises for mulatto slave Saul, run away from him in Rockbridge County. He was purchased from Mr. John Teakel on the Eastern Shore.

Samuel Beall at Richmond advertises various commodities for sale.

P. Muhlenburg, B[rigadier] G[eneral], advertises deserters from camp: Sgt. Frederick Snyder, John Burrow, Cpl. Valentine Akers, Augustine Akers, George Walthal, Henry Bowyer, Henry Lybook and J. Johnson, all from Montgomery County.

Richard Taylor advertises for slaves Marcus and Nanny (who was bought of Edward Cocke of Charles City, ran away before and lived as a free woman as Nanny Lymus in Hampton, has a husband belonging to Mr. Mastersin in New Kent).

William Ellis advertises for a runaway Negro Major.

Elliot Bohannon Jun. advertises a steer taken up in Culpeper County on Robinson River.

Offer of $1000 reward for a silver watch with Matthew Fernando on the face or plate, lost in Blandford or between that place and Col. William Call's plantation. Deliver to Bradley's tavern or Col. William Call's store, both in Petersburg.

Nat. Read, Capt., advertises deserters from Chesterfield Court House: Joseph Tyre of Buckingham, Berry Lewis of Halifax, James Robertson of Amelia County.

Josiah Ellis advertises for Negro Joe, who formerly belonged to Col. Adams, run away from him in Amherst.

William Thompson advertises a horse taken up in Pittsylvania County on Potter's Creek.

Rodham Tullus advertises a mare taken up in Fauquier near the head of Town Run.

25 November 1780

A Merchant writes "A wink to the wise is enough" concerning the credit of the United States and depreciated money.

Advertisement of sale of one-fourth of new schooner boat, Betsy Corbin, now lying at Fredericksburg. Apply to Smith, Bowdoin and Hunter at that place, or Hunter, Banks and Co. at Richmond.

Advertisement for rent of plantation in Spotsylvania County with large dwelling house. Apply to Maj. John Minor of Hanover County.

Advertisement of Negro slave for sale. Enquire of Mr. William Cary, merchant in York Town.

Advertisement of Negro slave for sale. Enquire of Miles Taylor of Richmond.

Samuel Nivins near Manchester advertises a Negro

woman slave for hire, and a waterman who has been a sailor many years, and for sale a collection of books on physick, surgery, chymistry, philosophy, logick and a set of Voltaire's works in 35 volumes.

John Brookingbrough in Essex County advertises for a single person to teach a few boys reading, writing and arithmetic.

George Dame in Gloucester County advertises for runaway Negro who will endeavor to pass as a free woman Lucy Blewford.

William Tunstall and Peter Saunders, executors, desire all persons having demands against the estate of John Rowland, dec., of Henry County to present them. Peter Saunders will treat with anyone during his stay at the Assembly in Richmond.

William Jones in Orange advertises for runaway Negro Jack. His sister belongs to Mr. Richard Hanson at Petersburg.

Loftin Newman in King William County advertises for runaway slave Iverson's Sam.

Elizabeth Seldon in Blandford advertises for runaway Negro Isaac.

William Rowlet advertises for mare strayed or stolen from him in Fredericksburg.

William Matthews advertises a horse taken up in Fauquier County.

William Duncan Junior advertises a sow taken up in Culpeper County in the Gourdvine Fork.

John Pendleton, Jun., C[lerk] G[eneral] C[ourt], certifies the prices of tobacco estimated by the Grand Jury at the last session of the General Court.

John Lyne at Richmond advertises money found lying on a table in the Treasury Office.

The Executors of John Alexander advertise for rent the plantation adjoining the town of Alexandria where Mr. Charles Jones now lives, on Potowmack River and Great Hunting Creek, of about 450 acres.

J. Nelson, M[ajor] V[irginia] L[ight] D[ragoons], advertises for Richard Leigh (soldier in 3rd Troop, State Cavalry, who was left sick in King and Queen County) and Thomas Fears (of the same troop, who had small pox on Pedee River) to repair to Richmond.

William Hill Serjeant at Petersburg advertises for gelding strayed from Col. Bannister's.

Anna Smith advertises for a heifer taken up in Culpeper.

Thomas Wright advertises a heifer taken up in Culpeper.

William Roach advertises a steer taken up in Fauquier County.

(To be continued)

A GUIDE TO THE COUNTIES

OF VIRGINIA

BOONE COUNTY
West Virginia
(Continued from v. 5, p. 78)

COURT RECORDS (at County Court House at Madison): Wills are complete from 1865 to the present. Each volume has its own index. Will Book A was destroyed during the War of 1861-65.

Deeds are complete from 1847 with the exception of Deed Book C which was destroyed in the War of 1861-65. There is a General Index 1847-1953 and another 1953-date. Deeds of Trust are complete from 1872 and have a general index.

There is a Surveyor's Entry Book for 1847-61 and Surveyors' Record books 1837-1953, 1901-13.

Releases of leins date from 1873 and have a general index.

Commissioner's Record books begin in 1881, each indexed separately. These contain court orders and minutes.

Marriage Register 1, 1873-1923, has no index. Succeeding registers, beginning in 1903, are separately indexed.

Birth records begin in 1865 and death records begin in 1888.

There are three volumes of Discharge Records for World War I and eleven volumes for World War II.

Land tax books remain for 1866-71 and from 1880 to the present.

BRAXTON COUNTY
West Virginia

Braxton County was formed in 1836 from Lewis and Nicholas counties. It then included its present area and parts of Clay and Webster counties. It was bounded on the north by Lewis County, on the west by Kanawha, on the south by Nicholas and on the east by Randolph. In 1849 a portion of Randolph County from the head of the right fork of Little Kanawha River to the top of Point Mountain was added to Braxton. In 1858 Clay County was formed from Braxton and Nicholas and in 1860 Webster County was formed from Braxton, Nicholas and Randolph counties. The Braxton-Webster border was adjusted in 1861.

Among the historical publications relating to Braxton County are John Davison Sutton, **History of Braxton County**

and Central West Virginia (Sutton, 1919) and Hardesty's
Historical and Geographical Encyclopedia ... (Braxton
and Gilmer cos. ed.; Chicago, 1883).

COURT RECORDS (at County Court House at Sutton):
Wills are complete from 1836 and there is a general index.
A separate series of inventories and settlements of estates begins in 1885.
 Deeds are complete from 1836. There are general indexes of grantors and grantees in several volumes. The series of Trust Deeds, with a general index, begins in 1880.
 A Land Entry Book is dated 1836-53. There are several volumes of Surveys, beginning in 1850.
 There is an Index of Guardians and Personal Representatives 1866-1903, naming administrators, executors and guardians. Court order books remain for 1867-72, 1876-92. Fiduciary orders begin in 1885.
 There are Bond books covering the years 1847-78, 1881-date.
 The marriage registers begin in 1836 and are complete to date.
 Birth and death records begin in 1853 and are complete to date. There is an index of Births, Marriages and Deaths 1853-86 and later volumes are indexed individually.

TAX LISTS: The Virginia State Library has personal property tax books of Braxton County for 1836-61. There are two books 1853-61. Land tax books from 1861 to the present are preserved at the County Court House.

CENSUS RECORDS: 1840 census, a single alphabetical list.
 1850 census, a single list.
 1860 census, a single list (post office, Braxton Court House).
 1870 census, for Clay Township (P.O. Salt Lick Bridge, Bull Town), Franklin Township (P.O. Braxton Court House, Perkins Mills, Holly River), Lincoln Township (P.O. Braxton Court House); Washington Township (P.O. Tate Creek).
 1880 census, for Birch District, Holly District, Kanawha District, Otter District, Salt Lick District.

POST OFFICES (established before 1890): Atkinson (1889-91).
 Beech Bottom (1858-66; fell into Webster County 1860); Belfont (1881-88, 1889-   ); Bensville (1881-82, name changed to Newville); Big Otter (1851-54; 1872-   , formerly Duck Creek, changed into Clay County); Birchtown (1852-66, name changed to Tate Creek); Bliss (1884-94);

Braxton Court House (1836-90, formerly Suttonville, name changed to Sutton); Brown's Mountain (1855-60); Buffalo Fork (1855-65); Bulltown (1825-64; before 1836 in Lewis County; 1865-1931); Burnsville (1874-   , formerly Laforme's Store).

Canfield (1888-   ); Caress (1888-   ); Carlisle (1888-91); Chapel (1881-   ); Confluence (1888-1907; changed into Lewis County 1890, back into Braxton County 1893 and again into Lewis County 1896); Copen (1884-   ); Corley (1888-   ); Crescent Mount (1847-49); Cushing (1880-80, 1881-82); Cutlips (1880-   ).

Daly (1886-89); Doctorsville (1884-   ); Duck Creek (1860-66; 1871-72, name changed to Big Otter; 1878-81).

Elmira (1881-1905, 1906-   ).

Fallsmill (1888-   ); Flatwoods (1830-   , before 1836 in Lewis County); Frame's Mills (1871-81, name changed to Frametown); Frametown (1860-66; 1881-   , formerly Frame's Mills).

German (1871-1905).

Hacker's Valley (1856-   , fell into Webster County 1860); Haymond's Mills (1839-42); Haymond's Store (1859-1866); Hettie (1888-   ); Holly River (1852-94, name changed to Holly); Home (1887-94); Hope (1889-1908).

Knawl's Creek (1870-71; 1873-94, name changed to Knawl).

Laforme's Store (1868-74, name changed to Burnsville); Little Birch (1881-   ); Little Otter (1860-1922, 1923-); Lloydsville (1879-1922).

Middleport (1852-83, fell into Webster County 1860); Milroy (1888-   ); Morley (1889-1904, name changed to Glendon).

Newville (1882-   , formerly Bensville).

Perkins' Mills (1855-87); Progress (1887-   ).

Rock Camp (1851-54, 1855-60).

Servia (1882-83, 1884-91, 1892-   ); Salt Lick Bridge (1853-1915); Shock (1881-83, 1884-1902); Sideling Hill (1856-59); Sleith (1886-   ); Stonecoal (1882-82); Strange Creek (1872-   ).

Tate Creek (1866-83, formerly Birchtown; 1885-93); Twistville (1872-1913); Two Lick Run (1856-66, 1867-69, 1875-75).

THE REVEREND DAVID MOSSOM

OF MASSACHUSETTS AND VIRGINIA

By Lundie W. Barlow
Boston, Massachusetts

In pre-Revolutionary times the colonists were in closer contact, and there was much more moving about, than is generally realized. The career of the Reverend David Mossom (1690-1767)[1] affords an interesting example of the numerous changes of residence during that period, predominantly between New England and the communities to the southward.

As a scholar from St. John's, Cambridge,[2] David Mossom was ordained a priest of the Church of England in 1718. He received the King's Bounty and was sent the same year by the Society for the Propagation of the Gospel to New England. There he became rector of St. Michael's Church, Marblehead, Massachusetts. He held that benefice about nine years and officiated also from time to time, apparently during vacancies, at Queen Anne's Chapel in Newburyport.[3] In 1727 the Reverend David Mossom was inducted rector of St. Peter's, New Kent County, Virginia, serving that church throughout the remaining forty years of his life.[4]

In 1735 Mr. Mossom acted as supply minister at Curles Church, Henrico Parish, then in the environs of Richmond, preaching there every fifth Sunday. For each sermon he was paid 480 pounds of tobacco, reckoned at about £2.5.0 sterling, a quite liberal honorarium worth in present

---

[1] *William and Mary College Quarterly*, 1st series, v. 5, pp. 78, 205-06. The years of his birth and death are from the legend, in Latin, on his tombstone in St. Peter's churchyard. He was born in Kent, England, a son of Thomas Mossom of Greenwich, chandler.

[2] *Ibid.*, pp. 205-06. The Cambridge records show that he was admitted sizar on 5 June 1705 but not that he was a graduate or gained a scholarship elsewhere, and no degree is stated in his epitaph.

[3] Frederick Lewis Weis, *The Colonial Clergy of New England, 1620-1776* (Lancaster, Mass., 1936), p. 147; Weis, *The Colonial Clergy of Virginia, North Carolina and South Carolina* (Boston, 1955), p. 37; *New England Historical and Genealogical Register*, v. 35, p. 163; John J. Currier, *Ould Newbury* (Boston, 1896), p. 382; information from the church records supplied by Charles C. Stockman 2d of Newburyport.

[4] Weis, loc. cit.; J. Staunton Moore, ed., *Annals of Henrico Parish* (n.p., 1904), p. 13; William Meade, *Old Churches, Ministers and Families of Virginia* (Philadelphia, 1857), v. 1, p. 386, v. 2, p. 490. The reason why David Mossom went to Virginia does not appear from the records examined.

purchasing power perhaps as much as $500.[5]

The Reverend Devereux Jarratt (1723-1801) of New Kent and Dinwiddie counties, Virginia, recorded in his autobiography that David Mossom was "a poor preacher, very near-sighted, and, reading his sermons, closely kept his eyes fixed on the paper, and his remarks seemed rather addressed to the cushion than to the congregation." This writer also told of a quarrel between the rector and the parish clerk——Mr. Mossom assailed the clerk from the pulpit during a sermon; the latter avenged himself by reading from the lectern these lines out of the Psalter: "With restless and ungoverned rage / Why do the heathen storm? / Why in such rash attempts engage / As they can ne'er perform?"[6]

Despite his reputed short-comings as a preacher, and his seeming quickness of temper, the Reverend David Mossom attained a proud distinction. Of it, however, he certainly was not cognizant at the time, and he did not live to realize its importance in history. On 6 January 1759 he read the stately phrases of the Form of Solemnization of Matrimony whereby a young parishioner, the widow Martha (Dandridge) Custis, became the wife of a twenty-six year old officer of the Virginia troops, Colonel George Washington of Mount Vernon.[7]

David Mossom married first Elizabeth —— (surname unknown), obviously in England as their first four children were born before the removal to America in 1718. Elizabeth Mossom died in 1737 and the widower married second Mary, widow of Henry Claiborne, who died in 1745, and third Elizabeth, daughter of Henry Soane and widow of Benskin Marston, who died in 1759. Mr. Mossom was the father of at least five sons and two daughters but the name seems to have petered out at the death, before 15 April 1823, of his grandson, Captain David Mossom III, a soldier of the Revolutionary War. There are, however, present generation descendants of the good parson through female lines.[8]

---

5 Moore, op. cit., pp. 13, Appendix, pp. 16, 18.
6 William and Mary College Quarterly, 1st series, v. 5, p. 81; Weis, The Colonial Clergy of Virginia ..., p. 27.
7 Douglas Southall Freeman, George Washington, A Biography v. 3 (New York, 1951), pp. 1-2.
8 Extracts from the Mossom family Bible, in William and Mary College Quarterly, 1st series, v. 5, pp. 66-67, v. 19, pp. 138-39; Virginia Half-Pay application papers of the heirs of Captain David Mossom, File R.16608, National Archives, Washington, D.C. One of the supporting documents in the Half-Pay file is a certificate of the Elizabeth City County Court, 29 May 1841, that Captain Mossom "died intestate leaving no issue, but an only aunt and the only near kindred, who was Mary Roe, who intermarried with James Cunningham" and that her descendants, named therein, "are the only heirs at law of the said David Mossom."

THE BOOKER FAMILY:

ADDENDUM

By Cameron Allen
East Orange, New Jersey

Additional information relating to the family of one of the children of James Booker and his first wife (Elizabeth Hubbard?) has been located since the article "The Booker Family of Petsworth Parish, Gloucester Co., Va., and South Farnham Parish, Essex Co., Va.," which appeared in this magazine, v. 5, pp. 51-64, was prepared for publication.

13. Mary^4 Booker (James^3, James^2, ---^{1}), born say 1746/7, married William Shapard (Sheppard), son of Samuel and Mary (Kavanagh) Sheppard and grandson of Robert and Jessica (Hubard) Sheppard.[1] His brother Samuel Sheppard refers to him only as "my brother William who moved to North Carolina" and gives no further information. On 12 Oct. 1762 "William Shepherd of the County of Essex" bought a tract on the branches of Green Creek in Cumberland Co., Va., bounding on the land of John Woodson, from one Thomas Wright.[2] On 27 June 1785 "William Shapard and Mary his wife and Samuel Shapard of the County of Cumberland" sold this tract to Richard Wilson.[3] Thereupon William and Mary with the bulk of their family moved on down to Granville Co., N.C., and settled near Mary's sister Amy (Booker) Webb.[4]

Mary (Booker) Shapard appears to have lived to participate in the move to North Carolina, but apparently predeceased her husband by a number of years. She failed to relinquish dower in any lands sold by him from 1799 on. William Shapard died intestate in Granville County sometime between 2 Feb. 1807, when he was grantor in a deed, and 20 Feb. 1808 when his administrator Francis Royster sold his "last known property."[5]

Despite the fact he left no will, he did on 2 Feb. 1807 make its practical equivalent, a deed of all his

---

[1] Account of his brother Samuel Sheppard, written 1792, in *William and Mary College Quarterly*, 2nd series, v. 7, pp. 174-80.
[2] Cumberland Co., Va., Deed Book 3, p. 374.
[3] Ibid., Deed Book 6, p. 317.
[4] It should be noted that some of the Shapard children seem to have retained Cumberland ties for years. On 8 Nov. 1797, for example, Miller Woodson of Cumberland appointed his "trusty friend Samuel B. Shapard" his attorney in fact to attend to some realty matters for him in Kentucky (ibid., Deed Book 8, p. 273).
[5] Granville Co., N.C., Wills, Inventories, Etc., v. 6, p. 422.

THE BOOKER FAMILY 173

property to trustees Thomas Shapard and Francis Royster in return for an annuity to be provided each Christmas by his children: "Samuel, Mildred, William(s?), Elizabeth Royster, James, William Lewis, Thomas, Mary, John, Anne, Barnett and Robert."[6] The punctuation in this list of children is seemingly very careless and consequently misleading.

Issue of William and Mary (Booker) Shapard, probably virtually all born in Cumberland Co., Va. (Shapard was the definite preference in spelling of this branch of the Sheppard family):

    i. Samuel B. Shapard, born say 1763.
    ii. Mildred Shapard, born say 1765. It seems probable that she is the Mildred Shepard who on 18 Dec. 1786 in Cumberland Co., Va., married Anderson Williams, despite William Shepard's assertion that she was the daughter of Samuel.[7]
    iii. Elizabeth H. Shapard, born say 1768, married (date of bond) 6 May 1789 in Granville Co., N.C., Francis Royster.[8] Royster's will, made 26 May 1818, was probated at May Court 1820.[9] His widow Elizabeth dated her will 13 Nov. 1840; it was proved at August Court 1842.[10] Issue: 1) Banister Royster; 2) Robert Royster; 3) Wiley Royster, d.s.p. 1860, Granville Co., N.C.; 4) Lettice Royster married (date of bond) 26 Dec. 1815 Joseph A. Norwood[11]; 5) Martha Royster married --- Farrow; 6) Stella Royster; 7) Mary B. Royster; 8) Marcus D. Royster married 1842 Frances Y. Webb; 9) Emily Royster; 10) William Royster.
    iv. James Shapard, born say 1770.
    v. William Shapard, Jr., born say 1773.
    vi. Lewis Shapard, born say 1775; in 1806 was of Caswell Co., N.C.
    vii. Thomas Shapard, born say 1777, married 1811 Fanny Bailey of Person Co., N.C. They resided in Person County for many years and then migrated to Tennessee, settling near Memphis.
    viii. Mary Shapard, born say 1780.
    ix. John S. Shapard, born say 1782, married 1808, Person Co., N.C., Elizabeth Vass, daughter of Philip and Elizabeth (Webb) Vass. They resided

---

6 Ibid., Deed Book T, p. 49.
7 Account of Samuel Sheppard, loc. cit.
8 Granville Co., N.C., Marriage Record, p. 163.
9 Ibid., Wills, Inventories, Etc., v. 8, p. 357.
10 Ibid., Wills, Inventories, Etc., v. 15, p. 301.
11 Ibid., Marriage Record, p. 155.

in Person Co., N.C., and Halifax Co., Va.
Issue: 1) Mary E. Shapard married 1830, Halifax Co., Va., Richard Carter; 2) Emily B. Shapard married 1838, Halifax Co., Va., Joseph A. Haden; 3) Martha T. Shapard.
- x. Anne Shapard, born say 1784, married (date of bond) 21 May 1804, Granville Co., N.C., Joseph Barnett.
- xi. Robert Shapard, born say 1786.

The data cited herein make it clear that Mary (Booker) Shapard was the eldest surviving child in James Booker's family and that the birth date estimated in the initial article was about ten years too late.

THE WELL DRESSED MILITIAMAN

Contributed by James F. Lewis
Callao, Virginia

The following loose paper was found in a file box marked Miscellaneous Papers, District Court, in the Circuit Clerk's Office of Accomack County, Virginia.

Ordered that the uniform of the Infantry of the 2nd Regiment be a blue coat lapelled with scarlet cuffs and cape edged with white lining white buttons and white Epaulett, three buttons to each cuff and four to each pocket flap, pocket to be inside white waistcoat without Skirts, white Pantaloons for Captains & subaltern, white waistcoat & breeches for field Officers and boots with red Tops, cocked hats for all the Officers with black Cockaids. Dated 5th day of Augt. 1799.

SOME VIRGINIA REVOLUTIONARY SOLDIERS

Contributed by William H. Dumont
Washington, D.C.

Not all Revolutionary soldiers who were living in 1818 when the first of the general pension laws was enacted made application for government assistance. Nor was this true in the case of some who were living after the more liberal Act of 1832 was passed. The following thirty-four Virginians are among those who do not appear in the Index of Revolutionary War pension applications. Eleven were living veterans who exchanged their Bounty Land Warrants between 1833 and 1836 for scrip which could be used at any land office for land in Ohio, Indiana and Illinois. The other twenty-three were veterans who assigned their Warrants to someone else at some date before 1830. It is not shown whether the latter were alive in 1830.

These names will be found in Volume NN of the old loan records of the Treasury Department, now in the National Archives. The veterans from Virginia who left heirs have appeared in The Virginia Genealogist, volumes 1 and 2.

Veterans who exchanged
their warrants for scrip

				page
Griffith Dickerson, Sr.	Corporal	CL	1833	31
Joseph Dixon	Matross	SL	1834	229
Daniel Edwards	Private	CL	1833	43
John Emerson	Lieut.	CL	1836	174
Robert Furguson	Private	CL	1836	176
John Hoy	Private	CL	1835	81
Richard K. Meade	Private	CL	1836	162
John Nail	Sergeant	CL	1836	162
James Nickers	Private	CL	1835	75
James Oast	Private	CL	1833	35
Bennet Pemberton	Private	SL	1835	78

Veterans who assigned
their warrants to others

Edward Baker	Private	SL	78
William Barnes	Private	SL	39
Artan Bennett	Gunner	SN	61
Henry Clayton	Private	SL	81
Robert Cowne	Captain	SL	64
William Creekmur	Private	CL	13
George Cummings	Private	SL	205
Hezikiah Freeman	Private	SL	179
George Glendeny	Sailor	SN	203
John Gordon	Captain	CL	77
Martin Heely	Captain	SL	68

Christopher Henry	Private	SL	54
Thomas Hust	Private	SL	138
John Jett	Seaman	SN	75
John Love	Sergeant	SL	78
Richard McCarty	Captain	SL	67
John McKinley	-	CL	191
Mathias Newtam	-	SL	264
John Reins	Private	CL	17
William Santee	Private	SL	17
Joseph Sellman	Private	SL	75
Benjamin Smith	Private	CL	135
Edward Stewart	Private	SL	78

CL - Continental Line; SL - State Line; SN - State Navy

SOME CULPEPER COUNTY MARRIAGES

Contributed by George H. S. King
Fredericksburg, Virginia

Philip Clayton served some years as deputy clerk of the Culpeper Co., Va., Court under Roger Dixon, Gentleman, Clerk. In the papers in the chancery suit Clayton vs. Gray, File #49, Fredericksburg District Court, there is a transcript of an account kept by Philip Clayton starting in 1750. The following excerpts are from these accounts:

1751
   By Finley Morrison for his marriage license
      & to the Governor   ₤ 1:0:0
   By John Bramham, Jr.   do   1:0:0
   By John Slaughter*   1:5:0

1754
   By John Woods   Marriage License fee   1:5:0
   By William Fields   do   to Governor   1:0:0
   By Thomas Oxford   do   do   1:0:0
   By William Hunton   do   and your fee   1:5:0
   By John Price   Marriage License fee to
      Governor   1:0:0

* There is no "do" here; these names are listed as shown.

There are other items showing fees for licenses, etc., but the names of the parties are not given.

BOOK REVIEWS

Wills and Administrations of Elizabeth City County, Virginia, and Other Genealogical & Historical Items, 1610-1800. Abstracted and compiled by Blanche Adams Chapman. [Smithfield, Va.] 1941. 302 pp. $10.00.
Isle of Wight County Marriages, 1628-1800. Compiled and edited by Blanche Adams Chapman. [Smithfield, Va.] 1933. 137 pp. $5.00 [To be reprinted upon demand]
Wills and Administrations of Isle of Wight County, Virginia, 1647-1800. Abstracted and compiled by Blanche Adams Chapman. [Smithfield, Va.] 1938. 3 vols. Each $10.00. [V. 2 and 3 to be reprinted if there are sufficient requests]
Wills and Administrations of Southampton County, Virginia, 1749-1800. Abstracted and compiled by Blanche Adams Chapman. [Smithfield, Va.] 1947-58. 2 vols. Each $10.00.
Surry County Records, Surry County, Virginia, 1652-1684. Abstracted by Elizabeth T. Davis. [n.p., n.d.] 206 pp. $10.00.

The late Blanche Adams Chapman devoted many years to research in the early Virginia records. Her work of abstracting the records of Elizabeth City, Isle of Wight and Southampton counties was praised at the time her books first appeared. The reprints of these volumes, which are now being prepared by her daughter-in-law Mrs. L. L. Chapman, Jr., will be welcomed by many who did not have an opportunity to secure them when they first were published.

Although many Elizabeth City County records have been lost, Mrs. Chapman points out in her preface that from 1688 to 1800 there is some kind of record in the Clerk's Office for each year. In addition to the wills and estate records, Mrs. Chapman has included abstracts of Elizabeth City County land patents, lists of county officers, Revolutionary War military and patriotic services and the few remaining marriage licenses, among many other items.

There were settlers in Isle of Wight County from the beginning of Virginia's history. The three volumes of wills and administrations consist of over 500 pages of abstracts. The book of marriages contains not only all marriage bonds and ministers' returns prior to 1800 but also 62 pages of marriages deduced from deeds and wills, the records of two Quaker meetings, and Isle of Wight references in the marriages of other counties.

The two Southampton County volumes contain 300 pages of abstracts. A number of connections with North Carolina are shown in the wills.

Mrs. Davis' Surry County volume is a very full abstract of some of the earliest Surry records. The original book is quite difficult to read and these abstracts provide important information about the beginnings of many Southside Virginia families.

All of these volumes are indexed. Those who have ancestors in the several counties would do well to secure the books while the reprints are available. The number being printed is limited. Copies of all can be secured from Mrs. L. L. Chapman, Jr., Magruder Road, Smithfield, Va.

The Dulin Family in America. Compiled by Roberta Dulin Stewart. Ann Arbor, Mich., Braun-Brumfield, Inc., 1961. x, 323 pp. $20.00.

The early generations of the Dulin (Duling, Dooling) family in Virginia are not clearly set forth in the records. Mrs. Stewart has studied the existing data and has produced an account of the family which sets forth the probable relationships. She is careful to indicate what is proved and what remains to be confirmed. Her explanations are thorough and well reasoned.

It would appear that there were three brothers, Robert Dooling of Essex County (whose son William settled in Fauquier County and whose son Thomas went to North Carolina), Philip Dooling of Westmoreland County (whose probable descendants are given), and William Dulin(g) of Fairfax County (who left a large family in Virginia and Kentucky). Numerous descendants of all three have been traced. Biographical information is frequently given and there are over forty photographs. Data on some other Dulin, Duling and Dowling families are given from American and European records. The book is indexed.

Copies can be secured from the author, 908 Malcolm Ave., Los Angeles 24, Calif.

The Broyles, Laffitte and Boyd Relatives and Ancestors of Montague Laffitte Boyd, Jr., M.D. [Atlanta, Ga., 1959]. 60 [8] 30 [4] 30 [3] pp.

The Laffitte and Boyd families both originated in South Carolina. The Broyles family descends from John Broyles, a member of the Germanna Colony of 1717. In a succeeding generation Ozey Robert Broyles of Pendleton, S.C., married Sarah Ann Taliaferro and information about her Taliaferro, Carter and Beverley ancestry has been included in this volume.

In the later generations Dr. Boyd has been successful in gathering much information about the family. His findings supplement and correct the account of the Broyles descendants in The Beverley Family of Virginia. Most of the data relating to the colonial ancestors have, however, been copied from other printed works and some familiar errors (such as the statement that the first Robert Taliaferro married the daughter of The Rev. Charles Grymes, rather than his step-daughter) are perpetuated.

Copies will be distributed by the compiler, Dr. Montague Laffitte Boyd, Jr., 2560 Habersham Road, n.w., Atlanta 5, Ga., for 50 cents (the cost of postage).

QUERIES

Each subscriber to The Virginia Genealogist is entitled to have one or more queries published, free of charge, but limited to a total of fifty words per year, exclusive of name and address. All queries must have a Virginia connection.

515. CRAIG. Want parents, brothers, wife of James Craig who paid taxes in Loudoun Co., Va., 1770 until death 1810. Sons were William, born 1759 (where?), Robert, Absalom, James, Samuel. Mrs. David Reichlein, Route 1, Box 53, Roy, Wash.

516. LUNDY-TYUS. Want parentage, ancestry, dates of birth of both Joshua C. Lundy and Polly Tyus, married 8 Sept. 1794, Greensville Co., Va. Also date of birth of their son Ethelred H. Lundy who married Sarah Turner 16 April 1824, Greensville Co. Mrs. H. D. Southerland, Jr., 47 Greenway Road, Birmingham 13, Ala.

517. THARPE-ALLENTHARPE. Want any data, especially Revolutionary service of men of these names who went to N.C. Want children of John Allentharpe and Thomas Tharpe, possibly of Stafford Co., Va. Will correspond. Mrs. Mildred T. Hope, 471 South Tacoma Pl., Kennewick, Wash.

518. HAMMAKER-HERR. David Hammaker (Hammacher, Haymaker) and wife Anna Herr were in Augusta Co., Va., 1788-95 and in Fredericksville Parish, Albemarle Co. in 1800. Want names of their children. Have proof there were daughters named Barbara and Anne. Were there sons named William, John, Samuel, Adam, Joseph? Will exchange data. Mrs. J. E. Schwartz, 300 South 29th Ave., Hattiesburg, Miss.

519. ROSS. Andrew Jackson Ross was born 30 Jan. 1833 Va. (where?), died 10 Aug. 1916, Dacoma, Okla., married 11 Jan. 1854, Tipton Co., Ind., to Lyle Elizabeth Tudor. Served in Civil War. Will appreciate anything about his parents, grandparents, brothers, sisters, etc. Tradition

says they are related to husband of Betsey Ross. Mrs. B. D. Stockwell, 1053 W. 27th St., San Bernardino, Calif.

520. VAUGHAN. Want date and place of birth in Va. of James Vaugh(a)n who served in Revolutionary War (want record of service). He later moved to Fayette Co., Ky., where he died Dec. 1837, a feeble old man. His wife (want name, date and place of birth) died the following year. Want names of children (older ones married in Va.); known sons were Henry and Cornelius.
   FIELD-CLARK. Col. John Field of Culpeper Co., Va., was killed at the battle of Point Pleasant, 10 Oct. 1774. His wife was Anna Rogers Clark. Want her parents, ancestry and all possible data regarding her. Mrs. Charles DeSpain, Box 54, Anchorage, Ky.

521. SMITH-HENRY-JOHNSON. Want ancestors and descendants of Roland Smith (1818-1889) and wife Elizabeth Henry (1822-1894); both died Madison Co., Ala. Also of John Johnson (born 1803, Va.); children Sarah 1830, Henry 1833, Lucy 1836, Mariah 1839, John 1842 were born N.C., George A. 1845, Ann 1847 were born Tenn., and Mary 1849 born Madison Co., Ala. James O. Vassar, Route 1, Box 83, Decatur, Ala.

522. POWELL-RAPLEY-LACY-LACEY-NETTLES-ROUZEE-JONES. Wish to find descendants of William Powell and Mary Tapley, living 1655, York Co., Va. Dates, locations and parents of William and Mary Nettles Lacy, living in Greenbrier Co., W.Va., 1780. Same for Thomas and Elizabeth (   ) Jones, living Bruton Parish 1752. And children of Thomas (died 1739) and Mary Rouzee Jones of Essex Co., Va. Miss Ruth E. Frey, 407 Marshall St., Paris, Ill.

523. BANE-BRYAN-DALE-SMITH-CHILDERS-HUNT-WOOLMAN. Want any data on ancestors of George Bane, Elizabeth Bryan (both born ca.1830); Madison Dale, Henry Smith, Angeline Childers and Luscinda Dale (all born ca.1812) in Rockbridge Co., Va. Also William Hunt and Mary Woolman (1720's), Fairfax Co., Va. Mrs. Howard Knutson, 3525 Kingswood Dr., Dayton 29, Ohio.

524. WHITE-McGEE-CATLETT-MILLS. Want information on John White, born 1757, married Priscilla Mills 1792 (who was she?). He resided Botetourt Co., Va.; was private in Capt. Beatty's co. at battle of King's Mountain 1780; lived with Caleb White in Germantown, Ky., 1840. Who was Caleb White, born 1793, married Elizabeth Catlett? Need information on Thomas McGee, Revolutionary War veteran, who resided in Preston Co., Va. Leonard R. McGee, 757 Hayes Ave., Hamilton, Ohio.

QUERIES 181

525. NEWMAN. Rebecca Evans of Charles City Co., Va. (received legacy from Reginald Evans 1656) married 1st Anthony Patram (son Francis born 1671), 2nd Charles Featherstone (chn. Charles and Anne), 3rd by 1680 Samuel Newman of Henrico Co., Va. Want names of Newman children and Rebecca's death date. Was Walter Newman (died Md. 1729) her son? Miss Grace Gaw, 102 South 3rd Ave., Cleveland, Miss.

526. ALLEN-ALLIN-ALLAN. Am gathering information on southern Allen-Allin-Allan families, especially the descendants of Richard Allen (died 1725) of New Kent and Hanover cos., Va., with view to publication. These given names are particularly distinctive among his early descendants: Drury, Young, Josiah, Grant, Howard, Stokes, Turner, Valentine, Darling, Pleasant, Jones, Reynold, Julius, Littlebury, Isham and George-Hunt, as well as the more commonplace William, David, Robert, Joseph, Benjamin. Desire correspondence with all interested. Cameron Allen, 682 S. Hampton Rd., Columbus 13, Ohio.

527. HARRIS-GLASS. Will of William Harris proved York Co., Va., 1739, names brother John, sisters Sarah and Mary Glass, heir-at-law John Glass, father-in-law William Bruce. Need parents and further information. Was this family originally from York Co., or is there a connection with the Isle of Wight family or Henrico family? Would also like information on Glass family.
PEMBERTON. Need parents and further information on Mary Pemberton, born ca.1718, married Joseph DeJarnette, bapt. 1716, Abingdon Parish, Gloucester Co., Va. They settled in Caroline Co., Va.
JORDAN. Need parents and further information on Mary Jordan, born ca.1706, first wife of John George. Son Robert's birth recorded in Middlesex Co., Va., 1727. Other children born in Caroline County. Issue: Robert, Reuben, John, James, Ann (married Robert Woolfolk II), Elizabeth, Sarah, Mary, Edney (married James Pemberton DeJarnette), another daughter.
WALKER. Need parents and further information on Anne Walker of Essex Co., Va. Married Christ Church, Middlesex Co. 18 Dec. 1783, George DeJarnette. They settled Pittsylvania Co., Va. First child, Henry Walker DeJarnette.
TRIBBLE. Need wife, parents, further information on Peter Tribble. Will, Essex Co., Va., 1738, names sons George, John, William; daughters Meany Hilles, Mary Brown.
VAUGHAN-COOK. Need parents and further information on Robert Vaughan in Amelia Co., Va., during Revolution. Married Elsie Motley. Said to have had brothers Thomas and Lewis. Daughter Martha married 1784, Amelia County, Thomas Cook. He was in Revolution from Lunenburg Co.,

Va., died in Charlotte Co., Va. Need parents and information on Thomas Cook. Mrs. Peter MacQueen, Jr., 408 Butler Drive, Clinton, N.C.

528. BONSIL-BONSEL(L)-BONSAL(L). Joseph Bonsal 2nd married Frederick Co., Va. (Hopewell Monthly Meeting) 4 June 1805 Phebe Ann Adams (born Va. 1788, where?), dau. of Joseph Adams and wife Mary. Want Mary's parentage and antecedents with dates. Mrs. Estella U. Service, 217 East Helen Ave., Modesto, Calif.

529. MOODY. Marshall Moody of Va. was in Giles Co., Tenn., by 1820, where his first wife died bef. 1820. He married 2nd Betsy ---. He died Haywood Co., Tenn., 1841; will mentions 3 chn. by first wife, William H., John M. Moody, and Rebecca Harwell; by second wife Betsy, Henry, David and James Moody. According to tradition in Miss., Wm. H. Moody was born 1814, Richmond, Va. He died in Miss., 1865. His children believed him to be a relation of Chief Justice John Marshall. Could his father Marshall Moody have been the John M. Moody who married Catherine Baker of Hanover and Richmond in 1813? Was he related to Moodys of New Kent Co., Va.? Miss Lucille Payne, Box 47, Olive Branch, Miss.

530. GINGER. If anyone wishes data on portions of the Ginger family (Ludwig or Lewis), the undersigned will be happy to give what information is at hand. This is not a request for exchange information. This family resided for a time in Rockbridge Co., Va. Mrs. John R. Lynch, Box 293, Chula Vista, Calif.

531. RHINE-RION. Want ancestry of Jane Rion (Jennie Rhine) of Rion Hall, W.Va., married Jacob Moler (died 1804), died 1826, Harper's Ferry. Chn.: John Darby, Charles, Adam, Henry, Nellie, Anna, Jacob, Ellen, Lydia, Elizabeth.
PANCOAST. Will pay $20 reward for names of William Harding Pancoast's parents and birth place. He married Lydia Barnett Moler at Harper's Ferry, W.Va., 1815; removed to Allegany Co., Pa.; to Knox Co., Ohio, ca.1823; was born a Quaker and was a "New Light" preacher; died 1826, Ohio. Chn. Jacob Manuel (born 1818, m. Charity Gray), Angelina (1824-1890), Miranda (m. 1850 Joseph Muscrove; resided Chicago), John L. (born 1826, resided Hastings, Mich.). Mrs. W. A. Dean, Magnolia, Texas.

532. BUTLER. Will exchange data on William Aaron Butler of Louisa Co., Va. Dr. James B. Butler, Box 1055, Jackson 5, Miss.

533. MORRIS. Mary Ann Morris, born ca.1736, will Henrico

QUERIES

Co., Va., 1799, married 1st Edward Curd, 2nd Joseph Lewis, Henrico Co. 1783. Who was William Morris, her father?

COOPER. Want parents of Nancy Cooper (Mrs. James Washington Reynolds) who died Cumberland Co., Va., 1836, aged 20.

CARTER. Want parents of William Carter (will, Prince Edward Co., Va., 1812). Children: Robert, William, Polly Collier, Nancy Blankenship, Elizabeth Toombs, Sally Dodd. Miss Mary W. Canada, 1312 Lancaster St., Durham, N.C.

534. BODINE. John Bodine, Revolutionary War captain, born ca.1765, Cranbury, Middlesex Co., N.J., married 16 Sept. 1790 Ann Taylor of Hillsborough Dist., N.C. Had eight children. One branch of Bodine family claims him as ancestor, saying he came from Shepherdstown, Va., to Bardstown, Ky. Another branch says he came from Shepherdstown, Ky., to Bardstown. All branches did come from a John Bodine, Bardstown, Ky., but he married Catherine Parker, dau. of Richard Parker. His will 1815 mentions wife Caty, sister Caty and children not named, but her will (dated 23 March 1832, proved 18 Oct. 1836) names "my several named connections namely Elizabeth Johnson who intermarried with Richard Johnson, Robert Bodine's two children namely John Bodine and Martin Bodine, Richard Bodine, Martin Bodine, sons of Addison Bodine and Marian Bodine, heirs of John Bodine deceased, William Evens and Catherine Evens now Catherine Sanders, heirs of Samuel Evens ..." There were at this same time a John Bodine in Nelson Co., Ky., who married Sarah Bailey and a John Bodine who married Nancy Finch of Edgar Co., Ill. (they sold land once owned by John Finch 1 June 1836). Can anyone help me separate and identify these various John Bodines? I am looking particularly for a John Bodine, born ca.1782, of N.C., fought in War of 1812, married Nancy A.----, into Texas 1825, with five children (sixth born in Texas), died Texas 1836.

SHINER. George Shiner was head of a family, 1790 census, Winchester, Frederick Co., Va.; married Rachel Lister (pronounced Lester according to older members of family); daughter of Cornelius and Sarah (   ) Lister. Who were parents, brothers, sisters of George Shiner? Where did he come from to Va.? Known children: George Huse, born 20 June 1797; Cynthia born ca.1800. Possible daughter Katurah; others? He and wife died 1800; children reared by grandmother Sarah Lister. Mrs. A. O. Bodine, 323 Neil Drive, Yuba City, Calif.

535. RANDOLPH. Reward of $10.00 for first proof of parentage of Jane Winifred Randolph who married --- Short,

probably ca.1700. Several of their children married in Franklin Co., Va. Mrs. C. B. Nolen, Ferrum, Va.

536. BAILEY. Josiah Bailey, born 6 Oct. 1779, Va., and wife Susannah Ballard, born 20 April 1781, Va., went to Clinton Co., Ohio, ca.1804. Need help to verify records. Interested in Bailey of Va.-N.C.-Ohio-Indiana; also Ballard of Va.-Ohio. Mrs. Warren Middleton, Ridgeville, Ind.

537. BRYANT. Want place of birth in Va. of William Bryant born ca.1784, married Catherine Lancisco of Hampshire Co. before 1807; also names of his parents. Also birthplace of Benjamin Bryant, born ca.1795, married Susan Harper. Both died in Ohio. Relationship not known. Mrs. N. P. Shelby, Route 2, Waynetown, Ind.

538. SEALE-SALE. Want names of parents of Anthony Seale (Sale), will 1781, and Jarvis Seale, born 1759, both in Prince William Co., Va. Jarvis served in Revolution and had a brother John (pension application). He married 1785 Nancy Ann Yarborough; died in Green Co., Ala. Mrs. R. B. McLeod, 509 Walnut St., Hattiesburg, Miss.

539. SLAUGHTER. Want information on the following descendants of the Slaughter family: 1) Sarah H. R. Bell married 1825 John Poindexter Shelton of Amherst Co., Va., and had Mary E. L. (m. George G. Curle), Lucy J., Sarah C. (m. Dr. Lorenzo D. Williams), Virginia R., Emily Frances (m. William Anderson Bellowe); 2) Lucy R. S. Bell (ca.1805-1883) married 1825 Obediah F. Reynolds of Buckingham Co., Va., and had Martha (m. Richard T. Cobb), William H., Frances (m. John W. Toney), Robert W., Sarah Elizabeth (m. George Abbitt), Victoria (m. George M. Gillespie), Ella O. (m. Richard A. Davis), Archer L., Isaac O.; 3) Francis Norvell Farrar of Amherst Co., Va., married 1841 Louisa Bryant; 4) Charles H. Spencer of Amherst Co. married 1830 Sarah Jane Camp; 5) Mary Lightfoot Slaughter married 1782 Robert Dudley Dawson of Amherst Co., Va., whose only known child Frances (1786-1823) married George Cofer of Bedford Co., Va.; 6) Tallyrand P. Brown of Kanawha Co., W.Va., married 1st Sarah Vincent, 2nd Sophia Forqueran, moved to Washington Co., Minn.; 7) Louellen Norton (born ca.1845) married Robert P. Shrewsbury of Malden, W.Va.; 8) James W. Poindexter (born 1827) of Bedford Co., Va., moved to Collin Co., Texas, after 1880; 9) Jane Brown (1824-1908) married Davis Hudson of Kanawha Co., W.Va.; 10) brothers John Covington (to Missouri), Robert Warren Covington (to Tennessee) and William D. C. Covington of Rockingham Co., Va. J. Fred Dorman, 2311 Connecticut Ave., n.w., Washington 8, D.C.

INDEX

Aaron, Richard	91
Abbins, James	91
Abbitt, George	184
Sarah Elizabeth (Reynolds)	184
Abingdon, Alexandria Co.	117
Abingdon Parish, Gloucester Co., Va.	52, 79, 144, 181
Abney, John	80
Abstracts of the Wills of the State of South Carolina	136
Accomack Co., Va.	116, 174
Adams, Col. ---	165
Benjamin	155
Dancy	18
David	18
Frederick	18
Joseph	182
Mary ( )	182
Phebe Ann	182
Richard	80, 118
William	18
Wily	18
Adams Creek, Caswell Co., N.C.	105
Adcocke, Joseph	80
Adderson, John	120
Thomas	124
Adventurers of Purse and Person	51
Air, Scotland	88
Air Mount, Va.	133
Akers, Augustine	165
Valentine	165
Albemarle Barracks	88, 120
Albemarle Co., N.C.	43
Albemarle Co., Va.	89, 95-96, 120, 123, 144, 164, 179
Albemarle Parish, Sussex Co.	142
Alden, Mary	93
Alegan, John	155
Aler, F. Vernon	33
Aler's History of Martinsburg and Berkeley County	33
Alexander, Jesse	122
John	166
Alexandria, Va.	48, 117, 166
Alford, John	80
Thomas	80
William	80, 86
see also Allford	
Allcock, John	155
Joseph	155
Richard	155
William	155
Alldin, ---	110
Elizabeth	72-73
Frances	72-73, 110
Frances (Williamson)	14, 71-73, 110
Alldin, John	9-11, 14-15, 69, 71-73, 110
Martha	72-73, 110
Mary	110
Alleghany Co., Va.	131, 133
Allegheny Co., Pa.	182
Allen, Benjamin	181
Cameron	51, 98, 172, 181
Daniel	18
Darling	181
David	181
Drury	181
George Hunt	181
Grant	181
Hamblin	18
Hannah	155
Henry	117, 164
Hiram	80
Howard	181
Isham	181
Jesse	80
Jones	181
Joseph	80, 181
Josiah	181
Julius	181
Littlebury	181
Mary	113
Pleasant	181
Reynold	181
Richard	18, 181
Robert	155, 181
Samuel	18
Stokes	181
Turner	181
Valentine	181
William	18, 80, 181
Young	181
see also Allin	
Allensworth, Jennie	48
Allentharpe, John	179
Alley, Isaiah	155
Allford, ---	110
see also Alford	
Allin, Isabella	59
Thomas	155
see also Allen	
Allison, Elizabeth Kelly [Mrs. Fred]	137
William	150
Alsup, Benjamin	118
Ambler, John	155
Amelia Co., Va.	18-27, 39, 94, 120, 122, 124, 135, 141, 143, 165, 181
"Amelia County, Virginia, 1800 Tax List"	18-27
American Antiquarian Society Proceedings	135
American Genealogist	50, 98

Amherst Co., Va. 47, 80-84, 86, 89, 125-30, 144-60, 164-65, 184
"Amherst County, Virginia, 1800 Tax List" 80-84, 125-30, 155-60
Amherst Parish, Amherst Co. 125
   80, 125
Amite County, Mississippi, 1699-1890 106
Amsterdam, Va. 133
Amsterdam Dist., Botetourt Co. 133
Amus, Joseph 155
Anderson, Ann ( ) 11-13
  Mrs. Blanford Towler 93
  Charles 18
  Churchel 18
  Claiborne 18
  Francis 18
  G. 123
  Henry 12, 18
  James 18
  Mary 60, 155
  Nelson 80
  Olivia Carrington 63
  Ralph C. 18
  Sarah ( ) 12
  Sarah (Goare) 73
  Thomas 155, 164
  William 11-13, 18, 108, 164
Andrea, Leonardo 93
Andrew, William 155
Anguies, James 155
  William 155
Ann Arbor, Mich. 92
Ann Arbor Publishers 92
"Ann (Herndon) Lea" 99-106
Annals of Henrico Parish 170
Annals of Southwest Virginia 132
Anson, John 5
Antilope (ship) 39
Anyan, George 18
Aplin, Thomas 155
Appomattox River 120
Arbuthnot, Dorothea 124
Arch Mills, Va. 133-34
Archer, John 18
  Peterfield 18
  Richard 18
  William 18
Arden, Berkeley Co., W.Va. 35
Arden Twp., Berkeley Co. 35
Arisman, Jacob 80
Arlington, William 155
Armistead, Henry 7-8, 109
  W. 163
  William 155
Armstrong, Benjamin 155
  Maj. William 148
  Zella 100
  family 96
Arrington, John 80

Arrington, Samuel 80
Ashbourn, Derbyshire 66-67
Ashe Co., N.C. 149-50
"Ashland," Essex Co., Va. 64
Ashton, Burditt 120
Ashurst, Jacob 18
Asselin, Francis 18
  Sally 18
Aston, Samuel 18
Athens, Tenn. 94, 149-50
Atkinson, James 18
  Joshua 18
Atkinson, W.Va. 168
Atkison, John 5
Atkisson, Josiah 155
Attkerson, Walker 155
Augusta, Ga. 46
Augusta Co., Va. 46, 89, 131, 137, 141, 151, 179
Austin, Aincy (Morton) Dear 153
  Andrew 150
  Angeline 149
  Anne (Reeves) 150
  Archibald Pruit 151-52
  Augustine S. 149
  Bartholomew 148, 150
  Bledsoe 149-50
  Champness 152-53
  Clisby 153
  Daniel 149
  Daniel B. 153
  David 149-50, 152, 154
  Edwin 151
  Eleanor (Fields) 150
  Eliza 154
  Elizabeth 149, 153
  Elizabeth ( ) 153
  Elizabeth (Oliver) 154
  Fanny 152
  Francis 153
  Franklin 149-50
  Garland A. 153
  George 150
  Hannah ( ) 147
  Isaiah 148-50
  Jackson 151
  James 149-50, 152, 154
  James R. 153
  Jane 150
  Jefferson 153
  Jesse 150
  John 147-52
  John W. 153
  Joseph 80, 147-48, 151-53
  Lacy 149-50
  Louisanne (Bryant) 150
  Lucinda 150, 153
  Lucy 152
  Margaret (Douglass) 150
  Maria (Brown) 147
  Martha 152
  Mary 151-52
  Mary (Maybee) 148

INDEX

Austin, Mary W.	154
Moses	147
Nancy	152
Nancy ( )	149
Owen	154
Pastey	152
Polly ( )	152
Prudence	151
Rebecca ( )	152
Rebecca (Hankins)	154
Richard	147, 151
Richardson	147, 151
Robert	149-50
Robert J.	153
Sarah	153-54
Saunders	148-49
Stephen	147-49, 151-52, 154
Stephen Fuller	147
Thomas	80, 148
Valentine	147, 151
Welthy (Prewitt)	151
William	148-53
Austin Genealogical Society	50
Austin Genealogical Society Quarterly	98
Avory, Hannah	18
Joel	18
Baber, Achillis	80
Bacon, Edmund	43
Langston	155
Ludwell	155
William	155
Bacon Bridge, S.C.	61
Baer, Mabel VanDyke	90, 130
Bagby, Daniel	155
Reuben	155
Bagge, Catharine ( ) Bannerman	116
Bailey, David	155
Fanny	56, 173
John	81
Josiah	184
Martha	92
Reuben	81
Samuel	81
Sarah (Lanier)	92
Susannah (Ballard)	184
Terisha	81
William	80, 86, 156
Baird and Gordon	119
Baker, Dr. ---	38
Albert Riftin	28
Andrew Ellis	28
Bushrod W.	29
Cliveous Albert	28-29
Edm.	110
Edward	175
Elizabeth	93
Henry	4
Herman Cliveous	28-29
Joseph Hart	28
Judith Terrell (Durrett)	29
Baker, Marie Lou (Hart)	29
Sara	95
William	16
Bald Knob, W.Va.	78
Baldwin, George	18-19
George W.	19
John	19
William A.	19
Baldwin Station, Va.	133
Ball, Henry	109
James	81
John	80
M. Dulaney	75
Sallie Lewis (Wright)	75
Sarah	62
Sarah (Owen)	65
William	81
Ballard, Anna	104
John	155
Susannah	184
Thomas	104
Ballardsville, W.Va.	78
Ballentine, John	163
Ballinger, Henry	155
James	155
Joseph	156
Baltimore, Md.	87, 121
Bane, George	180
John	116
Banks, ---	119, 165
John	39
Banister River	121
Bannerman, Catharine ( )	112, 115
Margaret	111-12
Dr. Mark	67, 111-12, 114-15
Bannister, Col. ---	166
Barber's Creek, Va.	133
Barbour Co., W.Va.	40
Barden, William	18
Bardstown, Ky.	183
Barger, Christian	80
Philip	80
Barker, John	155
Barlow, Lundie W.	94, 170
Barnes, Margaret	118
William	175
Barnet, John	112
Barnett, Alexander	80
Anne (Shapard)	174
Joseph	174
Nathan	80-81
Reason	80
William	80
Barr, David	4
Barret, John	39
Barrick, George	110-11
Barry, Cleo A.	96
Mrs. Raymond W.	92
Baskerville, John	87
Baskin, Margaret Pickens	140
Bass, Alexander	18
Edward	18

Bass, Ivan E.	140
John	19, 50
Mary	19
Tabitha ( )	50
Batchelder, Hannah	74, 114
James	74, 107, 114
John	74
Samuel	9-10, 74, 107, 110, 114
Sarah	74
William	74, 107, 112, 114
Bateman, Lucy D. ( )	138
Rebecah	46
Bates, William	124
Bath Co., Va.	131
Baugh, William	19
Baughan, Elizabeth (Booker)	62
Henry H.	62
Baytop, Capt. Thomas	54
Bayts, Elizabeth (Blanks)	93
Bazile, Judge Leon M.	44, 146
Beall, ---	119
Samuel	118-19, 165
Bean, George	121
John	116
Beattie family	137
Beatty, Capt. ---	180
Beaverdam Dist., Granville Co., N.C.	151
Bebee, Peter	80
Beck, Jessee	155
Beckley, John	163
Becknal, John	81
Nancy	81
William	80
Beddington, W.Va.	35
Bedel, Thomas	18
Bedford Co., Tenn.	153-54
Bedford Co., Va.	46, 120, 184
Bedford C.H., Va.	120
Bedington, W.Va.	35
Beech Bottom, W.Va.	168
Belcher, John	19
Thomas	19
Belches, James	163
Belfield, John	42
Dr. Joseph	42
Ruth (Sydnor)	42
The Belfield Family	42
Belfont, W.Va.	168
Bell, Capt. ---	11
Andrew	163
Claiborne	18
Drury	155
Humphrey	67, 109
John	18
Joseph	68
Lucy R. S.	184
Samuel	155
Sarah H. R.	184
family	146
Beller, George	4
Bellevue, Va.	133
Bellow, Thomas	81
Bellowe, Emily Frances (Shelton)	184
William Anderson	184
Belmont Co., Ohio	93
"Ben Lomond," Essex Co.	62-64
Benner, Henry	80
Bennett, Anne	95
Artan	175
Mrs. Edward J.	140
James	124
Benson, Mrs. H. L.	142
Bensville, W.Va.	168-69
Bentley, Capt. ---	124
Efford	19
William	19
Bently, Anna Salinda	94
Caroline	94
Mortimer	94
Nancy (Hunter)	94
Bere, Theo.	15
Berkeley, Edmund	69
Berkeley Co., W.Va.	33-36, 93, 119, 124
Berkeley Springs, W.Va.	35
Berks Co., Pa.	90
Bermuda	124
Berry, Addamson	81
Ann	17
Catharine A. (Lewis)	94
Docia	94
Mrs. Earl D.	94
John	11, 17, 69, 71, 80
Margaret (Sims)	94
Mary ( )	17, 69
Mary Jane (Lewis)	94
Matilda	94
Morris	94
Nancy	94
Peter	18
Steven	94
Thomas	18
William	17
William T.	94
Bery, John	15
Bethel, John	80-81
Martin	80
Nancy	81
Bettersworth, Richard	156
Betts, Samson	8
Thompson	109
Beverley, Harry	12
family	178
The Beverley Family of Virginia	178
Beverly town, Henrico Co.	85
Bevil, Claiborne	18
Joel	19
Lucy	19
Susanah	19
Bias, W.Va.	78
Biass, John	155
Roling	155
Bibb, Cary	80

INDEX

Bibb, Elizabeth	81
Henry	81
James	80
Martin	80, 155
Thomas	80
"Bible of Jonathan Durrett"	28-30
A Bibliography of Virginia	135
Biby, Jolley	156
Bidlack, Russell E.	92
Big Cole, W.Va.	78
Big Lick, Va.	133
Big Otter, W.Va.	168-69
Bigbyville, Tenn.	32
Bigg, Zach.	4
Biggs, Joseph	5
Birch Dist., Braxton Co., W.Va.	168
Birchtown, W.Va.	168-69
Black, James	5
William	39, 118
family	96
Black Creek, New Kent Co.	86
Blackburn, Capt. ---	15
John	4
Blackburne, William	69, 110
Blackley, Anne ( )	15
George	15
Robert	15, 74, 112
Blackly, Ann	70
Black's cabins, Ohio Co.	5
Blackstone Creek, Mecklenburg Co., Va.	39
Blain, Alexander	80
George	80-81
William	80
Blair, Allen	155
Archibald	88, 122
Capt. James	121
John	120
Bland, Anne (Bennett)	95
Richard	95
Theodorick	95
Bland, Va.	77
Bland Co., Va.	77-78
Bland C. H., Va.	77
Blandford, Va.	37, 86, 88, 165-66
Blankenship, Nancy (Carter)	183
Blankinship, Abel	156
Thomas	19
Blanks, Elizabeth	93
Henry	93
James	93
John	93
Joseph	93
Naomi ( )	93
Polly	93
Sarah	93
Tabitha	93
William	93
Blanton, Ann Elizabeth	28
Emmet Todd	28
Mary A.	29
Richard Alfred	28

Blasingame, John	52
Blewford, Lucy	166
Bliss, W.Va.	168
Blue Ridge, Va.	133-34
Blue Ridge Springs, Va.	133
Bluestone Creek, Mecklenburg Co., Va.	38
Blundell, Richard	50
Blunt, Charles	80
Bobbitt, John	155
Bodine, Mrs. A. O.	183
Ann (Taylor)	183
Catharine (Parker)	183
Elizabeth	183
John	183
Martin	183
Nancy A. ( )	183
Nancy (Finch)	183
Richard	183
Robert	183
Boggs, William	3
see also Bogs, Boogs	
Bogs, James	4
Bohannon, Elliot	165
Boler, Austin	81
John	81
Larkin	81
Bolling, Bailey	155
James	155
Thomas	120
Thomas T.	19
see also Bowling	
Bolt, Catherine	46
Catherine (Sutphen)	46
Charles	46
Ellis	46
Elmyra	46
Harrison	46
Helen K.	46
Loretta	46
William	46
William Amos	46
Bomar family	46
Bond, John	156
Bonet, Luis	4
Bonsack's Depot, Va.	133
Bonsal, Joseph	182
Phebe Ann (Adams)	182
Boogs, Alexander	3
Ezekel	3
Francis	3
John	4
see also Boggs, Bogs	
Booker, Amy	56-58, 172
Amy ( )	52-53
Ann	56
Ann (Throckmorton)	62
Caroline (Richardson)	62-63
Carrie	63
Daniel	19
Davis	18
Dorothy	62
Edmund	51, 122

Booker, Edward	51
Efford	18
Elizabeth	56, 62-63
Elizabeth (Eubank)	63
Elizabeth (Hubbard)	55-56, 172
Elizabeth Taylor	63
Elizabeth ( ) Wright-	55
Ellen	63
Emily	63
Erasmus Darwin	63
George Albert	63
George Tabb	62-63
J.	25
James	51-56, 62, 172, 174
James Webb	63
Joanna	56-57
John	19, 54
John E.	19
Judith	62
Judith (Dudley)	56, 62
Lewis	51-53, 56, 60-63
Lucy Landon (Page)	63
Margaret (Lowry)	51
Mary	56, 62, 172-74
Mary ( )	51, 53
Mary Garnett	63
Olivia Carrington (Anderson)	63
Parham	19, 27
Pink D.	19
Richard	51-52, 88
Richerson	19
Samuel Marion	63
Sarah	19, 94
Sarah H.	62-63
Thomas	52-53, 63
William	53, 62
William L.	63
William M.	18
"The Booker Family"	51-64, 172
"The Booker Family: Addendum"	172-74
Boone Co., W.Va.	78-79, 167
"Boone County, W.Va., Births, Marriages, Deaths, Wills and Inventories"	78
Booth, Capt. Thomas	163
Boothe, George	155
John	19
Matthew	18
Ross	99
Thomas	19
Borck, Henry	10
see also Burck, Burke, Burks	
Bosely, Miss ----	140
Botetourt, Va.	133
Botetourt Co., Va. 39, 96, 131-34, 163, 180	
Botetourt Parish, Botetourt Co., Va.	132
Botetourt Springs, Va.	133
Bott, James	18
Miles	18
Bottom, John	19
Lydda	19
William	19
Bourne, Henry	155
Boush, Arthur	163
Charles S.	163
Bowdoin, ---	165
John	119
Presson	85
Bowles, Charles	155
Elbourn	149
Elizabeth (Austin) Davis	149
Lucy	19
Bowling, Jesse	40
John	155
Powhatan	156
Sarah ( )	40
William	40
see also Bolling	
Bowman, John	81
Sherrod	81
William	80-81
Bowmar family	46
Bowyer, Henry	165
John	165
Boyd, George	164
Mrs. Hazel Mason	137
Montague Laffitte	178-79
family	178
Boyd's ferry, Dan River	164
Boyleston family	96
Bracket, Ben	19
Brackett, Ludwell	19
Bradley, ---	165
J.	17
James A.	19
Bradshaw, Felix	74, 108, 110
John	18
Judith ( )	108
Shadrack	80
William	19
Brame, Diana Howard (Clarke)	143
George Washington	143
Bramham, John	176
Branch, Christopher	118
Brand, Joseph	38
Brandywine, battle of	46
Branner, Peter	80
Brannum, Edward	156
Braudus, Edward	130
see also Broaddus	
Brawton, John	19
Braxton Co., W.Va.	167-69
Braxton C.H., W.Va.	168-69
Breckinridge, Va.	133-34
Breckinridge Co., Ky.	59-60
Breedlove, Richard	81
William	80
Brent, James	81
Brewster, Mrs. Edwin S.	143
Brian, Banister	18
see also Bryan	
Briant, Berry	155

INDEX

Briant, Finney	156
Lewis	155
William	156
see also Bryant, Bryent	
Briary Swamp, Middlesex Co.	8
Bridge, James	81
Bridges, Mrs. Margaret C.	139
Bridgwater, Charles	81
Jonathan	80
Samuel	80
William	80
Briscoe, Robert	85
Brish---, Nicholas	74
Bristow, Nicholas	8
William	113
Broaddus, Richard	18
see also Braudus	
Broadfoot, Charles	19
Broadway, Thomas	19
Broadway, Va.	118
Brock, Joseph	102
Michael	80
Brock, Rucker & Co.	155
Brockman, John	155
Bronaugh, Catey	146
Brooke, Dudley	123
Brooking, Vivion	19, 122
William	19
Brookingbrough, John	166
Brooks, James	80
Brown, ---	155
Adam	80
Bennet	19
Francis	51
Henry	119, 155
James M.	155
Jane	184
John	155-56
John R.	81
L. H.	139
Leroy	155
Maria	147
Mary (Tribble)	181
Peter	120
Rachel	156
Robert	11, 48, 65-66, 109
Sarah (Vincent)	184
Sophia (Forqueran)	184
Tallyrand P.	184
Thomas	80, 119
William	155
Zachariah	80
Brown, Brown & Co.	130
Brown, Rives & Co.	80
Browning, Emily (Booker)	63
George	63
Brownlow, John	117
Brown's Mountain, W.Va.	169
Broyles, Ozey Robert	178
Sarah Ann (Taliaferro)	178
The Broyles, Laffitte and Boyd Relatives and Ancestors of Montague Laffitte Boyd	178
Bruce, William	181
Brugh's Mill, Va.	133
Brumall, Thomas	80
Brumfield, John	120
Brumley, Austin	151
Thomas	151
Brumskil, John	19
Brunswick Co., Va.	92, 143, 147
Brunswick C.H., Va.	124
Bruton Parish	180
Bryan, Benjamin	123
Elizabeth	180
Elizabeth (Cole)	142
William	142
see also Brian	
Bryant, Benjamin	184
Catherine (Lancisco)	184
Louisa	184
Louisanne	150
Perminus	80
Susan (Harper)	184
William	184
see also Briant, Bryent	
Brydie, Brown & Co.	80, 155
Brydie, Brydie & Co.	130
Bryent, John	80
Martin	80
William	81
see also Briant, Bryant	
Bryn, Kezia	96
Buchanan, Andrew	94
Margaret	94
Samuel	94
family	137
Buchanan, Va.	133-34
Buchanan Dist., Botetourt Co.	133
Buckholder, Laurence	123
Buckingham Co., Va.	39, 144, 163-64, 165, 184
Buckingham road, Chesterfield Co., Va.	119
Buckley, Butler	140
Buckner, Col. Anthony	47
Catherine (Herbert) Gibbens	47
Bucks Co., Pa.	50
Bucky, John	5
see also Bukey	
Bucton, Va.	48
Buffalo Fork, W.Va.	169
Buffalo Lick Twp., Chariton Co., Mo.	142
Buffalora, W.Va.	78
Buford, Thomas	110
Bugg, Sherod	155
Bukey, John	5
family	50
see also Bucky	
Bukley, Susannah	156
see also Buckley	
Bulltown, W.Va.	169
Bunker Hill, W.Va.	35-36
Bunting, Richard	48
Burbridge, Easter ( )	141

Burbridge, Thomas	141
family	90
Burch, Francis	156
John	155
Burck, John	72
see also Borck, Burke, Burks	
Burdett, William	69-70
Burditt, William	17
Burford, Ambrose	155
Archerles	155
Daniel	156
James	155
John	155-56
Philip	155
William	156
Burger, Joseph	80
Burgess, Charles	67-68, 114
Burk, John	113
see also Borck, Burke, Burck	
Burke, Cleary (Fleming)	46
Mrs. Ella	46
Henry	46
Mary (McKinney)	46
Thomas	46
see also Borck, Burck, Burk	
Burke Co., Ga.	140
Burke's Garden, Va.	46
Burks, Charles	156
David	155-56
Elizabeth (Rowland)	96
Isham	96
John	96, 155-56
Lindsey	155
Mary (Davis)	96
Richard	155
Samuel	96, 156
Sarah ( )	96
William	155
"Burlington," King William Co., Va.	139
Burlington Co., N.J.	45
Burnett, Edmund	80
Elizabeth	144
Jacob	155
John	81
Lucy	144
Margaret (Maupin)	144
Micajah	80
Richmond	80
Roland	144
William	80-81
Burnett's Chapel Methodist Church	43
Burnley, Alexander	38
Richard	38
Burnsville, W.Va.	169
Burrow, John	165
Burrus, Charles	155
Joseph	155
Sarah	155
Burtin, James	80
Burton, Abel	19
Abraham	19
Burton, Allen	19
Belle	95
Camillus	95
Charles	95
Jane	150
John	19, 39
Laura	95
Lucy S. (Nelson)	95
Martin	87
Minerva	95
Peter	19
Philip	155
Samuel	18
Sarah Frances ( )	95
Thomas Nelson	95
Vetura	95
William	18
Burton's ferry, Mecklenburg Co., Va.	87
Burwell, Capt. ---	61
Anne	56
Lewis	109
Nathaniel	164
Butcher's Creek, Mecklenburg Co., Va.	38
Butler, Isaac	18
Dr. James B.	182
Lewis	124
William	18
William Aaron	182
Zachariah	19
Butt, Dr. Albert	138
Byass, Larkin	155
Bynum, Abigail	92
Byrd, Adam	38
Mary (Willing)	87
Byron, Va.	77
Cabell, Frederick	81
Hector	81
Landon	81
Margaret	81
Nicholas	81
Samuel J.	82
William	81
William H.	81
Cabell Co., W.Va.	78
Caldvill, John	5
Caldwell, James	3-5
John	5
Samuel	3
Calendar of Virginia State Papers	58
Call, William	38, 119, 165
Callaway, Dudley	156
Nancy	156
Calor, Charles	81
Cambridge University	170
Camden, Benjamin	81
Henry	156
Jabez	157
John	81
Micajah	156

INDEX

Camden, William	157	Carter, Jonathan Melzar	28
Cameron, Duncan	156	Mary Ann J.	28
Camm, John	157	Mary E. (Shapard)	174
Camp, Sarah Jane	184	Melzer	29
Camp Mountain	131	Nancy	183
Campbell, Aaron	157	Peter	156-57
Alexander	119	Polly	183
Ambrose	156	Richard	174
Andrew	81	Robert	183
Clyde	96	Sally	183
Francis	81	Shadrack	82
George	156, 81	Solomon	157
Hugh	157	Wallis Marion	28
James	81, 156-57	William	85, 156-57, 183
Joel	82, 157	William Porter	28
John	81, 156	family	178
Larrance	156	Carter Co., Tenn.	143
Peter	81	Cartmell, Thomas K.	33
Samuel	81, 156	Cartright, John	157
Wiley	156	Cartwright, Thomas	38
William	81, 88	Carty, see McCarty	
family	146	Cary, Daniel	81
Campbell Co., Va.	89, 144	Solomon	81
Canada, Mary W.	183	Thomas	37
Canfield, W.Va.	169	William	165
Canoy [Candy], John	3	Wilson Miles	53, 87
Cannon, Sarah (Hudson) Holder	94	Cary's warehouse	163
Thomas	94	Casey, Albert E.	99-100, 106
Cape Fear, N.C.	90	Cash, Bartlett	156
Cape Henry	37	Howard	156
Cardwell, Richard	20	James	156
Thomas	15	Joel	156
Caress, W.Va.	169	John	156
Carlisle, W.Va.	169	Peter	156
Carolina, Va.	133	Randolph	156
Caroline Co., Va.	29-30, 45	Samuel	81
	47, 88, 122-23, 181	William	156
Caroline C.H., Va.	85	Cashwell, Henry	81, 157
Cary, ---	163	Peter	157
Carpenter, Benjamin	19, 156	Cassels, William	20, 27
Eaton	156	Caswell Co., N.C.	99-105, 151, 173
Enoch	156	Catawba, Va.	133
Hensley	156	Catlett, Allie (King)	48
James	156	Ann (Gwathmey)	139
William	81	Elizabeth	180
Carr, ---	87	John	48
Archibald	4	Thomas	139
John	81	Catron, Mrs. Joris B.	143
Carre, Capt. ---	58	Cattail Swamp, Spotsylvania	
Carroll Co., Va.	46, 98	Co., Va.	102
Carter, Abigail (Durrett)	29	Cattuk, Clarke	82
Abraham	156	Caubin, James	81
Ann	102	Caufland, Benjamin	157
Apphia	81	Causanday, Peter	124
Charles	88, 157	Causer, Alice ( )	110
Edward	156	Anne	110
Elizabeth	183	Thomas	110
Elizabeth ( )	102	William	110
Ellenorah Hassentine	28	Cavaliers and Pioneers	91
George	102	Cecil, Kezia (Bryn)	96
Job	124	Rebecca (White)	96
John	156	Samuel W.	96
John Jarret	121	Cemetery Records of Marion County, Texas	137

Ceres, Va.	77
Chaffin, Joshua	19
Chalkley, Lyman	151
Chamberlayne, Churchill G.	52, 54
Chambers, David	5
Chambersburg, Pa.	139
Chamblin, Jane	130
Chandler, Martin	19
Chaney, Thomas	8, 71
Chap, W.Va.	78
Chapel, W.Va.	169
Chapline, Moses	5
Chapman, Benjamin	19
Blanche Adams [Mrs. L.L.]	177
James	102
John	19
Mrs. L. L., Jr.	177-78
William	4, 19
Chappell, Abner	19
Bob	20
John	19
Robert	19
Chariton Co., Mo.	142
Charlemont Dist., Bedford Co.	79
Charles City Co., Va.	88-89, 91, 95, 118, 165, 181
Charles Co., Md.	59, 139
Charleston Co., S.C.	136
Charlestown, Mass.	147
Charlotte Co., Va.	37, 46-47, 87, 95, 120, 122, 140, 182
Charlotte C.H., Va.	120
Chase, Ambrose	81
Chatham, Va.	47-48
Cheadle, Frances ( )	10
Robert	10
Thomas	10
Cheatham, Arthur	95
James	95
Josiah	82
Lenard	82
Margaret (Rudd)	95
Nancy (Hancock)	95
Obediah	95
Robert	82
Cheatham Co., Tenn.	57
Cheatwood, Daniel	157
Cherokee Lake, Hamblen Co., Tenn.	153
Chesterfield, Caroline Co.	85
Chesterfield Co., Va.	88, 95, 117-20, 164
Chesterfield C.H., Va.	121, 124, 163, 165
Chewning, John	81
see also Chowning	
Chicago, Ill.	182
Chickahominy River	118
Childers, Angeline	180
Childres, Benjamin	81
Childress, John	156
Joseph	156
Chisnal, Alexander	82
Chiswell, Nancy	75
Choate, Zippora	140
Chowning, George	11, 15, 66, 69, 71, 74, 109, 113
Janet	70
William	69-70, 74, 107, 112
see also Chewning	
Christ Church Parish, Middlesex Co., Va.	8, 10-11, 13, 16, 65, 67, 73, 112-15, 181
Christia, Hugh	156
Christian, Anthony	156
Charles	157
Drury	157
Henry	157
James	156-57
John	156-57
John H.	156
Robert	157
Walter	157
Christian Co., Ky.	43-44, 161-62
Chronicles of Old Berkeley	33
Chronicles of the Scotch-Irish Settlement	151
Chuney, Thomas	11
see also Cheney	
Church, Thomas	81
Churchill, Armistead	12
Churchman family	45
Claiborne, Henry	171
Mary ( )	171
Thomas	124
William	37
see also Cliborne	
Clark, Anna Rogers	180
Benjamin	19
Charles	114
Christopher	164
Edward	113
George	157
Henry	4
James	4, 156
Joseph	157
Julia R. (Jones)	46
Mrs. Leona A.	46
Lewis	20
Micajah	157
Samuel	87
W. R.	46
William	156-57
family	137
Clark Co., Ga.	95
Clark Co., Ky.	96
Clark Twp., Chariton Co., Mo.	142
Clarke, ---	164
David	81
Diana Howard	140
James	81, 143
John	81
Nathaniel	81
Sarah (Howard)	140
William	6
Clarke Co., Va.	89, 130

INDEX

Clarkson, David	81
James	81
Jesse	81
John	156
William	156
Clasby, William	81
Claxton, Charles	123
Clay, Charles	20
David	19
Edward	19
Jesse	20
Thomas	19
Clay Co., W.Va.	131, 167-68
Clay Twp., Braxton Co., W.Va.	168
Claybrook, Lucia	19
Mary	19
Samuel	19
Clayton, Henry	19, 175
John	156
John W.	157
Philip	176
Thomas	156
Clear Fork, Va.	77
Clement, Maude C.	152
Clements, David	156
Drury	156
Francis	157
Gersham	157
Isham	19
James	156
Jesse	157
John	20, 156
Joseph	19
Stephen	157
Thomas	156
William	20, 156
William W.	156
Cleyback, Henry	4
Cliborne, Leonard	19
see also Claiborne	
Clinton Co., Ohio	184
Clopton, Reuben	88
Robert	88
Clough, Richard	20
Cloverdale, Va.	133
Coats, Jeremiah	156
Cobb, Martha (Reynolds)	184
Richard T.	184
Cobbs, John	39
John C.	20
Thomas M.	20
Cocke, Absolem	81
Charles Francis	89
Edward	165
Stephen	20
Coddington, John Insley	31
Cofer, Frances (Dawson)	184
George	184
Coffee, Joel	117
Coffey, Edmund	81
Jordan	82
Reuben	81
William	81
Coghill, Frederick	122
Cole, Elizabeth	142
James	109
John	82, 142
Richard	142
Coleman, ---	119
Abraham	20
Archer	19
Benjamin	156
Burwell	19
Daniel	19
Ebenezer	20
Elizabeth	63, 157
George	157
Hawes	82
Jesse	20, 156
Joseph	20
Lindsey	156
Littlebury	156
Peter	149
Rebecca	141
Robert	20
Samuel	157
Solomon	20
Susannah	141
Thomas	157
William	20, 157
Coles, John	81, 120, 164
Coles Co., Ill.	146
College and Research Libraries	135
College Landing, Williamsburg, Va.	86
Colley, Thomas	20, 27
see also Collie	
Collie, Carter	47
Dona	48
Gidem (Hall)	47
J. W.	48
James	143
Johnnie	48
Mary Elizabeth	48
Nancy (Jennings)	143
Nannie	48
William R.	48
see also Colley	
Collier, Frances	46
Polly (Carter)	183
Collin Co., Texas	184
Collins, James	81
John	119
Colman, Jakem	4
Colonial Clergy of New England	170
Colonial Clergy of the Middle Colonies	36
Colonial Clergy of Virginia ...	170-71
Columbia, Tenn.	79
Columbia Co., Pa.	93
Columbia Co., Tenn.	32
Columbus, Ohio	62, 94
Colvert, Cornelius	119

Compton, Jeremiah	19	Cox, Judith (Booker)	62
Condon, David	96	Lucy (Estes)	94
Elizabeth (Scasbrook)	96	Reubin	156
Mary	96	Valentine	157
Coner, Daniel	81	Coxe, Rev. S. O.	44
Confluence, W.Va.	169	Crab Orchard, Ky.	77
Connell, John	4-5	Craddock, Asa C.	19
Conyers Springs, Va.	133	Charles	19
Cook, Martha (Vaughan)	181	Claiborne	19
Thomas	181-82	James	19
Cooke, Mordecai	86	Jean H.	20
Cooney, John	157	Samuel	20
Coon's Mill, W.Va.	78	Richard C.	20
Coons Store, W.Va.	78	Robert	20
Cooper, Charles	10	William C.	19
John	157	Craig, Absalom	179
John L.	20	James	179
Leonard B.	156	Robert	179
Nancy	183	Samuel	179
Robert	81	Thomas	120
Wills	119	William	179
Copen, W.Va.	169	Craig Co., Va.	131, 133-34
Corbin, Betsy	165	Craig's Creek, Va.	133
Corinth, Miss.	47	Cranbury, N.J.	183
Corley, W.Va.	169	Crank, Matthew	8
Cornwall Parish, Lunenburg Co.,		Crawford, Col. ---	3
Va.	147	Ann	81
"Corrections and Comments"	79	Charles	157
Corris, John	120	David	156-57
Couch, Edward	11	Dr. James L.	94
Coulter, Michael	156	John	94, 156
Counties of Christian and		John D.	157
Trigg, Kentucky	43	Margaret (Buchanan)	94
Courdy, Archi	69	Nathan	81
Cousins, Elizabeth	19	Nelson	156
John	19-20	Robert	12
John C.	19	Rev. William	81
Richard	20	William S.	157
Coverley, Thomas	20	Creamoore, Barnett	157
Covington, Fanny (Austin)	152	Creekmur, William	175
John	184	Creel, Charles	141
Robert Warren	184	Sarah ( )	141
William D. C.	184	Crenshaw, Anthony	19
Covington, Va.	133	Crescent Mount, W.Va.	169
Cowgill, Daniel	45	Crews, Anderson	156
Elizabeth	45	Archerlis	156
Elizabeth (Martin)	45	James	157
Frankie	45	John	156
George Washington	45	Joseph	156
Joseph	45	Lewis	156
Martin	45	Reuben	157
Nancy	45	Thomas	156
Sarah (Emerson)	45	Crisp, William	82
Cowley, Capt. Abraham	87	Crittenden Co., Ky.	162
Anne ( )	87	Crittenton, John	20
Cowl's ferry, Chickahominy		Critzer, Dora Bell	141
River	118	Croacher, William	157
Cowne, Robert	175	Crockett, David	47
Cox, Ann	20	Croker, Mrs. Cathryn	94
George	19	Crook, James	45
Henry	119	Mary (West)	45
Jacob	94	Crook, W.Va.	78
John L.	62	Crook Dist., Boone Co.,W.Va.	78

INDEX

Cross, Benjamin	4
John	4
Crouch, Mary	71
Crowder, Herod T.	20
John M.	19
William	20
Crutcher, Elizabeth (Pollard)	47
William	47
Crutchfield, E.	164
Fortunatus	122
John	122
William	71, 116
Cryser, John	81
Culpeper Co., Va.	45, 89, 93-94, 118
	122, 141-42, 165-66, 180
Culpepper, Agnes	140
Charles	140
Eleanor (Gilbert)	140
Elizabeth	140
John	140
Joseph Mallory	140
Margaret Pickens (Baskin)	140
Sampson	140
Cumberland Co., Va.	56-57, 121, 172-73, 183
Cumings, Angia	12
Cummings, Angelo	13
Eleanor ( )	13
George	175
Cunliffe, Foster	67-68
Cunningham, James	82, 171
Mary (Rose)	171
family	96
Curd, Edward	122, 183
Mary Ann (Morris)	182-83
Curle, George G.	184
Mary E. L. (Shelton)	184
Curles, Henrico Co.	120
Curles Church, Henrico Psh.	170
Currier, John J.	170
Curry, William	82
Curtis, Augustine	9
Charles	9
Chichester	9
James	10, 115
Janet (Austin)	147
John	15, 108-10, 112
Mary ( )	9
Richard	11
Susanah	107
Cushing, W.Va.	169
Custis, John Parke	117
Martha (Dandridge)	171
Cutlips, W.Va.	169
Dabney, Philadelphia (Gwathmey)	139
William	139
Dacoma, Okla.	179
Daggers, Va.	133
Daggers Springs, Va.	133-34
Dailey, Mrs. A. V.	93
Daily, Elizabeth (Baker) Rhodes	93
Jacob	93
Peter	93
Daingerfield, America (Edmunds)	162
Dr. J. F.	162
Marian Louise	162
Sally	161-62
see also Dangerfield	
Dalby, John A.	20
Dale, Luscinda	180
Madison	180
Daleville, Va.	133
Dallill, John	157
Daly, W.Va.	169
Dame, George	166
Dameron, Dunmoore	157
William	157
Damron, Littlepage	82
Michael	82
William R.	82
Dan River	164
Dandridge, Capt. ---	61
Martha	171
Nathaniel W.	120
Dangerfield, Leroy	82
see also Daingerfield	
Daniel, ---	115
Constant	8
Elizabeth	8
Garrett	8, 109
Henry	109
James	8, 116
Jeane	8
Phebe	112
Robert	8
Stephen	20
Travers	164
William	8
Daniell, Agatha	7
Ann	7
Elizabeth	7
James	109
John	7
Josiah	114
Mary	7
Mosely	7
Obadiah	7
Robert	7
Sarah	7
William	7, 114
Dannivant Creek, Charlotte Co.	37
Danville, Va.	100
Darkesville, W.Va.	35
Darnaby, Mildred	90
Nancy	90
Daubins, George	82
Daughters of the American Revolution	137-38
Library	43, 78
Magazine	50, 98, 136, 146
Davenport, Joseph	157

Davenport, Richard	39
see also Devenport	
Daverson, Giles	158
David, Thomas	20
Davidson Co., Tenn.	94
Davis, ---	72
Arther L.	157
Benjamin	5
Charles	157
Edmund	82
Elizabeth	157
Elizabeth (Austin)	149
Mrs. Elizabeth T.	177
Ella O. (Reynolds)	184
Isham	158
Israel	157
Jabus	82
James	149, 157
Jesse	82
Joel	82
John	11, 15, 69, 107, 157
John F.	157
Jonathan	151
Joshua	157
Lewis	157
Margaret	82
Mary	96
Mary (Austin)	151
Nicholas C.	157
Phillip	82
Richard	157
Richard A.	184
Thomas	124
William	10, 82, 124, 157-58
family	146
Dawkins, John	93
Nancy ( )	93
Dawson, Frances	184
Henry	82
John	82
John S.	82
Joseph	158
Martin	82, 157
Mary Lightfoot (Slaughter)	184
Nelson C.	157
Pleasant	157
Robert Dudley	184
William	157
Day, Mary Ann	157
Samuel	157
William	124
Dean, Mrs. W. A.	45, 182
see also Deen	
Deane family	45
Dear, Aincy (Morton)	153
Dearen, William	20
Dearing, Eliza (Austin)	154
Willis	154
Deaton, George	20
James	20
John	20
Levy	20
de Bernoux, Galvan	38
Deen, Jeremiah	157
Samuel	157
see also Dean	
Degge, John	111
Simon	111
Dehart, Jesse	157
John	158
Deisher's Mill, Va.	133
DeJarnette, Anne (Walker)	181
Edney (George)	181
George	181
Henry Walker	181
James Pemberton	181
Joseph	181
Mary (Pemberton)	181
Delany, David	20
Demsey, Tandy	82
William	82
Denning, Fannie Mary	75-76
Jane Hester	75-76
Dennis, George	68
Jesse	82
Denoon, John	15
Dent, Miss ---	47
Department of Archives and History, Raleigh, N.C.	60
Depriest, Langsdon	82
Descendants of William and Sarah (Poe) Herndon	99
DeSpain, Mrs. Charles	45, 180
Devenport, Richard	158
William	158
see also Davenport	
Dewauser, John	157
Dewhitt, Thomas	157
Dickerson, ---	120
Griffith	175
Thurston	82
Dickey, Capt. ---	141
James	82
Robert	20
Dickins, Frances (Moore)	60
Harriet Phillips	60
Jesse	60
Dickson, William	82
see also Dixon	
Dictionary of American Biography	135
Dier, Daniel	20
Thomas	20
William	20
Digges, Catherine	106
Edward	106
John	82
Diggs, William H.	82
Dik, James	4
Dillard, George	157
James	82, 157
John	82
Joseph	157
William	157
Dinsmore, William	82
Dinwiddie, Ann	82

INDEX

Dinwiddie, John	82	Duholm, Mrs. Lea F.	48
Dinwiddie Co., Va.		Dulhallow, Darby MacOwen	
	39, 95, 118, 120, 171	MacCarthy, Lord of	31
Dixon, Mrs. ---	123	Dulin, William	· 178
Elizabeth ( )	143	see also Dooling,	
Enoch	82	The Dulin Family in America	178
Henry	143	Dumfries, Va. 85, 87,	120
James	82	Dumont, William H.	175
John	82	Dunbars, Va.	63
Joseph	175	Duncan, Fleming H.	157
Roger	176	John	158
Tabitha	143	Joseph	82
William	82	William 157,	166
see also Dickson		Dunevant, Daniel	158
D'Neal, William O.	124	see also Dunnavant	
Doctorsville, W.Va.	169	Dunkum, Mary Jane	28-29
Dodd, John	82, 157	Dunnavant, Abner	20
Joseph	157	Frederick	20
Sally (Carter)	183	Philip	20
William	82	Samuel	20
Dodson, John Hackney	16, 110	Thomas	20
Mabell	16	see also Dunevant	
Rachel	16	Dunnington's Depot, W.Va.	35
Rebekah	16, 110	Dunmore Co., Va.	31
Doggett family	45	Dunstall, John	112
Dold, William	82	Dupriest, Nathan	20
Doliante, Mrs. William J.	143	Durham, Isaac	82
Donald, Robert	121	James	82, 163
Donald, Young & Co.	119	Thomas	20
Donaldson, Daniel	47	Durham, Conn.	147
Karenhappuck (Morehead)	47	Durrett, Abigail	28-29
Doncastle, Thomas	38	Albert	28-29
Dooling, Philip	178	Ann Elizabeth (Williams)	29-30
Robert	178	Ann Lewis	28
Thomas	178	Avah	30
William	178	Braxton Byrd	28-30
see also Dulin		Cammillus Durkee	30
Dorman, John Frederick	184	Charles Lewis	28
Douglass, Margaret	150	Claiborne	30
Dover, Va.	118	Eleanorah Ann Hazzeltine	30
Dowdy, Benjamin	20	Elizabeth	29
Marion L.	144	Elizabeth ( )	30
Dowling family	178	Elizabeth (Hines)	29
Dragon Swamp, Middlesex Co.	72-73	Elliott Vermanet	28-29
Drake, Boswell	20	Ellis	30
James	20	Everett Vermanet	28
William	20	Fannie	30
Draper Manuscripts	79	Ferenia	29
Dreisback, Catherine (Ginder)	93	Francis Braxton	30
Henry	93	Harvey John Thomas	28
Drennan, Mrs. Jerry	48	Jane Richard	30
Drumheller, Jacob	82	John Dunkum	30
Drummond, Henly	82	John Hines	29-30
Dry Fork Creek, Bland Co.	77	Jonathan	28-30
Dubois, ---	87	Jonathan Jackson	28-30
Duck Creek, W.Va.	168-69	Judith T.	28
Dudley, Dorothy (Tabb)	62	Judith Terrell	28-29
George	62	Kate Baker	28
James	69-70, 108, 110	Laurence Blanton	28
John	11	Margaret J. (Tompkins)	29-30
Judith	56, 62	Maria L. (Hester)	29
Robert	11, 69	Martha Ellen	28-29
Thomas	110, 116	Martin	29-30

Durrett, Mary A. (Blanton)	29
Mary Ann Johnson	28-29
Mary Elizabeth	28-30
Mary Elizabeth Tule	30
Mary Jane (Dunkum)	28-29
Mary Sophia	30
Mary Virginia	28
Mildred	30
Minor	30
Nancy (Hodges)	29
Oscar Fitzallen	28-29
Oscar George Price	30
Oscar Hines	30
Polly H. (Lively)	28-29
Rebecca (White)	29-30
Robert Henry	28
Robert William	30
Susan E. Jones	29-30
Susan Pauline	30
Thomas Jackson	30
William	29
William Albert	28
William Alfred	30
William Hines	28-30
William Jonathan	30
Dutch Hill Cemetery, Columbia Co., Pa.	93
DuVal, Samuel	85, 163
Eades, Isaac	82
William	82
Eads, Bartlett	158
Eagle Rock, Va.	133
Eanes, Henry	20
Earl Gregg Swem, A Bibliography	135
Early Marriages, Wills ... Botetourt County ...	132
Early Southwest Virginia Families	137
Early Virginia Immigrants	91
East, James	82
Easter, Francis	52
Matthew	20
Thomas	52
Easterby [Easterly], Richard	11
Eastree, Richard	110
see also Estree	
Eaton, William	121-22
Ebenezer Church, Bigbyville, Tenn.	32, 79
Ebenezer M.E. Church, Oak Hill, N.C.	59
Eckhardt, Mrs. W. R.	141
Eckstein, Samuel	62
Eddens, Capt. Samuel	61
Edenton, N.C.	87
Edgar Co., Ill.	183
Edgebrook, Va.	133
Edmondson, James	57
Mary	57
family	137
Edmunds, America	162

Edmunds, Anna (Greathouse)	161
Charles	82
Cornelia	162
Ealine Louise	162
Edward R.	161
Edwin Short	161-62
Eliza G. (Henry)	161
Eliza H.	161-62
Eliza Kennon (Randolph)	161
Eliza Randolph	162
George M.	162
Jack B. F.	161
James	82
John	82, 161
Marguerite	162
Martha A. E. M.	161
Martha (Short)	161
Mary P. (Green)	161
Nettie (Van Vlear)	162
Rolling	82
Sally (McAfee)	161-62
Samuel	82
Thomas	161
Thomas M.	162
Thomas McAfee	162
Thomas W. R.	161
William	20, 82
"Edmunds Family Bible"	161-62
Edwards, Ann	144
Benjamin Thrasher	118
Bessie Z.	48
Daniel	175
James	116
John	117
Margaret	117
Mark	118
Nell (Henton) [Mrs. A.L.]	89-90
Thomas	158
Eggleston, Edward	20
Joseph	20
Richard	20
William T.	20
Elbert Co., Ga.	94
Elizabeth City Co., Va.	87, 171, 177
Elk Creek, Grayson Co.	150
Elk Run, W.Va.	78
Elliott, Elizabeth	11
Robert	86
Ellis, Anne	107
Elizabeth	107
Francis	88, 163
Hezekiah	70, 107
James	20
John	20, 107, 158
Josiah	158, 165
Mary	107
Mary ( )	70, 107
Richard S.	82
Robert	107
Samuel	158
Sarah	107

INDEX

Ellis, Thomas	20
William	107, 158, 165
family	90
Ellison, Henry	85
Elmira, W.Va.	169
Elmore, Thomas	20
Embly, Luke	82
Emerson, Sarah	45
England, Charles	140
John	140
Joseph	140
William	158
Zippora (Choate)	140
English, Edward	143
"The English Origin of Randall Holt and Edward Normansell"	98
Enox, David	82
Mishek	82
Ens, Harbet	82
Eppes, Elizabeth	144
John	20
Essex Co., Va.	16, 51-52 54-60, 62-64, 93, 111 166, 172, 178, 180-81
Estep, Elisha	82
Estes, Lucy	94
Estree, Richard	107-08
see also Eastree	
Eubank, Elizabeth	63
George	158
John	158
Evans, Elisha	158
Pleasant	158
Rebecca	181
Reginald	181
Thomas	158
William	158
William F.	33
see also Evens, Evins	
Evens, Catherine	183
Samuel	183
William	183
see also Evans, Evins	
Everidge, Bright	121
Evins, Arnod.	4
Charles	82
James	82
John	82, 109
Ewers, Thomas	82
William	82
Fagg, William	21
Faircloth, Ephraim	124
Fairfax Co., Va.	87, 93, 139, 143, 178, 180
Falkner, Thomas	12, 107
Falling Waters, W.Va.	35
Falling Waters Twp., Berkeley Co., W.Va.	35
Falls plantation, Chesterfield Co., Va.	118
Fallsmill, W.Va.	169
"Family of John Tomlin"	130
Faris, William	21
see also Farriss	
Farley, Matthew	20
Peter	21
Stephen	21
William	20-21
Farmer, Charles	20
"Farmers Retreat," King and Queen Co., Va.	64
Farming, Reuben	4
Farnsworth, Henry	158
Farrar, Francis Norvell	184
Louisa (Bryant)	184
Farrell, Edward	71
Farrer, Fleming	82
John	83
Joseph	83
Parin	83
Samuel	21
Thomas	83
Farriss, James	143
see also Faris	
Farrow, Martha (Royster)	173
Farthing, Tabitha (Blanks)	93
Faulkner, Ellis	107
Faulks, Gabriel	122
Fauntleroy, Annette Lorhelle (Sisson)	62
Griffin	57
Dr. Henry	62
Mary (Booker)	62
Robert	62
Robert H.	62
Sarah (Ball)	62
Fauntleroy <u>Family</u>	62
Fauquier Co., Va.	47, 93, 96, 122, 142, 165-66, 178
Fayette Co., Ky.	45, 141, 180
Fayette Co., Ohio	143
Fearn, John	68, 71, 107
Fears, Thomas	166
Featherstone, Anne	181
Charles	21, 181
Rebecca (Evans) Patram	181
Felicity (ship)	39
Fenten, Zachariah	83
Fergason, Samuel	83
Ferguson, Joseph	21
Robert	21, 175
William	21
Fernando, Matthew	165
Field, Anna Rogers (Clark)	180
Col. John	180
Judith (Soane) Randolph	144
Peter	144
Fields, Eleanor	150
William	176
Filmer, Henry	50
<u>Filson Club History Quarterly</u>	135
<u>Fincastle, Va.</u>	131, 133
Fincastle Co., Va.	131
Fincastle Dist., Botetourt Co.	133

Finch, Edward	122
John	183
Nancy	183
Finley, John	5
Finney, Anne	13
Nancy	20
William	20
Finniewood, Va.	123
1st Virginia Regiment, Continental Line	37
Fishback, Harmon	122
Fisher, William	21
Fitsjerrald, Hugh	83
William	82
see also Fitzgerald, Fitzjerrald	
Fitspatrick, Edmund	83
John	83
Joseph	83
Thomas	82-83
William	83
see also Fitzpatrick	
Fitzgerald, Elizabeth (Booker)	63
Fitzjerrald, James	82
Jordan	82
see also Fitsjerrald	
Fitzpatrick, John	130
John E.	82
see also Fitspatrick	
Flanigan, Mary	139
Flat Branch, Henrico Co.	85
Flat Creek, W.Va.	78
Flat Creek, Amelia Co.	122
Flatwoods, W.Va.	169
Fleet, Henry	15
Fleming, Cleary [Clara]	46
Robert	21
Col. William	87
Fletcher, Christopher	158
Flood, Charles	83
John	158
Flower, William	158
Floweree, Arianna Adolpheus (Hanson)	96
Daniel	96
Floyd, James	158
Flukes, Va.	133
Fluvanna Co., Va.	38, 117
Forbes, Alexander	83
William	83
Ford, Catharine (Grace)	139
Christopher	121
Hezekiah	21
Jane (Milstead)	139
John	21, 139
Rachel (Spencer)	139
Samuel	21
Thomas	139
Waller	20
Foreman, Reuben	5
Fork Dale, Va.	133-34
Forkner, Spencer	82
Forqueran, Sophia	184
Forrest, Josiah	21
Fort Delaware	63
Fort LaFayette	63
Fort Pitt	3
Fortune, Benjamin	82
Eddy	82
Nicholas	82
Thomas	82
Zachariah	82
Forward (ship)	67
Foster, ---	39
Anthony	21
Booker	21
Claiborne	21
Joel	20
John	20
Larkin	21
Richard	20
Robert	20
William	20, 158
family	146
Foster, W.Va.	78
Foushee, Francis	86
Fouts, Andrew	5
Fox, John	52, 82, 163
Joseph	83
Samuel	82
William	82
Frame's Mills, W.Va.	169
Frametown, W.Va.	169
France, Edward	141
Francis, Edward	141
John	5
Francis Bonaventure (ship)	96
Franklin, James	158
Jeremiah	158
Joel	158
Reubin	158
Peachery	158
Samuel	158
Franklin Co., Pa.	139
Franklin Co., Va.	47, 89, 140, 184
Franklin Twp., Braxton Co., W.Va.	168
Fraser, Alexander	111-12
Frazer, Alexander	114
John	158
Walter	158
Frazier, Alexander	116
Frederick, Md.	121
Frederick Co., Md.	33, 96
Frederick Co., Va.	31, 33, 47-48, 89, 139, 182-83
Fredericksburg, N.Y.	61
Fredericksburg, Va.	6, 38, 76, 117, 119-20, 123-24, 165-66
Fredericksburg District Court	176
Fredericksville Parish, Albemarle Co., Va.	89, 179
Freeman, Douglas Southall	171
Hezekiah	175
Thomas	108

INDEX

Freeman, Will	21
Zachariah	83
"Freeman's," Dinwiddie Co.	121
Freeme, John	91
Freestone, George	113
Mary	113
French, James	121
Frey, Ruth E.	180
Friend, William	20
Fry, Charles Meriwether	143
Elizabeth (Leigh)	143
Elizabeth Speed (Smith)	143
Col..Joshua	143
Mary Margaret	143
Mary (Shorter)	143-44
Thomas Slaughter	143
Thomas Walker	143
Frye, George W.	144
Fugat, James	4
Fulcher, James	158
John	158
Fulsher, John	108
Fulton, Alexander	5
Gaines, Donna C.	75, 161
Gala, Va.	133
Galatia Church, Botetourt Co.	132
Galloway, David	120
Galt, ---	85, 87, 117, 121
William	158
Gandy, Elias	83
Ganotown, W.Va.	35
Gant, Robert	83
Gardiner, Ann Henshaw	33
Laurence B.	142
Mabel (Henshaw)	33
William	11
see also Gardner	
Gardner, Ann	7
Anne ( )	8
Eliza ( )	8
William	8, 71
Garland, Anderson	83
David	158
David S.	158
Griffin,	88, 164
Hudson M.	158
James	158
Spotswood	158
Garner, Joseph	158
Garnett, Booker	62, 64
David S.	64
Dorothy (Booker)	62
George S.	62
George William	63
Lewis H.	63
Muscoe	62-63
Sarah H. (Booker)	62-63
William A.	62
Garven, James	158
Gaskins, James	83
Thomas	58
Gates, Gen. Horatio	119, 124

Gates, Robert	124
Gatewood, Ransom	158
Reuben	158
William	158
Gausney, Henry	158
Gaw, Grace	181
Genealogical Book Co.	92
Genealogy of the Heston Family	89
General Court	166
Genito, Amelia Co.	19
George, Ann	181
David	7, 65, 70, 109
Edney	181
Elizabeth	181
Harry	65
James	65, 181
Jean	65
John	7, 65, 71, 109, 181
Mary	181
Mary (Jordan)	181
Reuben	181
Robert	8, 10, 12, 74, 113, 181
Salley	158
Sarah	181
George Washington	171
Georgia Department of Archives and History	79
German, W.Va.	169
Germantown, Ky.	180
Germantown, battle of	46
Gerrardstown Twp., Berkeley Co., W.Va.	35
Gerrardstown, W.Va.	35
Gibbens, Benjamin	47
Catherine (Herbert)	47
James-	47
John	47
Gibbs, John	13, 116
Mary ( )	13, 116
Miles	21
Thomas	21
William	21
Gibson, Abraham	93
Ann ( )	93
Gibson's warehouse, King George Co., Va.	121
Giddings, Rev. G. P.	161
Gifin, Daniel	4
Gilbert, Eleanor	140
Ezekel	83, 158
Henry	158
Giles, William	83
William B.	21
Giles, W.Va.	78
Giles Co., Tenn.	148
Giles Co., Va.	77, 131
Gill, James	21
John	21
Joseph	37
Gillam, Lettice	142
see also Gilliam	
Gillespie, Alexander	158

Gillespie, George	158	Goode, William	83
George M.	184	Goodman, ---	123
Mary Ann	46	Goodrich, ---	39
Sherod M.	158	Edmond	158
Victoria (Reynolds)	184	James	158
Gilliam, Archerbald	158	John	158
Jarrett	158	Samuel	158
John	120, 158	Thomas	158
Robert	120	Goodwin, Cornelius	158
William	21	George	158
Gilliland, Susannah	158	James	158
Gillinwaters, James	158	Micajah	158
Joshua	83	Thomas	83
Gillis Creek, Henrico Co.	124	Goodwyn, David	119
Gillock, Mrs. J. C.	144	Francis	21
Gilmore's Mills, Va.	133	Jesse	21
Ginder, Catherine	93	Solomon	21
Ginger, Ludwig [Lewis]	182	Goolsby, A. M.	48
Giroud, Honore	117	Mary Elizabeth (Collie)	48
Gist, Col. ---	121	Nancy ( )	48
Givens, Debrorah	144	Samuel	158
James	144	William Edward	48
Martha ( )	144	Goosely, William	119
Glass, Mary	181	Gordon, ---	119, 164
Samuel	4	Charles	21
Sarah	181	John	175
Glen Wilton, Va.	133	Thomas	119
Glendeny, George	175	William	12, 111-12, 116
Glendon, W.Va.	169	Gordon, W.Va.	78
Glengary, W.Va.	35	Gott, John K.	96
Gloucester, Va.	75-76	Gourdvine Fork, Culpeper Co.	166
Gloucester (ship)	39	Grace, Catherine	139
Gloucester Co., Va.	39, 51-55	Grace Furnace, Va.	133
	69, 75-76, 79, 86, 90, 108	Gracy, Mrs. David C.	98
	119-22, 144, 163, 166, 181	Grady, John Paul	141
Goalder, Elizabeth (Goare)	73	Graham, Richard	119-20
Goar, H.	37	Grainger Co., Tenn.	79, 152-53
Goare, Ann	73	Grange, John	10
Elizabeth	73	Grant, William	21, 188
Henry	73	Grant Co., Ky.	45
John	73	Granville Co., N.C.	
Jose	73		56, 59-60, 161, 172-74
Joseph	9, 15, 73-74	Grapefield, Va.	77
	107, 112, 116	Grass, Mrs. Frank	139
Lucretia	73, 107	Grassy Creek Presbyterian Church	
Lucretia ( )	74, 116	Granville Co., N.C.	59
Mary	73	Graves, Alexander	109
Sarah	73	Isabella (Lea)	99, 102-03
William	73	John	83, 99, 102-03
Godbee, John	70	John C.	143
Godbey, Mary	10	John Herndon	99, 103, 105
Going, Aaron	83	Mary	103
Landon	83	Nancy	99
Phillip	83	Nancy (Slade)	99
William	83	Richard	83
Gooch, Philip	158	"The Graves Family of Spotsylvania"	102-03
Thomas	141	Gray, ---	176
Goochland Co., Va.		Charity	182
	39, 119-20, 135, 141	Mrs. Frank S.	140
Good, Benjamin	158	James	39
Goode, Campbell	83	William	70
Daniel	83	family	45
Mary	21	Grayson Co., Va.	46, 148-50
Phebe	83		

INDEX

Grayson C.H., Va.	150
Great Hunting Creek	166
Greathouse, Anna	161
Green, Abraham	21
Caleb	21
John	124
Mary P.	161
Thomas	21
William	21
Green Co., Ky.	141
Green Creek, Cumberland Co.	172
Green Springs, Louisa Co.	163
Greenbrier Co., W.Va. 131, 144, 146,	180
Greene, Mrs. Anne G. 48,	143
Jarvis	143
Rev. John	143
Gen. Nathaniel	148
Greene Co., Ala.	184
Greeneville, Va.	150
Greensburgh, W.Va.	35
Greensville Co., Va. 140,	179
Greenvillage, Pa.	139
Greenwich, Kent, England	170
Greenwood, Thomas	16
Greer, George Cabell	91
John	4-5
Gregory, James	83
John	158
William	21
Gretter, William	87
Griffie, Benjamin	158
Griffin, Charles	83
Lady Christiana ( )	76
Cyrus	76
Cyrus Anstruther	75-76
Fannie Mary (Denning)	75-76
Fayette	76
Henry Stuart	76
J. S. B.	75
James Lewis Corbin	75-76
Jane Hester (Denning)	75-76
John	76, 83
John M.	83
John Mercer	75
John Tayloe	141
Julia Amy	76
Louisa	76
Mary ( )	76
Mary Anne	141
Mary (Lightfoot)	141
Mary Louisa	75
Mary Stuart	76
Robert	4
Samuel Stuart	75-76
Sarah (Lewis)	75-76
Thomas	76, 83
Thomas Stuart	75
"Griffin Family Bible, Gloucester County, Virginia"	75-76
Griffith, William	5
Grigg, Mary M. C.	139-40
Grimes, Moses	158
Grimes, Thomas	158
see also Grymes	
Grindstaff, Lewis	4
Grissom, Thomas	158
Grist, John	4
Grooms, John	158
Grymes, Rev. Charles	179
John 12-13,	116
see also Grimes	
Guhy, William	112
"A Guide to the Counties of Virginia" Berkeley County	33-36
Bland County	77-78
Boone County 78-79,	167
Botetourt County	131-34
Braxton County	167-69
Guide to the Study of West Virginia History	40
Guine, Tom	116
Guthery, William	158
Guthrie, Agg	47
Benjamin	47
David	47
Henry	47
James	47
John	47
Mary	47
Milley	47
Penelope	47
Penelope ( )	47
Ruth	47
Sally Ann	47
Wayne T.	47
Gutrie, William	14
Guttery, David	158
Edward	158
William	158
Guttrey, John 10, 74,	109
Gwathmey, Ann	139
Philadelphia	139
Maj. Philip	139
Hacker's Valley, W.Va.	169
Hackett, Thomas 10,	109
Hackney, William 16,	110-11
Haden, Emily B. (Shapard)	174
Joseph A.	174
Haestand, Elizabeth	139
John	139
Hager, John	159
Hager, W.Va.	78
Hail, Leonard	83
Hainesville, W.Va.	35
Hairston [Harston], Peter	117
Halifax, N.C.	86
Halifax Co., Va. 37, 46, 138, 147-48, 151-52, 164-65,	174
Hall, Capt. ---	6
Bolling	21
Gidem	47
Instant	21
John 21,	159

Hall, Judith (Shelton)	143	Hardaway, Daniel	21
Moses	159	Samuel	118
Thomas	22	Hardee, Joseph	8, 65
William	22, 159	Margaret ( )	109
William H.	143	Thomas	109
Hallitrom, Mrs. H. A.	141	see also Hardy	
Hallork, Capt. ---	120	Harden, Joseph	10
Hally, James	4	see also Hardin	
Hamblen Co., Tenn.	153	Hardesty, Richard	4
Hambleton, Andrew	159	Hardesty's Historical and Geo-	
James	84	graphical Encyclopedia	168
Milley	84	Hardin, George	8, 12, 69
Robert	84, 159	see also Harden	
William	84	Hardin Co., Tenn.	148-49
Hamerton, Pinchback	11, 66	Hardwick, Richard	159
Hamilton, Gilbert	111-12	Harding, Edward	84
William	163	George	111
Hamlet, Elias	159	John	83
Hamlett, Susanah	84	Hardy, Robert	83
Hamlin, William B.	21	see also Hardee	
Hamm, James	159	Hare, Richard	83
John	21	Robert	87
Stephen	159	William B.	83
William	21, 159	Haregrove, Hezekiah	83
Hammaker, Adam	179	Joseph	83
Anna (Herr)	179	William	83
David	170	Haroll, Thomas	84
John	179	Harford Co., Md.	36
Joseph	179	Harlin, Jesse	83
Samuel	179	Harlow, Agustin	83
William	179	Nathaniel	84
Hampshire Co., W.Va.	33, 184	Reubin	83
Hampton, Va.	165	Harmanson, John	39
Hancock, Anthony	95	Harper, John	21
Nancy	95	Henry	84
Sara (Baker)	95	Mrs. Robert William	140
Handsborough, Samuel	83	Susan	184
see also Hansborough		Harper's Ferry, W.Va.	35, 182
Handy, W.Va.	78	Harrelson, Mrs. F. G.	100
Hankins, Mary (Austin)	152	see also Haralson	
Rebecca	154	Harris, Amos	39
William	152-53	Benjamin	21, 83
Hannah, Salley	21	Edward	83
Hanover Co., Va.	6, 38	Elizabeth	83
44, 48, 59, 89, 118-20		James	83, 87
122, 147, 163-65, 181-82		John	10, 83, 181
Hanover County Police Benevolent		Matthew	83-84
Association	44	Nathan	83
Hanover Town, Va.		Reuben	83
37-38, 117, 122, 164		Schuyler	84
Hansborough, James	83	William	83-84, 181
Kezeah	84	William B.	84
see also Handsborough		William Lee	83
Hansford, John	159	family	96, 146
William	159	Harrison, ---	123
Hanson, Arianna Adolpheus	96	Capt. ---	124
John	96	Benjamin	58, 119
Richard	166	Benjamin, & Co.	86
Haralson, Herndon	101, 103-04	Col. Charles	61
Major	104	Edmund	21
Nancy (Lea)	103-04	George	159
Paul	104-05	James	158
see also Harrelson		John	159

INDEX

Harrison, Josiah	158
Nathaniel	21, 120
Nicholas	159
Reuben	158
Richard	159
Samuel	119
Mrs. Vivian P.	47
William	5, 21-22
Hart, Andrew	29
Marie Lou	29
Mary A. J. (Durrett)	29
Harter, Mrs. Bert	28
Hartless, Henry	159
James	159
Peter	159
Richard	159
William	159
Harwell, Lucy (Vaughan)	142
Rebecca (Moody)	182
Harwood, John	118
Col. William	88
Haselwood, John	143
Sarah (Jarvis)	143
Thomas	11, 71, 109
Hastings, Mich.	182
Hastins, Clayton	22
Elizabeth	22
Hatcher, Angelina	46
Hatter, James	83
John M.	83
Hatton, Richard	159
Haubstadt, Ind.	91
Haulee, Joseph	8
Haverstraw, N.Y.	58
Hawkins, David	22
Jesse	159
John	83
Joseph	159
Thomas	83
Hay, John	117, 119, 163
Haycock, Ebnezer	83
Hayes, James	21
see also Hays	
Haymaker, see Hammaker	
Haymakertown, Va.	133
Haymond's Mills, W.Va.	169
Haymond's Store, W.Va.	169
Haynes, Charles	159
Hardin	159
Jesse	159
Mary (Lewis)	144
Hays, Samuel	84
Thomas	84
see also Hayes	
Haywood, William	159
Haywood Co., Tenn.	182
Hedding, Benjamin	117
Hedges, Charles	4-5
Silas	5
Hedgesville, W.Va.	35-36
Hedgesville Twp., Berkeley Co.	35
Heely, Martin	175
Helm, John	140

Helton, George	83
Henderson, James	21
John	5, 83
Joseph	104
Major	104
Nathaniel	159
Peggie	159
Philadelphia (Lea)	104
Robert	83
Salley	159
Stephen	83
William	83
Henderson's, Va.	133
Hendrick, Benjamin	21
Garland	21
James	21
John	21
Zach.	21
Hendricks, Jesse	84
Peter	84
Henley, Leonard	159
Henrico Co., Va.	85, 87-89
	117-18, 120, 122, 140
	144, 146, 170, 181-82
Henrico C. H., Va.	124
Henrico Parish, Henrico Co.	170
Henry, Christopher	176
Eliza G.	161
Elizabeth	180
Elizabeth (Mitchell)	141
James	142
Rev. John Hall	141
Henry Co., Va.	89, 117
	123, 151, 153, 166
Henton, George	90
John	90
Mildred (Darnaby)	90
Nancy (Darnaby)	90
Thomas	90
William	90
Herbert, Catherine	47
William	86
Hern, Peter	21
Herndon, Ann	99, 104, 106
Catherine (Digges)	106
David	104
Edward	101-02, 104, 106
John Goodwin	99
Nancy	104
Sarah (Poe)	99
William	99, 101, 103, 106
The Herndon Family of Virginia	99, 106
Hero (ship)	119
Herr, Anna	179
Herrin, Jonathan	12
Herring, Jonathan	7
Hester, Maria L.	28-29
Hettie, W.Va.	169
Hevens, Sarah	11
Hewett, W.Va.	78
Hewittsville, W.Va.	78
Hewittville, W.Va.	78

Hewlings, Jacob W.	21
Hicksville, Va.	77
Hiden, Martha Woodroof [Mrs. Philip Wallace]	51, 102-03
Higginbotham, Aaron	159
Charles	159
James	159
Jesse	83
John	83, 159
Joseph	159
Moses	159
Reubin	159
William	159
High Court of Chancery	146
Hight, George	83
Matthew	83
Hignett, Mrs. Edelle Cox	94
Hildebrand, John	47
Hill, Ezekiel	158
J. Ed	79
James	21, 159
John	21, 159
Lodowich J.	79
Maddison	159
Miles	79
Nathaniel	83
Pleasant	83
Richard	116
Samuel	159
Tabitha (Pope)	79
Thomas	159
William	83, 86, 110
Hill, W.Va.	78
Hilles, Meany (Tribble)	181
"The Hills of Wilkes County, Georgia"	79
Hillsborough Dist., N.C.	183
Hilsman, James	22
Jose	21
Hilton, Matt	22
Moses	22
Hines, Abner	29
Elizabeth	29
Mary Elizabeth (Durrett)	29-30
Hinson, James	159
Joseph	159
Hipkings, James	12
Hipkins, John	74
The Historical Foundation and Its Treasures	138
Historical Foundation of the Presbyterian and Reformed Churches	31-32, 79, 138
Historical Genealogy of the Woodsons	57
Historical Hand-Atlas ... of Berkeley and Jefferson Counties	33
"Historical Sketch of Boone County"	78
History of Berkeley County	33
History of Braxton County	167
The History of Pittsylvania County	152
History of the Lower Shenandoah Valley Counties	33
Hobbs, Elizabeth Harrison	57
Hobbs Hole, Va.	61, 120
Hodges, Nancy	28-29
Hodgson, Richard	22
Hogg, John	159
Randolph	159
William F.	159
Holbrook, Jane (Smith)	36
Rev. John	36
Holder, Sarah (Hudson)	94
Holderness, Robert	15
Holland, Elizabeth Anne (Odom)	141
George Washington	141
Joseph	141
Mary Anne (Griffin)	141
Hollens Creek Cemetery, Hardin Co., Tenn.	148
Hollingsworth, Joseph	83
William	84
Holloway, John	21, 27, 119
Robert	159
Holly Brook, Va.	77
Holly Dist., Braxton Co.	168
Holly River, W.Va.	168-69
Holmes, Basil	119
Holt, Jesse	21
John	22
Joseph	122
Randall	98
Richard	22
Sarah	21
William	21
Holton, W.Va.	36
Home, W.Va.	169
Honey Farm, W.Va.	78
Hood, Abraham	21-22
Allen	21
Edward	21
John	22
Joshua	22
Nathaniel	143
Solomon	22
Hoofmire, John	83
Hooker, William	159
Hope, Mrs. Mildred T.	179
Hope, W.Va.	169
Hopewell Monthly Meeting	182
Hopkins, James	67, 83
Hopkinsville, Ky.	63
Horner, John	83
Horsburgh, Alexander	84
Horsley, John	84
Joseph	84
Martha	84
Robert	84
William	84
Horton, John	116
House, James	84
Houston Mines, Va.	133-34
Howard, Binjamin	159
George	159

INDEX

Howard, John	83
Sarah	140
William	159
Howel, John	22
Howell, Aaron	4
David	4
John	4
Spencer	21
see also Howl	
Howerton, Harritage	159
Howl, Absolam	159
see also Howell	
Howlett, William	22
Hoy, John	175
Hubard, Jessica	56, 172
Hubbard, Christopher	22
Elizabeth	55-56, 172
Johannah ( )	55
Huckstep, Samuel	159
Hudgens, William	84
Hudgings, Burwell	21
Hudgins, Drewry	84
Hudson, Davis	184
Francis E.	21
George	159
Jane (Brown)	184
Joshua	159
Leweling	21
Reubin	159
Richard	94
Rush	159
Sarah	94
Sarah (Booker)	94
William	21, 94
William C.	21
Hughes, Christopher	87
John	83
Moses	84
Thomas	39, 144
Hughs, Benjamin	22
Blackburn	21
John	21, 109
Nancy	21
William	159
Hundley, John	39
Joshua	22
see also Hunley, Hunly	
Hungar's Parish, Northampton Co., Va.	36
Hunley, Josiah	120
see also Hundley, Hunly	
Hunly, James	83
Hunt, Dorothy (Vaughan)	142
Mary	114
Mary ( )	114-15
Matthew	114-15
William	180
Hunter, ---	165
David	159
Nancy	94
Hunter, Banks & Co.	119, 165
Hunterdon Co., N.J.	50
Huntington, Samuel	122
Huntington, W.Va.	94
Hunton, William	176
Hurdle Mills, Person Co., N.C.	59
Hurt, Anderson	22
Hust, Thomas	176
Hutcherson, Charles	22
John	159
Independence, Va.	150
Indian Rock, Va.	134
Ingersoll, Mrs. R. E.	92
Ingram, Elizabeth	9
John	124
family	96
Inichan, Thomas	11
Innis, George	84
John	84
Thomas	84
Irish, Nathaniel	122
Iron Mound, Va.	134
Irvine, William	160
Isbell, Christopher	160
William	159
Zachariah	159
Isle of Wight Co., Va. 43, 174, 181	
Isle of Wight County Marriages	177
Ivy, Capt. William	163
Jackson, Abel	22
Burwell	84
Francis	22
Hannah	39
Isaac	94
Samuel A.	22
Wily	22
Jackson, Va.	133
Jackson Co., Tenn.	60
Jackson Co., W.Va.	131
Jacksonville, Fla.	93
Jacob, John	84
Jacobs, David	84
William	84
Jacode, Joseph	70
James, Richard	85
James City Co., Va. 51, 98, 103, 121	
James River, Va.	47, 134
James River	39, 87, 117, 119, 131, 163-64
Jamestown 350th Anniversary Historical Booklets	91, 135
Jamieson, George	87
"Jane (Smith) Holbrook of New Jersey and Virginia"	36
Jarratt, Rev. Devereux	171
Jarrell's Valley, W.Va.	78
Jarvis, John	160
Joseph	160
Sarah	143
Jefferson, John G.	22
Thomas	37
Jefferson, Texas	138

Jefferson Co., Ga.	95
Jefferson Co., Ky.	95
Jefferson Co., W.Va.	33, 35, 45
Jeffries, Elizabeth (Booker)	56
Richard	56
Jemeco	7
Jenkins, Bennett	160
John	160
Josiah	160
Lucy	159
Thomas	159
Jennings, Elizabeth Taylor (Booker)	63
Nancy	143
Robert	143, 160
Robert F.	63
Susanna ( )	143
Jennings Creek, Va.	134
Jester, Annie Lash	51
Jeter, Ambrose	22
John	22
Mary	19
Rodofil	22
Jett, John	176
Johns, Abraham	152
John A.	160
Joseph	154
Mary W. (Austin)	154
Patsy (Austin)	152
Patterson	160
Robert	159
Thomas	159
William	160
Johnson, Allen	22
Ann	160, 180
Bennet	22
Dennis	48
Elizabeth (Bodine)	183
George A.	180
Henry	180
J.	165
James	22
John	10, 159, 180
Jonathan	12, 68, 70-71
Lucy	180
Mariah	180
Philip	160
Richard	22, 183
Robert	22, 111
Sarah	180
Thomas	22
William	48
see also Jonson	
Johnston, Benjamin	84
Delinos	84
General	84
Isham	84
John	84
Peter	84
Samuel	84
Stephen	84
Thomas	84
William	84
Johnston, William C.	84
Joiner, Peter	159
William	159
Jolly, David	3-4
Henry	4, 22
John	3-4
Susanah	22
Jones, Agnes	22
Alexander	22
Angelina (Hatcher)	46
Ann	108
Archer	22
Charles	84, 166
David	46
David C.	22
Dorothy	142
Elizabeth ( )	180
Francis	22
George	22
Henry W.	22
Humphrey	16, 66
James	160
Jesse	84
John	22, 124
Julia R.	46
Littleberry H.	22
Mary (Rouzee)	180
Nelson	53
Nicholas	160
Peter	22
Richard	22, 108
Robert	22
Samuel	22
Susan E.	29-30
Susanah	22
Thomas	17, 84, 159, 180
Timandra E.	46
William	22, 159, 166
Rev. William D.	161
family	45
Jones Springs, W.Va.	35-36
Jonson, Rebeckah	110
see also Johnson	
Joplin, Mo.	95
Jopling, James	84
Jesse	84
John	84
Josiah	84
Thomas	84
Jordan, Mary	181
William	84
Jordey, ---	130
Journals of the Council of the State of Virginia	54, 57
Julian, W.Va.	78
Junction Store, Va.	133-34
Kanawha Co., W.Va.	78, 167, 184
Kanawha Dist., Braxton Co.	168
Kavanagh, Mary	55, 172
Kay, James	96
John	96
Mary (Pannill)	96

INDEX

Keey, Susanah	84	Knight, Augustine	160
Kegley, Frederick B.	131	John	160
Kegley's Virginia Frontier	131	William	160
Kelly, Kathrine ( )	10	Knorr, Catherine Lindsay (Smith)	
Patrick	10, 109	[Mrs. H. A.]	41-42
family	137	Knowles, Grace Fuller [Mrs.	
Kemp, Matthew 9, 12, 17, 69, 109		William Herbert]	146
Kendrick, Lucy (Austin)	152	Knox Co., Ohio	182
Thomas	152	Knox Co., Tenn.	153
Kennada, Jesse	160	Knutson, Mrs. Howard	180
John	160	Kue and Roberts	119
Kennedy, Susan	143	Kyle, Va.	134
Kennerly, Joseph	160		
The Kentucky Genealogist	146	Lackey, John	160
Kentucky Society D.A.R.	137	Lacy, Mary (Nettles)	180
Kenyon, family	142	John	23
Kernal, William	160	William	180
Kerr, ---	119	Lafayette Co., Miss.	60
John	22	Laffitte family	178
Mary (Graves)	103	Laforme's Store, W.Va.	169
William	84	Lagarde & Co.	123
Kersy, Edward	22	Laird family	96
Key, John	160	Lamb, James	87
Rice	160	Lambert, ---	86
William	84	Lancaster, Elizabeth	48
Keys family	137	Lancaster Co., S.C.	96
Kid, George	22	Lancaster Co., Va.	
Kidd, Daniel	70	12, 15, 57, 67, 124	
Elizabeth	69	Lancisco, Catherine	184
Frances	70	Landram, Thomas	160
James	84	Lane, Maj. Allen M.	86
John	70, 160	Garrett	160
Mary	70	Henry	160
Moses	8, 70	Joseph	160
Thomas	8, 70	William	160
William	70-71, 110, 115	Lanham, Benedict	125
Zachariah	84	John	125
Killand, Thomas	84	Joseph	125
Kimberlin Springs, Va.	77	Lanier, Sarah	92
Kimberling, Va.	77	Lankford, Charles	125
King, Allie	48	Lansdown, William	160
Archibald	160	Laporte, Bajien	38
George Harrison Sanford		Larke, John 13, 65, 69, 116	
40-41, 176		Larrance, Sarah	11
Jacob	84	Lashell, James	160
John	88	Lauger, Ethel	162
Majer	84	"Laurel Grove," Essex Co., Va.	
Zachariah	84	55-56, 62-63	
King and Queen Co., Va. 16-17		Lavender, Allen	125
63-64, 90, 101, 104-05, 166		Charles	125
King George Co., Va.		George	125
40, 96, 121, 142		Lavinder, Anthony	125
King William Co., Va.		John	160
10, 139, 163-64, 166		William	125
King William C.H., Va.	123	Lawhorn, George	160
King's Mountain	180	Henry	160
Kingston Parish, Mathews Co.	54	William	160
Kite, Elizabeth (Haestand)	139	Lawlen, Patrick	87
Henry	139	Lawless, Richard	160
Samuel	139	William	160
Kline, Catherine	139	Lawson, Phebe	112
Knawl, W.Va.	169	Robert	117
Knawl's Creek, W.Va.	169	William	113

Lay, Gideon		160	Leslie, Alexander	23
Laycock, Mercy		144	Lester, Riland	23
Layne, James		84	**Letters Home**	92
John		125	**Lewis, ---**	39
Thomas		84, 125	Capt. ---	123
William		84, 125	Anne	114
Lea, Ann (Carter)		102	Berry	165
Ann (Herndon)		99, 102-06	Catherine A.	94
Edmund		105	Charles A.	84
Elliot		105	Emily	144
Capt. Gabriel		105	Eusabious	114
Garnett		105	Harriet	144
George A.		99	James	94, 144
Hannah (Slade)		99	James F.	174
Henry		105	John	14-15, 88
Herndon		103		110, 114-15, 118
Isabella		99, 102-03	John A.	94
James		99-106	John Z.	118
John		102, 105-06	Joseph	183
John C.		99	Joshua	110
Lucy		103	Kitty Ann (Pendleton)	94
Rev. Luke		104	Louisa	144
Major		103-05	Margaret	144
Nancy		103-04	Mary	114, 144
Philadelphia		104	Mary Ann (Morris) Curd	183
Rebekka ( )		103	Mary (Hunt)	114
William		101-02, 105-06	Mary Jane	94
Zachariah		105-06	Nancy	144
see also Lee, Leigh			Nancy (Berry)	94
League, James		22	Nancy (Chiswell)	75
Leasburg, N.C.		105	Nicholas	118
Leath, Jesse		23	Robert	118, 144
Leatherbury, Jo.		116	Sarah	75-76, 144
Leatherwood Creek, Henry Co.		151	Susan Haden (Mason)	144
Ledemon, Peter		124	William	144
Ledgerwood, Agnes ( )		46	family	53
James		46	Lewis Co., W.Va.	167, 169
Mrs. W. L.		46	"Lewisville," Gloucester Co.	75
William		46	Lexington, Ky.	61
Lee, Charles		8, 86	Lexington, Va.	93
Dorothy ( )		8	Lexington Parish, Amherst Co.	155
Frank		160	Liberty (schooner)	118
James		160	Library of Congress	44
Richard		125	Lick Run, Va.	134
Richard Henry		119	Lick Run Bridge, Va.	133-34
Robert E.		50	Lightfoot, Armistead	118
Thomas		109	Mary	141
see also Lea, Leigh			Lightsville, W.Va.	36
Lee Co., Va.		94, 143	Ligon, Richard	22
Leeke, Staffordshire, Eng.		67	Thomas	23, 27
Leesburg, Va.		139	William	23
Leet, Daniel		3	Lillard, Mordica	125
Leftwich, Miss ---		104	Lilley, William	125
Legin, Frances		125	Linch, John	87
Leigh, Elizabeth		143	Lincoln, Edmands & Co.	161
Ferdinand		160	Lincoln Co., W.Va.	78
Richard		166	Lincoln Twp., Braxton Co.	168
Zachariah G.		22	Lindsay, Joyce H. [Mrs. James	
see also Lea, Lee			R.]	42
Lemley, Marie Perrin		142	Linis, William	119
Lemoin, Peter		125	Link, John Nicholas	141
Lennard, John		88	Margaret (Pence)	141
Leonirgan, John		160	Linley, Luke	37

INDEX

Linsley, Mrs. John C. W.	141	Lovern, Moses	22
Linton, William	12	Loving, George	84
Liske, John	4	James	84, 125
Lisle, John	96	John	84, 125
Turner	96	Joseph	125
Lister, Cornelius	183	Lunsford	125
Rachel	183	William	84, 125
Sarah ( )	183	Low, Benjamin	125
Lithia, Va.	134	Samuel	13
Litle, Harmon	23	Lowe, ---	123
Little Birch, W.Va.	169	Lower, Andrew	124
Little Georgetown, W.Va.	35-36	Henry	124
Little Kanawha River	167	Lowry, Margaret	51
Little Otter, W.Va.	169	Loyal, Paul	119
Little River	149	Lundy, Angelina	95
Liveley, James	160	Ethelred H.	179
Lively, Mark	160	Joshua C.	179
Polly H.	29	Polly (Tyus)	179
Liverpool, England	67-68, 119	Sarah (Turner)	179
Livingston, John	12	Lunenburg Co., Va.	
Lloyd, Absalom	143		119, 140, 147, 181
Elizabeth (Wells)	143	Lunenburg C.H., Va.	121
Mary Ann Luck (Wilson)	143	Lunsford, George	125
Lloydsville, W.Va.	169	John	125
Lobben, James	125	William	125
John	125	Lusk, Robert	160
Lobbin, William	125	Lyall, Ralph	114
"Local Notices from the Virginia		William	114
Gazette, 1780"	37-39	see also Lyell	
85-88, 117-24, 163-66		Lybook, Henry	165
Lockard, Philip	160	Lyell family	62
William	160	see also Lyall	
Locke, Jean (Walker)	67	Lyle, James	121
Martha (Vaughan)	142	Joseph	125
Locket, Jacob	23	Lyle and Banks	119
James	22	Lyleel, John	95
John	22	Sophia ( )	96
Josiah	23	Lyman, John	42
Lockey, Judith	144	Lymus, Nanny	165
Lockhart, Henry	44	Lynch, Mrs. John R.	182
Locust Bottom, Va.	133-34	Lyne, John	166
Locust Bottom Church, Botetourt		Lyon, John	125
Co., Va.	132	Peter	125
Loftin, Augustin	139	William	125
Mary M. C. (Grigg)	139-40		
Robert	66	Mabury, Elizabeth	140
Logan Co., Ill.	48	McAfee, Ethel Lauger	162
Logan Co., W.Va.	78	Georgia	161-62
London, James	160	Martha A.E.M.J.S. (Edmunds)	
John	160		161
Larkin	160	Sally	161-62
Lavender	84	family	96
London, England	66-67, 71	McAlester, Patrick	126
Long, Catherine E.	45	McAlexander, Alexander	125
William	160	David	125
Long Mountain, Bedford Co.	120	James	125
Lorton, Thomas	118	John	125
Loudoun Co., Va. 33, 45, 50, 179		McBride, Elizabeth (Lancaster)48	
Louisa Co., Va.44, 135, 163, 182		John	4, 48
Lourey, Jean	47	Martha	48
Love, Hannah [Honor]	147	Robert	48
John	176	Warren	48
Lovern, James	22	McCan, John	23

McCarter, John	81	McFarland, Mrs. Lindley J.	47
MacCarthy, Darby MacOwen	31	McGee, Leonard R.	180
Dermod MacOwen	31	Thomas	180
McCarthy, Samuel Trant	31	McGehee, Samuel	125
"MacCarthy-McCarthy-McCarty		McGinnis, Hiram	160
Notes"	31—32	Machen, Thomas 68-71,	107
The MacCarthys of Munster	31	McHendry, Joseph	3
McCarty, Andrew	32	McHenry, Joseph	5
Andrew Hervey	32	McIlwaine, H. R. 54, 57-58,	61
Benjamin	79	McIntosh, Col. John	119
Daniel	118	Gen. Lachlan	3
Darby	31	William 68,	116
David Franklin	32	McIntyer, John	4
Elizabeth L.	32	McKenny, Rev. ---	66
Hannah (Richardson)	31	McKinley, John	176
James	79	McKinly, William	5
James Reeves	32	McKinney, Mary	46
Jane Moriah	32	family	96
John Leroy	32	McLain, John	160
Minerva Cowan	32	McLaughlin, Barnet	142
Nancy Caroline	32	Charles	142
Richard	176	Sarah	142
Ruth ( )	32	Sarah (Terry)	142
Ruth Lovenah	32	McLeod, Mrs. R. B.	184
Sarah Susannah	32	McMeekin, James	4
William	79	McMetchen, William	4
William Wriley	32	McMinn Co., Tenn.	149
"McCarty Bible Records"	31	McMullon, Hannah	139
McCawn, Francis	124	McMurray, Samuel	160
James	124	McNairy Co., Tenn.	149
John	124	McNeil, Hector	23
Machen, Thomas 68-71,	107	McNight, John	126
McClain, Henry	125	William	126
James	126	McNulty, Catherine (Kline)	139
McClarren, John	23	Evelyn (Orr)	139
McClenachan, Col. Alexander	57	James	139
McCloud, Angus	160	John	139
McClue, Charles	126	Michael	139
McClure, John	126	Samuel	139
Robert	5	MacQueen, Mrs. Peter	182
McColloch, Am.	4	McRory, Lt.Col. George W.	93
George	4-5	James Henry	93
James	5	McVea, Christopher	23
John	5	McWane, Lewis	126
Samuel	5	McWilliams, William	3
see also McCulluck		Maddera, John	23
McConnell, Hugh	3	Madding, Rachel ( )	142
James	3-4	Thomas	142
John	4	Madison, W.Va. 78,	167
McConnico, Christopher 118,	123	Madison Co., Ala.	180
McCord, William	126	Madison Co., Ky.	144
McCoy, Daniel	126	Madison Co., Va.	89
Henry	105	Madison Mill, King and Queen	
McCracken, George E.	50	Co., Va.	101
McCulluck, Samuel	126	Madison's ordinary, Caroline	
see also McColloch		Co., Va.	122
McDonald, Archibald	125	Magann, John	160
Daniel	126	Joseph	160
Joseph	124	Magruder, Sarah	93
William	126	Main, Daniel	4
family	137	Philip	4
McDowel, Alexander	4	Majah, John	160
McDowell, Annie B.	132	Lucy	160

INDEX 215

Major, Anna (Ballard)	104	Martin, Isaac		3
Elizabeth (Mason)	104	James	125-26,	160
John	104	John T.		126
William	104	Joseph		126
Malden, W.Va.	184	Joshua Lanier		92
Mamson, Thomas	4	Martha (Bailey)		92
Manchester, Va.	39, 85	Moses		125
	117-19, 121, 164-65	Obadiah		160
Mann, Abel	23	Peter	126,	160
Abner	23	Pleasant		126
Cain	23	Rawley		48
Field	23	Rebecca		126
Joel	23	Reubin		125
Mary	23	Sherod		126
William	23, 27	Thomas		107
Manning, Ashley	94	Warner		92
Michael	94	William	23, 86, 95,	126
Mrs. Minnie	95	Martinsburg, W.Va.	33, 35-36	
Mansfield, William	73, 109	Mary (ship)		67
Marblehead, Mass.	170	Mason, Col. David		163
Mare, Alexander	125	Elizabeth		104
Marion, Gen. Francis	46	John	39,	144
Marion Co., Texas	137-38	Col. Lemuel		104
Markham, Bernard	117-19	Richard		39
Samuel	116	Polly Cary	52,	54
Marks, James	122	Susan Haden		144
Marr, Andrew	38	Massey, Thomas		126
John	160	Massie, John		125
"Marrable's," Dinwiddie Co.	121	Masters, Edward		125
Marriage Bonds and Ministers'		John		125
Returns of Surry County	41	Mastersin, ---		165
Marriage Bonds of Botetourt		Mathew, Mrs. ---		12
County	132	Mathews, James		126
Marriages of Amelia County	135	John	125-26	
Marriages of Henrico County	42	William	84, 125-26	
Marriages of Orange County	41	William P.		86
Marsden, ---	118	see also Matthews		
Marshall, Abraham	23	Mathews Co., Va.		54
Ferenia (Durrett)	29	Mattaponi River		101
John	23, 143, 182	Matthews, Robert		120
Mary (Parker)	140	William		166
Preston Holmes	140	see also Mathews		
Robert	23	Maupin, Daniel		144
Thomas	29	Margaret		144
William	23	Maury, James		119
William A.	140	Walker		87
Marston, Benskin	171	Maury Co., Tenn.		79
Elizabeth (Soane)	171	Mawbry, ---		39
John	116	Maxy, David		23
Martha McCraw Chapter, D.A.R.	137	May, William		4
Martiau, Mary	96	Maybee, Mary		148
Nicholas	96	William		148
Martin, ---	39	Mayes, Garner		23
Col. ---	39	see also Mays		
Abraham	160	Maynard, John	66-67	
Azariah	126	Mayo, John	9,	12
Bostin	124	Ruth ( )		9
Charles	126	Mays, Charles		125
Elizabeth	45	James	126,	160
George	126	Jesse		125
Gideon	126	John	126,	160
Henry	125-26	Joseph	125,	160
Hudson	126	Lewis		125

Mays, Richard	160
Robert	125, 160
William	160
see also Mayes	
Maysey, Mary	143
Meacham, James	66, 69, 107
John	109
Mead, David	23
Everard	23
Meade, Richard K.	175
William	170
Meadors, Ambrose C.	23
Anderson	23
Benjamin	23
Hezekiah	23
Isaac	23
Meadow Bridges, Hanover Co.	87-88, 163
Mechanicsburg, Va.	77
Mechanicsburg Dist., Bland Co.	77
Mecklenburg Co., N.C.	93
Mecklenburg Co., Va.	38-39, 87, 123, 140, 164
Mecklenburg C.H., Va.	37, 86, 122
Meek, Isaac	5
Megginson, Joseph C.	160
Meglason, James	23
Thomas W.	23
William	23
Meherrin River	119
Melton, John	126
Memphis, Tenn.	173
Mercer, Abraham	4
Hugh	76
Louisa (Griffin)	76
Meriweathers, William	23
Meriwether's Warehouse	37
Merritt, Thomas	160
Merry, John	71
Metcalf, Allen	5
Michall, Samuel	4
see also Mitchell	
Mickleburrough, Ed.	10, 69, 113
Middle Mountain, Va.	134
Middle Town, W.Va.	35
Middlebrook, N.J.	57-58, 61
Middleport, W.Va.	169
Middlesex Co., N.J.	183
Middlesex Co., Va.	7-17, 47-48, 65-74, 107-16, 181
"Middlesex County, Virginia, Wills, 1713-1734"	7-17, 65-74, 107-16
Middleton, Alexander	15
Mrs. Warren	184
Miles, John	160
Militia uniforms	174
Mill Creek, W.Va.	35-36
Mill Creek Church, Berkeley Co. W.Va.	35
Mill Creek Twp., Berkeley Co.	35
Mill Neck, Middlesex Co.	70
Miller, Dabny	23
Miller, Elizabeth ( )	116
John	110
Joseph	5
Martha Porter	136
Mary	57
Mary (Durrett)	30
Patrick	116
Simon	126
William	30
Miller's Tavern, Essex Co.	55
Millhier, Alexander	5
Mills, Henry	23
John	4
Levi	4-5
Priscilla	180
Milo, Mo.	46
Milroy, W.Va.	169
Milstead, Jane	139
Joseph	160
The Miner's Ten Commandments	92
Minitree, William	118
Minor, Maj. John	165
Mississippi Cemetery and Bible Records	29
Mississippi Genealogical Society	29
Mitchel, James	5
Mitchell, Archerles	160
Bolling	160
Elizabeth	141
Henry	141
James C.	23
John	4, 23, 141
Nancy	141
Pleasant	141
Polly	141
Rebecca (Coleman)	141
Robert	141
William	61
family	96
see also Michall	
Mitchell, W.Va.	78
Mitthall, James	5
Moalson, Richard	114
see also Moulson	
Mohler family	45
Moler, Adam	182
Anna	182
Charles	182
Elizabeth	182
Ellen	182
Henry	182
Jacob	182
Jane (Rion)	182
John Darby	182
Lydia Barnett	182
Nellie	182
Mollie, Va.	133-34
Monroe, Nelson	126
Monroe Co., W.Va.	131, 134, 141
Montague, Thomas	11, 71, 110
William	16-17, 68, 109
Montgomery, James	80, 126

INDEX 217

Montgomery, John Scott	126
Montgomery Co., Ky.	137
Montgomery Co., Tenn.	57
Montgomery Co., Va.	96, 131, 137, 148-50, 165
Moody, Betsy ( )	182
Catherine (Baker)	182
David	182
Capt. Edward	164
Henry	182
James	182
John M.	182
Marshall	182
Philip	85
Rebecca	182
William H.	182
Moor, Edward	23
Moore, Caroline T. [Mrs. H. A.]	136
Cecil	139
Daniel	52
Elizabeth	139
Frances	60, 139
Gilbert	139
Isabel	139
J. Staunton	170-71
John	139, 160
John Lean	139
Lettisha	126
Matthew	139
Thomas	139
Zachariah	139
see also Moor, More	
Moorhead, Joseph	5
see also Morehead	
Moorman, Elizabeth	60
Moran, Elijah	125
John	125
Nicholas	125
More, Carter	23
see also Moor, Moore	
Morehead, John Motley	103
Karenhappuck	47
see also Moorhead	
The Morehead Family	103
Moreland, Andrew	126
Morgan, Daniel	143
Elizabeth	112
Morgan Co., W.Va.	33, 35-36
Morgin, John	23
Martha	23
Simon	23
William	23
Morley, W.Va.	169
Morrill cemetery, Carroll Co., Va.	98
Morris, Conrad	126
Isaac	23
John	23, 126
Mark	143
Mary Ann	182
Moses	23
Philip	141
Morris, Silvanus	23
Tabitha	23
Walter	23
William	23, 39, 183
Zachariah	23
see also Morriss	
Morrison, Finley	176
James	125
Robert	126
Thomas	126
William	125
Morriss, George	160
Thomas	160
see also Morris	
Morristown, N.J.	58
Morton, Aincy	153
Edmund	23
Joseph	147
Mosbey, John	125
William H.	125
Mosby, Daniel	126
Moseley, John	11, 15
Marvell	15, 70-71
see also Moslay, Mosley, Mossley	
Moses, Samuel	126
Moslay, John	70
Mosley, John	66
see also Moseley, Moslay, Mossley	
Moss, John	86
Mossley, John	74
Marvel	109
see also Moseley, Moslay, Mosley	
Mossom, David	170-171
Elizabeth ( )	171
Elizabeth (Soane) Marston	171
Mary ( ) Claiborne	171
Thomas	170
Mother Earth, Land Grants in Virginia, 1607-1699	91
Motley, Elsie	181
Mottley, John	23, 27
Joseph	23
Moulson, Richard	68, 113
William	113
see also Moalson	
"Mount Pleasant," King George Co., Va.	121
"Mount Pleasant," Powhatan Co.	87
Mount Sidney, Va.	141
Mt. Zion Church, Berkeley Co.	35
Mounts, Providence	5
Mountain Home, Va.	133
Mountain Union, Va.	134
Mouth of Cow Pasture, Va.	134
Mouth Short Creek, W.Va.	78-79
Mowrey, Christiana ( )	141
Lewis	141
Moxley, Daniel	141
Mary (Spurling)	141
Nathaniel	141

Moxley, William	141	Nelson Co., Va.	48, 89
Mud River, W.Va.	79	Nemon, Cutlip	126
Muhlenburg, Gen. Peter		Nesmith, Alex	30
	121-22, 165	Nettles, Mary	180
Mulberry Island, Warwick Co.	50	Nevil, James	126
Mummey, John	121	Lewis	126
Munford, Mary	23	Zachariah	126
Robert	123	Nevils, Levy	23
Munford, Va.	134	Nevitt, James	4
Murphey, James	126	Nevius, America (Edmunds)	
Murray, William	23, 61	Daingerfield	162
see also Murry		H. V. D.	162
Murrel, Cornelius	126	New, Anthony	61
John	126	New Bridges, Hanover Co.	38
Murrell, Emily (Lewis)	144	New Castle, Va.	37
Jesse	126	New Castle, Botetourt Co.	134
Murrough, Lewis	124	New England Historical and	
Murry, David	10	Genealogical Register	
James	10		170-71
see also Murray		New Hanover County Court	
Muscrove, Joseph	182	Minutes, Part 3	90
Miranda (Pancoast)	182	New Kent Co., Va.	39, 86, 101
Muse, William	160		103-04, 141, 147
Muter, George	38, 85, 124		165, 170-71, 181-82
Myres, John	4	New London, Va.	120
William	4	New Market, Amherst Co.	80
		New Market, Shenandoah Co.	62
Nace, Va.	134	New River	148-50
Nail, John	175	New River Plantation, Grayson	
Nall, Andrew	94	Co., Va.	150
Docia (Berry)	94	New Windsor, N.Y.	61
George	94	New York Weekly Herald	76
Larkin	94	Newburyport, Mass.	170
Matilda (Berry)	94	Newby, Jesse	23
Nalle, Martin	93	Newman, John	23, 126
Mary (Alden)	93	Loftin	166
Nansemond Co., Va.	141	Rebecca (Evans) Patram	
Napier, John	95	Featherstone	181
Patrick	117	Rice	23
Thomas	38	Samuel	181
Nash, Thomas	126	Walter	181
Nash Dist., Caswell Co., N.C.	151	Newsom, David	146
Nation, Mrs. S. J.	95	Newsom News	146
National Archives	58, 61	Newtam, Mathias	176
National Genealogical Society		Newton, Frances	92
Quarterly	98, 146	Thomas	85, 119
Naylors Hole, Va.	62	Newtown, Princess Anne Co.	87
Neal, Thomas	102	Newville, W.Va.	168-69
see also Neel, Neil		Nichol, James	161
Neel, Eurie Pearl Wilford [Mrs.		Martha A.E.M.J.S. (Edmunds)	
Courtland Moore]	43-44	McAfee	161
"Nehocknay," Essex Co.	111	Martha Eliza	161
Neice, Jacob	126	Nicholas, Robert C.	38
Neil, Archer	23	Nicholas Co., W.Va.	130, 167
John	23	Nichols, ---	47
see also Neal, Neel		Nickers, James	175
Nelley, Aaron	126	Nimmo, Robert	126
Bennett	126	William	126
Nelson, Maj. J.	166	9th Virginia Cavalry, C.S.A.	
Lucy S.	95		63-64
Thomas	58, 67	Nisbitt, Will	116
Nelson, W.Va.	79	Nivins, Samuel	165
Nelson Co., Ky.	183	Nixon, Henry	71, 109

INDEX

Noble, Austin	23
John	23
Joseph	23
Joshua	23
Stephen	23
Nolen, Mrs. C. B.	184
Norborne Parish, Berkeley Co.	34
Norcutt, William	8
Norfolk, Va.	76, 85
Norfolk Co., Va.	48, 140, 163
Norman, Elizabeth	68-69
Jane ( )	69
Moses	74
Robert	68—69
Thomas	68-69, 74
Normansell, Edward	98
Norris, J. E.	33
North, ---	119
North Mountain, W.Va.	36
North Mountain Depot, W.Va.	35
Northampton Co., Va.	36, 139
Northampton C.H., Va.	39
Northern Neck	89
Northumberland Co., Va.	58, 118, 120, 122, 146
Norton, John Hatley	117, 119
Louellen	184
Norwood, Joseph A.	173
Lettice (Royster)	173
Samuel	124
Noted Southern Families	100
Nourse, James	79
Nugent, Nell Marion	91
Nully, Joseph	4
Nutall, Ann	60
Oak Hill, N.C.	59
Oakton, W.Va.	36
Oakwood Cemetery, Jefferson, Texas	138
Oakwood Cemetery, Richmond, Va.	146
Oast, James	175
O'Banion, Brian	79
Obenshain, Va.	133-34
Ober, James	123
Odom, Elizabeth Anne	141
O'Donnell, Mrs. James E.	139
O'Driscoll family	31
Official Letters of the Governors	58
Offutt, Nathaniel	126
Ogdin, Ignatius	4
Ogilby, Richard	24
Oglesby, Jesse	126
Peter	126
Ohio Co., W.Va.	3-6, 50, 93
"Ohio County Legislative Petitions"	3-6
Ohio Records and Pioneer Families	44
Ohio River	3-4
Old, Winney	24
Old Churches, Ministers and Families	170
Old Hickory, Va.	154
Old Homes and Families of Nottoway	146
Old Town Twp., Grayson Co.	150
Oliver, Elizabeth	154
Oneal, Cathrine	113
Opequon Creek	33
Opequon Twp., Berkeley Co.	35
Orange, N.Y.	37
Orange, W.Va.	79
Orange Co., N.C.	102, 104-06
Orange Co., Va.	41, 45, 87, 93-95, 166
Oriskany, Va.	134
Orr, Evelyn	139
Orrill, Lawrence	110, 115
Osborne, Abner	24
Mrs. C. D.	142
Christopher	93
John	24
Jonathan	93
Joseph	24
Sarah (Magruder)	93
Osborne's warehouse	37, 86, 119
Otken, Frances Powell	99-100
Otter Dist., Braxton Co.	168
Ould Newbury	170
Our Webb Kin of Dixie	60
Overbee, Jeremiah	39
Overstreet, Benoni	24
Overton, Mary	24
Moses	23
Richard	24
Owen, Anne	65
Augustine	13, 65, 68
Christopher	65
Clemonds	65
Constant	65
Elizabeth (Webb)	59
Isabella (Allin)	59
Jacob	65
James	65
John	65, 107-08
Mary	65
Mary ( )	107
Patrick	107
Ruth	12
Ruth ( )	107-08
Sarah	65
Thomas	59
William	12, 15, 65, 68, 107-08, 110, 116
Owens, David	126
John	126
Levy	126
Mary	126
Owin, Augt.	108
Christopher	108
John	9
William	9
Oxford, Thomas	176

Pace, Benjamin		113	Patrick, John	127
Page, Dillard		127	Patterson, Alexander	127
Edmund		127	Angelina	142
Francis	24,	127	Charles	126
Gabriel		126	David	127
Linsey		127	Deborah (Givens)	144
Lucy Landon		63	Elizabeth	127, 142
Page Co., Va.		89	Frances	142
Pain, Frances ( )		102	James	142, 144
John		102	John	142
William		12	Joseph	142
Painter, John		127	Mary A. (Snider)	142
Pamplin, James		127	Penelope	142
Leroy		127	Thomas	142
Robert		127	Virginia	142
William		127	William	142
Pamunkey River	37,	117	Patton, Thomas	126
Pancoast, Angelina		182	Pattonsburg, Va.	133-34
Charity (Gray)		182	Paulett, Thomas	24
Jacob Manuel		182	Paull, Jacob	5
John L.		182	Payne, Mrs. ---	67
Lydia Barnett (Moler)		182	Mrs. A. K.	138
Miranda		182	Benjamin	127
William Harding		182	Lucille	182
family		45	Peachy, Thomas Griffin	124
Panel, Luke		127	Pearc, William	5
see also Pannel, Pannill			Pechtall, Henry	4
Pankey, John		163	Pedee River	166
Pannel, Benjamin		127	Peed, James	96
see also Panel, Pannill			Pemberton, Bennet	175
Pannill, Mary		96	Mary	181
Parish, Samuel		126	Pence, Margaret	141
see also Parrish			Rebecca	141
Parish Lines, Diocese of Southwestern Virginia		89	Pendleton, Edmund	85
			John	166
Park, Mrs. ---		119	Kitty Ann	94
Catherine ( )		86	Micajah	127
Edward		86	Pendleton, S.C.	178
Parker, Catharine		183	Pendleton Co., W.Va.	142
George		162	Penn, Thomas	126
Marguerite (Edmunds)		162	Wilson	126
Mary		140	Pentecost, Dorsey	3
Richard		183	Peoria, Ill.	162
Parr, Henry		4	Perin, Isaac	24
Nathan		4	Perkins, Samuel	127
Parrish, James P.		126	Perkins Mills, W.Va.	168-69
Mrs. Marie		30	Perkinson, Archer	24
see also Parish			Claiborne	24
Parrock, David		127	Elizabeth	24
John		127	Isham	24
Parrott, Richard		109	John	24
Parsons, Major		24	Thomas	24, 27
Polly (Blanks)		93	Perrett, Robert	8
Parton, William		24	Perrin, William Henry	43
Pasley, Hugh		127	Perrott, Catherine	16-17
John		127	Catharine ( )	8
Patillo, Ann (Webb)		60	S. F.	46
Rev. Henry		60	Timandra E. (Jones)	46
John Franklin		60	Person Co., N.C.	
Mary (Anderson)		60	56, 59-60, 95, 104, 173-74	
Patram, Anthony		181	Petaluma, Calif.	139
Francis		181	Peters, Elisha	126
Rebecca (Evans)		181	James	127

INDEX

Peters, Zachariah 126
Petersburg, Va. 38, 86, 88, 118, 123, 141, 163, 165-66
Peterson, Joseph 103
  Lucy (Lea) 103
  Martha K. 95
  Robert Karl 36
  Temperance 95
Petsworth Parish, Gloucester Co., Va. 51-54, 56
Petty, Rebecca 93
  Thomas 93
Peyton, Catey (Bronaugh) 146
  Cuthbert H. 146
  Henry 85
  Thomas 163
Peytona, W.Va. 78-79
Peytona Dist., Boone Co. 78
Phelps, John 39
Philadelphia, Pa. 31, 58, 75-76, 87, 147
Philips, --- 123
Phillips, Emanuel 127
  George 127
  John 126
  Johnston 127
  Joseph 127
  Leonard 127
  Lucy 24
  Nancy 127
  Thomas 101
  Zachariah 126-27
Pierce, Miss --- 46
  Capt. --- 61
  Joseph 88
Pierce and Wilson 119
Pigg, George 127
  Hezekiah 121
Pigg Run, Henry Co. 123
Pilkinton, William 24
Pine Dale, Va. 134
Pinkston family 146
Pitchford, John 24
Pitt, William 38
Pittsylvania Co., Va. 47-48, 93, 121-22, 140, 142-43, 147-48, 151-54, 165, 181
Pleasants, John 87
  Thomas 120
Plough, Henry 127
  Phillip 127
Pluckemin, N.J. 61
Plume, William 119
Pocahontas Co., W.Va. 131
Pocahuntus, Va. 117
Poe, Sarah 99
Poindexter, James W. 184
Point Mountain, Braxton Co. 167
Point Pleasant, Va. 77, 180
Pointer, William 37, 86
Pollard, Ambrose 24
Pollard, Elizabeth 47
  George 24
  Joe 24
  John 24
  Leah 24
  Richard C. 127
  Thomas 24
  Zachariah 24
Pomfret, Amy 60
Ponten, Joel 126
Ponton, Francis 24
  John 24
  William 126
Pope, Burrell 79
  Priscilla (Wooten) 79
  Tabitha 79
Poropotank River 53
Poropotank Warehouse 54
Port Royal, Va. 88, 121
Portobacco Swamp, Essex Co. 51
Portsmouth, Va. 85-86, 124
Poston, Mrs. Elenor E. 95
Potomac River 33, 47, 86, 121, 164, 166
Potomac Run, Stafford Co. 86
Potter's Creek, Pittsylvania Co., Va. 122, 165
Potts, Philip 11
Pound, Va. 150
Powel, Benjamin 126
  Seymore 126
Powell, Abraham 24
  Esther Weygandt 44-45
  Lucus 127
  Mary 127
  Thomas 88
  Mary (Tapley) 180
  Nathaniel 127
  Richard 24
  Robert 24
  William 24, 180
  Winney 24
Powhatan Co., Va. 18, 87, 163
Pratt, John Lee and Lillian Thomas, Foundation 40
  Thomas 127
Prayton, Archibald 124
  Jonathan 124
Preston Co., W.Va. 180
Prewitt, Mrs. L. D. 93
  see also Pruit
Price, James 16
  Jane 16
  John 9, 16-17, 66, 176
  Prentiss 31, 79
  Randolph 120
  Robert 16
  Samuel 16
  T. 66
  Thomas 16-17
  William 16

Pride, Elizabeth	24
Francis	24, 27
John	24, 27
Thomas	24
Priller & Cary	163
Prince, Francis	128
Prince Edward Co., Va. 46, 94, 117-18,	183
Prince Edward C.H., Va.	121
Prince William Co., Va. 93, 146,	184
Princess Amelia (ship)	67
Princess Anne Co., Va. 87,	138
Proffett, David	127
Jesse	127
John	127
Randolph	127
Progress, W.Va.	169
Pruit, Ann	151
Daniel	151
Lucy	151
Welthy	151
see also Prewitt	
Puckett, Samuel	126
Pugh, Frederick	127
James	127
John	127
Thomas	127
Pulliam, Elizabeth	60
Elizabeth (Wilson)	60
John	60
Purcell, Valentine Vernon	50
see also Pursell	
Purcellville, Va.	50
Purckett, Jacob	126
Purefoy, family	51
Pursell, Thomas	50
see also Purcell	
Purvis, Charles	126
George	127
William	127
"Putney," New Kent Co.	37
Qualls, Angeline (Austin)	149
Henry	149
Quarles, Isaac	24
Nathaniel	164
Queen Anne's Chapel, Marblehead, Mass.	170
Rachell (brigantine)	117
Racine, W.Va.	79
Raiborne, George	24
Raine, Elizabeth	57
Raines, Richard	95
Theodosia	95
Rains, Presley	127
Rakestraw, Robert	120
Ramapo, N.J.	58
Ramsey, James	127
William	87
Randolph, Ann (Edwards)	144
Eliza Kennon	161
Randolph, Elizabeth (Eppes)	144
Henry	144
Jane Winifred	183
Judith (Lockey)	144
Judith (Soane)	144
Sarah (Swann)	144
Thomas	25
Thomas M.	119, 164
William	144
Randolph Co., W.Va.	167
Rankin, Rev. Jesse	59
Rappahannock Co., Va.	89
Rappahannock River 89, 121,	124
Ratcliffe, Dr. C. S.	162
Georgia (McAfee)	162
Read, Nat.	165
Thomas	11
Reade, Ann ( )	48
Charles	48
Elizabeth	48
Elizabeth ( )	48
Elizabeth (Tomkies)	48
Dr. John	48
Thomas	74
Ready, Isham	127
Rebecca Furnace, Va.	133-34
<u>Records</u> <u>of</u> <u>Gloucester</u> <u>Co.</u>, <u>Va.</u>	52
<u>Redd, John</u>	123
Reddy, Ann Waller	42
Reed, Alexander	127
Jonathan	127
Reese, Isham	141
Susannah (Coleman)	141
Reeves, Anne	150
George	150
Henry	163
Jane (Burton)	150
William	150
<u>Register</u> <u>of</u> <u>Saint</u> <u>Paul's</u> <u>Parish</u>	40
Reichlein, Mrs. David	144, 179
Reid, Andrew	124
Henry	127
Samuel	127
Reins, John	176
William	24
Renown (ship)	119, 123
Repass, Va.	77
Repeto, James	127
Peter	127
"Research in the West Virginia Collection"	98
"The Reverend David Mossom of Massachusetts and Virginia"	170-71
Revercomb, Jacob	50
Reves, Robert	127
Revley, ---	39
Revolutionary war deserters	37
Reynolds, Archer L.	184
Ella O.	184
Frances	184
Isaac O.	184

INDEX

Reynolds, James Washington 183
  Lucy R. S. (Bell) 184
  Martha 184
  Nancy (Cooper) 183
  Obediah F. 184
  Robert W. 184
  Sarah Elizabeth 184
  Victoria 184
  William H. 184
Rhea, Archibald 127
Rhine, see Rion
Rhoads, John 16
  William 110
  see also Rhodes, Roads, Rodes
Rhodes, Elizabeth (Baker) 93
  John 109, 111
  Randolph 15
  see also Rhoads, Roads, Rodes
Rice, Jacob 15
Richard and Coleman 119
Richardson, Caroline 62-63
  Elizabeth (Coleman) 63
  Hannah 31
  Thomas 63
  Turner 119
Richeson, Col..Holt 58, 122
Richmond, Va. 5, 37-39
  41, 43, 48, 60, 85-88
  117-19, 121-24, 138, 141
  146, 163-66, 170, 182
Richmond Co., Ga. 95
Richmond Co., Va. 42, 58, 62, 142
Ridd, John 8
Ridgway, John 112
Riffe, Andrew Lewis 42
Riggs, Benjamin 47
Rio Mills, Va. 134
Rion, Jane 182
Rion Hall, W.Va. 182
Risin, Elery 24
  Richard 24
Rison, John 24
Ritchson, Edward 4
Rivers, Elizabeth (Vaughan) 142
Roach, Elizabeth 25
  John 24
  Joseph 25
  William 166
Roads, John 11
Roane, Spencer 60
  William 58
Roane Co., W.Va. 131
Roanoke, Va. 47
Roanoke Co., Va. 131-34
Roanoke Red Sulphur Springs, Va. 133
Roanoke River 87, 123
Roaring Run, Va. 133-34
Roberts, --- 119
  Alexander 24, 127
  Henry 127
  Jacob 24
  John 24, 127

Roberts, Joseph 127
  Pleasant 25
  Zachariah 127
Robertson, Archibald 88
  Bridge 24
  Christopher 119
  Elizabeth 24
  George 24
  James 24, 165
  John 24
  John A. 25
  Leroy 127
  Levy 127
  Nathan 24
  Peter 25
  William 24, 120
Robertson Co., Tenn. 57
Robins, Joseph 116
Robinson, --- 66
  Benjamin 68
  Christopher 12-13, 74, 111, 116
  Henry 12
  John 8-10, 12, 68, 74
  W. Stitt 91
  William 15
Robinson River 165
Rock Camp, W.Va. 169
Rockbridge Co., Va. 96, 124, 131
  134, 143, 146, 164, 180
Rockett's landing, Richmond 86
Rockingham Co., N.C. 151, 153
Rockingham Co., Va.
  90, 139-40, 143, 184
Rocky Gap, Va. 77
Rocky Gap Dist., Bland Co. 77
Rocky Point, Va. 134
Rocky Point Mills, Va. 134
Rocky River Presbyterian Church 93
Roddey, Samuel 120
Rodes, Charles 127
  David 127
  see also Rhoads, Rhodes, Roads
Roe, Mary 171
Rogers, William 24
Roller, Carrie (Booker) 63
  Rev. Robert Douglas 63
Ronald, --- 124
  William 163
Roper, Jesse 117
Rose, Charles 127
  Jacob 4
  John 127
  Margaret 127
  Patrick 127
  William 37
Ross, Andrew Jackson 179
  Betsey 180
  David 119, 123
  John 3
  Lyle Elizabeth (Tudor) 179
Ross, Shore & Co. 119, 123

Rossert, Henry	127
Rouzee, Mary	180
Rowan, Mrs. M. B.	47
Rowan Co., N.C.	90, 148
Rowe, Benjamin	9
John	11
Ruth	9
Rowland, Elizabeth	96
John	166
Zachariah	119
Rowlet, George	24
Thomas	24
William	166
Royall, John	24
Joseph	24, 27
Royster, Banister	173
Elizabeth H. (Shapard)	173
Emily	173
Frances Y. (Webb)	173
Francis	56, 172-73
Lettice	173
Marcus D.	173
Martha	173
Mary B.	173
Robert	173
Stella	173
Wiley	173
William	173
Rubincam, Milton	50
Rubsamen, Jacob	118
Rucker, ---	155
Brice	24
John	127
Joshua	24
Lemuel	24
Pleasant	24
Reuben	24
Rudicil, Jacob	127
Rudd, A. Böhmer	43
Margaret	95
Runyon, Isaac	96
Robert	96
Russel, C.	37
Russell, Daniel	67
Rutherford Co., N.C.	141
Rutherford Co., Tenn.	154
Ryan, Edmund	13
see also Rion, Ryon	
Ryburn family	137
Rynes, Samuel	119
Ryon, Charles	127
Phillip	127
William	127
see also Rion, Ryan	
Sadler, Anna	25
James	25
John	109, 112
Robert	25
Samuel	25
St. Eustatia	38-39, 119-20, 123, 163
St. George's Parish, Harford Co., Md.	36
St. George's Parish, Spotsylvania Co., Va.	102
St. John's, Newfoundland	75
St. John's College, Cambridge	170
St. Lawrence Dist., Caswell Co., N.C.	106
St. Martin's Parish, Hanover Co., Va.	89
St. Michael's Church, Marblehead, Mass.	170
St. Peter's Parish, New Kent Co., Va.	104, 170
St. Stephen's Parish, King and Queen Co., Va.	101
Salem, N.J.	36
Salem, Va.	134
Salem Co., N.J.	36
"Salisbury," Chesterfield Co.	164
Salisbury Dist., Rockingham Co., N.C.	151
Salisbury Furnace, Va.	134
Salt Lick Bridge, W.Va.	169
Salt Lick Dist., Braxton Co.	168
Salt Petre Cave, Va.	133-34
Saltillo, Tenn.	149
Samms, James	102
San Francisco, Calif.	162
Sanders, Bill	150
Catherine (Evens)	183
George	107
Jane (Austin)	150
John	16, 110, 128
Peter	127
Richard	127
Sandifer, Matthew	25
Sandusky Plains, Ohio	3
Sandy River, Pittsylvania Co.	151, 153
Sankford, Benjamin	147
Santee, William	176
Sarah and Mary (ship)	67
Satchel, William	139
Saunders, Don Sebastine	115
Peter	166
Savage, John	128
W.	87
Savannah, Ga.	76
Sayre, Daniel	25
Scasbrook, Elizabeth	96
Col. John	96
Mary (Martiau)	96
Schwartz, Mrs. J. E.	179
Scoggin, James W.	143
Rev. John	143
Scott, Capt. ---	124
A. E.	141
Alexander	4
Elizabeth	128
Frances (Collier)	46
George	25
Capt. James	46
John	122
John L.	25
Joseph	25

INDEX

Scott, Mildred 46
  Samuel 25
  Sarah 25
  Thomas 25
  Thompson 25
Scott Dist., Boone Co., W.Va. 78
Scrabble, W.Va. 35-36
Scruggs, John 128
  Samuel S. 128
  Timothy 128
Seabrook, Nicholas B. 38
Seale, Anthony 184
  Jarvis 184
  John 184
  Nancy Ann (Yarborough) 184
Seaman, Jonah 5
Sears, John 109
Seawell, John 121
Seay, Abraham 25, 127-28
  Dudley 25
  James 25, 128
  John 128
  Joseph 128
  Moses 25
  Samuel 143
2nd Richmond Howitzers, C.S.A. 64
Seblee, John 71
Seddon, Va. 77
Seddon Dist., Bland Co. 77
Segar [Seager], John 65-66, 71, 109
  Oliver 16
  William 8, 11, 109
Selden, Mrs. --- 86
Seldon, Elizabeth 166
Sellman, Joseph 176
Serjeant, William Hill 166
Servia, W.Va. 169
Service, Mrs. Estella U. 182
Servies, James A. 75, 135, 161
7th Virginia Regiment 58
Shackelford family 90
Shanghai, W.Va. 35-36
Shanklin, Edward 143
Shapard, Anne 173-74
  Elizabeth H. 56, 173
  Elizabeth (Vass) 56, 173
  Emily B. 174
  Fanny (Bailey) 56, 173
  James 173
  John S. 56, 173
  Lewis 173
  Martha T. 174
  Mary 173
  Mary (Booker) 56, 172-74
  Mary E. 174
  Mildred 173
  Robert 173-74
  Samuel B. 172-73
  Thomas 56, 173
  William 55, 172-73
  see also Sheppard, Shepherd
Sharon, Va. 77-78

Sharon Dist., Bland Co. 77
Sharon Springs, Va. 77
Sharp, Sarah 93
Sheets, Va. 133-34
Shelby, Mrs. N.P. 184
Shelby Co., Ky. 139-40
Sheldon Cemetery, Milo, Mo. 46
Shelton, Clough 128
  Emily Frances 184
  George 143
  John Poindexter 184
  Judith 143
  Lucy J. 184
  Mark 143
  Mary ( ) 143
  Mary E. L. 184
  Mary (Goare) 73
  Sarah C. 184
  Sarah H. R.(Bell) 184
  Thomas 128
  Virginia R. 184
Shenandoah Co., Va. 62, 90
Shenandoah Valley Pioneers 33
Shepherd, Augustine 128
  John 128
  Moses 4
  William 4
  see also Shapard, Shepperd
Shepherdstown, Ky. 183
Shepherdstown, W.Va. 183
Sheppard, Anne (Burwell) 56
  Elizabeth 55
  James Booker 56
  Jessica (Hubard) 56, 172
  Mary (Kavanagh) 55, 172
  Robert 56, 172
  Samuel 56, 172-73
  see also Shapard, Shepherd
Sherman Dist., Boone Co. 78
Shetler, Charles 40, 98
Shields, Mrs. C. W. 99
  James 128
  John 128
  Robert 128
Shiner, Cynthia 183
  George 183
  George Huse 183
  Katurah 183
  Rachel (Lister) 183
Shirkey's, Va. 134
"Shirley," Charles City Co. 88
Shock, W.Va. 169
Shockoe Hill Cemetery, Richmond, Virginia, Register of Interments 43
Shore, --- 119
  Thomas 123
Short, Jane Winifred (Randolph) 183
  Martha 161
Shorter, John 74
  Mary 143-44
Showers, Lloyd I. 146

Shrewsbury, Louellen (Norton)	184
Robert P.	184
Shuffield, Stephen	25
Shugart, Earl B. C.	94
Elizabeth (Woodward)	94
Shurley, Thomas	113
Sibley, Mrs. R. E.	47
Robert	47
Siddens, William	128
Sideling Hill, W.Va.	169
Silent Dell, Va.	134
Sillies, James	124
Simmons, Agatha Aimar	136
Vinson	25
Sims, Ann	11
John	94
Margaret	94
Martha ( )	93
Rebecca (Petty)	93
Thomas	93
William	93
Sinking Creek, Va.	134
Sisson, Annette Lorhelle	62
Skelton, James	13
John	128
Joseph	128
Skinner, William	86
Skipwith, Sir Peyton	123
Slade, Hannah	99
John	100
Nancy	99
Slash Branch, W.Va.	79
Slaughter, A.	86
John	176
Mary Lightfoot	184
Sleith, W.Va.	169
Small, Mrs. Cecil I.	96
William	128
Smith, ---	117-18
Abraham	128
Amy (Pomfret)	60
Amy (Webb)	60
Ann	113, 115
Ann ( )	11, 109
Ann Hunt	60
Anna	166
Anthony	25
Augustine	11-12, 74, 128
Austin	128
Benjamin	176
Cary	113, 115
Charles	142
Childers	128
Clary	114
Covington	25
Dinah	113
Edward	113
Elizabeth	112-13
Elizabeth ( )	14
Elizabeth (Alldin)	72-73
Elizabeth (Henry)	180
Elizabeth Speed	143
Smith, Francis	128
Frederick	117, 164
Henry	4, 128, 180
Isaac	58
Dr. J. K.	162
James	4, 13, 60
	112-13, 115-16, 124
James Webb	60
Jane	36, 112
John	10, 14-15, 25, 36
	72-74, 110-15, 128, 164
Joseph	65, 71, 121, 128, 143
Josias	128
Lettice (Gillam)	142
Margaret	113
Mary Margaret (Fry)	143
Mary (Webb)	60
Col. Maurice	60
Oswald	113, 115
Richard	110
Robert Nelson	143
Roland	180
Salley	128
Samuel	36, 38, 60
Sterling	25
Thomas	4, 11, 25, 109
William	111-13, 115, 128, 143
Mrs. William H.	139
Smith, Bowdoin & Hunter	165
Smith Co., Tenn.	60, 149
Smithey, John	25
Joshua	25
Robert	25
Smith's Clove, N.Y.	58, 61
Smyth Co., Va.	78
Smyth family	137
Sneed, Claiborne	25
Sneling, Aquila	11
Snelson, Robert	128
Snider, John	128
Mary A.	142
Snyder, Frederick	165
Soane, Elizabeth	171
Henry	171
Judith	144
Society for the Propagation of the Gospel	170, 36
Soderberg, Mrs. Gertrude L.	144
Soho, W.Va.	36
"Some Culpeper County Marriages"	176
Some Marriages in Montgomery County, Kentucky	137
"Some Virginia Revolutionary Soldiers"	175
Sons of the American Revolution Library	44
South Branch, Potomac River	47
South Farnham Parish, Essex Co., Va.	51, 55, 60
South Quay, Richmond	117
Southall, Henry H.	25

INDEX

Southall, James	25
John	25
Stephen	25, 86, 124
Southampton Co., Va.	39, 92, 95, 117, 164, 174
Southerland, Mrs. H. D.	179
Southren, Edward	109
"Southside Virginia Austins"	147-54
Southworth, Thomas	73
William	10
Sparrer, John	128
Spears, Richard	5
Speer, Amelia	90
Spence, Thomas Hugh	79, 138
Spencer, Charles	184
James	128
John	127
Mildred (Scott)	46
Rachel	139
Samuel	128
Sarah Jane (Camp)	184
William	128
Spinner, John	25
Spotsylvania Co., Va.	66, 88-90, 102-05, 118, 165
Spratt, John	52
Sprigg, ---	5
Jac.	4
Spring Grove Church, Granville Co., N.C.	59
Spring Mills, W.Va.	36
Springwood, Va.	134
Spurling, Mary	141
Stafford, Co., Va.	39-40, 86, 93, 164, 179
"Staggland," Spotsylvania Co.	66
Stamper, Mary ( )	110
Powell	14
Powels	110
Stanard, ---	8
W.	74, 113
William	11
Stanback, John	25
Stanley, Mrs. Eugene A.	47
Staples, John	128
Joseph	128
Samuel	128
Staten, Elijah	128
Statham, Charles	128
Thomas	128
Staubach, Mrs. Arnold	95
Staunton, Va.	48
Staunton River	118
Stephenson, Avah (Durrett)	30
Stevens, Alice ( )	102
James	102, 128
Jeremiah	102
John	128, 144
Polly (Tomkies)	144
Richard	8, 110
Stewart, Edward	176
James	93
Stewart, John	93
Roberta Dulin	178
Sarah ( )	93
Stiff, Jacob	11, 69, 71, 107, 110
Stine, Mrs. Edwina Warren	146
Stinson, Mrs. Paul F.	140
Stirpes	98
"Stock Hill," Essex Co.	64
Stockman, Charles C.	170
Stockton, Thomas	128
Stockton, Calif.	162
Stockwell, Mrs. B. D.	180
Stoddard, North and Kerr	119
Stone, Mrs. ---	86
Stonecoal, W.Va.	169
Stonham, George	128
Henry	128
Stony Creek, Dinwiddie Co.	118
Storrs, Joshua	87, 119
Stott, James	25
Rawleigh	25
Strachan, Alexander G.	118
Strange Creek, W.Va.	169
Stratten, Benjamin	12
Strawberry Creek, Pittsylvania Co., Va.	153
Stricker, George	5
Strickler, Joseph	128
Stricklin, Joseph	128
Stringer, Daniel	25
Strom, Va.	134
Strutten, William	128
Stubbs, Francis Smith	144
John Segar	144
Sarah Jane (Tomkies)	144
Thomas	120
Sudberry, John	25
Suffolk, Va.	37
Suffolk (ship)	37
Sullivan, Mary	38
Summers, Lewis P.	132
Summers Co., W.Va.	131
Sumner Co., Tenn.	141
Sumter, Gen. Thomas	46
Surry Co., N.C.	148-49
Surry Co., Va.	41, 92, 95, 120, 144, 174
Surry County Records ... 1652-1684	177
Surry C.H., Va.	39, 41
Sussex, N.J.	147
Sussex Co., Va.	142
Sutler, John	128
Sutphen, Catherine	46
Sutton, Christopher	9, 111
John Davison	167
Sutton, W.Va.	79, 168-69
Suttonville, W.Va.	169
Swan, Matthew	92
Swann, Sarah	144
Swearingen, Van	3, 5
Sweet Springs, Va.	134, 163
Swem, Earl Gregg	43, 135

Sweny, Daniel	69
Swepston, John	37, 86
Swift Creek, Chesterfield Co.	120
Sydnor, Ruth	42
Tabb, Dorothy	62
Frances	25
Frances C.	25
Harriot	25
John	25
Marianna	25
Polley	25
Sarah ( )	76
Seigniora	25
Tabler, W.Va.	36
Talbert, Ann	99-100, 103-04
see also Talbot, Talburt	
Talbot, Miss ---	99-100
Thomas H.	117
see also Talbert, Talburt	
Talburt, John	102
Margaret ( )	102
see also Talbert, Talbot	
Taliaferro, Judith	129
Richard	54
Robert	11, 179
Sarah Ann	178
Talley, Abner	25
Elkannah	163
Grief	25
John	25
Peyton	25
Robert	25
Tankard, Stephen	86
Tanner, Robert	25
Tapley, Mary	180
Tarr, see Torr	
Tate, James	116
Tate Creek, W.Va.	168
Tayloe, Col. ---	88, 164
John	118
Taylor, Angelina (Lundy)	95
Ann	183
Benjamin	7, 109, 128
Blackgrove	25
Dudley	61
Col. Henry	95
James	38
John	95
Martha K. (Peterson)	95
Miles	165
Richard	6, 119, 165
Temperance (Peterson)	95
William	95
Tazewell Co., Va.	46, 77, 96
Teakel, John	165
Tease, William	128
Tenant, John	115
Terbet, John	15
Terry, Henry	142
Margaret ( )	142
Sarah	142
family	147

Texas State Genealogical Society	98
Thacker, Edwin	10, 72, 74, 116
Henry	15, 74
Tharpe, Thomas	179
Thilman, Paul	11, 109
13th Virginia Regiment	3
Thomas, Cornelius	128
John	129
Mary Jane	59
Norbon	128
Philip	59
Samuel	123
Thomasin family	142
Thompson, Mrs. Arthur A.	143
Bartlett	128
Catherine E. (Long)	45-46
Charles	122, 129
David	25
James	128
John	118, 128-29
Joseph	128
Patton James	46
Pleasant	128
Rebecca	152
Thomas	25
Waddy	129
William	122, 152, 165
Thompsons, Mainly of Hanover and Louisa Counties	44
Thomson family	44
Thornton, Lewis	124
Meux	53
Col. Peter Presley	118, 155
Thoroughfare Mountain	122
Thorp, James	129
William	129
Three Forks, Pittsylvania Co.	121
Throckmorton, Ann	62
Thurmond, Charles	129
Goodrich	129
Thwart, Capt. William	119
Tiberghier, Charles	5
Tignal, William	11
Tilford, James	128
Tilly, John	17
Tilman, Thomas	128
Tilson's Mill, Va.	77
Timberlake, Benjamin	69
Elizabeth	69
Frances	69
Francis	13, 69, 71
Henry	69
John	69
Joshua	110
Richard	69, 88
Sarah	69
Sarah ( )	69, 71
Tindle, Lewis	129
Tinker Knob, Va.	134
Tinkling Spring Church, Augusta Co., Va.	46
Tipton Co., Ind.	179

INDEX

Tolbert, see Talbert, Talbot	
Tomahawk, W.Va.	35-36
Tomahawk Spring, W.Va.	36
Tomes, Edward T.	128
Joseph	128
Tomkies, D. Simpson	48, 79, 144
Elizabeth	48
Lewis	79
Polly	144
Sarah Jane	144
Tomlin, Elizabeth	130
George	130
Jane (Chamblin)	130
John	130
Mary	130
Reuben	130
Sarah	130
William	130
Tompkins, Margaret J.	29-30
Tomson, Mary ( )	71, 107
Samuel	71
William	71, 107
Toney, Frances (Reynolds)	184
John W.	184
Tooley, Charles	128
Elizabeth	128
John	128
Toombs, Elizabeth (Carter)	183
Torr, Levi	47
Mary (Troxel)	47
William	47
Towar, Alexandria	75
Towles, Oliver	114
Stokeley	9-11, 15, 110, 114-15
Town Run, Fauquier Co.	122, 165
Townes, Allen	25
Armistead	25
James	25
John	25
Townson, Charles	128
Trace Fork, W.Va.	79
Trail, Abraham	129
Charles	128-29
Edward	129
Luraina	128
Thomas	128-29
Traverse, William	4
Travis, Scott	4
Tredway, Moses	118
Tredway's Ordinary, Manchester, Va.	39
Trent, Alexander	25
Tribble, George	181
John	181
Mary	181
Meany	181
Peter	181
William	181
Trigg, Abraham	10
Trigg Co., Ky.	43-44
Trinity, Va.	134
Troutsville, Va.	134
Troutville, Va.	133-34
Troxel, Mary	47
True Blue, Va.	134
Truehart, Daniel	118
Truly, John	25
Sam	25
Trusler, John	128
Truxall, Mrs. H. R.	140
Tryall, David	128
"Tuckahoe," Goochland Co.	119
Tuckahoe Creek, Henrico Co.	85
Tucker, Absalom	25
Anderson	25
Edward	67-68
John	25
Nelson	25
Robert	85
St. George	119
Thomas	25
Tugel, Henry	14-15, 110, 115
Tuke, Thomas	15
Tullos, Rodham	122, 165
Tunstall, Joseph	124
William	166
Turberville, George	86
"Turkey Island"	144
Turner, James	124, 128
James L.	128
John	129
Sarah	36, 179
Stephen	128
Terisha	128
W. R.	146
Tustin, Mary (Flanigan)	139
Samuel	139
Turtle Creek, W.Va.	79
Twistville, W.Va.	169
Two Lick Run, W.Va.	169
Twyman, George	110
Tyler, Martha	141
Tyler's Quarterly	54, 102-03
Tylor, Col. ---	123
Tyre, Joseph	165
Tyree, Jesse	129
Nathan	128
Reuben	129
William	129
Zachariah	128-29
Tyrer, Frank	50
Tyus, Polly	179
Uline, Benr.	5
Union Dist., S.C.	152
University of North Carolina	59
Upper James, Va.	134
Upper Machodoc Warehouse, King George Co.	121
Urbanna, Va.	9, 11, 66, 74
Vaden, Henry	26
Vaiden, Dora Bell (Critzer)	141
Harry C.	141
Dr. Joseph C.	140-41
Martha (Tyler)	141

Vaiden, William H.	141	Virginia State Library	3, 35
Valley Forge, Pa.	58	43-44, 54, 58, 62, 77-78, 89	
Van, W.Va.	79	92, 131-32, 135, 146, 168	
Van Clevesville, W.Va.	35-36	Bulletin	135
Van der Veer, Cornelis Jansz		Vivion, Eliza ( )	17
	90-91	John	17
Vandeveer, Amelia (Speer)	90		
John	90	Waddel, Jacob	27
W. W.	90—91	Waddil, Carter	26
The Vandeveers of North Carolina		Waddington family	142
Kentucky and Indiana 90-91		Wade, Nathaniel	129
Vanduvall, Daniel	37	Walden, John	26
Vanmeter, Hannah	5	Walford, Dr. ---	8
John	5	Walke, Hannah	26
Van Vlear, Nettie	162	Walker, Alexander McDonald	90
Vass, Elizabeth	56, 173	Ann	66-68, 181
Elizabeth (Webb)	56, 173	Catherine	66, 68
Philip	56, 59, 173	David	67
Vassar, James O.	180	Elizabeth	13
Vasser, Peter	26	Emma Jane [Mrs Wilburn]	137
Richard	26	George	26, 112, 114
Vaughan, Anne	142	Mrs. George B.	94
Cornelius	180	Jacob	47
Dorothy	142	James	8, 11, 66, 68
Dorothy (Jones)	142	Jean	67
Elizabeth	142	John	66, 68
Elsie (Motley)	181	Mary	26
Fielding	142	Richard	9, 66, 68, 113, 115
George	129	Thomas	67
Henry	180	Walker Creek, Franklin Co.	47
James	25, 180	Wall, Thomas	123
John	25	Wallace, Rev. B. J.	161
Judith	142	Eliza H. (Edmunds)	162
Lewis	25, 181	W. P.	162
Lucy	142	Walls, John	11
Martha	142, 181	Walne, Peter	50
Nicholas	26	Walters, James	129
Patrick	26	John	129
Robert	26, 181	Walthal, Bartley	26
Thomas	142, 181	Christopher	26
William	129, 142	Daniel	26
Willis	26	Francis	26
Venable, Elizabeth (Raine)	57	George	165
John	57	Henry	26
Martha Ann	57	John	26
Venice (brig)	86	Lucy	27
Vermillion Co., Ill.	62	Peter	26
Vesnel, ---	117	Richard	26
Vestry Book of Petsworth Parish		William	26
	52	Waltham, Bridget	116
Viar, Robert	129	Walton, Amos	144
William	129	Ann ( )	144
Vigust, James	129	Eleanor	144
Vincent, Sarah	184	Elijah	144
Vines, John	129	Elisha	144
Virginia Gazette 53, 55, 58, 61		Elizabeth	144
Virginia Genealogical Society 146		George	144
Bulletin	146	James	144
Virginia Historical Index	135	Jane	144
Virginia Historical Society	44	Jesse	27
Virginia Magazine of History and		Job	144
Biography 50, 54, 75, 135		John	144

INDEX

Walton, Margaret ( ) 144
   Mercy (Laycock) 144
   Nancy 144
   Sherwood 27
   William 144
Walton, Ga. 94
Waltrip, Joseph 26
Ward, Rowland 26
   William 26
Ward's Fork, Charlotte Co. 87
Warden, Rebecah (Bateman) 46
   Thomas 46
Ware, Thomas 129
Waring, T. 109
   Thomas 11
Warner, Jacob 129
   James 129
   William 129
Warren, Donald 123
   Sampson 154
   Sarah (Austin) 154
Warren Co., Tenn. 148
Warren Co., Va. 48, 89
Warriner, William 26
Warwick, Abram 129
   John 129
Warwick, Chesterfield Co. 117, 163
Warwick Co., Va. 87-88, 96
Washington, George 171, 37
   George Steptoe 79
   John 86
   John Perrin 79
   Martha (Dandridge) Custis 171
   Susannah ( ) 79
   William 148
Washington Co., Ky. 94
Washington Co., Md. 33
Washington Co., Minn. 184
Washington Co., Pa. 3
Washington Co., Va.
   46, 94, 137, 143, 149-50
Washington Dist., Boone Co. 78
Washington Dist., Tenn. 79
Washington Twp., Braxton Co. 168
Waskey's Mills, Va. 133-34
Waters, William 26
Watkins, Benjamin 129
   John 129
   Peter 27
   Sarah (Blanks) 93
   William 129
   family 96
Watkinson, Capt. John 67-68
Watt, Thomas 129
Watts, Charles 129
   Stephen 129
Waugh, Andrew 26
Wayne Co., Ind. 143
Wayne Co., Tenn. 148-49
Weatherford, William 26
Webb, Amy 60
   Amy (Booker) 56-59, 172
   Ann 60

Webb, Ann Hunt (Smith) 60
   Ann (Nuttall) 60
   Elizabeth 56, 59, 173
   Elizabeth (Moorman) 60
   Elizabeth (Pulliam) 60
   Frances Y. 173
   George 37, 163
   Giles 144
   Harriet Phillips (Dickins) 60
   Isaac 60
   James 57, 60
   John 56-60
   Lewis 60
   Mrs. Lynn T. 46
   Mary 60
   Mary (Edmondson) 57
   Mary Jane (Thomas) 59
   Sarah (Swann) Randolph 144
   Susanna 60
   Thomas 59
   W. J. 60
   William 59-60
Webb's Ferry, Pamunkey River 37
Webster, Anthony 26
   Edward 26
   John 26
   Peter 26
   William 26
Webster Co., W.Va. 167-69
Weedon, Gen. George 122
Weis, Frederick Lewis 36, 170-71
Welch, Mrs. William H. 96
Welch-Welsh-Walsh 50
"The Well Dressed Militiaman" 174
Wells, Aaron 5
   Abraham 5
   Charles 5
   Elizabeth 143
Wesson, John 120
West, Bransford 129
   Francis 129
   H. H. 95
   James 129
   Robert 95
West Fork, W.Va. 79
West Liberty, W.Va. 5
West River, Anne Arundel Co., Md. 100
West Virginia Review 78
West Virginia University
   30, 40-41, 98
Westbroke, Joshua 124
Westbrook, Elizabeth (Mabury) 140
   Thornton 140
Westbrooks, William 129
Westham, Henrico Co.
   85, 122, 124, 163
Westmore, --- 87
Westmoreland Co., Va.
   86, 93, 146, 178
Westmoreland C.H., Va. 88
Weston, John 71, 108, 111
"Westover," Charles City Co. 87

Wetzel, Mrs. Fred J.	93
Weymouth, England	67
Wharton, Elizabeth	142
Elizabeth ( )	142
Leonard	142
Sarah ( )	142
Susan	142
Walker	142
William	142
Wheeler, Clement	93
Jacob	129
Sarah (Sharp)	93
Whig, Richmond, Va.	43
Whistler, Ann	66
Betty	66
Wil	66
Whitaker, Edward	11
Peter	150
White, Caleb	180
Conyers	129-30
Elizabeth (Catlett)	180
Elizabeth (Durrett)	29
John	180
Joseph	129
Priscilla (Mills)	180
Rebecca	29-30, 96
William	29
Zachariah	129
White Plains, N.Y.	58, 61
Whittingham, Hebr.	109
Whitworth, Clayborne	39
Rowland	26
Thomas	164
Wiatt, John	52
Wiesegar, Daniel	163
Wigglesworth, John	11
Wilcox, Edmund	129
Wild, see Wyld	
The Wilford-Williford Family	43
Wilkerson, Anne (Vaughan)	142
Daniel	27
Edward	26
Wilkinson, Joseph	26
Reuben	120
William	26
Wilkinson Co., Miss.	139
Wilkes Co., N.C.	141
Wilks, Benjamin	37
William and Mary, College of	39
48, 75, 120, 123, 135, 161	
William and Mary Quarterly	
56, 135, 170-72	
William Parks Club Publications	
	135
Williams, Anderson	173
Ann Elizabeth	29-30
Christian	116
Frederick H.	26
Howard	115
Jane	113
Jeremiah	5
John	4, 10
Kathleen Booth [Mrs. E. Burton]	135
Williams, Dr. Lorenzo D.	184
Mildred (Shapard)	173
Philip	27
Robert Murphy	103
Sarah	138
Sarah C. (Shelton)	184
Shadrack	4
Tobias	95
Williams and Murphy Records	103
Williamsburg, Va.	
38, 75-76, 85-87, 117, 121	
Williamson, Abigail (Bynum)	92
Benjamin	14
Frances	14
Jacob	26
Jeremiah	4
John	4, 92
Lancelot	26
Martha	14
Moses	4
Robert 13-15, 73-74, 107, 112	
Williford, John	43
Willingham Bridges, Lunenburg Co., Va.	119
Willis, Francis	119
Isaiah	140
John	124
Rhody	140
Richard	72
Wills, Elias	96
James	129
John	26, 129
Mary (Condon)	96
Thomas F.	27
Willis	129-30
Wills, Cowper & Co.	37
Wills and Administrations of Elizabeth City County	177
Wills and Administrations of Isle of Wight County	177
Wills and Administrations of Southampton County	177
Willson, Aaron	4
Alexander	26
Archer	26
Daniel	26
John	26-27
Matthew	27
Richard	26
Thomas	26
Tom B.	26
Tom F.	26
William	26
see also Wilson	
Willoughby, Joshua	129
Wilmington, N.C.	90
Wilson, ---	119
David	66
Elizabeth	60
John	143
Mary Ann Luck	143
Richard	172
Samuel	5
Solomon	119

INDEX

Wilson, Virginia — 137
Wilton, Richard — 39
Wily, John — 26, 120
Winchester, Va. — 139, 183
Wingfield, Josiah — 130
  see also Winkfield
Wingo, Churchel — 26
  John — 26
Winkfield, Josias — 129
  Robert — 129
  Thomas — 124
  see also Wingfield
Winston, John — 26
  Mary Ann (Gillespie) — 46
  Robert — 46
  William — 27, 88, 111
Winters, Henry — 4
Wisconsin Historical Society — 79
Wise Co., Va. — 150
Witt, David — 129
  Jenney — 129
  John — 129
Witten family — 96
Womack, A. Elizabeth (Yancey) — 99-100, 104
Wood, E. B. — 46
  Jacob — 129
  Jesse — 129
  Josiah — 129
  Richard — 129
  Samuel — 129
  Capt. Thomas — 56
  William — 26, 67, 129
Woods, Andrew — 4-5
  James — 129
  John — 176
  Robert — 4
Woodson, Benjamin — 57
  Booker — 57
  Elizabeth — 57
  Elizabeth ( ) — 57
  Elizabeth Harrison (Hobbs) — 57
  Elizabeth (Raine) Venable — 57
  Henry Morton — 57
  James — 57
  Joanna (Booker) — 56-57
  John — 56-57, 121, 172
  Joseph — 26
  Joseph Nathaniel — 57
  Martha Ann (Venable) — 57
  Mary (Miller) — 57
  Miller — 172
  Patrick — 117
  Patsy ( ) — 57
  Peter — 57
  Rene — 117
  Sukey ( ) — 57
  William — 120
Woodward, Elizabeth — 94
  Henry — 37
  William — 37
Woody, Augustin — 129
  Benjamin — 129

Woody, George — 129
Wooldridge, Robert — 163
Woolfolk, Ann (George) — 181
  Robert — 181
Woolman, Mary — 180
Wooten, Mrs. James R. — 95
  Priscilla — 79
Worden, see Warden
Worrell, Anne Lowry — 132
Worsham, --- — 27
  Betsy G. — 27
  Daniel — 27
  Elizabeth — 26
  George — 26
  Henry — 26
  Peter — 26
  Thomas — 27
  William — 27
Wortham, George — 13
Worton, Abra. — 110
Wray, Henry G. — 140
  James — 26
  Thomas — 26
  Thomas Jefferson — 140
Wright, Abby ( ) — 76
  Achilles — 129
  Ambrose — 55
  Andrew — 129
  Archibald — 55
  Augustin — 129
  Benjamin — 129
  David — 129
  Elizabeth (Sheppard) — 55
  Elizabeth (Woodson) — 57
  Harry — 13
  Henry — 15
  James — 129-30
  Jesse — 129
  John — 26, 121, 129
  Jordan — 129
  Linsey — 129
  Mary Louisa (Griffin) — 75-76
  Minos — 129
  Pleasant — 26
  Reubin — 26
  Richard — 129
  Robert — 26, 129
  Sallie Lewis — 75
  Samuel — 26
  Stephen — 26, 76
  Stephen Orren — 75-76
  Thomas — 26-27, 129, 166, 172
  William — 57, 118, 129
Wyatt, Frances (Newton) — 92-93
  William — 93
Wyld, Ann B. — 56
  Ann (Booker) — 56
  Elizabeth H. — 56
Wylie family — 96
Wyncoop's Spring Run, Berkeley Co., W.Va. — 33
Wynne, Angelica — 95
  Anne — 95

Wynne, Cornelia	95
Lucretia	95
Martha	95
Mary ( )	95
Robert	95
Thomas	95
Wyoming Co., W.Va.	131
Wysor family	96
Wythe Co., Va.	46, 77, 147, 159-50
Yancey, A. Elizabeth	99
Bartlett	99
Nancy (Graves)	99
Yanceyville, N.C.	100, 103
Yancy, Charles	130
Yarborough, Nancy Ann	184
Yates, Bartholomew	9, 67-68, 113
York Co., Va.	51, 89, 96, 104, 120, 144, 180-81
Yorktown, Va.	61, 67, 75-76, 88, 164-65
Young, ---	119
Capt. Henry	58
Younger, James	51
Younghusband, Isaac	87
Zane, Ebenezer	3

www.ingramcontent.com/pod-product-compliance
Lightning Source LLC
Chambersburg PA
CBHW071711160426
43195CB00012B/1646